AMERICA'S
Wonderful
LITTLE
HOTELS
& INNS
1992

The South

D1027381

States Covered in this Edition

Alabama	Louisiana
Arkansas	Mississippi
Florida	North Carolina
Georgia	South Carolina
Kentucky	Tennessee

Also in this Series

America's Wonderful Little Hotels & Inns, U.S.A. and Canada
America's Wonderful Little Hotels & Inns, New England
America's Wonderful Little Hotels & Inns, The Middle Atlantic
America's Wonderful Little Hotels & Inns, The Midwest
*America's Wonderful Little Hotels & Inns, The Rocky Mountains
and The Southwest*
America's Wonderful Little Hotels & Inns, The West Coast
Europe's Wonderful Little Hotels & Inns, Great Britain & Ireland
Europe's Wonderful Little Hotels & Inns, The Continent

AMERICA'S
Wonderful
LITTLE
HOTELS
& INNS
1992

The South

Edited by Sandra W. Soule

Associate Editors:
Nancy P. Barker
June C. Horn
Kirstin O'Rielly
Mary Ann Boyle

Contributing Editors:
Suzanne Carmichael, Susan Waller Schwemm,
Linda F. Phillipps, Jennifer Klipstein, Ulla Olofsson

Editorial Assistants:
Neil Horn
Jeffrey Soule

St. Martin's Press
New York

This book is dedicated to the people who take the time and trouble to write about the hotels and inns they've visited, and to my children—Hilary and Jeffrey—my husband, and my parents.

ISBN 0–312-06284-2

First Edition

10   9   8   7   6   5   4   3   2   1

Maps by David Lindroth © 1992, 1991, 1990, 1989, 1988, 1987 by St. Martin's Press

Contents

Acknowledgments

I would like again to thank all the people who wrote in such helpful detail about the inns and hotels they visited. To them belong both the dedication and the acknowledgments, for without their support, this guide would not exist. If I have inadvertently misspelled or omitted anyone's name, please accept my sincerest apologies.

I would also like to thank Hilary Rubinstein, who originated the concept for this series. Also thanks to my helpful and supportive editor, Anne Savarese; to my colleagues Nancy Barker, June Horn, Kirstin O'Rielly, and Mary Ann Boyle; to Neil Horn, my invaluable assistant; to Suzanne Carmichael, Susan Schwemm, Nancy Debevoise, Linda Goldberg, and Diane Wolf, my colleagues in the field; to John Blewer, April Burwell, Marjorie Cohen, Dianne Crawford, Arlyne Craighead, Willis Frick, Frank Hepler, Stephen Holman, Keith Jurgens, Dave Kendall, Jim & Tina Kirkpatrick, Zita Knific, Pat and Glen Lush, Betty Norman, Carolyn Mathiasen, Carolyn Myles, Ed Okie, Janet Payne, Mary Louise Rogers, Joe Schmidt, Jeanne Smith, Lee Todd, James and Janice Utt, Wendi Van Exan, Hope Welliver, Gay Whitehead, Diane Wolf, Rose Wolf, and the many others who went far beyond the call of duty in their assistance and support; and to Melania Lanni, for without her help, I'd never get anything done.

Introduction

Reading the Entries

Each entry generally has three parts: a description of the inn or hotel, quotes from guests who have stayed there, and relevant details about rooms, rates, location, and facilities. Occasionally you may find that no general description is given or that the factual data is incomplete. There are two reasons for this: Either the descriptions supplied by guests made this unnecessary, or the facility failed to supply us with adequate information because of time limitations or other problems.

Please remember that the length of an entry is in no way a reflection of that inn or hotel's quality. Rather, it is an indication of the type of feedback we've received both from guests and from the innkeepers themselves. Some hotel owners are totally unaware of this guide; others take an active role in encouraging their guests to write.

Wherever a location is of particular tourist interest, we've tried to include some information about its attractions. If we have only one listing for a town, this description usually falls within the body of the entry. If there is more than one inn or hotel listed for a town, the description of the town and information about its location precede the individual entries.

In some areas the magnet is not a particular town but rather a compact, distinct region. Travelers choose one place to stay and use it as a base from which to explore the area. But because this guide is organized by town, not by region, the entries are scattered throughout the chapter. When this applies, you will see the name of the region noted under the "Location" heading; check back to the introduction for a description of the region involved. For example, inns and hotels in Bucks County, Pennsylvania, start with Erwinna near the beginning of the chapter and extend to Upper Black Eddy at the end, but the description of the area itself is found at the beginning of the chapter.

The names at the end of the quotations are those who have recommended the hotel or inn. Some entries are entirely or largely quoted from one report; if several names follow the quotation, we have distinguished the writers of the quoted material by putting their names first. Some writers have requested that we not use their names; you will see initials noted instead. *We never print the names of those who have sent us adverse reports, although their contributions are invaluable indeed.*

Although we have tried to make the listings as accurate and complete as possible, mistakes and inaccuracies invariably creep in. The most significant area of inaccuracy applies to the rates charged by each establishment. In preparing this guide, we asked all the hotels and inns to give us their 1992 rates, ranging from the least expensive room in the off-season to the most expensive peak-season price. Some did so, while others just noted the 1991 rate.

Since the process of writing and publishing a book takes nearly a year, please don't rely solely on the figures printed. *You should always double-check the rates when you make your reservations; please don't blame the hotel or this guide if the prices are wrong.* On the other hand, given the current level of inflation, you should not encounter anything more than a 5% increase, unless there has been a substantial improvement in the amenities offered or a change of ownership. Please let us know immediately if you find anything more than that!

If you find any errors of omission or commission in any part of the entries, we urgently request your help in correcting them. We recognize that it takes extra time and effort for readers to write us letters or fill in report forms, but this feedback is essential in keeping this publication totally responsive to consumer needs.

Inngoers' Bill of Rights

We've read through a lot more brochures for inns and hotels than the average bear, and can attest to the fact that not one makes mention of its possible drawbacks, however slight. And rightly so. A brochure is paid advertising, no more obligated to provide the full picture—both pros and cons—than a TV ad for diet soda. Furthermore, unlike this guidebook, *which accepts no fee of any kind for an entry,* most inn guidebooks charge a listing or membership fee of some kind, making them basically paid advertisements. Despite brochure promises and glowing listings in other books, we all know that perfection isn't possible in this world, but we feel that (despite the irate reactions of some innkeepers) complete and honest reporting will give readers *reasonable* expectations, ones that are often surpassed in the best of hostelries.

On the other hand, although perfection may not be on the menu, as guests (and customers), travelers have the right to expect certain minimum standards. These rights are especially important in hotels and inns at the top end of the rate scale; we don't expect as much from more modestly priced places, although it certainly is often received.

So, please use this Bill of Rights as a kind of checklist in deciding how you think a place stacks up on your own personal rating scale. And, whether an establishment fails, reaches, or exceeds these levels, be sure to let us know. These rights are especially important because of the financial penalties levied by most establishments; with the exception of the larger hotels, nearly every establishment listed in this book requires a substantial advance deposit, yet travelers have little or no recourse if facilities prove to be substandard. We would also hope that innkeepers will use this list to help evaluate both the strong points and shortcomings of their own establishments, and are grateful to those who have already done so.

The right to suitable cleanliness. An establishment that looks, feels, and smells clean, with no musty or smoky odors. Not just middle-of-the-room clean, but immaculate in all the nooks and crannies—under the radiators, in the dresser drawers, out on the balconies. Rooms should be immaculate prior to check-in, and kept as close as possible to that standard during your stay. You also have the right to prompt maid service, and should not have to wait until mid-afternoon for your room to be made up.

The right to suitable room furnishings. A comfortable bed with a firm mattress and soft pillows (preferably two per person), fresh clean linens, and blankets is a minimum. On *each* side of a double or larger-size bed should be a reading lamp (minimum 60 watts; ideal are three-way bulbs), along with a night table (or its equivalent) giving you a place to leave the bedtime necessities—a glass of water, a box of tissues, your eyeglasses and watch. Two comfortable chairs with good reading lights are a welcome addition, as are a well-lit mirror and readily accessible electric outlets in a room without a private bath. A well-equipped room also has adequate storage space for clothes, both in drawers and closets, along with extra pillows and blankets and a rack for your luggage.

The right to comfortable, attractive rooms. Guest rooms and common rooms that are not only attractive, but livable as well. Not just a visually handsome museum set piece, but a place where you'd like to spend some time reading, chatting, relaxing. You should be as comfortable as you are at home, without having to do any of the work to make yourself so.

The right to a decent bathroom. Of course, cleanliness heads the list here, followed by reliable plumbing, adequate and even supplies of hot water, decent lighting, an accessible electric outlet with wiring that can take a hair dryer, a fixed or hand-held shower added to old-fashioned tubs, a shelf or table for toiletries, and an ample supply of soft, absorbent towels. In more expensive accommodations, an "amenities kit" is a reasonable expectation.

The right to privacy and discretion. In even the most familial of inns, you are entitled to conduct private conversations in common rooms, and even more private ones in your own room—and you have the right *not* to hear the equally private conversations of your neighbors. The right to discretion precludes prying hosts' questions about one's marital status or sexual preference. A truly offensive intrusion on a guest's privacy is the practice of displaying proselytizing religious brochures, tracts, and signs.

The right to good, healthful food. Fresh nutritious food, ample in quantity, high in quality, attractively presented, and graciously served in enjoyable smoke-free surroundings—whether the offering is a cup of coffee and a roll, a seven-course gourmet dinner, or anything in between. An end to dessert masquerading as breakfast and ample supplies of brewed decaffeinated coffee and herbal teas is applauded. Freedom from pretentious menus written in fractured French menuspeak would be a welcome companion.

The right to comfortable temperatures and noise levels. Rooms should be reasonably cool on the hottest of summer nights and warm on the coldest winter evenings. Windows that open, screens without holes, fans, air conditioners, and heating systems that run quietly are all key; although not always possible, individually controlled thermostats are ideal. In locations where traffic noise is a problem, double- or even triple-glazed windows, drapes, and landscaping should all be in place.

The right to fair value. People don't stay in inns or small hotels because they are cheap, which is good, because very few of them are. What is expected, though, is a good value, with prices that are in reasonable relation to the facilities offered and to the cost of equivalent accommodation in the area. This right extends to the times when things go wrong. Even when the problem is beyond the innkeepers' control, guests have the right to an apology at the minimum, and restitution at the maximum, depending on the situation. Guests do not have the right to perfection, but they have the right to innkeepers who are concerned and solicitous when a problem arises.

The right to genuine hospitality. Owners and staff who are sincerely glad you've come, and who make it their business to make your stay pleasant and memorable without being intrusive. Innkeepers who help guests to get to know each other when appropriate and who leave the less sociable to their own thoughts. Resident owners are best, resident staff is often acceptable; someone should be readily available for emergencies around the clock.

The right to a caring environment and little luxuries. Seeing that the little extras have been attended to—asking about pet allergies and dietary restrictions, making dinner reservations, providing inside and accurate information on area activities and events. Offering afternoon or evening refreshments, and welcoming new arrivals with refreshments appropriate to the season. Leaving a personal note, fresh flowers, or candies to greet guests is another way of saying welcome. Being there to provide toothpaste or a toothbrush to guests who have forgotten theirs at home. A good hostelry is more than accommodation. It's an end in itself, not just a means to an end. Amenities are more than imported soaps; innkeepers who are attuned to guests' needs and wants, anticipating them before they're even expressed, are the most important amenity of all.

The right to personal safety. Facilities in large cities need to be located in reasonably safe neighborhoods, with adequate care given to building security. Where caution, especially at night, is advisable, innkeepers have an obligation to share this information with guests.

The right to professionalism. Running an inn or hotel is not a business for amateurs, and guests have the right to receive requested brochures promptly, after one request, and to have their room reservations handled efficiently and responsibly. Check-in and check-out should be smooth, with rooms available as confirmed.

The right to adequate common areas. One of the key distinctions between a motel and an inn is the existence of at least one common room where guests can gather to read, chat, or relax, free of any pressure (implied or otherwise) to buy anything.

The right of people traveling alone to have all the above rights. Those traveling alone usually pay just a few dollars less than a couple, yet the welcome, services, and rooms they receive are often less than equal.

The right to a reasonable cancellation policy. Before booking, get the details. Penalties levied for a cancellation made fewer than 7–14 days before arrival is relatively standard at most inns; the 2–7 day policy found at many Western inns is preferable. Most inns will refund deposits (minus a processing fee) even after the deadline if the room is rebooked. We feel that all should offer the chance to rebook within a few months as an alternative to cancellation penalties. To be avoided are inns with policies such as this: "On cancellations received less than 45 days in advance, the deposit [approximately 50%] is not refundable, whether the room is re-rented or not."

Of course, there is no "perfect" inn or hotel, even when every provision of the bill of rights is met, since people's tastes and needs vary so greatly. But one key phrase does pop up in the hotel/inn reports over and over again, whether the writer is describing a small hotel in the city or a country inn: "I felt right at home." This is not written in the literal sense—a commercial lodging, no matter how cozy or charming, is never the same as one's home. What is really meant is that guests felt as welcome, as relaxed, as comfortable, as they would in their own home. One writer put it this way: "Where does one start in describing this inn? With mixed feelings. (It's a wonderful place, and I don't want the world to discover and spoil it.) But I'll tell you about this grand hideaway. It's clean, quiet, isolated, warm, and comfortable. The fireplaces work and the owners seem intent on making your stay happy. They describe dinner specials with smiles, remember you from trip to trip, and are willing to help in any way they can. The unique qualities of each room make you want to try them all. It's a wonderful place. Please don't take my room."

What makes for a wonderful stay?

We've tried our best to make sure that all the hotels and inns listed in this guide are as wonderful as our title promises. Inevitably, there will be some disappointments. Sometimes these will be caused by a change in ownership or management that has resulted in lowered standards. Other times, unusual circumstances, which can arise in the best of establishments, will lead to problems. Quite often, though, problems will occur because there's not a good "fit" between the inn or hotel and the guest. Decide what you're looking for, then find the inn that suits your needs, whether you're looking for a casual environment or a dressy one, a romantic setting or a family-oriented one, a vacation spot or a business person's environment, an isolated country retreat or a convenient in-town location.

We've tried to give you as much information as possible on each hotel or inn listed, and have taken care to indicate the atmosphere each inn-keeper is trying to create. After you've read the listing, write, if there is time, for a copy of the establishment's brochure, which will give you more information. Finally, feel free to call any inn or hotel where you're planning to stay, and ask as many questions as necessary.

Inn etiquette

A first-rate inn is a joy indeed, but as guests we need to do our part to respect its special qualities. For starters, you'll need to maintain a higher level of consideration for your fellow guests. Century-old Victorians are noted for their nostalgic charms, not their sound-proofing; if you come in late or get up early, remember that voices and footsteps echo off all those gleaming hardwood floors and doors. If you're going to pick a fight with your roommate, pull the covers up over your head or go out for a walk.

If you're sharing a bath, don't dawdle, tidy up after yourself, and dry your hair back in your room. If you've admired the Oriental carpets, antique decor, handmade quilts, and the thick fluffy towels, don't leave wet glasses on the furniture, put suitcases on the bed, or use the towels for wiping the snow off your skis or car. After all, innkeepers have rights too!

Hotels, inns . . . resorts and motels

As the title indicates, this is a guide to exceptional inns and hotels. Generally, the inns have 5 to 25 rooms, although a few have only 2 rooms and some have over 100. The hotels are more often found in the cities and range in size from about 50 to 200 rooms.

The line between an inn or hotel and a resort is often a fine one. There are times when we all want the extra facilities a resort provides, so we've added a number of reader-recommended facilities to this edition.

You'll also find that we've listed a handful of motels. Although they don't strictly fall within the context of this book, we've included them because we received letters strongly endorsing their positive qualities, particularly their concerned and involved owners and friendly atmosphere, two qualities usually lacking in even the best of motels. A number of these recommendations have come for properties in the Best Western chain. Please don't be put off by this; Best Western is a franchise operation, with no architectural unity from one property to the next. Those listed in this guide have substantial architectural or historical appeal and concerned, professional management.

Although we do not provide full coverage of hotel chains, we do want to point out that the Four Seasons and Ritz-Carlton hotels are almost impossible to beat at the luxury end of the spectrum. Readers consistently rave about their unbeatable combination of unparalleled service and plush accommodation.

Rooms

All hotel and inn rooms are not created equal. Although the rooms at a typical chain motel or hotel may be identical, the owners of most of the establishments described in this book pride themselves on the individuality of each guest room. Some, although not all, of these differences are reflected in the rates charged.

More important, it means that travelers need to express their needs clearly to the innkeepers when making reservations and again when checking in. Some rooms may be quite spacious but may have extremely small private baths or limited closet space. Some antique double beds have rather high footboards—beautiful to look at but torture for people over six feet tall! Many inns are trading their double beds in for queens and kings; if you prefer an oversize bed, say so. If you want twin beds, be sure to specify this when making reservations and again when you check in; many smaller inns have only one or two twin-bedded rooms.

Some rooms may have gorgeous old bathrooms, with tubs the size of small swimming pools, but if you are a hard-core shower person, that room won't be right for you. Many others have showers but no baths, which may be disappointing if you love a long, luxurious soak in the tub. If you are traveling on business and simply must have a working-size desk with good light, speak up. Some rooms look terrific inside but don't look out at anything much; others may have the view but not quite as special a decor. Sometimes the best rooms may look out onto a main road and can be quite noisy. Decide what's important to you. Although the owners and staff of the hotels and inns listed here are incredibly hard-working and dedicated people, they can't read your mind. Let your needs be known, and, within the limits of availability, they will try to accommodate you.

Our most frequent complaints center around beds that are too soft and on inadequate reading lights. If these are priorities for you (as they are for us), don't be shy about requesting bedboards or additional lamps to remedy the situation. Similarly, if there are other amenities your room is lacking—extra pillows, blankets, or even an easy chair—speak up. Most innkeepers would rather put in an extra five minutes of work than have an unhappy guest.

If your reservation is contingent upon obtaining a particular room, make this very clear to the innkeeper. Some inns will not accept such reservations, feeling that they are too difficult to guarantee. Those that do accept them have an obligation to meet their guarantee; if circumstances prevent them from following through on the promised room, make it clear that you expect some sort of remuneration—either the return of your deposit or a reduction in the price of another room.

If you really don't like your room, ask for another as soon as possible, preferably before you've unpacked your bags. The sooner you voice your dissatisfaction, the sooner something can be done to improve the situation. If you don't like the food, ask for something else—in other words, you're the guest, make sure you get treated like one. If things go terribly wrong, don't be shy about asking for your money back, and be *sure* to write us about any problems.

What is a single? A double? A suite? A cottage or cabin?

Unlike the proverbial rose, a single is not a single is not a single. Sometimes it is a room with one twin bed, which really can accommodate only one person. Quite often it is described as a room with a standard-size double bed, in contrast to a double, which has two twin beds. Other hotels call both of the preceding doubles, although doubles often have queen- or even king-size beds instead. Many times the only distinction is made by the number of guests occupying the room; a single will pay slightly less, but there's no difference in the room.

There's almost as much variation when it comes to suites. We define a suite as a bedroom with a separate living room area and often a small kitchen, as well. Unfortunately, since suites are now a very popular concept in the hotel business, the word has been stretched to cover other setups too. Some so-called suites are only one large room, accommodating a table and a separate seating area in addition to the bed. If you require a suite that has two separate rooms with a door between them, specify this when you make reservations.

Quite a few of our entries have separate cabins or cottages in addition to rooms in the main building. In general, a cabin is understood to be a somewhat more rustic residence than a cottage, although there's no hard-and-fast rule. Be sure to inquire for details when making reservations.

What is a B&B anyway?

There are basically two kinds of B&Bs—the B&B homestay and the B&B inn. The homestay is typically the home of an empty nester, who has a few empty bedrooms to fill, gaining some extra income and pleasant company. B&B inns are run on a more professional basis, independently marketed and subject to state and local licensing. Guests typically have dedicated common areas for their use, and do not share the hosts' living quarters, as in a homestay. We list very few homestays in this guide. Full-service or country inns and lodges are similar to the B&B inn, except that they serve breakfast and dinner on a regular basis, and may be somewhat larger in size; dinner is often offered to the public as well as to house guests. The best of all of these are made special by resident owners bringing the warmth of their personalities to the total experience. A B&B is *not* a motel that serves breakfast.

Making reservations

Unless you are inquiring many months in advance of your visit, it's best to telephone when making reservations. This offers a number of advantages: You will know immediately if space is available on your requested dates; you can find out if that space is suitable to your specific needs. You will have a chance to discuss the pros and cons of the available rooms and will be able to find out about any changes made in recent months—new facilities, recently redecorated rooms, nonsmoking policies, possibly even a change of ownership. It's also a good time to ask the innkeeper about other concerns—Is the neighborhood safe at night? Is there any renovation or construction in progress that might be disturbing? Will a wedding reception or other social function that might affect your use of the common areas or parking lot be in progress during your visit? If you're reserving a room at a plantation home that is available for public tours, get specifics about the check-in/out times; in many, rooms are not available before 5 P.M. and must be vacated by 9 A.M. sharp. The savvy traveler will always get the best value for his accommodation dollar.

If you expect to be checking in late at night, *be sure to say so;* many inns give doorkeys to their guests, then lock up by 10 P.M.

We're often asked about the need for making advance reservations. If you'll be traveling in peak periods, in prime tourist areas, and want to be sure of getting a first-rate room at the best-known inns, reserve at least three to six months ahead. This is especially true if you're traveling with friends or family and will need more than one room. On the other hand, if you like a bit of adventure, and don't want to be stuck with cancellation fees when you change your mind, by all means stick our book in the glove compartment and hit the road. If you're traveling in the off-season, or even midweek in season, you'll have a grand time. But look for a room by late afternoon; never wait until after dinner and hope that you'll find something decent.

Payment

Many innkeepers don't like plastic any better for payment than they do for decorating. Some accept credit cards for the initial deposit but prefer cash, traveler's checks, or personal checks for the balance; others offer the reverse policy. Still others have accepted credit cards as a part of modern living. When no credit cards are accepted at all, you can settle your bill with a personal check, traveler's check, or even (!) cash.

When using your credit card to guarantee a reservation, be aware that some inns and hotels will charge your card for the amount of the deposit only, while others will put a "hold" on your card for the full amount of your entire stay, plus the cost of meals and incidentals that you may (or may not) spend. If you're using your card to reserve a fairly extended trip, you may find that you're well over your credit limit without actually having spent a nickel. We'd suggest inquiring; if the latter is the procedure, either send a check for the deposit or go elsewhere.

Rates

All rates quoted are per room, unless otherwise noted as being per person. Rates quoted per person are usually based on double occupancy, unless otherwise stated.

"Room only" rates do not include any meals. In most cases two or three meals a day are served by the hotel restaurant, but are charged separately. Average meal prices are noted when available. In a very few cases no meals are served on the premises at all; rooms in these facilities are usually equipped with kitchenettes.

B&B rates include bed and breakfast. Breakfast, though, can vary from a simple continental breakfast to an expanded continental breakfast to a full breakfast. Afternoon tea and evening refreshments are sometimes included, as well.

MAP (Modified American Plan) rates are often listed per person and include breakfast and dinner. Only a few of the inns listed serve lunch, although many will prepare a picnic on request for an additional charge.

State and local sales taxes are not included in the rates; the percentage varies from state to state and is noted in the introduction to each state chapter or in the individual listing. When budgeting for your trip, remember that taxes can easily add 10–15% to the cost of your travels.

When inquiring about rates, always ask if any off-season or special package rates are available. Sometimes discounted rates are available *only* on request; seniors and AAA members often qualify for substantial discounts. During the week, when making reservations at city hotels or country inns, it's important to ask if any corporate rates are available. Depending on the establishment, you may or may not be asked for some proof of corporate affiliation (a business card is usually all that's needed), but it's well worth inquiring, since the effort can result in a saving of 15 to 20%, plus an upgrade to a substantially better room. Another money-saving trick can be to look for inns in towns a bit off the beaten path. If you stay in a town that neighbors a famous resort or historic community, you will often find that rates are anywhere from $20 to $50 less per night for equivalent accommodation. If you're travelling without reservations, and arrive at a half-empty inn in late afternoon, don't hesitate to ask for a price reduction or free room upgrade. And of course, watch for our ¢ symbol, which indicates places which are a particularly good value.

If an establishment has a specific tipping policy, whether it is "no tipping" or the addition of a set service charge, it is noted under "Rates." When both breakfast and dinner are included in the rates, a 15% service charge is standard; a number of B&Bs are also adding on 10%, a practice which sits poorly with us. When no notation is made, it's generally expected that guests will leave about 5 to 10% for the housekeeping staff and 15% for meal service. A number of inns have taken to leaving little cards or envelopes to remind guests to leave a tip for the housekeepers; this practice is spreading, as are reader complaints on the subject. Reported one reader: "An envelope was left out for tips for the chambermaids, a practice I dislike very much. I would much rather they paid their employees a living wage and add a service charge if they must. I don't wish to be told that the maids rely on my generosity to pay their rent." If you welcome a no-tipping policy and object to solicitation, be sure to let the innkeeper know.

A few readers have indicated that they feel some innkeepers have taken advantage of the current popularity of B&Bs with a disproportionate increase in their rates: "I've encountered a few American B&Bs without a private bath and serving only a barely adequate continental breakfast that charge two people as much or more than a good chain motel would. Granted, there's a more personal touch, but given the lack of motel amenities, I think the price should be somewhat lower. Even some B&Bs with private baths and considerable charm are, I fear, suffering delusions of grandeur when pricing themselves in the range of a grand hotel." (AD) We agree; judging from recent feedback, so do many of you. Opinions?

Deposits and cancellations

Nearly all innkeepers print their deposit and cancellation policies clearly on their brochures. Deposits generally range from payment of the first night's stay to 50% of the cost of the entire stay. Some inns repeat the cancellation policy when confirming reservations. In general, guests canceling well in advance of the planned arrival (two to four weeks is typical) receive a full refund minus a cancellation fee. After that date, no refunds are offered unless the room is rented to someone else. A few will not refund *even if the room is rented,* so take careful note. If you're making a credit card booking over the phone, be sure to find out what the cancellation policy is.

We would like to applaud many of the inns of the Northwest, where only two to seven days' notice of cancellation is required, and would love to see other areas follow suit. We also feel that even if you cancel on short notice, you should be given the opportunity to rebook within a reasonable time period rather than lose your entire deposit.

Sometimes the shoe may be on the other foot. Even if you were told earlier that the inn at which you really wanted to stay was full, it may be worthwhile to make a call to see if cancellations have opened up any last-minute vacancies.

Minimum stays

Two- and three-night minimum weekend and holiday stays are the rule at many inns during peak periods. We have noted these when possible, although we suspect that the policy may be more common than is always indicated in print. On the other hand, you may just be hitting a slow period, so it never hurts to ask if a one-night reservation would be accepted. Again, cancellations are always a possibility; you can try calling on a Friday or Saturday morning to see if something is available for that night.

Pets

Very few of the inns and hotels listed accept pets. When they do we've noted it under "Extras." On the other hand, over one-half of the country inns listed in this book have at least one dog or cat, sometimes more. If you are highly allergic to animals, *we strongly urge that you inquire for details before making reservations.*

Children

Some inns are family-style places and welcome children of all ages; we've marked them with our ♙ symbol. Others do not feel that they have facilities for the very young and only allow children over a certain age. Still others cultivate an "adults only" atmosphere and don't even welcome children at dinner. When inns and hotels do not encourage all children, we've noted the age requirement under the heading "Restrictions." If special facilities are available to children, these are noted under "Facilities" and "Extras." If an inn does not exclude children yet does not offer any special amenities or rate reductions for them, we would suggest it only for the best-behaved youngsters.

Whatever the policy, you may want to remind your children to follow the same rules of courtesy toward others that we expect of adults. Be aware that the pitter-patter of little feet on an uncarpeted hardwood floor can sound like a herd of stampeding buffalo to those on the floor below. Children used to the indestructible plastics of contemporary homes will need to be reminded (more than once) to be gentle with furniture that dates back 100 years or more.

For some reason, Southerners seem to be more tolerant of children than are New Englanders. Of the dozens of exquisitely decorated, antique-filled inns in the South, there are very few that exclude kids. In the North, nearly all do! And California innkeepers apparently would prefer it if children never crossed the state borders at all! Most inns there won't take any children under 12, and some are strictly for adults only.

State laws governing discrimination by age are affecting policies at some inns. To our knowledge, both California and Michigan now have such laws on the books, although this was rarely reflected in the brochures sent to us by inns in those states. Some inns get around age discrimination by limiting room occupancy to two adults. This discourages families by forcing them to pay for two rooms instead of one. Our own children are very clear on their preferences: although they've been to many inns that don't encourage guests under the age of 12, they find them "really boring"; on the other hand, they've loved every family-oriented place we've ever visited.

Porterage and packing

Only the largest of our listings will have personnel whose sole job is to assist guests with baggage. In the casual atmosphere associated with many inns, it is simply assumed that guests will carry their own bags. If you do need assistance with your luggage—because you have a bad back, because your bags are exceptionally heavy, or for any other reason at all—don't hesitate to say so; it should be gladly given. Ideally, innkeepers and their staff should ask you if you need help, but if they forget, don't suffer silently; just say "Could you give us a hand?"

If you're planning an extended trip to a number of small inns, we'd suggest packing as lightly as possible, using two small bags rather than one large suitcase. You'll know why if you've ever tried hauling a 50-pound oversize suitcase up a steep and narrow 18th-century staircase. On the other hand, don't forget about the local climate when assembling your wardrobe. In mountainous and desert regions, day- and nighttime temperatures can vary by as much as 40 degrees. Also, bear in mind that Easterners tend to dress more formally than Westerners; if you'll be traveling in New England or the South, men should pack a tie and jacket, women a skirt or dress.

Meals

If you have particular dietary restrictions—low-salt, vegetarian, or religious—or allergies—to caffeine, nuts, whatever—be sure to mention these when making reservations and again at check-in. If you're allergic to a common breakfast food or beverage, an evening reminder will ensure that you'll be able to enjoy the breakfast that's been prepared for you. Most innkeepers will do their best to accommodate your special needs, although, as one innkeeper noted tartly, "we're not operating a hospital."

In preparing each listing, we asked the owners to give us the cost of prix fixe and à la carte meals when available. An "alc dinner" price at the end of the "Rates" section is the figure we were given when we requested the average cost, in 1992, of a three-course dinner with a half bottle of house wine, including tax and tip. Prices listed for prix fixe meals do not include wine and service. Lunch prices, where noted, do not include the cost of any alcoholic beverage. Hotels and inns which serve meals to the public are noted with the ✕ symbol.

Dinner and lunch reservations are always a courtesy and are often essential. Most B&B owners will offer to make reservations for you; this can be especially helpful in getting you a table at a popular restaurant in peak season and/or on weekends. Some of the establishments we list operate restaurants fully open to the public. Others serve dinner primarily to their overnight guests, but they also will serve meals to outsiders; reservations are essential at such inns, usually eight or more hours in advance.

Quite a number of restaurants require jackets and ties for men at dinner, even in rather isolated areas. Of course, this is more often the case in traditional New England and the Old South than in the West. Unless you're going only to a very casual country lodge, we recommend that men bring them along and that women have corresponding attire.

Breakfast: Breakfast is served at nearly every inn or hotel listed in this guide. Those that do not, should. No inn is truly "wonderful" if you have to get in your car and drive somewhere for a cup of coffee and a roll, and early-morning strolls should be the choice of the guest, not the host! Nor do we consider the availability of coffee and tea alone an appropriate substitute.

The vast majority of lodgings listed include breakfast in their rates. Whenever possible we describe a typical breakfast, rather than using the largely meaningless terms "continental" or "full" breakfast.

Continental breakfast ranges from coffee and store-bought pastry to a lavish offering of fresh fruit and juices, yogurt and granola, cereals, even cheese and cold meats, homemade muffins and breads, and a choice of decaffeinated or regular coffee, herbal and regular tea. There's almost as much variety in the full breakfasts, which range from the traditional eggs, bacon, and toast, plus juice and coffee, to three-course gourmet extravaganzas.

We've received occasional complaints about the lack of variety in the breakfasts served. No one likes to have pancakes three days in a row, and doctors advise against having eggs every day. Sweet breads and muffins are the only breakfast offering at some establishments, yet many guests prefer a roll or slice of toast. As one reader put it: "Bed and breakfast hosts seem to think that in order for a breakfast to be special, it has to be sweet. They should make plain toast or unsweetened rolls available to guests without the guest having to ask for them. People feel funny about making special requests—they don't want to cause trouble. What about diabetics? What about people like my husband who simply don't care much for sweets? There are plenty of good things for breakfast that don't have to be made with sugar." We agree. Do make your preferences known!

Lunch: Very few of the inns and hotels listed here serve lunch. Those that do generally operate a full-service restaurant, and you'll see some mention of it in the listing. Quite a number of B&B inns are happy to make up picnic lunches for an additional fee. We've noted this where we know about it; if we haven't, just ask if they can make one for you.

Dinner: Meals served at the inns listed here vary widely from simple home-style family cooking to gourmet cuisine. We are looking for food that is a good, honest example of the type of cooking involved. Ingredients should be fresh and homemade as far as is possible; service and presentation should be pleasant and straightforward. We are not interested in elaborate and pretentious restaurants where the descriptions found on the menu far exceed the chef's ability to prepare the dishes.

13

Here's how one of our readers put it, reporting on an inn in Virginia: "The inn had changed owners from our first to our second visit, a few years later. Although the rooms were much improved, the food was not. Dinner was of the type I describe as 'American pretentious,' the sort of ambitious would-be haute (and haughty) cuisine that a regional inn without a fine professional chef and kitchen staff is ill-advised to attempt. The innkeepers would have been much better off keeping the old cooks who were still in the kitchen the first time we visited, preparing the same delicious Southern home cooking they'd been doing for at least 30 years." *(Ann Delugach)*

Drinks

With a very few exceptions (noted under "Restrictions" in each listing), alcoholic beverages may be enjoyed in moderation at all of the inns and hotels listed. Most establishments with a full-service restaurant serving the public as well as overnight guests are licensed to serve beer, wine, and liquor to their customers, although "brown-bagging" or BYOB (bring your own bottle) is occasionally permitted, especially in dry counties. Bed & breakfasts, and inns serving meals primarily to overnight guests, do not typically have liquor licenses, although most will provide guests with setups, i.e., glasses, ice, and mixers, at what is often called a BYO (bring your own) bar.

Overseas visitors will be amazed at the hodgepodge of regulations around the country. Liquor laws are determined in general by each state, but individual counties, or even towns, can prohibit or restrict the sale of alcoholic beverages, even beer.

Smoking

Most of the larger inns and hotels do not have any smoking restrictions, except to prohibit cigars and pipes in dining rooms; restrictions at smaller establishments are becoming quite common. Where prohibitions apply we have noted this under "Restrictions." When smoking is prohibited in the guest rooms, this is usually for safety reasons; when it's not allowed in the common rooms, it's because your hosts don't care for the smell. A growing number of inns prohibit indoor smoking entirely. We suggest that confirmed smokers be courteous or make reservations elsewhere. One reader noted with dismay that although smoking was not specifically prohibited at one inn, no ashtrays were in evidence, making her feel very uncomfortable about lighting up. When making reservations at larger hotels, nonsmokers should be sure to ask if nonsmoking rooms are available. Such rooms, which have been set aside and specially cleaned, have become common.

Physical limitations and wheelchair accessibility

We asked every innkeeper if the hotel or inn was suitable for the disabled, and if yes, what facilities were provided. Unfortunately, the answer was often no. A great many inns dating back 80 years or more have far too many steps and narrow doorways to permit wheelchair access. If you do not need a wheelchair but have difficulty with stairs, we urge you to mention this when making reservations; many inns and small hotels have one or two rooms on the ground floor, but very few have elevators. Similarly, if you are visually handicapped, do share this information so that you may be given a room with good lighting and no unexpected steps.

Where the answer was positive, we have noted under "Extras" the facilities offered. In some cases the response was not nearly as complete as we would have liked. Wheelchair access (via ramp) to inn and hotel restaurants tends to be better than guest room accessibility. City hotels often have street-level entrances and, of course, elevators. Some innkeepers noted that ground-floor guest rooms were wheelchair accessible but did not note whether that applied to the bathrooms, as well. Please do inquire for details when making reservations, and please share your findings with us.

Air-conditioning

Heat is a relative condition, and the perceived need for air-conditioning varies tremendously from one individual to the next. If an inn or hotel has air-conditioning, you'll see this listed under "Rooms." If it's important to you, be sure to ask when making reservations. If air-conditioning is not available, check to see if fans are provided. Remember that top-floor rooms in most inns (usually a converted attic) can be uncomfortably warm even in relatively cool climates.

Transportation

A car is more or less essential for visiting most of the inns and hotels listed here, as well as the surrounding sights of interest. Exceptions are those located in the major cities. In some historic towns, a car is the easiest way to get there, but once you've arrived, you'll want to find a place to park the car and forget about it.

If you are traveling by public transportation, check the "Extras" section at the end of each write-up. If the innkeepers are willing to pick you up from the nearest airport, bus, or train station, you'll see it noted here. This service is usually free or available at modest cost. If it's not listed, the innkeeper will direct you to a commercial facility that can help.

Parking

Although not a concern in most cases, parking is a problem in many cities, beach resorts, and historic towns. If you'll be traveling by car, ask the innkeeper for advice when making reservations. If parking is not on-site, stop at the hotel first to drop off your bags, then go park the car. In big cities, if "free parking" is included in the rates, this usually covers only one arrival and departure. Additional "ins and outs" incur substantial extra charges. Be sure to ask.

If on-site parking is available in areas where parking can be a problem, we've noted it under "Facilities." Since it's so rarely a problem in country inns, we haven't included that information in those listings.

Christmas travel

Many people love to travel to a country inn or hotel at Christmas. Quite a number of places do stay open through the holidays, but the extent to which the occasion is celebrated varies widely indeed. We know of many inns that decorate beautifully, serve a fabulous meal, and organize all kinds of traditional Christmas activities. But we also know of others, especially in ski areas, that do nothing more than throw a few token ornaments on a tree. Be sure to inquire.

Is innkeeping for me?

Many of our readers fantasize about running their own inn; for some the fantasy may soon become a reality. Before taking the big plunge, it's vital to find out as much as you can about this very demanding business. Experienced innkeepers all over the country are offering seminars for those who'd like to get in the business. While these can be very helpful, they tend to be limited by the innkeepers' own experience with only one or two inns. (Some examples are the Chanticleer in Ashland, Oregon; the Wildwood Inn in Ware, Massachusetts; the Wedgwood Inn in New Hope, Pennsylvania; the Lord's Proprietors Inn in Edenton, North Carolina; and the Big Spring Inn in Greeneville, Tennessee; see entries for addresses.) For a broader perspective, we'd suggest you contact Bill Oates (P.O. Box 1162, Brattleboro, VT 05301; 802–254–5931) and find out when and where he'll be offering his next seminar entitled "How to Purchase and Operate a Country Inn." Bill is a highly respected pro in this field and has worked with innkeepers facing a wide range of needs and problems; his newsletter, *Innquest,* is written for prospective innkeepers looking to buy property. Another good source is Pat Hardy and Jo Ann Bell, publishers of *Innkeeping Newsletter,* as well as a number of books for would-be innkeepers. They also offer a biannual workshop in Santa Barbara, California, entitled "So, you think you want to be an innkeeper?" For details contact them at P.O. Box 90710, Santa Barbara, CA 93190; 805–965–0707.

For more information

The best sources of travel information in this country and in Canada are absolutely free; in many cases, you don't even have to supply the cost of a stamp or telephone call. They are the state and provincial tourist offices.

For each state you'll be visiting, request a copy of the official state map, which will show you every little highway and byway and will make exploring much more fun; it will also have concise information on state parks and major attractions.

Ask also for a calendar of events and for information on topics of particular interest, such as fishing or antiquing, vineyards or crafts; many states have published B&B directories, and some are quite informative. If you're going to an area of particular tourist interest, you might also want to ask the state office to give you the name of the regional tourist board for more detailed information. You'll find the addresses and telephone numbers for all the states and provinces covered in this book in Appendix 4, at the back of this book.

You may also want to contact the local chamber of commerce for information on local sights and events of interest or even an area map. You can get the necessary addresses and telephone numbers from the inn or hotel where you'll be staying or from the state tourist office.

If you are one of those people who never travel with less than three guidebooks (which includes us), you will find the AAA and Mobil regional guides to be helpful references. The Mobil guides can be found in any bookstore, while the AAA guides are distributed free on request to members. Both series cover hotels, restaurants, and sightseeing information, although we find the AAA guides offer wider coverage and more details. If you're not already an AAA member, *we'd strongly urge you join before your next trip;* in addition to their road service, they offer quality guidebooks and maps, and an excellent discount program at many hotels (including a number listed here).

We'd also like to tell you about a guidebook that makes a delightful companion to our own. *The Traveler's Guide to American Crafts,* by contributing editor Suzanne Carmichael, is divided into eastern and western editions. Suzanne leads readers to the workshops and galleries of outstanding craftspeople in every state.

Guidebooks are published only once a year (or less frequently); if you'd like to have a more frequent update, we'd suggest the following:

The Discerning Traveler (504 West Mermaid Lane, Philadelphia, PA 19118; 215–247–5578), $50, 8 issues annually, $6 single copy. Picks a single destination in the New England, Mid-Atlantic, or Southern states and covers it in real depth—sights, restaurants, lodging, and more. The authors have published two delightful books on the subject as well.

Uncommon Lodgings (P.O. Box 181329, Dallas, TX 75218; 214–343–9766) $15.95, 11 issues annually, $1.50 single copy. Lots of information on inns all over the country, from a delightfully opinionated editor; an excellent value.

Innsider (821 Wanda, Ferndale, MI 48220; 313–541–6623) $18, 6 issues annually. Country inns, B&Bs, historic lodgings; inn-depth articles & lots of pictures; also recipes, book reviews, misc.

Country Inns/Bed & Breakfasts (P.O. Box 182, South Orange, NJ 07079; 800–435–0715) $15, 6 issues annually. As above. Exceptional photography and paper quality.

Glossary of Architectural and Decorating Terms

We are not architectural experts, and when we started writing *America's Wonderful Little Hotels & Inns,* we didn't know a dentil from a dependency, a tester from a transom. We've learned a bit more since then, and hope that our primer of terms, prepared by associate editor Nancy Barker, will also be helpful to you.

Adam: building style (1780–1840) featuring a classic box design with a dominant front door and fanlight, and accented by an elaborate surround or an entry porch; cornice with decorative moldings incorporating dentil, swag, garland, or stylized geometric design. Three-part Palladian-style windows are common.

antebellum: existing prior to the U.S. Civil War (1861–1865).

Arts and Craft movement: considered the first phase of the Modern movement that led to the Prairie style (1900–20) of Frank Lloyd Wright in Chicago, and the Craftsman style (1905–30) of the Greene brothers in Southern California. In the Arts and Craft style, historical precedent for decoration and design was rejected and ornamentation, while not eliminated, was "modernized" to remove any trace of its historic origins. It features low-pitched roofs, wide eave overhangs, and both symmetrical and asymmetrical front façades.

carpenter Gothic: *see* country, folk Victorian.

chinoiserie: imitation of Chinese decorative motifs; i.e., simulated Oriental lacquer covering pine or maple furniture. See also Chinese Chippendale below.

Chippendale: named for English furniture designer, Thomas Chippendale, of the Queen Anne period (1750–1790); the style varies from the Queen Anne style more in ornamentation than overall form, with more angular shapes and heavier carving of shells, leaves, scrolls. Chinese Chippendale furniture employs chiefly straight lines, bamboo turnings, and as decoration, fluting, and fretwork in a variety of lattice patterns.

Colonial Revival: building style (1880–1955) featuring a classic box design with a dominant front door elaborated with pilasters and either a pediment (Georgian-style) or a fanlight (Adam-style); double-hung windows symmetrically balanced, frequently in adjacent pairs.

corbel: an architectural member that projects from a wall to support a weight and is stepped outward and upward from the vertical surface.

Corinthian: column popular in Greek Revival style for support of porch roofs; the capitals are shaped like inverted bells and decorated with acanthus leaves.

cornice: projecting horizontal carving or molding that crowns a wall or roof.

country, folk Victorian: simple house form (1870–1910) with accents of Victorian (usually Queen Anne or Italianate) design in porch spindlework and cornice details. Also known as carpenter Gothic.

Craftsman: building style (1905–1930) with low-pitched, gabled roof and wide, unenclosed eave overhang; decorative beams or braces added under gables; usually one-story; porches supported by tapered square columns that frequently extend to ground level.

dentil: exterior or interior molding characterized by a series of small rectangular blocks projecting like teeth.

dependencies: buildings that are subordinate to the main dwelling; i.e., a detached garage or barn. *See* also garçonnière.

Doric: column popular in Greek Revival style for support of porch roofs; the simplest of the three styles, with a fluted column, no base, and a square capital.

Eastlake: architectural detail on Victorian houses, commonly referred to as "gingerbread." Typically has lacy spandrels and knob-like beads, in exterior and interior design, patterned after the style of Charles Eastlake, an English furniture designer. Eastlake also promoted Gothic and Jacobean Revival styles with their strong rectangular lines; quality workmanship instead of machine manufacture; and the use of varnished oak, glazed tiles, and unharmonized color.

Eclectic movement: architectural tradition (1880–1940) which emphasized relatively pure copies of Early American, Mediterranean, or Native American homes. This was an opposing tradition to the free stylistic mixtures of the Victorian era.

faux: literally, French for "false." Refers commonly to woodwork painted to look like marble or another stone.

Federal: *See* Adam.

Franklin stove: metal heating stove which is set out into the room to conserve heat and better distribute it. Named after its inventor, the American statesman Benjamin Franklin; some designs resemble a fireplace when their front doors are open. Commonly called a woodstove today.

four-poster bed: variation on a tester bed but one in which the tall corner posts, of equal height, do not support a canopy. Carving of rice sheaves was a popular design in the Southern states, and signified prosperity.

gambrel roof: a two-slope, barn-style roof, with a lower steeper slope and a flatter upper one.

garçonnière: found on antebellum estates; a dependency housing unmarried male guests and family members.

Georgian: building style (1700–1830) featuring a classic box design with a dominant front door elaborated with pilasters and a pediment, usually with a row of small panes of glass beneath the crown or in a transom; cornices with decorative moldings, usually dentil.

Gothic Revival: building style (1840–1880) with a steeply pitched roof, steep gables with decorated vergeboards, and one-story porch supported by flattened Gothic arches. Windows commonly have pointed-arch shape.

Greek Revival: building style (1825–1860) having a gabled or hipped roof of low pitch; cornice line of main and porch roofs emphasized by a wide band of trim; porches supported by prominent columns (usually Doric).

half-tester bed: a bed with a low footboard and a canopy projecting from the posts at the head of the bed. Pronounced "half tee'-stir."

Ionic: column popular in Greek Revival style for support of porch roofs; the caps of the column resemble the rolled ends of a scroll.

Italianate: building style (1840–1885) with two or three stories and a low-pitched roof with widely overhanging eaves supported by decorative brackets; tall, narrow windows arched or curved above with elaborate crowns. Many have a square cupola or tower.

kiva: stuccoed, corner beehive-shaped fireplace common in adobe homes in Southwestern U.S.

Lincrusta (or Lincrusta-Walton): an embossed, linoleum-like wallcovering made with linseed oil, developed in 1877 in England by Frederick Walton.

lintel: horizontal beam, supported at both ends, that spans an opening.

INTRODUCTION

mansard roof: having two slopes on all sides with the lower slope steeper than the upper one.

Mission: building style (1890–1920) with Spanish mission-style parapet; commonly with red tile roof, widely overhanging, open eaves, and smooth stucco finish. In furniture, the Mission style is best represented by the work of designer Gustav Stickley. Using machine manufacture, he utilized simple, rectangular lines and favored quarter-sawn white oak for the rich texture of the graining.

Palladian window: typically a central window with an arched or semicircular head.

Pewabic (tile): glazed tiles made in the Detroit, Michigan, area, in the first half of the 1890s, whose unique manufacturing process has been lost.

Prairie: building style (1900–1920) with low-pitched roof and widely overhanging eaves; two stories with one-story wings or porches; façade detailing that emphasizes horizontal lines; massive, square porch supports.

post and beam: building style based on the Medieval post-and-girder method, where upper loads are supported by heavy corner posts and cross timbers, not the thin internal walls below. In contemporary construction, the posts and beams are often left exposed on the interior.

Queen Anne: building style (1880–1910) with a steeply pitched roof of irregular shapes; an asymmetrical façade with one-story porch; patterned shingles, bay windows, single tower. In furniture design the Queen Anne (more accurately known as Baroque) style was prevalent from 1725 to 1750, characterized by a graceful, unadorned curve of the leg (known as cabriole) and repeated curve of the top crest and vase-form back (splat) of a chair. Sometimes the foot was carved as a claw grasping a ball. Carved shells or leaves were added as a decorative element.

quoin: wood, stone, or brick materials that form the exterior corner of a building and are distinguishable from the background surface because of texture, color, size, material, or projection from it.

rice-carved bed: *See* four-poster bed.

Richardsonian Romanesque: building style (1880–1900) with masonry walls of rough, squared stonework and round-topped arches over windows, porch supports, or entrances; round tower with conical roof common.

Second Empire: building style (1855–1885) with mansard roof adorned with dormer windows on lower slope; molded cornices above and below lower roof, and decorative brackets beneath eaves.

Shaker: style of furniture constructed by the religious commune of Shakers that represents their belief in simplicity. The finely crafted pieces are functional, without ornamentation. Chairs have ladder backs, rush seats, and simple turned legs; tables and cabinets are angular, with smooth surfaces.

Sheraton: named for English furniture designer, Thomas Sheraton, of the Federal period (early 1800s); style marked by straight lines, delicate proportions, wood inlays, and spare use of carving; legs characteristically are tapered with reed carving.

Shingle: building style (1880–1900) with walls and roofing of continuous wood shingles; no decorative detailing at doors, windows, corners, or roof overhang. Irregular, steeply pitched roof line and extensive porches common.

spandrel: decorative trim that fits the top corners of doorways, porches, or gables; usually triangular in shape.

Spanish Colonial: building style (1600–1900) of thick masonry walls (either adobe or rubble stone covered with stucco), with low pitched or flat roof, interior wooden shutters covering small window openings, and multiple doorways. Pitched roof style often has half-cylindrical tiles; flat style has massive horizontal beams embedded in walls to support heavy roof of earth or mortar. Internal courtyards or cantilevered second-story porches are common.

Stick: building style (1860–1890) with a steeply pitched, gabled roof, usually with decorative trusses at apex; shingle or board walls interrupted by patterns of boards (stickwork) raised from the surface for emphasis.

tester bed: a bed with a full canopy (the tester), supported at all four corners by tall posts. Pronounced "tee'-stir."

Territorial: a variation of the Spanish Colonial building style found in New Mexico, western Texas, and Arizona. The flat roof and single story are topped by a protective layer of fired brick to form a decorative crown.

transom: usually refers to a window placed above a doorway.

trompe l'oeil: literally, French for "to trick the eye." Commonly refers to wall paintings that create an optical illusion.

Tudor: building style (1890–1940) with steeply pitched roof, usually cross-gabled; decorative half-timbering; tall, narrow, multi-paned windows; massive chimney crowned with decorative chimney pots.

vergeboard: decorative trim extending from the roof overhang of Tudor, Gothic Revival, or Queen Anne-style houses.

vernacular: style of architecture employing the commonest forms, materials, and decorations of a period or place.

viga(s): exposed (interior) and projecting (exterior) rough-hewn wooden roof beams common in adobe homes in Southwestern U.S.

wainscoting: most commonly, narrow wood paneling found on the lower half of a room's walls.

widow's walk: a railed observation platform built above the roof of a coastal house to permit unobstructed views of the sea. Name derives from the fate of many wives who paced the platform waiting for the return of their husbands from months (or years) at sea. Also called a "captain's walk."

Windsor: style of simple chair, with spindle back, turned legs, and usually a saddle seat. Considered a "country" design, it was popular in 18th and early 19th century towns and rural areas. Often painted to give consistency to the variety of local woods used.

For more information:

A Field Guide to American Houses (Virginia & Lee McAlester, New York: Alfred A. Knopf, 1984; $19.95, paperback) was an invaluable source in preparing this glossary, and is highly recommended. Its 525 pages are lavishly illustrated with photographs and diagrams.

Clues to American Architecture (Marilyn W. Klein and David P. Fogle, Washington, D.C.: Starrhill Press, 1985; $6.95, paperback) is a handy affordable 64-page pocket guide to over 30 architectural styles, from the Colonial period to contemporary construction. Each is clearly described in easy-to-understand language, and illustrated with numerous detailed sketches. Also in the same style and format is *Clues to American Furniture* (Jean Taylor Federico, Washington, D.C.: Starrhill Press, 1988; $6.95), covering design styles from Pilgrim to Chippendale, Eastlake to Art Deco. If your bookstore doesn't stock these titles, contact Starrhill directly (P.O. Box 32342, Washington, D.C. 20007; 202–686–6703).

Regional itineraries

Contributing editor Suzanne Carmichael has prepared these delightful itineraries to lead you from the best-known towns and cities through beautiful countryside, over less-traveled scenic highways to delightful towns and villages, to places where sights both natural and historic outnumber the modern "attractions" which so often litter the contemporary landscape.

To get a rough idea of where each itinerary will lead you, take a look at the appropriate map at the back of this book. But to really see where you'll be heading, pull out a detailed full-size map or road atlas, and use a highlighter to chart your path. (If you're hopeless when it comes to reading maps, ask the AAA to help you plan the trip with one of their Triptiks.) Some of our routes are circular, others are meant to be followed from one end to another; some are fairly short, others cover hundreds of miles. They can be traveled in either direction, or for just a section of the suggested route. You can sample an itinerary for a weekend, a week, or even two, depending on your travel style and the time available. For information on what to see and do along the way, refer to our state and local introductions, and to a good regional guidebook. For a list of places to stay en route, see the list of towns at the end of each itinerary, then refer to the entries in the state chapters for full details.

Ocean Auto Cruise: Cruise back roads cooled by sea-breezes, loll on ocean beaches, and explore both historic southern towns and barrier islands along the south's prettiest stretch of ocean. Begin in gracious Charleston, South Carolina, where pastel houses peek out from behind lacy iron gates and horse-drawn carriages clomp by on cobblestoned streets. Visit revolutionary era and 19th-century homes, stroll the walkways at Charles Towne Landing park, and peruse items for sale at City Market (especially the Gullah Blacks' sweetgrass baskets).

Head south on Route 17 to South Carolina's Low Country and resort islands. Pause first in Beaufort, where Spanish explorers stopped 100 years before the Pilgrims landed at Plymouth Rock. Absorb the town's 18th century atmosphere as you walk past palmetto trees and moss-covered oaks. Before turning south, take Route 21 to Hunting Island State Park, where you can climb to the top of a 140-foot lighthouse for superb island, ocean, and mainland views.

Continue south on Route 170 to Route 17 and the Georgia border, detouring if you wish on Route 278 to Hilton Head Island, the largest sea island between New Jersey and Florida and a popular, though crowded, resort area. Savannah welcomes you to Georgia. A town of public squares (21 of them) with the country's largest urban historic district, Savannah was founded in 1733 as the seat of our 13th colony.

Route 17 now meanders slowly south through sleepy villages, across river channels and towards the area's famous Sea Islands. Turn east from Victorian Brunswick to visit Saint Simons Island, a vacation center with lush resorts and sophisticated shops. Or continue south, then turn east on Route 50 to Jekyll Island where you can "hyde" away on golden beaches or bicycle through stands of stately palms. Another detour, just north of the Florida border, is to take Route 40 to St. Marys where you can ferry to Cumberland Island National Seashore to glimpse wild horses, collect shells, and swim on pristine beaches.

It's time to explore northeastern Florida. To maintain your vacation mentality, leave Route 17 and skirt north of urban Jacksonville by turning east at Yulee on Route 200, to Route A1A which runs south along barrier beaches for 105 miles. Turn north first to Fernandina Beach, famous for its Victorian architecture and infamous as an early 19th-century haven for pirates and smugglers. South on Route A1A is Amelia Island, the only area in the U.S. to have been governed under eight different flags.

Follow Route A1A to St. Augustine, the end of your ocean auto cruise. A center of Spanish influence since 1513, St. Augustine is the oldest U.S. city. Be sure to visit the restored Spanish quarter, as well as Castillo de San Marcos, a rock fortress made from coquina, a local limestone of shells and coral.

Sample southern hospitality at accommodations in these towns (in order of the appearance above): Charleston and Beaufort (South Carolina); Savannah, Saint Simons Island, Jekyll Island and St. Marys (Georgia); Fernandina Beach, Amelia Island, and St. Augustine (Florida). Orange Park, south of Jacksonville, is another northeastern Florida option.

Appalachian Highland Routes: North Carolina's Highland area is known for its beauty: ancient weathered and rounded mountains, gentle pastures, waterfalls and tumbling trout-filled streams, hillsides vivid with wild flowers. Equally enduring are the legacies of the Cherokee Indians and the craft traditions of the area's Appalachian residents. We suggest both a northern and a southern loop route, both starting in Asheville.

Before setting off on either journey, pause in Asheville to visit the impressive Biltmore Estate, with its gardens and winery. Start your northern journey by following I-40 and Route 70 onto the Blue Ridge Parkway, a 470-mile road tracing mountain ridges north to Virginia. Numerous overlooks and attractions dot the parkway. Look particularly for The Folk Art Center (Milepost 382; ½ mile north of Route 70) which offers an excellent introduction to regional crafts, and Craggy Gardens (Milepost 364.6, 17 miles northeast of Asheville) which are spectacular in spring.

Take short detours from the parkway to see the double waterfalls at Linville Falls, and Blowing Rock's unusual rock formation. Leave the parkway at Route 16 to head northwest through Glendale Springs, then turn south on Routes 221 and 194. Wind through small Appalachian hamlets such as Banner Elk, continuing south on Route 19E. Pass through Spruce Pine, then take a short detour north to Penland, home of the famous Penland School of Crafts and its impressive gallery. Return to Route 19E, continuing past Burnsville to Mars Hill. Follow Route 213, then Route 251 back to Asheville (or drop south from Mars Hill on Route 19 for a high-speed return to the city).

Begin your southern loop in Asheville by heading west on Route 19 through the picturesque Great Smoky Mountain foothills and small towns such as Clyde. Detour several miles south to Waynesville for a peek at the Museum of North Carolina Handicrafts, then return to Route 19. Continue to Cherokee, home of the eastern branch of the Cherokee tribe. Just north, on Route 441, visit Oconaluftee Indian Village, a reconstructed 1750 Cherokee town where residents create top-notch crafts (available for purchase at Qualla Arts & Crafts, next door).

From here you may want to detour south on Route 441 along the Tuckasegee River to Dillsboro, and Sylva (note the architecture of the county courthouse). Return to (or continue on) Route 19 through Bryson City, at the southern edge of the Great Smoky Mountains National Park. Just past Lauada, turn north on Route 28 to Robbinsville, on the shore of Lake Santeetlah, near excellent white-water rafting on the Naantahala River. From here follow Route 129 south, turning (south again) on Route 141 to Brasstown, home of the John C. Campbell Folk School, best known for its stable of talented woodcarvers.

Go north from Brasstown to Route 64 and head east. You'll pass through scenic countryside and, just before Highlands, near five waterfalls in the Cullasaja River Gorge. Further along, Cashiers and Lake Toxaway are popular resort areas. Continue north passing through Brevard, known as 'Land of the Waterfalls.' Follow Route 280 which runs alongside the southern boundary of the Pisgah National Forest back to Asheville.

Recommended accommodations in this area can be found in (in order of appearance above) Northern Loop: Asheville, Black Mountain (just east of Asheville), Blowing Rock, Glendale Springs, Banner Elk, Spruce Pine, Burnsville, and Mars Hill; Southern Loop: Asheville, Clyde, Waynesville, Dillsboro, Sylva, Bryson City, Robbinsville, Highlands, Cashiers, Lake Toxaway and Brevard.

Lower Mississippi River Route: Bustling river cities and small, languid towns, Confederate and Acadian-French historical sites, plantation mansions and sugarcane fields all vie for travelers' attention along the lower Mississippi River. Our route takes you from Jackson, Mississippi, to New Orleans through a variety of settings. Plan to spend three to five days on this route, leaving yourself plenty of time to enjoy New Orleans too.

Begin in Jackson, the state's capital, where you can see Confederate trenches in Battlefield Park, and visit Mynelle Gardens botanical park. Head west on Route 20, a superhighway that will whisk you to Vicksburg and your first glimpse of the mighty Mississippi. Known for its Civil War sites, Vicksburg also has several plantation mansions open to the public.

Turn south on Route 27 to the Natchez Trace Parkway, which stretches 500 miles from Natchez to Nashville, Tennessee. Originally a footpath used by rivermen to "trace" their way back north after taking goods down river, today the two-lane road passes green fields, forests, huge rhododendrons, and flocks of wild turkeys. Take the parkway south to Natchez, stopping to see Port Gibson's historic homes. Overnight in Natchez, and tour plantation homes, Natchez-Under-the-Hill, and the Grand Village of the Natchez Indians.

Head south on Route 61, driving past pecan orchards and oak trees dripping with Spanish moss. Make your first Louisiana overnight in St. Francisville to see Rosedown Plantation, then take a short detour up Route 965 to the Audubon State Commemorative Area. Leave St. Francisville via Route 10 south continuing to the river's edge. Board a small car ferry here to cross the Mississippi, then follow Route 10 to Route 415 which winds behind river dikes, through sugarcane fields and rice paddies, and past signs advertising "fried pig tails."

Turn east on Route 190, following it through Baton Rouge, then picking up Route 30 south of the Old State Capitol. Turn south on Route 75 which follows the river's oxbow turns. At Carville head again to river's edge and another car ferry which will take you across the Mississippi to White Castle. From here scenic Route 1 travels along Bayou Lafourche past Napoleonville to Thibodaux in the heart of Louisiana's "sugar belt."

Take Route 24 south to Houma, a historic Cajun city laced by seven bayous and more than 50 bridges. Walk through the local historic district, embark on a boat tour of nearby bayous and swamps, or stroll by the Intercoastal Waterway which begins south of Tallahassee, Florida, and stretches to Brownsville, Texas. Before heading to New Orleans on Route 90, an optional detour (128 miles round-trip) is for those who like to "go to the end of the road." Take Route 1 south as it parallels Bayou Lafourche and ends at Grand Isle State Park on the Gulf of Mexico, near the entrance to Barataria Bay.

Overnight accommodations in this area include ones in the following towns (in order of their appearance above): Jackson, Vicksburg, Natchez (Mississippi); St. Francisville, White Castle, Napoleonville and New Orleans (Louisiana).

Where is my favorite inn?

In reading through this book, you may find that your favorite inn is not listed, or that a well-known inn has been dropped from this edition. Why? Two reasons, basically:

—In several cases very well-known hotels and inns have been dropped from this edition because our readers had unsatisfactory experiences. We do not list places that do not measure up to our standards. Feel free to write us for details.

—Others have been dropped without prejudice, because we've had no reader feedback at all. This may mean that readers visiting these hotels and inns had satisfactory experiences but were not sufficiently impressed to write about them, or that readers were pleased but just assumed that someone else would take the trouble. If the latter applies, please, please, do write and let us know of your experiences. We try to visit as many inns as possible ourselves, but it is impossible to visit every place, every year. Nor is the way we are received a fair indication of the way another guest is treated. This system only works because of you. So please, keep those cards, letters, and telephone calls coming! As an added incentive, we will be sending free copies of the next edition of this book to our most helpful respondents.

Little Inns of Horror

We try awfully hard to list only the most worthy establishments, but sometimes the best-laid plans of mice and travel writers do go astray. Please understand that whenever we receive a complaint about an entry in our guide we feel terrible, and do our best to investigate the situation. Readers occasionally send us complaints about establishments listed in *other* guidebooks; these are quite helpful as warning signals.

The most common complaints we receive—and the least forgivable—are on the issue of dirt. Scummy sinks and bathtubs, cobwebbed windows, littered porches, mildewed carpeting, water-stained ceilings, and grimy linens are all stars of this horror show.

Next in line are problems dealing with maintenance, or rather the lack of it: peeling paint and wallpaper; sagging, soft, lumpy mattresses; radiators that don't get hot and those that could be used for cooking dinner; windows that won't open, windows that won't close, windows with no screens, decayed or inoperable window shades; moldy shower curtains, rusty shower stalls, worn-out towels, fluctuating water temperatures, dripping faucets, and showers that only dribble top the list on our sh-t parade.

Food complaints come next on this disaster lineup: poorly prepared canned or frozen food when fresh is readily available; meals served on paper, plastic, or worst of all, styrofoam; and insensitivity to dietary needs. Some complaints are received about unhelpful, abrasive, or abusive innkeepers, with a few more about uncaring, inept, or invisible staff. Innkeeping complaints are most common in full-service inns when the restaurant business can dominate the owners' time, leaving guest rooms and overnight guests to suffer. More tricky are questions of taste—high Victorian might look elegant to you, funereal to me; my collectibles could be your Salvation Army thriftshop donation. In short, there are more than a few inns and hotels that give new meaning to the phrase "having reservations"; fortunately they're many times outnumbered by the many wonderful places listed in this guide.

Criteria for entries

Unlike some other very well known guidebooks, *we do not collect a membership or listing fee of any kind from the inns and hotels we include.* What matters to us is the feedback we get from you, our readers. This means we are free to write up the negative as well as the positive attributes of each inn listed, and if any given establishment does not measure up, there is no difficulty in dropping it.

Key to Abbreviations and Symbols

For complete information and explanations, please see the Introduction.

¢ Especially good value for overnight accommodation.

♙ Families welcome. Most (but not all) have cribs, baby-sitting, games, play equipment, and reduced rates for children.

✗ Meals served to public; reservations recommended or required.

🕇 Tennis court and swimming pool or lake on the grounds. Golf usually on grounds or nearby.

Rates: Range from least expensive room in low season to most expensive room in peak season.

Room only: No meals included; European Plan (EP).

B&B: Bed and breakfast; includes breakfast, sometimes afternoon/ evening refreshment.

MAP: Modified American Plan; includes breakfast and dinner.

Full board: Three meals daily.

Alc lunch: À la carte lunch; average price of entrée plus nonalcoholic drink, tax, tip.

Alc dinner: Average price of three-course dinner, including half bottle of house wine, tax, tip.

Prix fixe dinner: Three- to five-course set dinner, excluding wine, tax, tip unless otherwise noted.

Extras: Noted if available. Always confirm in advance. Pets are not permitted unless specified; if you are allergic, ask for details; *most innkeepers have pets.*

We Want to Hear from You!

As you know, this book is only effective with your help. We really need to know about your experiences and discoveries. If you stayed at an inn or hotel listed here, we want to know how it was. Did it live up to our description? Exceed it? Was it what you expected? Did you like it? Were you disappointed? Delighted? Have you discovered new establishments that we should add to the next edition?

Tear out one of the report forms at the back of this book (or use your own stationery if you prefer) and write today. *Even if you write only "Fully endorse existing entry" you will have been most helpful.*

Thank You!

Alabama

Grace Hall, Selma

There's much to see and do in Alabama, from Huntsville's Alabama Space and Rocket Center to historic Mobile, and the gorgeous gardens at Bellingrath. To sample Gulf Coast beaches, drive south from Mobile to Dauphin Island, a scenic sliver of land where you can rent boats, swim, and watch huge ships enter Mobile Bay. In northern Alabama visit Russell Cave National Monument, an enormous limestone cave that was used as a seasonal shelter by people beginning in 6500 B.C. Birmingham, a major commercial center, is also known for the unusual "geologic walkway" carved into a mountain at Red Mountain Museum. Curiosity seekers can travel to Scottsboro, in the northeastern corner of the state. The self-proclaimed "Lost Luggage Capital of the World," bargain hunters can sift through racks of unclaimed luggage—from sunglasses to downhill skis at the "Unclaimed Baggage Center."

   Information please: The Dancy-Polk House Inn (901 Railroad Street, N.W., Decatur 35601; 205–353–3579) features two spacious, antique-furnished bedrooms and offers a continental breakfast. Situated 70 miles north of Birmingham, the inn is 20 minutes west of the Rocket and Space Museum in Huntsville. Another possibility is the **Stamps Inn** (100 First Avenue, N.E., Arab 35016; 205–586–7038) in the mountain lakes region of northeast Alabama, 30 miles south of Huntsville. Built in 1936, this inn offers antique decor in its four guest rooms; lunch is served every weekday. In east central Alabama, 40 miles north of Columbus, Georgia is the **Hill-Ware-Dowdell Mansion** (203 Second Avenue SW, Lafayette 36862; 205–864–7861), a Greek Revival antebellum mansion. Its four guest rooms are furnished with period reproductions, and rates include breakfast and evening refreshments.

Rates listed below do not include state sales tax of 7½%, unless otherwise noted.

ANNISTON

Textile mills and blast furnances were built in Anniston after the Civil War to help the region recuperate from the ravages of war. Today it's better known as the home of Fort McClellan; although the fort's Chemical Corps Training Command is off-limits to civilians, those intrigued by peculiar museums can make an appointment to visit the Chemical Corps Museum, tracing the history of chemical warfare (we don't think Saddam Hussein has yet signed the guest book). More appealing is Anniston's Museum of Natural History, best known for its bird collection (but the kids will want to see the Egyptian mummies, of course). Anniston is located in northeastern Alabama, one hour's drive east of Birmingham via I-20, and about two hours west of Atlanta, Georgia.

Noble-McCaa-Butler House
Tel: 205–236–1791
1025 Fairmont, 36201

The Noble House was built in 1886 by Anniston's founding family, and remained in the family until 1989, when it was purchased by Robert and Prudence Johnson. Now restored to its original Victorian appearance, the inn is listed on the National Register of Historic Places. Rates include welcoming beverages and breakfast.

"This charming old-fashioned home is painted dark red with white trim. The grounds are spacious and attractively landscaped. The inn is immaculate—its shiny wooden floors and period antiques are enhanced by light floral prints and clever decorated touches. In one of the upstairs rooms, for example, the bathroom floor was painted green, with lovely flowers painted on the floor and continuing up the wall. The original gas chandelier in the dining room has been converted for electricity." *(Jeanne Smith)*

Open All year.
Rooms 1 suite, 5 doubles—3 with private bath, 3 with a maximum of 6 people sharing bath. All with radio, TV, desk.
Facilities Dining room, parlor, study with piano. Extensive porches. Boating, fishing nearby.
Location 6 blocks from center, at corner of 11th & Fairmont. From I-20, exit at Hwy. 21 (Quintard Blvd.) drive N toward Anniston. At 10th St., go right (E). At 3rd light, go left (N) on Fairmont to inn on right.
Restrictions No smoking. "Well-behaved children only."
Credit cards Amex, CB, DC, MC, Visa.
Rates B&B, $120 suite, $90–100 double. 3-day minimum during races. Corporate rate, $68–92.
Extras Airport/station pickups. Wheelchair access.

The Victoria ¢ 👫 ✗
Tel: 205–236–0503
1604 Quintard Avenue, P.O. Box 2213, 36202

Built in 1888 and listed on National Register of Historic Places, The Victoria wears its name well, with a three-story turret, beautiful stained and etched glass windows, a conservatory, and colonnaded verandas. Restored and expanded in 1985, the inn consists of the original building, housing the Kirby House restaurant and three suites, plus a recently constructed annex which wraps around a courtyard and swimming pool.

"A real winner with well-decorated rooms and an exceptional restaurant. Though bordered by busy streets at front and back, its setting on a hill surrounded by trees and well-kept flower beds seems to insulate it from traffic noise. Our room in the annex was attractively furnished with period reproductions, including a king-size bed with a brass headboard, complemented by white wicker furniture—a chaise longue, glass-topped table and several chairs. We also saw the rooms in the original house, which are handsomely decorated with antiques. We found a newspaper awaiting us outside our door each morning, chocolates on our pillows at night. There were young bellmen dressed in black vests and crisp white shirts at every turn. Everyone we encountered seemed to be there just to please us." *(Jeanne Smith)*

"Our room in the new wing was charming with a bay window, lots of white wicker and pretty prints. It was so spacious and inviting that we elected to have breakfast at the table in our room. Dinner was highlighted by moist and flavorful blackened swordfish. The staff is caring and efficient." *(Ruth & Derek Tilsley)*

Open All year.
Rooms 3 suites in main house, 45 doubles in annex. All with private bath, telephone, TV, air-conditioning.
Facilities Restaurant, bar/lounge, swimming pool, art gallery, valet parking.
Location 60 m E of Birmingham. From I-20, take Oxford/Anniston exit; go 4 m N on Quintard (Hwy. 21/431) to inn. Make a U-turn at 17th St. & enter from Quintard.
Credit cards Amex, MC, Visa.
Rates Room only, $75–140 suite, $54–64 double. Extra person, $10. Children under 12 free.

ASHVILLE

Roses and Lace Inn ¢   *Tel:* 205–594–4366
Highway 231, P.O. Box 852, 35953   205–594–4660

When you see the lace curtains at every window, and the well-chosen use of rose-covered fabrics and wallcoverings scattered throughout this recently opened B&B, a Queen Anne Victorian house built in 1890, it won't take you long to understand its name. Looking at the heart pine woodwork, stained glass windows, crystal chandeliers, Victorian decor, and handmade quilts, you'll have a hard time imagining the hard work of the Sparks family, removing countless layers of black, olive, mustard, and white paint, and adding such modern essentials as central heat and air-conditioning. Shirley and Mark Sparks own and run the inn, but Mark's entire family helped with its restoration and decorating. Now a "painted lady," the exterior combines soft shades of cream and lavender. Shirley notes that guests especially like to relax in the swing and the rockers on the wraparound veranda, sipping a tall glass of ice tea and nibbling home-baked cookies, after a "shop 'till you drop" day at the Boaz outlet center 30 miles north.

"The Sparks made us feel just like family. In fact, Shirley was happily chattering away in the kitchen with my children when my husband and I finally got up. She cheerfully accommodated our picky eater at breakfast, while we feasted on fresh fruit and juice, homemade cinnamon rolls, bacon, and our choice of cheese omelets or French toast. Our rooms were spacious and clean, stocked with everything we needed. Blueberry pie (my husband's favorite) was available for late-night snacking in the kitchen. I remember the sorry state of this house a few years ago; now listed on the National Register of Historic Places, it's hard to believe it's the same place." *(Lynn Edge)*

Open All year.
Rooms 4 doubles—2 with private bath and/or shower, 2 with maximum of 4 people sharing bath. All with air-conditioning, fan. 1 with TV, deck.
Facilities Dining room, parlor with baby grand piano, guest laundry, porch. 11 acres. Tennis nearby.
Location NE AL, 40 m NE of Birmingham. 3½ blks S of Rte. 231 in center of town.
Restrictions No smoking. Traffic noise in front rooms.
Credit cards MC, Visa.
Rates B&B, $55–75 double, $45–65 single. Extra person, $10. No tipping please.
Extras Airport/station pickups.

BIRMINGHAM

Information please: Twenty minutes east of Birmingham is the **Country Sunshine B&B** (Route 2, Box 275, Leeds 35094; 205–699–9841) a ranch-style home with four guest rooms, each decorated in a different motif—country, Oriental, French, and art nouveau. Owner Kay Rice will even board your horses with her own. Reports appreciated.

The Tutwiler Hotel 🛏 ✕   *Tel:* 205–322–2100
Park Place at 21st Street North, 35203   800–866–7666

With the opening of the Tutwiler Hotel, Birmingham can at last boast of a luxury hotel of historic distinction. Built in 1914, the Tutwiler was restored in elegant and luxurious style, with antique reproduction furnishings created especially for the hotel. The restaurant is equally plush, serving classic American cuisine in an environment meant to simulate that of a private club. "Polite and helpful personnel; excellent restaurant." *(BJ Hensley)* "Luxurious, very European, with good food." *(Rita Langel)* "Ideal for those who like small hotels, fine courteous service, and an outstanding in-house restaurant. We stayed here several years ago and were delighted to find the same caring staff and gracious atmosphere on a return visit. Other appealing features include the convenient valet parking, and the location across from a beautiful park and within walking distance of the excellent Birmingham art museum." *(HJB)*

31

Open All year.

Rooms 52 suites, 96 doubles—all with full private bath, telephone, radio, TV, desk, air-conditioning. Extra amenities on Club floor.

Facilities Lobby, restaurant, lounge with weekend evening entertainment, terrace, patio. Free valet parking. Guest passes to health club with Nautilus, swimming pool, tennis, racquetball.

Location Downtown.

Restrictions No smoking in some guest bedrooms.

Credit cards Amex, CB, DC, Discover, MC, Visa.

Rates Room only, $144–169 suite, $133 double, $118 single. Extra adult, $15; children under 18 free in parents' room. Weekend rate. Prix fixe dinner, $27. Alc breakfast, $4–13; alc lunch, $12; alc dinner, $50.

Extras Wheelchair access; 6 rooms specially equipped for disabled. Airport/station pickups. Crib; babysitting by prior arrangement. Member, Historic Hotels of America.

FAIRHOPE

Fairhope makes an ideal base for touring Mobile and the Alabama coast. It's a charming little town, with appealing shops, a lovely park and fishing pier on Mobile Bay, and several enjoyable restaurants. Within an easy drive are the sugar sands of the Gulf beaches, Fort Morgan and the ferry across the bay, and the dozens of factory outlet shops of Riviera Centre. Golf, tennis, and horseback riding are all available through the Grand Hotel (see below).

Fairhope is located on the Eastern Shore of southern Alabama, 15 miles southeast of Mobile. Take I-10 E across Mobile Bay to Route 98 south. Follow 98 south for 8 miles, then turn right at sign for Fairhope/Point Clear, and follow road (Section Street) into Fairhope.

Also recommended: Although at over 300 rooms, really rather big to merit a full entry, we wanted to share the comments of well-traveled contributors about the elegant old **Grand Hotel** (Route 98, Point Clear 36564; 800–544–9933 or 800–228–9290) on the bay in nearby Point Clear, now owned by Marriott. "Grounds are beautiful, with live oaks and magnolias everywhere. Public areas are lovely, with water views, vaulted ceilings, bricks and beams visible, pegged floors." *(SHW) Glen Lush* wrote to say that "our corner room had spectacular sunset and water views. The Boardwalk offers a mile-long walk between the water and beautiful homes; the energetic can rent a bike and take the two-mile path into town. " Also: "Comfortable rooms, remarkable facilities, in a typical big-hotel atmosphere." *(Rita Langel)* "Housekeeping responded to our request for additional pillows and hangers with great efficiency. Service at breakfast was delightful one morning, lackadaisical the next." *(SWS)* Also: "We stayed in one of the new, standard-hotel-style rooms added by Marriott and were disappointed; overall, it was too big, too anonymous for our tastes." *(JMS)*

Reader tips: "Fairhope has a delightful selection of restaurants. We heard good things about Maggie's Bistro and The Wash House, but didn't have a chance to try them. We'd highly recommend the Old Bay Steamer for huge platters of steamed shrimp, crab, crawfish, and oysters at very reasonable prices. For wonderful water views and an inexpensive meal, go to the spanking clean Yardarm, right on the fishing pier. For great buys on casual cotton clothes for women and children, stop at the Aiella Bella outlet, next door to the Mershon Court B&B." *(SWS)*

The Guest House B&B ¢ 👫   *Tel:* 205–928–6226
63 South Church Street, 36532

"Painted dusty rose with white trim, The Guest House is a turn-of-the-century home, listed on the National Register of Historic Places and restored in 1990 by Betty Bostrom. The extensive and expensive restoration covered both aesthetic and structural details; the windows, for example, were replaced, at a cost of $19,000, to improve insulation, while the front door and adjacent side panels now sparkle with handsome stained glass windows originally made for a nearby church. A large side porch has white wicker chairs and tables, making it an inviting spot to enjoy the complimentary wine and cheese served in the early evening. It overlooks a large concrete patio with a fountain; this area is often set up for weddings and parties. At the back corner of the yard is a little cottage, charmingly furnished with a high wooden bed (supplied with steps) and an unusual antique rocker. With one exception, the inn's common areas are furnished with fine antiques—mostly family heirlooms—in superb condition. "Miz Betty" prepares a full breakfast each morning—perhaps fresh melon and berries, waffles and sausage—usually served at one or two of the half-dozen large round tables in the function room between the dining room and the porch. This area is also used for group luncheons on the Mobile area bus tours. The guest rooms are upstairs, and are light and lovely with floral print bedspreads and coordinating wall and window treatments; a closet or armoire is available for clothes storage; some but not all have a bureau as well.

"Betty Bostrum is a warm, friendly, and down-to-earth hostess; innkeeping is a full-time professional job for her and she's invested her considerable energies into making this inn a success." *(SWS)*

Open All year.
Rooms 1 cottage, 4 doubles—all with private bath and/or shower, TV, clock/radio, air-conditioning.
Facilities Dining room, meeting room, parlors, porch, patio, bicycles.
Location 4 blocks from bay, 2 blocks from downtown.
Restrictions Smoking discouraged.
Credit cards MC, Visa.
Rates B&B, $79 cottage, $65 double.
Extras Crib.

Mershon Court B&B Inn ¢   *Tel:* 205–928–7398
203 Fairhope Avenue, 36532

The Mershon house has been a landmark in this small seaside village since the turn-of-the-century when it was home and office for Dr. C.L. Mershon, the area doctor and a community leader. It was restored as a B&B by Susie Glickman, Dolly Parton's long-time personal secretary. In mid-1991, Susie decided to return to Dolly's staff, and has put the inn up for sale; at press time, the inn was being managed by a salaried innkeeper. Susie—a charming and friendly hostess—was still there when we visited, so make careful inquiries when booking. Rates include a breakfast of juice, coffee, and freshly baked blueberry, banana, or raisin bran muffins.

"The inn is built with gray stucco and white trim, surrounded by a lovely yard with a gazebo and swimming pool, and lots of flowers. Susie is a cat lover and in addition to her long-haired Siamese—Valentine, cat motifs are scattered throughout the decor. The common rooms are pleasantly furnished with traditional decor, and are comfortable places to sit and relax. The guest rooms are sunny and airy, with some antique pieces. My favorite is at the front of house, done in blue and white one with an enormous four-poster rice bed and matching armoire." *(SWS)* More reports needed.

Open All year.
Rooms 4 doubles—2 with private bath and/or shower, 2 with a maximum of 4 people sharing bath. All with air-conditioning, fan. 2 with deck.
Facilities Dining room, living room, game room, porch, swimming pool. 2 blocks to Mobile Bay and shopping areas. Swimming, boating, fishing nearby.
Location In center of Fairhope, turn right off Section St. onto Fairhope Ave. 1 block to downtown.
Restrictions No smoking. No children.
Credit cards MC, Visa.
Rates B&B, $55–69 double, $45–59 single. 2-night weekend minimum. Midweek corporate rates.

GREENSBORO

Information please: If you're traveling on I-20/59 between Birmingham and New Orleans, you might enjoy an overnight stop at **Kirkwood** (111 Kirkwood Drive, Eutaw 35462; 205–372–9909) 90 miles southwest of Birmingham, and about 20 miles northwest of Greensboro. Construction of this antebellum plantation house was halted in 1860 by the Civil War. Although continuously occupied, the building was not completed until it was bought and restored by the present owners in 1972. Furnished primarily with original antiques, two guest rooms are available and rent for $75 including breakfast. Reports appreciated.

"Blue Shadows" Guest House ¢ 👫   *Tel:* 205–624–3637
Route 14, RR 2, Box 432, 36744

After traveling the world as a pilot for TWA, Thaddeus May and his wife Janet were inspired to offer the same type of B&B accommodation in Alabama that they had enjoyed abroad. Their fifty-year-old home is shaded by mature trees, and is decorated eclectically with antiques and contemporary furnishings. Their guest house was originally built to accommodate their visiting children and grandchildren, but is now open to B&B guests as well.

Janet notes that "we seem to attract people who want a quiet elegant place to relax, take long walks, fish, or sit on the deck." She also notes that those seeking entertainment may enjoy their tree-climbing Sheltie (neighborhood cats may not find it as amusing!). Breakfast is continental, "unless I feel like doing otherwise," and afternoon tea or sherry is served. Located in the "Black Belt" (a reference to the richness of the region's prairie soil), Greensboro blossomed during the reign of "King Cotton" and the antebellum homes that dot the area are a testimony to the wealth of the early cotton growers. The Mays will gladly help with sightseeing plans; the nearby towns of Eutaw, Demopolis, Selma, and Gainesville should not be overlooked in your search for the antebellum and other historic areas.

"Relaxing atmosphere, with fresh fruit, flowers, and lots of reading material in your room." *(Mrs. Betty Hedberg)* "Rural ambiance; clean spacious rooms; intelligent, witty, gracious hosts; superior breakfast, ample kitchenette." *(Thomas Young)* "Great service; very cozy and warm. Janet and Thad are friendly, interesting hosts. Sara, their delightful dog, led us on the nature trail, but was never obtrusive or bothersome." *(Lance Bond)*

Open All year. Closed Thanksgiving week.
Rooms 1 guest house with private bath, living room, bar, kitchenette; 2 doubles in main house share 1 bath. All with radio, TV, air-conditioning, ceiling fan.
Facilities Breakfast room, living room with piano, library with TV/VCR stereo; sun parlor. 320 acres with nature trail, gardens, pecan and fruit orchard, barn, bird sanctuary, children's play equipment, picnic area. Private lake for fishing, boating. 2 m jogging trail. Golf, tennis privileges at local club.
Location W central AL. 35 m S of Tuscaloosa, 90 m W of Birmingham, Montgomery. 3 m NW of Greensboro, on Rte. 14.
Restrictions No smoking. Children welcome in guest house.
Credit cards None accepted.
Rates B&B, $55 cottage, double, $50 single. Extra person, $5.
Extras Crib, babysitting.

MENTONE

Nippersink Lodge ¢   *Tel:* 205–634–3610
Lookout Mountain, 35984   205–634–4255 (home)

The "Highlands," as northeastern Alabama is called, is composed of the plateaus and ridges of the Appalachian Mountains; Lookout Mountain is one of the two prominent ridges (Sand Mountain being the other) in the southern formation. DeSoto Falls with its 100-foot drop, and the Little River Canyon, with a depth of 600 feet are two popular natural attractions. The damming of the Tennessee, Alabama, Coosa, and Tallapoosa Rivers has given the Highlands an abundance of man-made lakes for water sports.

Heavily wooded and somewhat cooler and less humid than its sea level neighbors, Lookout Mountain has long been a popular spot for summer homes and camps. At an elevation of 2200 feet, The Nippersink Lodge was built in 1934 as a retreat for a Tennessee family, and given its name (a Cherokee word for "little river") due to its riverside location, ¼ mile upstream from DeSoto Falls. Constructed of native stone, cedar, and hickory, the lodge has been accepting paying guests since 1944 when two teachers decided to try their hand at innkeeping. Over the years, the original main lodge was supplemented by the addition of two cottages (one named "Hope" because at the time they hoped they could pay for it!) and their adventure proved successful.

Owned by Geraldine and Ed Disney since 1976, the inn is very much a family-run enterprise, with their two children, Therese and Desmond, and their families all pitching in to help. Geraldine explains that "Nippersink is not for everyone, nor do we want it to be. It's a place where you can relax, take walks, play cards, read, and visit with friends both old and new."

Rates include all meals, served at 8 A.M., noon, and 6:00 P.M. respectively.

"A delightful place off the beaten path, away from the 18-wheelers on the main drag, and yet near most Mentone attractions: the falls, park, ski and golf resort." *(Mary B. Morgan)* "Mentone is a quaint place in a lovely setting; autumn is a lovely time to visit." *(RM)* More comments please.

Open May through Oct.
Rooms 2 4-bedroom cabins, 9 doubles—all with private bath.
Facilities Dining room, living room with fireplace, screened porch,
Location NE AL. 75 m E of Huntsville. From Birmingham, take I-59 to Exit 231. Go S on Hwy 117, 5 m to Mentone. At top of mountain turn right at yellow light to Cty. Rd. 89 (DeSoto Pkwy.). Go 3 m to sign for DeSoto Falls/Nippersink Lodge. Turn left & go 1 m to inn.
Restrictions No smoking. "Not oriented for children."
Credit cards None accepted.
Rates Full board, $75 double, $38 single. 2-night weekend minimum. Midweek rates.

MOBILE

Reader tip: "Although Mobile has some museums and sights of interest, we preferred staying in Fairhope, about 15 miles away across the bay. In contrast to Mobile, we found Fairhope to be clean, safe, and friendly, and just as convenient for touring the area." *(MW)*

Information please: A newly opened B&B in the heart of Mobile's historic district is the **Church Street Inn** (505 Church Street, 03602; 205–438–3107) located on Queen Anne Row, so-named because of the three turn-of-the-century Queen Anne style homes built by a wealthy cotton merchant. One of these is now a B&B, offering four guest rooms, an extended continental breakfast, and afternoon sherry. Reports please.

Malaga Inn ¢ ✕   *Tel:* 205–438–4701
359 Church Street, 36602

The Malaga Inn, listed on the National Register of Historic Places, was originally two separate town houses built by two brothers-in-law in 1862, when the Civil War was going well for the South. When it was converted into a hotel, about 25 years ago, a wing was added to connect the two buildings, enclosing a courtyard.

"The inn has a large reception area, with most of the guest rooms surrounding a central courtyard with a fountain. Our spacious room had two big four-poster beds, a roomy armoire, marble fireplace, ceiling fan, and hardwood floors. We had access to a balcony trimmed with wrought iron. The bath was fairly small, but clean." *(MFD)*

"With 14-foot ceilings, wide-board floors, and a New Orleans-style balcony, our room was grand yet comfortable. Seafood selections in the hotel restaurant were fresh and unusual, and served with care." *(Allison & Bob Young)* "Although they cost slightly more, I'd recommend a room in one of the original townhouses. Their antique flavor is more pronounced; those overlooking the courtyard have a motelish feeling. Our meal was pleasant and inexpensive; the elderly woman who served us made it feel like we were lunching at grandma's house." *(SWS)*

Areas for improvement: "Although a charming place, the inn's slightly frayed gentility will strike some as romantic, others as shabby."

Open All year.
Rooms 3 suites, 37 doubles—all with full private bath, telephone, TV, desk, air-conditioning.
Facilities Restaurant, lounge, garden courtyard with fountain, swimming pool.
Location AL Gulf Coast. Church Street historic district.
Credit cards Amex, DC, Discover, MC, Visa.
Rates Room only, $125 suite, $55–65 double, $48–55 single, plus 10% tax. Extra person, $5. Alc lunch, $5–12; alc dinner, $15–25.
Extras Elevator for wheelchair access. Crib.

PRATTVILLE

Plantation House B&B ¢   *Tel:* 205–361–0442
752 Loder Street, 36067

Prattville is named for Daniel Pratt, inventor of the cotton gin; Pratt Industries buildings, dating from 1850, are still in use producing cotton gins to this day. Built in 1832 and known as the "Hadnot Plantation," it is a clapboard over brick structure, with a portico and four columns typical of the Greek Revival style. John and Bernice Hughes bought the house in 1989, after a devastating fire destroyed the rear of the building, and restored it as a B&B. The result is a happy combination of 19th century southern charm and 20th century comfort; the antique furnishings and nine fireplaces (not all working) are enhanced by central air-conditioning and thermal sound insulation.

"Impeccably kept, richly furnished in period pieces, and beautifully decorated, this B&B is set under huge trees." *(Mr. & Mrs. Joseph C. Abfalter)* "A winding staircase takes you up to the guest rooms, both of which offer lovely views of the grounds. Our room—the Master Bedroom—had a queen-size four-poster bed, hardwood floor, and a huge bathroom with a Jacuzzi. A continental breakfast of homemade muffins, croissants, juice, and coffee is served in a small breakfast area overlooking the grounds and the koi pond where fish swim in lazy circles. Bernice and John are friendly and charming, more than willing to answer questions and be of service. The state capital, Montgomery is an easy drive away, and offers the Alabama Shakespeare Festival, the zoo, and the Civil Rights Memorial." *(Glenn & Delane Goggans)*

Open All year.
Rooms 2 doubles—both with full private bath, telephone, TV, desk, air-conditioning, fan, balcony. 1 with working fireplace, whirlpool tub.
Facilities Library with fireplace, books; two lounges, sun porch. 4 1/2 acres with swimming pool, hot tub. Swimming, boating, fishing nearby.
Location Central AL, Autauga County. 10 m NW of Montgomery. 1 m from downtown. Exit I-65 at Main St. & drive toward town. After passing Hwy. 31, watch for Loder St. Turn right on Loder & watch for inn on right.
Restrictions No smoking in guest rooms. No children under 12.
Credit cards MC, Visa.
Rates B&B, $55–60 double, $50–60 single. 10% senior, AAA discount. Weekly rates. Family rates.

SELMA

Reader tip: "Major Grumbles restaurant a major disaster. Unless there's been a change of chef or management, opt for anything else."

Grace Hall   *Tel:* 205–875–5744
506 Lauderdale Street, P.O. Box 1014, 36701   *Tel:* 205–875–9967

After 1850, Alabama architecture is typified by a mixture of the older Greek Revival neoclassicism with "newer" Victorian trends. Listed on the National Register of Historic Places, Grace Hall exemplifies this eclecticism. Rates in this restored mansion, owned by Coy and Joey Dillon, include refreshments on arrival, a tour of the mansion, and a full breakfast. A recent morning feast featured fresh fruit compote, freshly squeezed orange juice, omelets filled with sautéed vegetables, bacon, homemade croissants, and banana nut bread. Dinners, available by prior arrangement, might include citrus salad with poppyseed dressing, Hungarian pork chops, cheddar tomatoes, and cranberry mold, with Italian cream cake for dessert.

"Beyond a doubt one of the most beautiful restored mansions—public or private—that we have ever seen. Mrs. Dillon is a lovely hostess. She provided a list of historic sites, made our dinner reservations, and told us the history of the house while she showed us through it. Breakfast, served in the smaller of the two dining rooms, was delicious, highlighted by homemade biscuits and gravy." *(Betty Jayne Hensley)* "Even better on a return visit than it was the first time." *(BH)* "Well worth a detour for this well-documented restoration. Rooms lovely. Loquacious hostess." *(John Blewer)*

Open All year.
Rooms 1 suite, 6 doubles—all with full bath and/or shower, telephone, TV, desk, air-conditioning, ceiling fan, fireplace. 3 rooms in annex.
Facilities Dining room, double parlor, library, family room with TV, all with fireplace; porches, patio, English garden with fountain. 1/2 m to water sports.
Location Central AL. 50 m S of Montgomery. 90 min. from Birmingham. 2 blocks from center. Follow signs to Chamber of Commerce; inn is across street.

Restrictions No smoking. No children under 6.
Credit cards MC, Visa.
Rates B&B, $110–135 suite, $65–100 double, $55–95 single. Extra person, $15. Prix fixe lunch $17; dinner, $35. Alc dinner, $55.
Extras Airport/station pickup, $25. Hungarian spoken.

TALLADEGA

The Governor's House ¢   *Tel:* 205–763–2186
Embry Cross Road, Rte. 6, Box 392, 35160   205–763–3336

When people mention a "mobile home," they're usually don't have an 1850 Greek Revival house in mind, but that's just what the Governor's House became for the short trip from downtown Talladega to its present location on Meadowlake Farm, overlooking Logan Martin Lake. Built by Alabama Governor Lewis Parsons, Mary Sue and Ralph Gaines moved the building onto their farm in 1990, restoring it as a B&B and furnishing it with family antiques and quilts. Guests enjoy watching the farm's horses, Hereford cattle, chicken, and pet goats, or trying their luck at fishing in the lake and bass-stocked pond. Rates include a breakfast of juice, fruit, homemade breads, breakfast meat, eggs, and grits. *(MW)*

"A clean, comfortable, and attractive home, with warm, gracious, and accomodating hosts. Best of all is the setting, on a knoll overlooking the lake, surrounded by rolling pastureland. The long front porch is furnished with white wicker and a swing—a serene place to relax." *(Cheryl Stone)*

Open All year.
Rooms 1 guest house, 3 doubles—1 with private shower bath, 2 with maximum of 4 sharing bath. All with radio, desk, air-conditioning, fan.
Facilities Dining room with fireplace, living room with fireplace, TV, books, porch. 7-acre grounds with antique shop; 157-acre farm. Lake adjacent to farm with boat ramp, fishing pier, swimming.
Location E central AL. 35 m E of Birmingham, 15 m W of Anniston, 105 m W of Atlanta, GA. From I-20, take Exit 165, and go S 2 m on Embry Cross Rd. 6 m W of Alabama International Motor Speedway and Hall of Fame.
Restrictions No smoking. No children under 12.
Credit cards None accepted.
Rates B&B, $60–70 double, $55–65 single. Family rates. Prix fixe lunch, $7.50; prix fixe dinner, $15. Inquire for guest house rates.
Extras Airport/station pickups, $25.

Arkansas

The Heartstone Inn, Eureka Springs

Rugged mountain individualism is one of the first things that comes to mind when Arkansas is mentioned. Although the Ozarks are a very old mountain chain and not terribly high, the terrain is rough and transportation was, until quite recently, very difficult. Distinctive crafts, cuisine, and culture developed as a result, much of which has been preserved through the Ozark Folk Center, located in Mountain View (see listing). Many famous springs dot this region of northwestern Arkansas as well, particularly Hot Springs National Park, 55 miles southwest of Little Rock, and Eureka Springs, in the north.

If you want to add sparkle to your Arkansas trip, visit Crater of Diamonds State Park, southeast of Hot Springs—it's America's only public diamond-hunting field. Outdoor enthusiasts generally head to the state's rivers for white-water canoeing or a fight with a largemouth bass, while amateur spelunkers visit what experts call the greatest cave find of the 20th century, Blanchard Springs Caves near MountainView.

Information please: Little Rock, the state capital, is a clean and modern city; we'd appreciate any recommendations for hotels or inns of character here, other than the cloned facilities of the major chains. In fact, we would be pleased to receive more recommendations for this whole state. A possibility in the northeastern corner of Arkansas is the **Washington Street B&B** (1001 South Washington, Siloam Springs 72761; 501–524–5669). Built in 1901, owner Ruby Lawson saved it from the wrecking ball in 1982. Siloam Springs sits on the Arkansas/Oklahoma border, 60 miles southwest of Eureka Springs. Reports please!

Rates do not include 7% state sales tax, or additional local taxes.

ALTUS

St. Mary's Mountain Guest House ¢   *Tel:* 501—468—4141
501 St. Mary's Mountain Road, P.O. Box 100, 72821

"Innkeeper Joy Wilcox is a delight and is mayor of the little town of Altus. We enjoyed sitting on our balcony overlooking the mountains, enjoying the wine of a local vineyard; we selected the bottle from a variety of the complimentary wines and juices chilling in the common room refrigerator. The rooms of this modest hostlery were very clean and simply decorated. Breakfast included coffee, fresh fruit and juice, and delicious hot blueberry coffee cake. The area has great potential, with several wineries open for tours and tastings. The largest—Wiederkehr—has a good German restaurant, where meals are served in an old wine cellar. We took Highway 23 to Eureka Springs, and thought it was much more scenic than the highly touted Highway 7." *(Shirley Dittloff)*

Open All year.
Rooms 3 doubles, each with private bath and/or shower, radio, air-conditioning, fan, balcony, coffee pot. 1 with TV.
Facilities Common room with telephone, TV, library, guest refrigerator, microwave. Hiking, golf, canoeing nearby.
Location E central AR. 100 m NW of Little Rock, 40 m E of Ft. Smith. From I-40, take Exit #41 to Hwy. 186. Go 5 1/2 m S to Altus. Inn is on right, N of town, 1 m past Wiederkehr's Winery.
Restrictions No children under 12.
Credit cards Amex, Discover.
Rates B&B, $39 double, $30 single. Extra person, $8. Discounts for groups reserving all rooms.
Extras Wheelchair accessible.

EUREKA SPRINGS

Eureka Springs is the site of natural springs first discovered by the Indians, then lost for decades until rediscovered in the 1850s by a local doctor. The curative powers of the spring waters soon became renowned, and by the 1880s this hillside town boasted dozens of hotels. As the decades passed and medicine advanced, the town was forgotten and its Victorian charms thus preserved. The local Historic District Commission now stands guard to make sure that nothing is changed without its approval.

Local attractions include dozens of art galleries and mountain craft shops, the steam train ride through the Ozarks, the Passion Play, and the Pine Mountain Jamboree. Beaver Lake and the Buffalo and White rivers are nearby for swimming, boating, fishing, and canoeing.

Eureka Springs is located in northwest Arkansas, 50 miles northeast of Fayetteville, 200 miles northwest of Little Rock, and 100 miles south of Springfield, Missouri. It is best reached via Highways 62 or 23.

Information please: The **Old Homestead**, once a boarding house, even perhaps a bordello, is a century-old stone house across from the

41

historical museum, restored as a four-guest-room B&B (82 Armstrong, 72632; 501—253—7501). The **Piedmont House** (165 Spring Street, 72632; 501—253—9258) was built as an inn in 1880. The eight guest rooms combine antique decor with such modern amenities as private baths and air-conditioning; the inn offers off-street parking and a location within walking distance of the downtown historic area. A convenient spot if you're traveling with children is the **Elmwood House**, built in 1886 (110 Spring Street, 72632; 501—253—7227). Located in the downtown historic district, its four suites are each equipped with kitchens.

Another possibility is the **Crescent Cottage Inn** (211 Spring Street, 72632, 501—253—6022), a distinctive pink Victorian home built by the first governor of Arkansas. Restored in 1977, this B&B contains four antique furnished bedrooms overlooking the surrounding countryside. Listed in earlier editions, we need more feedback before reinstating it as a full entry.

If you're looking for a more private setting, we'd love to know what you think of **Bonnybrooke Farm Atop Misty Mountain** (Rte. 2, Box 335A, 72632; 501—253—6903), four miles from town. Three luxurious cottages are set on a 20-acre farm, amid huge oaks and rock gardens; each is equipped with a firepalce and double Jacuzzi, equipped kitchen, TV/VCR, radio and tape player, queen-size bed, and antiques. Even more isolated is the **Mountain Pines Cabin** (P.O. Box 1355, Harrison 72602; 501—420—3575), a three-bedroom log home, built in 1855 and set high atop Gaither Mountain, overlooking the Buffalo National River. It's just about an hour's drive east of Eureka Springs, not far from where scenic Route 7 joins Route 62. Owners Mike and Karen Nabors can advise you on the best spots for hiking and berry-picking, and provide guests with a continental breakfast highlighted by seasonal fruits, flowers, and vegetables.

Dairy Hollow House ♦ ✕
515 Spring Street, 72632

Tel: 501—253—7444
800—562—8650

When the doors of Dairy Hollow House opened in 1981, it was one of the first bed & breakfast inns in the state. Since then innkeepers Crescent Dragonwagon (she adopted the name after moving to Arkansas at age 18) and her husband, Ned Shank, have developed a nationwide reputation for their "Nouveau Zarks" cuisine, combining classic French and Oriental techniques with the Ozarks' best regional ingredients. Given the number of both B&Bs and restored buildings now thriving in Eureka Springs, it's clear to see that Ned (a former president of the Eureka Springs Preservation Society) and Crescent have successfully demonstrated that tourism and historic preservation can be allies, not enemies. After years of innkeeping, it's delightful when Ned and Crescent say: "We love innkeeping and the town of Eureka Springs and each other. This make us enthusiastic, and it is this that touches our dear guests, who are—as we like to say—'travelers, not tourists.' "

The Dairy Hollow House now encompasses the Farmhouse in the Hollow, a fully renovated 1880s farmhouse highlighted with in-room fireplaces, handmade quilts and period antiques; The Main House, housing three suites with fireplaces; Constance Cottage, one house down on

Spring Street; and the Restaurant at Dairy Hollow, on the garden level of the Main House. The central reception area is here also, next to the restaurant.

In addition to her inn-keeping abilities, Crescent Dragonwagon is a children's book and cookbook author. Meals here are a highlight, and breakfast specialties (delivered to your room) include fresh fruit or juice, German baked pancakes with fresh berry sauce, or perhaps shirred eggs Mornay and chicken-apple sausages, accompanied by homemade jams and jellies, gingerbread muffins, or blueberry coffee cake. Dinner is a six-course repast; fresh fruits, vegetables (either wild or cultivated), game and fish are used whenever possible, and a typical menu might include smoked trout mousse; bean soup with Arkansalsa and crème fraiche; buttermilk skillet cornbread; five-lettuce salad; venison with cranberry Cumberland sauce; chocolate bread pudding with raspberry sauce and whipped cream.

Ken & Jo Pottinger wrote to endorse the accuracy of our current write-up on the DHH: "If we were serious about world peace, we'd take up a collection to send the head of nations, a few at a time, to the DHH. It's impossible to stay tense there. Exquisite food; unobtrusive and attentive staff, graceful surroundings, and fine quiet touches of comfort and convenience make it an extraordinary experience. Crescent and Ned are splendid innkeepers; we suggested a few minor improvements—a hook for robes in the bath, a tray for taking drinks to the porch or deck, and both are now in place."

Open Inn open all year. Restaurant closed Jan.; open weekends only Feb. 1–March 15.
Rooms 5 suites, 3 doubles—all with private bath and/or shower, air-conditioning, fireplace, kitchenette, coffee maker. 4 rooms with desk. 2 rooms with Jacuzzi, TV. 1 with deck.
Facilities Parlor with games, library; dining room; lobby. Suites have private living rooms. Music entertainment holidays/festivals. 3 acres with flower gardens, woods, hot tub, children's games. 15 min to river for water sports, fishing.
Location 1 m from town.
Restrictions Light sleepers should request Farmhouse rooms. Smoking restricted.
Credit cards Amex, CB, DC, Discover, MC, Visa.
Rates B&B, $125–155 suite, $105–125 double, $100–120 single, plus optional $2–5 daily for service. Extra person, $15. 2-3 night minimum weekends/holidays. Off-season discount for longer stays. Mystery weekend packages. Prix fixe dinner, $39, plus 15% service.
Extras Restaurant is wheelchair accessible. Airport pickup by prior arrangement, $40. Crib, babysitting available.

Five Ojo Inn ¢   *Tel: 501–253–6734*
5 Ojo Street, 72632

Built in the 1890s, this comfortable Victorian home was bought by Paula Kirby Adkins a century later. After a typical 9 A.M. breakfast of eggs Benedict, sausages, potatoes O'Brien, sweet rolls, cheesecake, juice and juice, guests can relax on the front porch before taking the short trolley ride downtown.

"Despite our late arrival we were met with a warm hug and a big smile.

A warm, cozy room and a thoughtful basket of snacks put us in the perfect state of mind for a most romantic weekend." *(Eldon Arnold)* "Our room combined quaint period furnishings with the luxury of a fireplace and Jacuzzi. A wonderful breakfast and the warmth of our hostess rounded out a perfect trip." *(Lorna & Mike Weible)*

"My little cottage was very well-equipped, with a little kitchen nook, shower, built-in closet, and a comfortable bed; it was an ideal balance of rustic and modern features. Of course, the real gem here is the innkeeper, Paula, who made me feel very much at home." *(Rainier Valdellon)* "We relaxed in our comfortable cabin and woke to coffee and a lovely view; in the evening we unwound in the Jacuzzi and enjoyed a peaceful chat by the fire." *(Denise & Pat Bembenek)*

Open All year.
Rooms 2 cottages, 6 suites, 1 double—all with private bath and/or shower, radio, TV, air-conditioning, fan, refrigerator, coffee-maker. 3 suites with double whirlpool tub. Cottages with deck.
Facilities Breakfast room. 1½ acres with gardens, hot tub, picnic area. Golf nearby. Near lakes, rivers for swimming, boating, fishing.
Location Historic District.
Restrictions No smoking. No children under 14.
Credit cards Discover, MC, Visa.
Rates B&B, $59–105 cottage or suite, $59–95 double, $55–90 single. Extra person, $20. No tipping. 2-3 night weekend/holiday minimum.

Heart of the Hills Inn ¢
5 Summit Street, 72632

Tel: 501–253–7468

Built in 1883, Heart of the Hills was bought by Jan Jacobs Weber in 1986. She has restored its original woodwork, furnishing her B&B with period antiques, including many family heirlooms. In addition to a full breakfast of fruit, a hot entrée, and breakfast meat (served on the deck and porch in good weather), rates include homemade chocolates, fresh flowers, and an evening dessert. "We stayed in the Hearts & Flowers Cottage, a detached, restored carriage house. Our room had a queen-size brass bed, and every conceivable amenity, including an extra bed for a child. Dessert is served each night and the breakfasts are full and wonderful. Jan is a native of the area, and couldn't have been more charming or helpful." *(James Johnson)* "All of the antiques in the inn have sentimental value to Jan. She can tell you whose they were and where they came from; for example, her grandfather's wire rimmed glasses sit atop a book in the cottage. We loved sitting on the front porch swing, stargazing and chatting. The trolley stops right at the front door, taking you downtown in a moment."*(Cheryl LeBlanc)* "Excellent food and service. The inn is in a lovely neighborhood and we enjoyed walking around to see the other old homes." *(Janet Fisher)*

Open All year.
Rooms 1 cottage, 1 suite, 2 doubles—all with full private bath, TV, air-conditioning, fan, refrigerator, coffee maker. Cottage with CD player, deck, microwave.

Facilities Breakfast room, living room, porch with swing. Near White River for fishing, swimming.
Location 4 blocks to downtown. From Hwy. 62 W, turn right at high school onto Kingshighway to inn on left.
Restrictions No smoking. Children welcome under 1 or over 7.
Credit cards MC, Visa.
Rates B&B, $60–80 cottage/suite, $55–65 double, 50–60 single. Extra person, $10. Weekly rates. 2 night weekend/holiday minimum.
Extras Airport pickup. Crib.

The Heartstone Inn and Cottages ¢ ♦♦   Tel: 501–253–8916
35 Kingshighway (Highway 62B), 72632

Innkeepers Iris and Bill Simantel have owned this Victorian B&B inn since 1985. The rooms are decorated with antique and reproduction furniture and decorative country touches—including plenty of hearts. We've heard from many Heartstone guests, all unanimous on the warmth of their hosts, the immaculate facilities, the high-quality service, the delicious breakfasts, and the convenient location. Many noted that the Heartstone was their first B&B experience, but certainly not their last.

"Iris and Bill welcomed us as long-lost friends. They did more than we ever expected—providing candid restaurant suggestions, giving us directions to save time, and supplying us with blankets (unasked for) to stay warm and dry at an outside event we attended. Iris gave us a tour of the five bedrooms in the main house, the three newer and larger rooms in the ranch-style annex (attached by wood-planked decking), the nearby guest cottage, and the small Victorian home at the edge of their property. Our room was furnished with period antiques, hand-crocheted doilies, 'Auntie Lou' what-knots, and luscious rose bath towels.

"In the morning, guests gather for coffee or tea on the deck overlooking the wooded hollow behind the house. Promptly at nine, Bill invites all to breakfast. Delicate china place cards indicate our room numbers, signaling a thoughtful seating arrangement where table companions are sure to have something in common. Each morning we feasted on fresh fruit, sausage or bacon, fresh home-baked bread (different each morning), and a hot entrée—from egg souffle with raspberry sauce, to German apple pancakes, to strawberry blintzes. As soon as all have been served, Iris emerged from the kitchen to share some of her culinary secrets with us. Guests go their different ways during the day, but most gravitate back to the shaded deck in the afternoon for iced tea or lemonade." *(Linda Logsdon, and others)*

"The exterior of the inn is inviting and colorful. Hanging pots of Boston ferns sway lazily above the long front porch, and huge crocks spill over with salmon-colored geraniums. Our room, the Bridal Suite, was decorated with an old lace wedding dress and dried bridal bouquet; a queen-size bed was covered with a red, white, and blue quilt in the double wedding-band pattern. I enjoyed a peek into the other guest rooms, which included a pink one with white wicker furniture, another in soothing shades of peach and pale blue, and still another decorated in a patriotic theme with lots of country crafts and a white iron bed." *(Mr. & Mrs. J.D. Rolfe)* "The inn is very quiet with lots of birds singing and no traffic sounds; the parking is reserved with excellent lighting for security. Our room was spotless, and the bath had plenty of hot water." *(Carol Hawksley)* "The capable staff, Danny and Susan, were friendly and genuinely interested in making our stay a pleasant one." *(Catherine & Fred Schnaffner, also SD)* "Our two girls, ages 4 and 6, were treated with a special breakfast and lots of conversation with Bill and Iris." *(Diana Morin)*

Open Feb. 1–late Dec.
Rooms 1 2-bedroom cottage, 1 1-bedroom cottage, 1 suite, 9 doubles, all with full private bath, TV, radio, air-conditioning, ceiling fans. 4 rooms in annex.
Facilities Dining/breakfast rooms, guest lounge with piano, stereo, games, veranda, deck; massage therapy. Off-street parking. Live music during May, Sept. festivals.
Location Historic district, 4 blocks to downtown. City bus stop near house.
Restrictions No smoking. Children welcome in annex rooms.
Credit cards Amex, MC, Visa.
Rates B&B, $68–92 cottage, $67–77 suite, $55–67 double. Extra person, $15. Reduced charge for children under 5. 2-3 night weekend/holiday minimum. Tipping appreciated.
Extras Crib available.

Singleton House ¢   *Tel:* 501–253–9111
11 Singleton, 72632

Barbara Gavron, who has owned the century-old Singleton House since 1984, describes her light and airy guest rooms as being "whimsically decorated with an eclectic collection of antiques, folk art, and unexpected treasures." Breakfasts differ each day; in addition to fresh fruit and juice, they might include buttermilk waffles and home-baked muffins, or quiche with toasted herb bread.

"Homey, simple, clean, with an old-fashioned Victorian charm. The highlight for me is the Victorian garden. Although small it has all the required ingredients—rock paths lined with wild flowers and perennials, arches with morning glories, a weeping willow over the goldfish pond, and a wonderful collection of 50 bird houses. I love to have breakfast on the balcony overlooking the bird-filled garden. From the garden there is a shaded path down the hill to shops and cafés." *(Diane Minden)* "Barbara is friendly and helpful. She makes you feel like you're returning to Grandma's house as one of the family. A delightful and unpretentious B&B." *(Kathryn Bechen)* "Though small, my room was bright and comfortable; the entire house is extremely clean. Ms. Gavron is warm, witty, professional and entertaining." *(Patsy Maxwell)*

Open All year.
Rooms 1 cottage, 1 suite, 3 doubles—4 with private bath and/or shower, 1 with shared bath. All with air-conditioning, some with radio, TV, desk, fan, balcony. 1 with kitchenette.
Facilities Breakfast room, living room with TV, nature library, guest kitchen, porch. Garden with fishpond, picnic area, limited off-street parking.
Location Historic district, off Rte. 62B; Singleton is between Pine and Howell. 1 block to shops.
Restrictions No smoking.
Credit cards Amex, Discover, MC, Visa.

Rates B&B, $65–75 suite, $55–65 double. Discount for 4-night stay. 3-night minimum holiday/festival weekends. 2-night minimum in cottage year-round.

HEBER SPRINGS

Oak Tree Inn ¢ ♦♦   *Tel:* 501–362–7731
Vinegar Hill and Highway 110 West, 72543

Owner Freddie Lou Lodge reports that although the inn's design is a New England-type colonial, all materials used in its 1983 construction are from Arkansas. Rooms are decorated with antiques and traditional furnishings. The inn is an adults-only retreat, but Mrs. Lodge now offers family-style accommodation in four lakeside condominiums and four river cabins.

"Gracious hostess, lovely and interesting guests, and a comfortable, homelike atmosphere. Desserts and coffee are enjoyed in the evening around the fireplace, and guests are always treated to outstanding break-fasts." *(Mrs. David Garrett)* "Each room is named after someone important in the history of Heber Springs, and each is charming in its own right. All were immaculate. Ours was named after a local doctor, and had a lovely bathroom, wonderful queen-size bed, fireplace, a beautiful Oriental rug, a ceiling fan, wood shutters, sofa, and every possible convenience one could want." *(Phyllis Berlin, also Mr. & Mrs. Oscar Strid)*

"We were impressed with the inn's solid construction and detailing. The decor is relaxed elegance—fine antiques without the stuffy, 'don't touch' look." *(Dr. & Mrs. Lloyd Langston, also Mary Pruitt)* "Breakfasting on the patio was a delight." *(Mary Ann Allison)*

Open All year.
Rooms 4 1- & 2-bedroom condos, 4 cottages with bedroom and sleeping loft—all with kitchen, fireplace; condos with TV. 6 doubles in inn with private whirlpool baths, fan; 3 with desk, 5 with fireplace.
Facilities Common room. 1 acre with garden; swimming pool, 2 tennis courts adjacent. Swimming, boating, fishing in Greers Ferry Lake 1 block away. Tennis, hiking, trout fishing nearby. Canoe for guest use.
Location Ozarks, 60 m N of Little Rock. From Little Rock, take Rte. 67 NE to Hwy. 5, then N to Rte. 25 to Heber Springs. Inn is about 1 m W of Heber Springs on Rte. 110.
Restrictions Smoking and children permitted in condos/cottages.
Credit cards None accepted.
Rates Room only, $130 condo, $100 cottage. Inn, B&B $65–75 double; single rate on request. Extra person, $10. 2-night minimum in condos/cottages. Weekly rates.
Extras Airport pickups.

HELENA

Edwardian Inn ¢ ♦♦   *Tel:* 501–338–9155
317 South Biscoe, 72342

In 1904 cotton broker William A. Short built his family their dream house at the then-extraordinary cost of over $100,000. The Shorts were not the only prosperous family in town; Helena is known for its historic houses, both antebellum and postbellum. Most of the building's original beauty, such as the fine hardware and the beveled and leaded glass in the transoms, was uncovered in the restoration, along with the handsome oak paneling and the intricate woodwork.

"Upon arrival we were greeted graciously by owner Cathy Cunningham and innkeeper Geri Steed, and were quickly made to feel at home." *(Mr. & Mrs. E.L. Bartolotti)* "Our room was furnished with period pieces and appointed with modern conveniences. The air conditioner was both effective and quiet; the bath was modern and in excellent condition. The restoration retained all of the original features, including the woodwork in the entrance hall and the inlaid wood 'carpets.' " *(Ronald C. Eastes)*

"All the rooms are beautiful, but ours had a bed with a headboard made from a church pew, an enormous bath, a glassed-in sitting area with a window seat, and access to the balcony porch. The delicious continental breakfast included homemade cinnamon rolls and carrot cake." *(Sally Garrison)* "Especially enjoyable is the sunny kitchen/dining room, complete with linen tablecloths and napkins, and fresh flowers." *(Margaret Holaway)*

"Just as you've described it. Try dinner at Evelyn's Southern Charm (922 Miller Street). Evelyn is a warm, friendly hostess—we'd give it an 'A'." *(Yvonne Miller, also LW)*

Open All year.
Rooms 3 suites, 9 doubles, all with full private bath, telephone, radio, TV, air-conditioning, fan. Some with desk, fireplace.
Facilities Breakfast/sunroom. 5 m to lake for fishing, swimming.
Location SE AR, on Mississippi River, 70 m S of Memphis, TN.
Credit cards Amex, MC, Visa.
Rates B&B, $59 suite, $50 double, $44–50 single. Extra person in room, $10. Children under 12 free in parents' room. 10% senior discount.
Extras Wheelchair accessible. Small pets permitted. Crib, babysitting available.

HOT SPRINGS

A visit to Hot Springs will allow you to take your place in a long line of tradition; records indicate that the Indians used this site 10,000 years ago. The springs reached their height of popularity in the 19th century, and the area became a national park in 1921. Although not as popular as they once were, the bath houses are still well worth a visit; the naturally hot water will soothe your aching muscles after a day of hiking or horseback riding in the surrounding Zig Zag Mountains. Several lakes—Catherine, Hamilton, and Ouachita—are nearby for all water sports.

Hot Springs is located in central Arkansas, 55 miles southwest of Little Rock.

Information please: We need recent feedback to reinstate the reasonably priced **Stillmeadow Farm** (111 Stillmeadow Lane, 71913; 501–525–9994) for a full entry. A reproduction 1740 New England-style saltbox, this post-and-beam home was built to be a bed & breakfast inn, and is decorated entirely in antiques. Breakfast consists of juice, fresh fruit, home-baked muffins, homemade jams and jellies, and coffee. The 70 acres surrounding the house provide a quiet setting, ten miles from town.

We're also curious about a 5,000-square-foot Victorian mansion called **Dogwood Manor** (906 Malvern Avenue, 71901; 501–624–0896). Built in 1884, and restored 100 years later, the original woodwork and leaded glass windows are complemented by antiques. Rates for the five guest rooms range from $50–75, and include a continental breakfast. Reports welcome.

Vintage Comfort B&B Inn ¢   Tel: 501–623–3258
303 Quapaw Street, 71901

The Vintage Comfort Inn is a handsome Queen Anne Victorian maintained by the same family through three generations. Current owner and innkeeper, Helen Bartlett, restored the home in 1988 with a blend of old world style and modern practicality. After a breakfast of orange juice, eggs baked with mushrooms, bacon, cheese, and herbs, and orange pecan muffins with homemade apple butter, guests can relax on the veranda or stroll past Bath House Row and on into Hot Springs National Park.

"Helen is the best part of Vintage Comfort. Her warmth and caring demeanor become apparent immediately, and they carry over to the house itself. Rooms are large and airy, painted with muted, soothing colors. The entire place feels fresh and comfortable. Charm sits in every corner. Nutritious and delicious breakfasts arrive beautifully served." *(Sharon Morgan)* Additional comments welcome.

Open All year.
Rooms 1 suite, 3 doubles—all with private tub or shower, air-conditioning, fan. 2 with desk.
Facilities Living room, sitting room with TV and library, dining room, veranda. Off-street parking.
Location 3 blocks from center. From Central Ave. turn onto Market St. then left onto Quapaw St. Within walking distance of National Park hiking trails.
Restrictions No smoking. No children under 6.
Credit cards MC, Visa.
Rates B&B, $65 suite, $55–65 double, $45 single. Extra person, $10. 10% senior discount. 2-night weekend minimum Feb.–April.
Extras Station pickups free. Airport pickups $15. Hot Springs shuttle.

Williams House ¢   Tel: 501–624–4275
420 Quapaw, Hot Springs National Park, 71901

Listed on the National Register of Historic Places, this imposing 1890 brownstone-and-brick Victorian has been owned since 1980 by Mary and Gary Riley. Rooms are decorated with family antiques and lots of plants. Mary notes that "attention to detail and comfort are important to us, as is guest privacy." Rates include full breakfast; traditionalists will be relieved to know that eggs with ham, bacon, or sausage are always available; more adventurous palates will want to try the daily special, ranging from eggs Benedict to pecan waffles. *(BR)*

"Mary and Gary Riley are wonderful hosts. The house is filled with antiques the Rileys have gathered, and the food was excellent." *(Heather Fletcher)* "One of the highlights of a visit here is in the evening, when Mary tells us what the next day's breakfast special will be, and we choose our menu." *(Norman Garneau)* "Despite a late arrival, Mrs. Riley directed me to an excellent restaurant nearby. The Rileys have just the right touch, enough attention to be accommodating but not annoying." *(Gary Milam, also Lillie Galvin)*

Open All year.
Rooms 2 suites, 4 doubles—4 with private bath and/or shower, 2 with maximum of 4 people sharing bath. All with radio, most with air-conditioning. 2 rooms in carriage house.
Facilities Dining room, living room with fireplace, baby grand piano; family room with games, TV; porches. 1/2 acre with patios, picnic table. Indoor heated pool at YMCA next door. Walking distance to Bath House Row. Several lakes nearby for fishing, swimming, boating.
Location 4 blocks from center, at corner of Orange and Quapaw. From Bath House Row, go S on Central Ave., right on Prospect, left on Orange.
Restrictions Traffic noise might disturb light sleepers. No smoking in common rooms. No children under 7.
Credit cards Amex, MC, Visa.
Rates B&B, $70–85 suite, $55–85 double, $45–80 single. Extra person, $10. 2-night weekend minimum March, April.
Extras Pets permitted by prior arrangement.

LANGLEY

Country School Inn ¢ 👫   *Tel:* 501–356–3091
Highway 84 & 369, P.O. Box 6, 71952

Eddy and Charlotte Jo Ayers say that people come to their inn "to enjoy the simple things in life. The inn is very comfortable, not elegant. A place to let your hair down." Built as a schoolhouse in 1945, the Ayers turned the classrooms into guest rooms in 1986, the former auditorium into the lounge and dining area, and the stage into the kitchen; all are decorated with antique furniture, quilts, tools, plants, and memorabilia. Nearby is the Albert Pike Recreation Area in the Ouachita Mountains, ideal for fishing and hiking.

"The dining area has tables set with Depression glass and old china. The Ayers are more than hospitable; visiting with them around the wood-burning stove was like coming home again." *(Johnna McClain)* "Breakfasts are good, service excellent, and the Ayers' three-legged dog, Jack, is everyone's friend." *(Nora & Mel Lands)*

"Charlotte is everywhere at once, yet also knows when to make herself scarce." *(Elizabeth Holt)* "Rooms are clean, comfortable, and stocked with extra amenities such as current magazines, and mints." *(Ann Clayton)* "A treat was spotting bald eagles from the inn's grounds, and fishing for rainbow trout in the river." *(Mary Tollson)* "The vintage 1950s gymnasium next door is ideal for a therapeutic game of basketball" *(Gail & Gary Bryant)* More comments welcome.

Open Feb. through Dec.
Rooms 2 suites, 2 doubles (some sleeping 8), 1 "dorm" room, 1 single—all with private bath and/or shower, desk, air-conditioning, fan.
Facilities Dining/living room with fireplace, piano, stereo, TV/VCR, games. Gym next door for basketball, volleyball; 3 acres with playground for badminton, horseshoes, swings, barbecue grill, picnic table. Hiking, fishing, water sports at nearby state park, lakes, rivers. Ample parking for trailered boats.
Location Pike County, bordering Ouachita National Forest. 50 m from Hot Springs. From Hot Springs, take Hwy. 70 to Salem, then follow Hwy. 84 to Langley. Inn at intersection of Hwy. 84 and Hwy. 369.
Restrictions No smoking.
Credit cards MC, Visa.
Rates B&B, $45–50 suite, $37–40 double, $32–37 single. Extra person, $6. Discount for children, groups.
Extras Ramp for wheelchair access. Pets welcome with prior approval. Crib.

MORRILTON

Tanyard Springs Resort 🏃 ✕   *Tel:* 501–727–5200
Rte. 3, Box 335, 72110   800–533–1450

Named for the tanning yards that once occupied this site, this cluster of hand-crafted log cabins was built by Jim and Jane Fruge starting in 1983. Rustically handsome yet equipped with every modern convenience, each cabin has a totally different decor and theme—two even have a wagon and a stagecoach converted into beds. The resort is set in the woods atop Petit Jean Mountain close to the many outdoor pleasures of Petit Jean State Park. Also on the premises is Adrienne's Restaurant, serving such continental dishes as chicken Marsala and poached salmon, as well as trout baked in Creole pecan sauce, a favorite of the Fruges' native Louisiana. Although an ample wine list is available, guests will want to sample plenty of water from the resort's historic spring. This water was once bottled and sold widely, both for its pure taste and exceptionally low mineral content. *(FC)* Additional reports needed.

Open All year.
Rooms 13 1- to 2-bedroom cabins—all with private bath and/or shower, radio, desk, air-conditioning, ceiling fan, kitchen, barbecue grill, patio or porch. Some with sleeping loft.
Facilities Restaurant, bar/lounge. 180 acres with game room, general store, deli, laundry, bait shop, bicycles, miniature golf, horseback riding, volleyball, picnic area. Swimming, tennis, golf nearby.
Location 16 m SW of Morrilton, 57 m NW of Little Rock. From Little Rock, take Hwy. 40 N to Morrilton. In Morrilton, take Rte. 9 S to Rte. 154 and turn right. Turn left at 1st road on left, resort is on the left.
Credit cards Amex, MC, Optima, Visa.
Rates Room only, $110–185 cottage. Extra person in room, $25. MAP rates on request. Children's, family rates. 10% AARP discount. Continental breakfast, $5.50; alc lunch, $6.50; alc dinner, $32.
Extras Airport pickup from landing field on mountain. Cribs, babysitting available. French, Italian, Arabic spoken.

MOUNTAIN VIEW

It's difficult to imagine how isolated Mountain View was until the beginning of the 1970s—no paved roads, no trains, no scheduled buses. Then, in 1973, the Ozark Folk Center opened, bringing with it improved transportation. Dedicated to preserving the local culture, the center offers daily demonstrations of indigenous crafts, music and dance, storytelling, and cooking. The perfect balance to a day spent absorbing cultural history is a good dose of natural history, exploring the fantastic formations in the Blanchard Springs Caverns, 15 miles northwest of town, in the Ozark National Forest.

Also recommended: Although really not an inn, *Carol Moritz* wrote to recommend the **Ozark Folk Center Lodge** (State Rte. 382, 72560; 501–269–3871) as a pleasant and very reasonably priced motel at around $40 nightly. "The single-level octagonally shaped buildings have a bungalow feel, many with a private view of the woods from two walls of windows. It's different from the usual motel experience, and is an easy walk to the crafts area, music show, and restaurant (I wasn't impressed with the last). Lodge guests get a discount on admission to the crafts area."

The Commercial Hotel ¢ 👫   *Tel: 501–269–4383*
Courthouse Square, P.O. Box 72, 72560

Back in the old days a man traveling on business was a "commercial traveler"; an establishment that catered to such travelers was a commercial hotel. Today, of course, the warm and inviting Commercial Hotel, whose full name includes the subtitle, "A Vintage Guesthouse," doesn't seem very businesslike at all, with its relaxed and welcoming atmosphere, handmade curtains and dust ruffles, original iron beds and dressers, and immaculate baths. In 1982 Todd and Andrea Budy bought and fully renovated the hotel, now listed on the National Register of Historic Places. Rates include a buffet breakfast of juice, tea, and coffee, plus pastries and muffins from the Hearthstone Bakery which shares the hotel. The bakery claims to be "famous for four or five blocks around" for its freshly baked breads, pastries, cookies, and light lunches, all using fresh eggs, quality grains and flours, and real chocolate and nuts.

Mountain View is a mecca for local musicians, many of whom congregate on the hotel's front porch—even the local tax assessor was a lunchtime regular. Summer weekends, especially Saturday nights, see many outdoor concerts and dancing on the courthouse lawn.

"Spotlessly clean, with the warmest of receptions. Freshly baked breakfast breads and cakes—apricot is my favorite. Andrea provided introductions to the other guests, stimulating great conversations, yet providing quiet at the right times." *(Cheryl Schaerer)* "Though simple in construction, everything is perfectly functional. Musicians are welcome on the porch during the day, but are never a problem at night." *(Brode Morgan)*

Open All year. Open November–April by advance reservation only.
Rooms 3 suites, 5 doubles—3 with private shower, 5 rooms share 2 baths. Some with desk, all with air-conditioning.

Facilities Lobby, bakery with dining area, gift shop, wraparound porch with frequent live music. 1 shaded acre. Pool, tennis, hiking, caves, rock-climbing nearby. Short drive to White River, Sylamore Creek, Greers Ferry Lake, for fishing, swimming, float trips.
Location N central AR, Stone Cty. 100 m N of Little Rock, 150 m W of Memphis, TN. Hwys. 66, 9, 5/14 all lead to Courthouse Sq.; Inn on sq. at corner of Washington and Peabody Sts. 1 m from Folk Center.
Restrictions No smoking. "Dry county."
Credit cards Amex, MC, Visa.
Rates B&B, $52–69 suite, $38–53 double, $33–46 single. Extra person, $4. No charge for children under 6 in parents' room.
Extras Limited wheelchair accessibility. Cribs available. Very limited French.

PINE BLUFF

Reader tip: "Restaurant scene in Pine Bluff is desolate. We settled on Chinese at the Fu Mei—a cut above average." *(JB)*

Margland II Bed & Breakfast
703 West Second Street, 71601

Tel: 501–536–6000

A restored Victorian home on a quiet residential street, each suite at Margland has a different decor—French, Victorian, wicker, Pennsylvania Dutch, or country. Guests have a choice of continental or full breakfasts, brought to their room, served in the dining room, or on the terrace.

"Our room was beautifully decorated with antiques, and each morning the Little Rock paper was delivered with our coffee. Breakfast the first day included fresh fruit salad, freshly squeezed orange juice, hash brown potatoes, eggs Benedict, or blueberry pancakes; on the second, quail, grits, and biscuits were added to the menu. At night a plate of homemade chocolate chip cookies, fresh strawberries, and mints were left in our room. Wanda is the heart and soul of the place and a perfect hostess. She did everything to make our stay comfortable, even making fresh lemonade." *(Sidney Flynn)* "Endorse existing entry; though very expensive for the area, it was excellent in all respects. Our room was large and nicely appointed, with good reading lights." *(John Blewer)*

Open All year.
Rooms 6 suites with whirlpool bath, telephone, TV/VCR, air-conditioning, ceiling fans. 3 with loft bedrooms.
Facilities Dining room, living room, terraces, gardens.
Location C AR. 43 miles SE of Little Rock.
Credit cards None accepted.
Rates B&B, $93 double.

WOOSTER

Patton House Inn ¢
Highway 25, P.O. Box 61, 72181

Tel: 501–679–2975

When it was built in 1918 by Jim and Elsie Patton, this gracious home was considered a "showplace" for miles around. Old-timers claim that it was the first house in Wooster with indoor plumbing, and it was among the first to get electricity in the early 1920s. It has always stayed in the Patton family; present owner Mary Lee Patton Shirley has occupied the house since 1978, turning it into a B&B in 1989. Rates include early morning coffee, and a buffet breakfast of sausage souffle, English muffins, fresh fruit plate, and French toast sticks.

"Lovely colors, with fine carpeting and antiques throughout. We had the two upstairs bedrooms, each equipped with good mattresses and a handsome balance of solid and flowered bedspreads, drapes, and upholstery. A delicious breakfast was served on quality china; the food could win a blue ribbon at the fair! The ample grounds and location well back from the road makes for a quiet, peaceful setting." (Jack Marshall)

Open All year.
Rooms 3 doubles—1 with private bath, 2 with maximum of 4 people sharing bath. All with TV, air-conditioning. 1 with refrigerator, balcony.
Facilities Dining room, living room, library with TV, 3 porches, deck. 6½ acres. 3 lakes nearby for water sports.
Location Central AR, 40 m N of Little Rock. Take I-40 N to Conway. Go N on Rte. 25 8 m to Wooster. Hwy 25 turns right at Wilcox Grocery. Inn is 3rd house on right, opposite First Baptist Church.
Credit cards MC, Visa.
Rates B&B, $50 double, $40 single. Extra person, $15.
Extras Small pets permitted by prior arrangement.

We Want to Hear from You!

As you know, this book is only effective with your help. We really need to know about your experiences and discoveries. If you stayed at an inn or hotel listed here, we want to know how it was. Did it live up to our description? Exceed it? Was it what you expected? Did you like it? Were you disappointed? Delighted? Have you discovered new establishments that we should add to the next edition?

Tear out one of the report forms at the back of this book (or use your own stationery if you prefer) and write today. *Even if you write only "Fully endorse existing entry" you will have been most helpful.*

Thank You!

Florida

Chalet Suzanne, Lake Wales

There *is* a real Florida apart from giant theme parks, condo developments, and endless chains of cloned hotels and motels. It's just not that easy to find, so please be sure to share the good news whenever you discover something special. There are B&B inns in many areas, as well as older hotels of character that are being restored; we've added many of them to this edition, and would like to hear of more.

Although theme parks, beaches, and retired family members are three popular reasons for visiting Florida, we'd like to suggest some less-well-known Florida highlights. In the southeast, visit the tranquil Japanese flower gardens at the Morikami Cultural complex west of Delray Beach, or drop by a professional polo match in the Palm Beach area (you might even glimpse the Prince of Wales here). On the Gulf Coast, travel back roads to find isolated coastal inlets, drop by the Salvador Dali Museum in St. Petersburg, or visit unspoiled Honeymoon and Caladesi Islands that are maintained as state parks.

Although best known for its theme parks, Central Florida also boasts miles of grassy prairies, flowering fruit groves, horse farms, 1400 lakes, and the world's largest sandy pine forest. Southwest of Gainesville, on the Gulf Coast, escape to Cedar Key, a sleepy Victorian fishing village and art colony. In Northeast Florida don't miss the Spanish flavor of St. Augustine, the oldest city in the United States. Less-visited, the Florida Panhandle, in the northwest, offers miles of sugar-white sand, rolling hill country near Tallahassee, the Alaqua Vineyards (one of only four wineries in the state), and an unusual mixture of Creole, Victorian, and other architecture in Pensacola's Seville Historic District.

Rates do not include 6% Florida sales tax, plus additional local taxes where applicable. Peak season rates in most of Florida generally extend from December 1–15 through May 1–15; off-season rates are considerably lower. Do remember that August and September are the height of the tropical storm/hurricane season, so it might be best to avoid these months when planning a trip.

Reader tip: "Distinguish yourself from the average tourist by remembering that conch is pronounced *konk*."

Information please: On the east coast, the **St. Regis Hotel** is a century-old inn, restored in period with modern amenities and an inviting restaurant with a continental menu (509 Seabreeze Boulevard, Daytona Beach 32018; 904–252–8743). Let us know what you think.

AMELIA ISLAND

Amelia Island's only town is Fernandina Beach, at its north end, but since the two addresses appear to be used interchangeably, and the island name is better known, we've listed our entries here. Amelia Island is located in the northeast corner of Florida, just south of the Georgia border, and 35 miles north of Jacksonville. Activities focus on the area's wide sandy beaches, with ample opportunities for swimming, boating, and fishing, but golf and tennis are available as well. The scent of the sea is sometimes mixed with the less appealing odor of the island's paper mills, but this doesn't seem to bother the island's many enthusiasts.

Reader tip: "The historic district of Fernandina Beach feels the way Key West did 25 years ago. Many interesting shops and good places to eat; the townspeople are exceptionally friendly." *(Joe & Sheila Schmidt)*

Information please: David and Susan Caples, original owners of the 1735 Inn (see below) wrote to tell us about their newly built inn, the **Elizabeth Pointe Lodge** (82 South Fletcher Avenue, P.O. Drawer 1210, 32034; 904–277–4851). Constructed in an 1890s Nantucket shingle style, with a maritime theme, the inn has 20 guest rooms with B&B rates ranging from $75–150, most with ocean views (the sand dunes are just steps away).

In nearby Jacksonville, the **House on Cherry Street** (1844 Cherry Street, Jacksonville 32205; 904–384–1999) is a colonial-style home built in 1912 overlooking the St. John's River. Each of its four guest rooms has a private bath, and rates include evening wine and hors d'oeuvres and such elegant breakfast entrées as eggs Benedict or eggs with spinach and artichokes. Reports most appreciated.

For additional listings in the area, see Georgia, **Cumberland Island** and **St. Mary's.**

The Bailey House ¢   *Tel:* 904–261–5390
28 South 7th Street, P.O. Box 805, 32034

The Bailey House is an 1895 Queen Anne Victorian, listed on the National Register of Historic Places. The house was built by Effingham W. Bailey for his bride. She was given a choice of a modest home with fine furnishings, or an elaborate one with the furnishings to come. She very clearly chose the latter—the Bailey House is a profusion of turrets, gables, bays, fish-scale decoration, and many stained glass windows. It took three years to complete at the then-outrageous price of $10,000.

Diane and Tom Hay have owned the Bailey House since 1982 and have decorated it with period antiques; Ken Nolan is the manager.

Everybody's tastes are different, which may account for the two very different reader reports this year: "A delightful light airy home with ceiling fans and beautiful stained glass windows. Our room, the Victorian, had marble-topped furniture and a small sitting area. It was comfortably furnished, supplied with magazines, with good bedside lamps by which to read them. The bathrooms had antique fixtures which functioned as well as modern ones. We relaxed on the porch and in the parlor, and enjoyed a breakfast of home-baked bran muffins, good coffee, juice, and fresh fruit salad in the dining room. Our host offered interesting insights about the area along with good tips about restaurants and shops. Both he and his wife seemed genuinely concerned with our comfort. We were a bit surprised by the heavy industry in the area; there are two paper mills just outside of town. There were some distant rumbles from one of the plants, but with the central air-conditioning it was not disturbing." *(Amy Peritsky)*

Another reader (who visited during the same month) was less positive: "Our bedroom was not comfortable. It needed a painting, new linens, and overall freshening up." More reports required.

Open All year.
Rooms 1 suite, 3 doubles—all with private bath and/or shower, TV, air-conditioning, ceiling fans. Suite with fireplace.
Facilities Dining room, reception hall with fireplace, parlor with organ, Victrola, books, games; veranda with porch swing. Regular and tandem bicycles. 2 blocks to lighted tennis courts. Swimming, fishing, surfing, marina, horseback riding, golf nearby.
Location Historic district. From I-95, go E on A1A to Centre St. Turn left on Centre St., then left onto 7th St. to inn on left.
Restrictions No smoking. No children under 10.
Credit cards Amex.
Rates B&B, $105 suite, $75–95 double. Extra person, $10. Weekly rates. 2-day holiday weekend minimum.
Extras Local airport pickups. French spoken.

Florida House Inn ¢ ✕   *Tel:* 904–261–3300
20 & 22 South 3rd Street, P.O. Box 688, 32034   800–258–3301

One-time Florida resident Thomas Alva Edison is said to have remarked that: "Invention is 1% inspiration, 99% perspiration." When you see the "before" and "after" pictures of the newly opened Florida House, you may decide that restoring an old inn follows a similar ratio. In the summer of 1991, Karen and Bob Warner completed a total renovation of the Florida's oldest surviving (but just barely) hotel. During the 19th century, its many famous guests included General Ulysses S. Grant, plus assorted Rockefellers and Carnegies; in those days, the inn had 25 guest rooms and no indoor plumbing. Rates include a full southern breakfast; also available is a restaurant offering "boarding house" style dining.

"Friendly service; charming homey decor; clean, cozy rooms with good lighting and new plumbing with strong showers. An excellent breakfast is served on the back porch, with the enjoyable company of both innkeepers and guests. Sipping afternoon lemonade on the wooden rockers of the second floor porch was equally pleasant. The town is delightful, and everything is in walking distance—unless you'd rather take the horse-drawn buggy." *(Shirley Hall)* "The resurrected spirit of this historic stop-over is embodied in its new owners. Their genuine warmth promotes an instant rapport with guests. The inn itself balances Jacuzzi tubs and central air-conditioning with four-poster beds, quilts, and claw foot bathtubs. The shade of time-twisted oaks makes the old porches an inviting place to gather over morning coffee or evening wine." *(Michael & Jeanne Green)* And from a frequent contributor: "Clean rooms furnished with a variety of antique reproductions. We visited when they had just opened, and although not all rooms were done, we'd say that Florida House has the potential to become a very good inn." *(JS)* More comments welcome.

Minor niggle: "Probably fixed by now, but when we visited, the halls echoed a bit."

Open All year.

Rooms 2 suites, 9 doubles—all with private bath and/or shower, telephone, radio, TV, air-conditioning, fan. Most have desk; 2 with fireplace, 3 with Jacuzzi tub. 8 rooms in North Bldg. 3 rooms in South Bldg.

Facilities Restaurant, pub with fireplace, TV; living room with books; parlor. VCR available on request. Off-street parking. Tennis, golf nearby. 2 m from Atlantic Ocean for boating, fishing, swimming.

Location Historic District. From I-95, take A1A exit to Amelia Island, Fernandina Beach. A1A turns into 8th St. once you are on the island. Follow 8th St. to the intersection of 8th St. and Centre St. Turn left on Centre St. Go 5 blocks to South 3rd St. Turn left on S. 3rd St. Florida House Inn is ½ block from Centre on the left.

Restrictions No smoking. Children by prior arrangement.

Credit cards All major credit cards.

Rates B&B, $125 suite, $55–85 double. Extra person, $10. 10% senior, AAA discount. 2-3 night holiday weekend minimum.

Extras Limited wheelchair access. Airport pickups. Crib. Limited Spanish spoken.

The 1735 House ¢ ♦
584 South Fletcher Avenue, 32034

Tel: 904–261–5878
800–872–8531

Built in the 1920s, the inn sits on a narrow strip of land sandwiched between the beach and the road—it's just 100 yards from the water at high tide. The inn was purchased in 1987 by Gary and Emily Grable. We've heard from a great many guests of this inn, and most have been delighted with its atmosphere, the hospitality of the innkeepers, the accommodations, the breakfasts, and the beachside setting.

"The 1735 House is a delightful, rustic, converted old white clapboard house directly on the ocean. From your suite you look directly into the surf. When there are stormy seas, your bedroom window is lighted regularly by the lighthouse beacon, while the spray of the sea steams through the windows at night. In the morning, at the time you've requested, a wicker breakfast basket is left at your door with an awakening knock and the morning paper. It is hard to concentrate on current events with the vista of a freighter or shrimp trawlers on the horizon, and porpoises playing near the shore.

"We visited twice in the last year, and on both occasions our rooms were clean, well designed, and outfitted for a beach stay. The friendly staff supplied us with information on restaurants and area activities. I had a chance to speak with Gary Grable and he was ready to chat or lend advice." *(Dave Perry)* "We enjoyed sitting on the ocean-side patio, reading, and watching birds and surfers." *(Frank Heymann)* "Lots of room to stretch out, friendly people, large towels, great rates." *(Terry Rainey)* "Breakfast, with two bright yellow thermos jugs filled with hot coffee, and with fresh squeezed orange juice, warm cinnamon rolls, and fresh sliced peaches, was a treat to both the eye and the palate." *(Anne DeCamillo)* "Conveniently located near the delightful old town of Fernandina Beach, or the newer amenities of Amelia Plantation, with quaint restaurants, good food, fun shops, antiquers' heaven." *(Annalou Wren, and others)*

Areas for improvement: We have also had a few reports that housekeeping and maintenance can be erratic at times, and that a few additional decorating touches would be desirable. "Floor rugs would have been kind to my bare feet, and I couldn't get the air-conditioner to work." Also: "Perhaps their regular housekeeper was on vacation, but our suite could have used a good scrubbing, starting with the windows!" And: "Perhaps we hit a bad day, but we were never really welcomed by the staff." "A light in the shower would have been helpful—it was really dark." "Amazingly, our room was spotless, without a grain of sand, yet some furnishings needed dusting. Our towels were changed but the bed was never made during our two-night stay. Our room, the Captain's Suite, could have used better lighting and a bedroom mirror."

On the plus side, Gary noted that they are pleased to provide unsweetened baked goods for breakfast upon request.

Open All year.
Rooms 5 suites, 2-bedroom lighthouse—all with private shower, radio, TV, desk, air-conditioning, ceiling fan, refrigerator, coffee maker. 3 with kitchenette.
Facilities Kitchen privileges, games, patio. Off-street parking. Beach front for swimming, fishing; boogie boards, lawn chairs. Golf, tennis, surf-cast and deep-sea fishing, boat charters, horseback riding nearby.
Location NE FL, at GA border. 35 m N of Jacksonville. 2 hrs. S of Savannah, GA. Take I-95 to Fernandina Beach–Amelia Island exit, proceed E on Hwy. A1A, 15 m to Amelia Island. Cross bridge and turn right at 2nd traffic light (Sadler St.). Continue on Sadler to end, turn left on S. Fletcher Ave., 2 m to inn.
Restrictions Traffic, kitchen noise in some rooms. No children under 6.
Credit cards Amex, Discover, MC, Visa.
Rates B&B, $85–95 suite, $85 double. Extra person, $5. 10% senior, AAA discount. Tipping discouraged.
Extras Airport/station pickups.

APALACHICOLA

Although once a major Gulf port, Apalachicola is now a very sleepy town, with shrimp and oysters being the primary cash crops. Here's how one reader describes this little town in the Florida Panhandle: "It's near un-crowded Gulf beaches and is still basically undiscovered, except for the seafood festival in November each year. The town is a part of old Florida that shouldn't be missed. Pick up a copy of the walking tour guide and enjoy!" *(April Burwell)*

Information please: Another possibility is **Magnolia's** (116 Avenue E, 32320; 904–653–8905), a guest house built in 1926, on grounds shaded by magnolia and pecan trees. The reasonable rates include continental breakfast; the three guest rooms share two baths.

For an additional listing in the area, see **St. George Island.**

Gibson Inn ¢ ✗   *Tel:* 904–653–2191
100 Market Street, P.O. Box 221, 32320   904–653–8282

A large blue building surrounded by two-story white verandas and topped by a cupola, the turn-of-the-century Gibson Inn dates from the town's glory days. Restored in 1983, the inn overlooks the water and St. George Island. Rooms are furnished in period, with four-poster beds, ceiling fans, antique armoires, brass and porcelain bathroom fixtures, and claw-foot tubs. Its popular restaurant serves three meals a day, from a full range of standard breakfast favorites, to a lunch of fried oysters, to a dinner of seafood gumbo, Grecian spiced shrimp with feta cheese, and chocolate bourbon pecan pie.

"The Gibson brought us back to turn-of-the-century days, with its wraparound verandas well supplied with rockers and wicker chairs. Con-siderable money was put into its restoration. Most rooms have four-poster beds; ours had a TV in the armoire, two chairs, and a writing table. We had delicious shrimp at an inexpensive local seafood restaurant." *(April Burwell)*

"Our third-floor corner room was beautifully furnished, with a luxuri-ous bath and excellent bedding. Breakfast was good and filling, and they were happy to make a change for me. We enjoyed the inn cat too." *(Imogene Tillis)* "This town is truly the Old Florida I remember from the 1930s. The friendly desk clerk offered helpful suggestions, and we en-joyed a dinner of fresh local snapper. The staff was quick to fix a slow drain in our bathtub. We enjoyed the Gorrie Museum, devoted to the ice-making machine, developed to help yellow fever victims, and we discovered a tiny weaving shop tucked above a jewelry store." *(HB)*

And a word to the wise: "The rooms vary greatly; some on the courtyard are quite dark, so try to walk through the inn and pick your favorite." An area for improvement: "Better lights for reading in bed."

Open All year.
Rooms 1 suite, 29 doubles—all with private bath, telephone, TV, air-condition-ing, ceiling fan.
Facilities Restaurant, bar with weekend entertainment, lobby, verandas, gift/craft shop. Swimming, shelling, fishing, marina nearby.
Location FL Panhandle. Center of town, 1 block from waterfront. 75 m SW of Tallahassee, 60 m SE of Panama City, at corner of Hwy. 98 and Avenue C.
Credit cards MC, Visa.
Rates Room only, $105–110 suite, $60–85 double. Extra person, $5. Senior,

group, AAA, military discounts. Package rates. Alc breakfast, $2.75–7; alc lunch, $6–12; alc dinner, $17–32. 2-night holiday minimum.
Extras Pets permitted, $5. Crib.

The Pink Camellia Inn ¢   *Tel:* 904–653–2107
145 Avenue E, 32320

A pink brochure, pink stationery, and yes, a pink-painted inn all describe the Pink Camellia, a B&B opened in 1988 by Bill Barnes and Carole Jayne. The innkeepers are both artists, and their work is on display throughout the house. Bill and Carole did an eight-month restoration of the inn, adding the required modern conveniences. At the same time, they decorated the light and airy rooms with period antiques and contemporary paintings and pottery. Wake-up coffee is available early; later a full breakfast is served family-style in the dining room. A typical menu might include fresh strawberries and kiwi, blackberry coffee cake, and crabmeat and zucchini fritatta.

"Quiet setting, exceptionally clean. Delicious food pleasantly served. The owners do their utmost to make you feel comfortable." *(Mr. & Mrs. Karl Holzapfel)* "Beautifully decorated. A wonderful porch for relaxing. The owners make a great team." *(Debbie & Pat Gosney)* "It's a great place to explore on a sunny or rainy day, with beautiful colors, objets d'art—all magical and mysterious. Rooms are comfy and restful, with music filling the air. I've never had so much good food in a B&B: a three-course breakfast, late afternoon hors d'oeuvres of paté and cheese, and late evening dessert and coffee." *(Tom Caldarola, also Joe & Sheila Schmidt, and others)* "The bright (almost hot) pink house catches your eye right away. On the porch, simple wooden furniture is imaginatively painted, piquing the curiosity. A warm greeting by the owners and friendly smiles soon melted away any hesitation. These Yankee artists offer the openness and warmth of Southern hospitality. After-dinner conversation over a glass of wine was a delightful ending to the day. Early in the morning, outside our door was a Chinese red teapot with bright yellow cups on a quaint tray. Later we enjoyed a breakfast of fresh fruit and blueberry pancakes with a choice of syrups. We spent the day buying Christmas presents from the many craftspeople and artists in this old-fashioned town." *(Shirley Matthews)*

Open All year.
Rooms 1 suite, 3 doubles—all with private bath, telephone, air-conditioning.
Facilities Living room, dining room, common room with TV, library; wraparound porches, balcony. Gardens, deck. Tennis nearby. Beaches, marina nearby.
Location FL Panhandle. In historic district. Corner of 12th St. and Hwy. 98. 4 blocks from waterfront, 7 blocks from downtown.
Restrictions No smoking.
Credit cards Amex, Discover, MC, Visa.
Rates B&B, $75 suite, $65–75 double, $60–70 single. Extra person, $15. Less 10% for room only. 2-night holiday weekend minimum. Champagne weekend package.
Extras Airport pickups. Pets permitted by prior arrangement.

CAPTIVA ISLAND

For a change of pace from shell collecting and lazing on the wonderful beaches, spend time hiking, canoeing, or bicycling in the "Ding" Darling National Wildlife Preserve in Sanibel, or cross the causeway back to Fort Myers to visit the winter home of Thomas Edison. You can see his home, research labs, and 14-acre botanical gardens. Captiva recently spent millions of dollars restoring its beach, and current reader reports are ecstatic.

For additional area listings in the area, see **Sanibel Island**.

Reader tip: "Favorite restaurants are the Mad Hatter, and Bellini for pasta. We very much preferred Captiva to Sanibel; it had a much more natural authentic feel to it." *(MBO)*

'Tween Waters Inn 🏃 ✕ 🛶
Captiva Drive, P.O. Box 249, 33924

Tel: 813—472—5161
In FL: 800—282—7560
In U.S.: 800—223—5865

Set on a narrow strip of land between the Gulf of Mexico and Pine Island Sound, the 'Tween Waters Inn was started as a one-cabin operation in 1926. A variety of cottages was added over the years, but the whole inn was nearly bulldozed in the 1970s to make way for a condominium complex. Instead, the inn was bought in 1976 by Rochester Resorts, which has attempted to preserve the best features of the old while adding all the facilities most travelers expect in a luxury resort. While far from perfect, most readers are pleased with the hotel.

"The setting is less commercial than I thought possible in Florida. You can rent a canoe at the inn to go on a canoe trail through a nearby nature preserve, and you can walk a long way down the Gulf beach without seeing any buildings. The shelling is wonderful, as is the bird watching." *(Pamela Mack)*

"This old resort consists of many cottages and two large motel-type buildings overlooking either the Gulf of Mexico or Pine Island Sound. The cottages are quite nice, but the only ones that really have a water view face the highway." *(SN)* "Good service, very clean, lots of attention paid to our kids." *(Steve Shipps)* "We followed your recommendation for the 'Tween Waters, and were delighted we did. Our room overlooked the marina, and the newly restored beach was gorgeous." *(Mary Beth O'Reilly)* "An excellent place for vacationing with small children. They have many amenities—washer/dryer for guest use, small refrigerators in the rooms— to help ease the strains of traveling with kids. The staff is very good at keeping the busy pool area clean, and we enjoyed a performance at their little theater."*(Jane Mattoon)* "Since we love the water and the beach, the location between the Gulf of Mexico and the bay was great. The pool is lovely, the food good, and the grounds are well kept. "*(Pauline Wyrie)* "Our room in the main inn had a breathtaking view overlooking the Gulf of Mexico, though disturbed a bit by highway noise. We had a screened-in deck that allowed us to enjoy the sunsets as we examined our shell collections and enjoyed the cool ocean breezes. Our room was simple in style but comfortable, with such extras as a refrigerator, hair dryer, and free cable movie channel. Best of all was its location just a few minutes walk from the gorgeous, private, and shell-covered Captiva Beach. We found the restaurant to be prohibitively expensive at breakfast ($22 for two continental breakfasts), and used our refrigerator to store breakfast and lunch fixings." *(Thomas & Linda Fontana)*

Areas for improvement: "Despite your earlier reports, we thought the food was overpriced and just passable." Also: "Parking is barely adequate." And: "Our cottage room was very old and lacked character and decor. The walls were thin and we could hear everything going on in the next room."

Open All year.
Rooms 10 suites, 83 doubles, 51 cottages—all with private bath and/or shower, telephone, TV, air-conditioning. Many with refrigerator, hair-dryer, kitchenette, screened porch, balcony.
Facilities Dining room, lounge with live entertainment, game room, laundry facilities. 13 acres with marina, heated swimming pool, 3 tennis courts, shuffleboard, private beach on Gulf, fishing; boat, canoe, bicycle rentals.
Location SW FL. 25 m W of Ft. Myers.
Restrictions Significant traffic noise in Gulf-side rooms, cottages.
Credit cards MC, Visa.
Rates Room only, $80–235 suite or cottage, $75–185 double, $70–90 single. Extra person, $15. 3–night holiday and/or winter minimum. No charge for children under 12. 7–night packages, midweek specials. Alc breakfast, $7–15; alc lunch, $10–15; alc dinner, $20–30. Package rates.
Extras Public areas wheelchair accessible; some cottages specially equipped for disabled. Pets permitted by prior arrangement in some cottages. Crib.

CEDAR KEY

"Cedar Key is the way Florida used to be before the tourists found it—quiet, unflashy. Minimal tourist traffic, quaint, uncrowded, a great area for birds and other natural joys. The old cemetery has shell-covered graves, nesting osprey, and historic tombstones. Also good restaurants, shell mounds, wildlife refuges, and historic walking tours. There's a marina, museum, park, fishing pier. A pleasant spot to visit as a destination or as a stopover, and not far from Manatee State Park." *(Celia McCullough & Gary Kaplan)*

The Island Hotel ✗   *Tel:* 904–543–5111
2nd & B Streets, P.O. Box 460, 32625

Moving in 1980 from upscale Greenwich, Connecticut to laid-back Cedar Key was quite a change for Marsha Rogers, owner of the Island Hotel. Listed on the National Register of Historic Places, the inn was built of cypress faced with tabby, a mixture of lime rock and crushed oyster shells. Rates include a full breakfast—perhaps fresh fruit with cinnamon and pecans, and scrambled eggs with poppy seeds. Marsha notes that "our hotel is rustic, authentic, not trendy. It's not for everyone. The folks that love it and return are artists, and folks who want to step out of the fast lane and back in time."

"We were warmly greeted and shown through the hotel. The simple furnishings range from old to antique but all was clean and comfortable. It's far from being a 'Laura Ashley-style' inn, but we thought its slightly funky atmosphere gave us a real taste of the old Florida. The restaurant is superb, with an excellent choice of seafood and vegetarian dishes, home-baked breads, and attentive service." *(CM)* "Reflects the mood of greater days gone by, in a slow-paced, slightly seedy, present." *(Betty Richards)*

Open All year. Restaurant closed Tues., Wed.
Rooms 10 doubles—6 with private bath and/or shower, 4 with maximum of 4 sharing bath. All with air-conditioning, fan, some with desk.
Facilities Restaurant, café with bar, TV, VCR, games, library; screened porch, verandas. Courtyard, backyard. 1 block to swimming, boating, fishing.
Location W coast, N FL. 53 m SW of Gainesville. Midway between Tampa-St. Pete & Tallahassee. Enter keys on Rte. 24 via 4 small bridges. Go left at 1st stop sign to inn 2 blocks further on left.
Restrictions Light traffic noise on weekend nights. No smoking. No red meat served.
Credit cards Discover, MC, Visa.
Rates B&B, $104 suite, $90–104 double, $80–90 single. Extra person, $10. Child portions in dining room. 2-night weekend minimums. Alc dinner, $35.
Extras Limited wheelchair access in restaurant. Airport/station pickups, $35–50. Spanish spoken.

COCONUT GROVE

Information please: Also of interest to the business traveler is the **Grand Bay Hotel** (2669 South Bayshore Drive, Coconut Grove, Miami 33133; 800–327–2788), an elegant 180-room hotel overlooking Biscayne Bay. The atmosphere is one of European elegance, with relaxing lounges and fine restaurant, the Grand Café. Reports?

Coconut Grove is about ten minutes from downtown Miami. For additional area entries, see **Coral Gables, Miami, and Miami Beach.**

Mayfair House ✗
3000 Florida Avenue, Coconut Grove, 33133

Tel: 305–441–0000
In U.S. 800–433–4555
In FL: 800–341–0809

Despite its relatively bland concrete exterior, the Mayfair's designers spared no effort or expense to create a dark haven of luxury inside. Common areas are eclectically decorated with everything from French tapestries to Oriental furnishings to New Wave stained glass—more than one guest has been reminded of the fantastic work of Barcelona's Antonio Gaudi. Guest rooms are equally lavish if slightly more conventional, with Art Deco-style beds, dramatic fabric patterns, and Italian marble bathrooms. Complimentary caviar and paté is served with cocktails in the Tiffany Lounge amidst Oriental rugs, overstuffed sofas, and sculptural brass floor lamps, while dinner is served at the more restrained Grill. For late evening entertainment, check out the Ensign Bitters nightclub where Miami's social elite go to dance and unwind.

"Miami is not an easy place to find a good hotel. There are lots of plastic ones near the airport and downtown, and many absolutely awful ones on the beach. Although not small, the Mayfair is very personable, with excellent facilities and refined, attentive service. The hotel is part of a large, modern concrete shopping center, which makes some of the rooms a little noisy if there is an affair in the ballroom, but also makes it very safe (a rarity in Miami). It is convenient to the small shops, boutiques, and restaurants of Coconut Grove. On arrival you are whisked to an office, handed a glass of champagne or orange juice, and the formalities are taken care of quickly and quietly; there is no check-in desk. Even the smallest and least expensive rooms are very large with giant bathrooms, four telephones, two TV sets and a private hot tub outside on the patio. Quick room service, a nice rooftop pool, and complete concierge service completes the amenities. The concierge was unusually helpful and not at all snooty." *(Willis Frick)* Additional reports helpful.

Open All year.
Rooms 182 suites—all with full private bath, Japanese hot tub whirlpool, telephone, radio, TV, desk, air-conditioning, refrigerator, terrace. 50 with antique piano.
Facilities 2 restaurants, bar/lounge, lobby, roof garden/sun deck, swimming pool, solarium. Tennis, golf, boating, fishing nearby. Valet parking, 24-hour room service.
Location 20 min. from airport, 10 min. from downtown Miami. $\frac{1}{2}$ block from Biscayne Bay. From South Bayshore Dr., turn away from water onto Mary St. to hotel at corner of Mary & Florida in Mayfair in the Grove shopping complex.
Restrictions Early morning noise from service alley might disturb light sleepers; also in some rooms during functions.
Credit cards Amex, Discover, MC, Visa.
Rates Room only, $140–500. Extra person, $35. Alc breakfast, $8–18; alc lunch, $8–20.
Extras Wheelchair access; some rooms equipped for disabled. Crib. German, Spanish spoken.

CORAL GABLES

For additional area entries, see also **Coconut Grove, Miami, and Miami Beach**.

The Colonnade Hotel ✕
180 Aragon Avenue

Tel: 305–441–2600
800–533–1337

A 1920s Mediterranean masterpiece, the Colonnade has been elegantly restored; its guest rooms have dark mahogany furniture, softly lit with brass lamps, and all the amenities one expects from a deluxe hotel. The hotel's art deco restaurant, the Cafe Aragon, has been winning raves from the local press for its French nouvelle cuisine.

"A first-rate facility, with prices to match. Public spaces are spectacular. Doc Dammer's Saloon is excellent for casual eating, and the Aragon is first-rate. The rooms are luxurious and well maintained. Located in the

FLORIDA

heart of Coral Gables, the hotel is within easy walking distance of shops, movies, and fine restaurants." *(Sheila & Joe Schmidt)*

Open All year.
Rooms 17 suites, 140 doubles, all with full private bath, telephone, radio, TV, desk, air-conditioning.
Facilities Restaurant, saloon with entertainment, lobby. Heated swimming pool, hot tub. Tennis nearby.
Location 8 m from downtown Miami.
Credit cards Amex, DC, MC, Visa.
Rates Room only, $195 suite, $139 corporate, $129 weekend rate. Extra person, $20. Alc lunch, $10–25; alc dinner, $25–50.
Extras Wheelchair access. Airport/station pickups. Dutch, French, German, Spanish, Portuguese spoken.

Hotel Place St. Michel ✕ ♁   *Tel:* 305–444–1666
162 Alcazar Avenue, 33134   800–247–8526

Built as an office building in 1926, and converted into the Hotel Seville shortly thereafter, the hotel was a favorite of high rollers (a racetrack was nearby) and such celebrities as Hedda Hopper, Douglas Fairbanks, and Gloria Swanson. Following a typical pattern, the hotel fell into decay in the 1950's, but was totally restored and refurbished in 1979 by Stuart Bornstein and Alan Potamkin. The hotel is well known for its restaurant and bar, among Miami's best and most popular.

"The hotel is close enough to the airport to avoid most of the traffic, and it has an outstanding restaurant. The menu is French with creative Florida touches, and the service and presentation were faultless. The reasonable rates include a continental breakfast, the morning paper, and a basket of fresh fruit. The hotel was built in 1929 with a Moorish tiled entry hall and has been restored faithfully to the period, with arched ceilings and art nouveau chandeliers. It's decorated in turn-of-the-century furnishing with parquet floors, new plumbing, room-darkening drapes, and silver ice buckets. Most of the rooms are on a side street but even on the main street the air-conditioning drones out the noises. Shoppers will love the fact it's a quick walk to the shop-laden Miracle Mile." *(MAA)* More reports required.

Open All year.
Rooms 3 suites, 24 doubles—all with private bath and/or shower, telephone, radio, TV, air-conditioning, ceiling fan. Some with desk.
Facilities Restaurant, piano bar, roof-top garden, concierge, free parking. Swimming pool, health club nearby.
Location From U.S. 1, go N on Ponce de Leon Ave. to inn at corner of Alcazar. 7 min. from Miami Int'l Airport; 10 min. to downtown. 3 blocks to Miracle Mile.
Credit cards Amex, DC, MC, Visa.
Rates B&B, $110–125 suite, $85–105 double, $75–90 single. Extra person, $10. No charge for children under 12. 10% senior, AAA discount. Alc lunch, $10–12; alc dinner, $30–35.
Extras Wheelchair access. Crib, babysitting. French, German, Spanish, Portuguese, Arabic spoken.

DELRAY BEACH

Seagate Hotel & Beach Club ✕   *Tel:* 407–276–2421
400 South Ocean Boulevard, 33483   800–233–3581

A waterfront location on Florida's "Gold Coast" combined with a 400-foot white sand beach, and comfortable, attractive accommodations make the Seagate a good choice. The Beach Club restaurant offers such entrées as shrimp scampi, veal steak Alaska, broiled chicken breast, and shrimp creole. Nearby are Boca Raton and Palm Beach for shopping, championship polo, tennis, Jai Alai, horse racing, and nightlife.

"The Seagate is located in an expensive residential area on the land side of the 'A-1-A,' a 25-mph road that runs between the Intracoastal Waterway and the ocean. Hotel guests are welcome at the private beach club across the street, with a salt water swimming pool, and a monthly schedule of activities. Our suite overlooked the hotel courtyard and swimming pool, but was well screened by palm trees, flowers, and lush tropical foliage. It was decorated in soft peach tones with flowered chintz on the sofa and chairs of the living room. The kitchen was fully equipped (even a dishwasher) and coffee and tea supplies were replenished daily; maid service was good. The full bathroom, with big wall mirrors, also had a separate dressing room with sink, vanity, and closet. Lots of thick towels and toiletries were provided. Everything was clean and the individual thermostat and ceiling fans kept the rooms fresh. The staff was friendly and helpful, but it's the quiet location and the gorgeous beach that would bring us back." *(June & Dick Horn)*

Minor niggle: "A bedside table and lamp on *both* sides of the bed."

Open All year.
Rooms 59 suites, 11 doubles—all with private bath, telephone, radio, TV, air-conditioning, ceiling fan, fully equipped kitchen, balcony. Some with desk.
Facilities Restaurant, bar/lounge with TV/VCR, laundry facility. Valet parking for restaurant and beach club. Private lots for guests. 2 pools—1 heated. Jacuzzi. On beach for swimming, boating, windsurfing.
Location Palm Beach County. 20 m S of W. Palm Beach on Rte. A1A. 1 m to center of town.
Credit cards Amex, DC, MC, Visa.
Rates Room only, $69–425 suite, $59–142 double. Extra person, $15. 10% senior, AAA discount. ALC lunch, $7; alc dinner, $40.
Extras Wheelchair access. Crib.

DUCK KEY

Hawk's Cay 🏃 ✕ 🎿   *Tel:* 305–743–7000
Mile Marker 61, Marathon 33050-9757   In FL: 800–432–2242

Originally built in the late 1950s as the Indies Inn, the hotel was rebuilt and renamed in 1983 (at a cost of $15 million), then renovated in 1988. It's an ideal place for those who like their resorts with a full range of activities for both adults and children. The result, although designed to the last throw pillow, is surprisingly soothing and inviting. Like most of the Keys, Duck Key, a 60-acre island, has no beach, but a sand-bordered lagoon has been created to fill the gap.

"An enjoyable family getaway. The terrific tennis pro got us excited about tennis again, and the kids stayed busy with the numerous activities and were never underfoot. If you wanted to find a peaceful spot, the salt water lagoon was ideal, since most of the little kids stayed over at the swimming pool. The breakfast (served from 7:30 to 10 A.M.) is enormous and lavish, with a complete buffet complemented by eggs or whatever cooked to order. Fruit, juice, eggs Benedict, waffles, bagels, croissants—all was good and plentiful. The staff is very courteous and helpful, yet non-obtrusive; the many activities were well-run. Our room was comfortable but not luxurious, ample in size and clean, with an adequate bathroom. The resort's setting is especially nice; most places in the Keys are crammed one next to the other, while Hawk's Cay is more isolated, with a greater feeling of privacy." *(Angela & Jim Foote)*

"If you're travelling with the kids and would prefer more privacy, ask about their 2-bedroom condo units. The weekly condo rental rate costs less than two rooms at the hotel; while breakfast is not included, you are free to take advantage of all the resorts facilities." *(RK)*

Open All year.
Rooms 16 suites, 161 doubles—all with full private bath, telephone, TV, desk, air-conditioning, fan. All with balcony; some with refrigerator.
Facilities 4 restaurants, bar/lounge with entertainment nightly, meeting rooms, game center, library. 60 acres with 8 tennis courts, tennis instruction, heated swimming pool, Aquasize, massage, 2 hot tubs, sheltered cove with sand beach, marina, dolphin training facility, charter fishing, glass-bottom boat excursions, scuba diving, snorkeling, children's play equipment, bicycles, jogging trail with par course, children's program in summer. Free shuttle to golf course nearby.
Location S FL, middle Keys, just off Mile Marker 61. 90 m S of Miami, 8 m N of Marathon on Rte. 1.
Credit cards Amex, DC, Discover, MC, Visa.
Rates B&B, $225–700 suite, $130–320 double. Extra person, $30. Children under 12 free. $2/day service for housekeeping staff. Midweek packages. Tennis, fishing, dive, honeymoon, family packages. Alc lunch, $9; alc dinner, $25.
Extras Wheelchair access; some rooms equipped for the disabled. Airport/station pickups; rental cars. Crib, babysitting. French, Spanish, German, Italian spoken.

FORT LAUDERDALE

The Riverside Hotel ♚ ✕   *Tel:* 305–467–0671
620 East Las Olas Boulevard, 33301   Outside FL: 800–325–3280
                                           In FL: 800–421–7666

A gracious taste of "old Florida" awaits visitors to the Riverside. Bordered by Las Olas (the waves) Boulevard, filled with fine shops and restaurants, the shaded grounds of the Riverside have changed little since the hotel was built over 50 years ago.

"Like many tourist brochures, the Riverside's reflects reality—but slightly enhanced. The New River is an attractive stream; the pool is lovely, but far from Olympic, and so on. But the guest rooms are genuinely large, and the restaurants spacious. In addition to the interior courtyard, there is a sizable lawn adjacent to the pool. The lawn and pool are across a small quiet street, but parents should be aware that it's there. The pool had no lifeguard, but there was a friendly attendant whose primary function seemed to be as a bartender. We saw several rooms in the original building, constructed in 1936; they were spacious, spotless with updated wiring, and new vanities in the baths. The oak furniture is original to the hotel and beautiful. A typical room had a desk and lamps on either side of the bed. All rooms have tiny refrigerators in the closets. Suites on the second floor open on to a deck overlooking the interior courtyard. Few, if any rooms appear to face the street, which probably gets noisy on shopping days. We were taken with the unusual tile work in the hallways. Red, earth-tone tiles are enhanced by small hand-painted tiles interspersed throughout. Room numbers are on hand-painted tiles, too. Given the quality of the hotel, and its location in a fashionable shopping area, we thought the rates were very reasonable. The distance to the beach (about two miles) is probably a factor in keeping room rates down." *(Diane Wolf)*

"Rooms are clean and comfortable. The furniture is original, dating back to 1936; ask for a room with a river view. The delightful pool area is across a small road, and is on the river." *(Sheila & Joe Schmidt)*

Open All year.
Rooms 116 suites and doubles—all with private bath and/or shower, telephone, radio, TV, desk, air-conditioning, mini-refrigerator. Some with patio or deck.
Facilities 2 restaurants, lobby with fireplace, courtyard, meeting room. Gardens with heated swimming pool, private marina on river. Concierge, room service.
Location Downtown, 2 m W of Rte. A1A. 10 min from airport. From airport, take Rte. 84 E to U.S. Rte. 1 and go N, crossing river. Turn right on Las Olas Blvd. to hotel on right at SE 4th Ave.
Restrictions No smoking in some rooms.
Credit cards Amex, CB, Discover, MC, Visa.
Rates Room only, $95–275 suite, $70–150 double, $70–135 single. Extra person, $10; no charge for children under 16 in parents' room. Alc breakfast, $5–8; alc lunch, $8; alc dinner, $20–25; 18% service.

HOLMES BEACH

Information please: About 25 miles southeast of Holmes Beach is the 70-year-old **Crescent House** (459 Beach Road, Siesta Key, Sarasota 34242; 813–346–0857), a pleasant, reasonably priced B&B near Crescent Beach, with some of the whitest sand in the world just across the street. Its three guest rooms have private baths and color TVs, and the $90 rates include a breakfast of freshly squeezed orange juice, homemade muffins and scones, fresh fruit, yogurt, and cereal. Another possibility is the **Pepperberry House** (P.O. Box 841, Sarasota 34230; 813–951–0405), a Key West-style house on the Hudson Bayou.

Harrington House B&B   *Tel:* 813–778–5444
5626 Gulf Drive, 34217

If you've scoured the Gulf Coast for a B&B with a beach in its backyard, search no more, the Harrington House, a 1920s-era stucco building on Anna Maria Island, has seven miles of powdery white sand starting only a few feet from its door. If you're chilled after watching a brilliant Gulf sunset from one of the inn's balconies, join owners Jo and Frank Davis for a cup of hot chocolate before the fireplace in their living room with its eight-foot open-beam ceiling, then climb the original pecky cypress staircase to your room. Guest rooms, with names like Renaissance, Sunset, and Primrose, are decorated with floral wallpapers, reproduction furniture, ceiling fans, and lace curtains. You'll need to swim a few early morning laps in the pool to work up an appetite for the full breakfast of stuffed French toast or perhaps eggs Benedict.

"Friendly and warm hosts who never intrude on your privacy. The house is spotless and the beds comfortable. Most rooms have a view of the Gulf, including the dining room, where breakfasts of stuffed French toast or salmon quiche are served on pretty china." *(Catherine & Sam Bowers)*

Open All year.
Rooms 7 doubles, 1 cottage—all with private bath and/or shower, telephone, radio, TV, desk, air-conditioning, fan. Some with refrigerator, deck.
Facilities Dining room, living room with fireplace, piano, TV/VCR, stereo, library; porch, deck. 1½ acres on beach with swimming pool. Kayaks, bicycles available. Off-street parking.
Location Central Gulf Coast. 45 m S of Tampa, 25 m NW of Sarasota, 5 m W of Bradenton. On Anna Maria Island (the first island south of Tampa Bay).
Restrictions No smoking. No children under 13.
Credit cards Amex, MC, Visa.
Rates B&B, $79–125 double. 10% AAA discount. Minimum stay required summer weekends.
Extras Some rooms equipped for the disabled. Airport/station pickups.

INVERNESS

Crown Hotel ¢ ✕   *Tel:* 904–344–5555
109 North Seminole Avenue, 32650   Outside FL: 800–82–CROWN

The Crown began its existence as Inverness's first store nearly a century ago. It later became a hotel and was moved to Main Street. Around 1925, it was moved again, to its present location; later, the owners enlarged it by adding a third floor to the bottom of the hotel, and a fourth to the top! By 1980, the building was on the verge of collapse. Closed for 18 months and $2,000,000 worth of restoration, it was purchased by Jill and Nigel Sumner in 1990. The inn is decorated in the Florida version of an English country inn, with brass beds and reproduction Chippendale dressers and side chairs; a sweeping free-floating staircase along with a reproduction set of the crown jewels highlight the lobby. The inn's pub serves casual American fare, along with English favorites such as fish and chips and steak and kidney pie, while the more formal Churchill's restaurant offers continental specialties.

"The decor does give the impression of make-believe Victorian, since everything is a brand-new reproduction. This can hardly be considered a fault, in view of the recent complete restoration and reasonable rates. The lit-up facade of the hotel at night was a visual romantic treat. Our light breakfast included one of the most delightful fruit concoctions we've ever had, together with excellent muffins and coffee. We'll be back to go hiking in the nearby state forest." *(FH, also BJ Hensley)*

"Fully endorse existing entry. This charming small-town hotel is especially popular on weekends with couples from Florida's larger cities. We enjoy strolling the sidewalks around the hotel. The rooms, though somewhat small, are convenient, comfortable, and reasonably priced. We always feel pampered in the dining room, where good food is served well. The breakfast, now included in the rates, was as reported by *FH* last year; we prefer this to the heavier fare offered formerly." *(HB, also Sherrill Brown)* "We enjoyed playing checkers on the game table near the elegant second-floor staircase. We had an excellent dinner of venison and beef filet; although the price was a bit steep, the meal was pleasing." *(Thomas & Linda Fontana)*

Minor niggle: "We reserved the suite for an anniversary treat, but it was really just two adjoining hotel rooms, and did not have the luxurious feel of a properly designed suite. The bedroom was lovely, but the 'sitting room' was furnished with a futon and some straight-backed Victorian-style chairs."

Open All year.
Rooms 1 suite, 30 doubles, 2 singles—all with private bath and/or shower, telephone, TV, air-conditioning. Some with desk.
Facilities Restaurant with weekend entertainment, pub, parlor with fireplace. Swimming pool. Jogging trail, lakes, canoeing, golf nearby.
Location W central FL, 75 m N of Tampa, 75 m E of Orlando. Take I-75 to Hwy. 44. Go W for 16 m to town.
Credit cards Amex, MC, Visa.
Rates B&B, $115 suite, $65–70 double, $55–60 single. MAP, $95–115 double, $60–70 single. Extra person, $6. Rollaway bed, $6. Senior, AAA discount. "Crown Jewel" package rates. Prix fixe dinner, $11–13. Alc lunch, $7; alc dinner, $25.
Extras Crib.

ISLAMORADA

Cheeca Lodge 🛶 ✕ 🎣

Tel: 305–664–4651
800–327–2888

Mile Marker 82, Overseas Highway,
P.O. Box 527, 33036

We have resisted for several years, but as usual are putting reader opinion before any arbitrary size distinctions. Or maybe one should consider that the "Wonderful" in our title takes precedence over "Little" in the title of this series. Whatever the case, several well-traveled readers (and avid fishermen) have pointed out that Cheeca is indeed a special place. Spiffed up by a multi-million-dollar restoration several years ago, the rooms are luxurious, the food first rate, the service excellent, the atmosphere quite elegant, and the fishing superb. Those who prefer to stay on terra firma will enjoy the three swimming pools, private beach, six lighted Laykold tennis courts, and Jack Nicklaus–designed, par 3 nine-hole golf course.

"A quality rehabilitation of an old hotel. The warmth and charm of the public spaces and fine outdoor facilities make it an excellent resort." *(Joe & Sheila Schmidt)* "The package rate for our suite included unlimited tennis and golf, and we thought it was an excellent value. We had a small problem with the sofa-bed in the living room, and the staff solved the problem quickly and effectively." *(Ron Kahan)*

A suggested improvement: "The resorts' two restaurants are quite elegant; a snack bar where you could take the kids for a quick bite would be helpful."

Open All year.
Rooms 60 suites, 143 doubles—all with full private bath, telephone, radio, TV, VCR, air-conditioning, fan, refrigerator. Most with balcony or deck.
Facilities 2 restaurants, lounge with piano entertainment, TV. 27 acres with 3 swimming pools, 5 Jacuzzis, private beach, 6 tennis courts, 9-hole golf course. Summer/holiday children's program, playground, sailing, snorkeling, snorkel trail, windsurfing, scuba, deep-sea fishing.
Location Florida Keys, 75 S of Miami. Rte. 1, Mile Marker 82.
Credit cards All major credit cards accepted.
Rates Room only, $150–450 suite, $125–400 double. Extra adult, $25. Children under 16 free in parents' room. Minimum stay required holiday, special event weekends. Alc lunch $16.50, dinner $29.50. Package rates.
Extras Wheelchair access. Round-trip airport transfers, $125 for van. Crib, baby-sitting. Spanish, German, French, Italian spoken.

KEY LARGO

Jules' Undersea Lodge   *Tel:* 305–451–2353
P.O. Box 3330, 51 Shoreland Drive, 33037

Every hotel listed in this guide is unique, but this one is in another league altogether. Named for Jules Verne, the lodge rests 30 feet (not 20,000 leagues) beneath the water's surface in Key Largo Undersea Park. Built as an underwater research habitat in 1971 and put into mothballs three years later, the lodge was bought by Neil Monney in 1984 and converted to "the world's only underwater hotel." Guests stay overnight in private suites with 42-inch windows—the ultimate in water views. A full breakfast and dinner is served on board. There is an array of high-tech diversions. Uncertified divers will need to arrange for a three-hour resort diving course before descending to the lodge, and all should be aware that flying and diving don't mix; allow 12–24 hours between the two.

"A once in a lifetime experience. The resort is five fathoms below the surface in a lagoon, but the tethered breathing lines make diving effortless. I'd recommend renting your own movie tapes ahead of time as their selection is limited." *(Dianne Crawford)* "The lodge's high rates reflect the high costs of converting the lab into a hotel and its ongoing operational costs; don't expect a super-luxurious environment." *(MA)* "To maximize your diving time, check-in early. In the past year, the lodge has been moved to a new position, where the water is clearer." *(AF)* More reports (bubble, bubble) welcome.

Open All year.
Rooms 2 doubles, with maximum of 4 sharing bath. All with telephone, air-conditioning, VCR, stereo/CD, refrigerator, intercom to Command Center.
Facilities Common area with galley kitchen, marine radio, telephone, stereo/CD, microwave, radio communication with Command Center. Dive-port with "moon-pool" entrance. Guided day/night excursions by prior arrangement. Free parking shore side.
Location 2 m from Key Largo. 1 hr. S of Miami. From Key Largo, take Transylvania Ave. to mile marker 103.2 (Shoreland Dr.). 1/2 m off highway.
Restrictions No smoking, no alcohol, no hair dryers. No children under 12.
Credit cards Amex, MC, Visa.
Rates MAP, $195–295 per person. Resort diving course, $75 for first person, $50 for each additional person.
Extras Spanish, German spoken.

Largo Lodge ¢
101740 Overseas Highway, 33037

Tel: 305–451–0424
800–IN–THE–SUN

"Not far from John Pennekamp Underwater Park, Largo Lodge is made up of a half-dozen duplex cottages, each with a kitchen/dining and living room area, a separate bedroom with two double beds, and a screened porch. The units are fairly close together, and were spotlessly clean. The grounds are lushly landscaped, and the dock has many comfortable lounge chairs, and is romantically lit at night. Guests enjoy a picnic dinner and watch the sun go down, or feed the resident ducks. The manager is very friendly and warm, and has lots of brochures and a lending library of paperbacks. Although the walls are painted concrete blocks, and the furnishings basic motel stuff, the rooms are comfortable, and our unit had such unexpected extras as a full-length mirror on the bathroom door and very thick towels. The atmosphere is very peaceful and relaxing, although you can hear the highway noise (as you can almost everywhere in Key Largo). Nearby are restaurants, grocery stores, and a seafood retailer." *(Linda Bamber)* More reports needed.

"The Keys are filled with places that are either very expensive, or are absolute dives. At this friendly little place, we found the perfect medium." *(AF)* More comments please.

Open All year.
Rooms 6 cottages—all with TV, air-conditioning, ceiling fan, kitchenette, screened porch. Pay phone on premises.
Facilities Dock and ramp for ocean, backwater fishing; swimming; diving, snorkeling nearby.
Location On Rte. 1, 1 m from Pennecamp Coral Reef Park.
Restrictions No children. Traffic noise might disturb light sleepers.
Credit cards MC, Visa.
Rates Room only, $85 double. Extra person, $10.

KEY WEST

Key West is the southernmost city in the continental United States, located 161 miles south of Miami. The completion of the Overseas Highway in 1938 brought major changes to Key West. No longer a sleepy fishing village, the town is often filled with tourists and hustlers; its gay population is estimated at 25 percent. International travelers discovered its allures and are providing a foreign accent to the goings-on. Key West is currently riding an upscale wave, with a gentrifying trend away from tacky T-shirt shops and dive bars to quality clothing and art stores. It's not a place people are neutral about. One of our readers wrote that "Key West is lovely—unlike any other place I've been in America. Sophisticated and funky. There is something for everyone. Even the tacky is interesting." *(Elaine Malsin)* Another reported that: "Key West is a tourist trap, overcrowded and crawling with escapees from the north, but that's what's so endearing about it. The Key West Aquarium and Audubon House are well worth visiting, but the fabled sunset festival—complete with fire-eaters, jugglers, and fortune tellers—at Mallory Dock is over-rated. It's a faded re-make of San Francisco in the sixties, with lots of unemployed actors but without the spontaneity and freshness to make it work, especially if you remember what the real thing was like. Good food here though, which was hard to find elsewhere in the Keys." *(Wayne Braffman)*

If the sun and water overwhelm, some other Key West sights of interest include Ernest Hemingway's Home, Key West Lighthouse Museum, Wrecker's Museum, and Mel Fisher's exhibit of sunken treasure. Those who feel their stay will be incomplete without a taste of key lime pie (or two or three), may want to sample the offerings at the Deli Restaurant, the Buttery, Pier House, or Sloppy Joes; remember the real thing is *never* green or thickened with gelatin—it's yellow, creamy, and sweet.

A word of advice about navigating in the Keys—the Florida Keys' Overseas Highway (U.S. 1) is studded with 126 mile markers starting at the corner of Fleming and Whitehead streets in Key West and ending near Florida City. Watch for the small green signs with white writing, found on the right shoulder of the road, since they're often used as reference points when directions are given.

Budget travelers should note that hotel rates are substantially lower from June through November, with the exception of holiday weekends.

Reader tips: "Probably the best restaurant in Key West, and one of the most expensive, is Louie's Backyard. Fabulous food served in a dining room or on a deck overlooking the ocean." *(Sheila & Joe Schmidt)* "Our favorite restaurants included the early-bird dinner at the Café Marquesa, a best buy, and the Savanah, a southern-style place with reasonable prices." *(Michael Miller)* "Our innkeeper suggested Fort Zachary Taylor Beach, which is beautiful and quiet, but is very rocky, with a sharp drop-off into the water. The next day, we rented bicycles and headed over to Smathers Beach for soft sand and shallow, calm waters." *(Laura Prizzi)*

Information please: The Artist House (534 Eaton Street, 33040;

305–296–3977) is a Victorian home, complete with gingerbread trim, etched-glass windows, and a turret, updated with the addition of air-conditioning and a Jacuzzi. Each of the five guest rooms have antique and reproduction furnishings accented with hand-painted period wallpapers. It's located in historic Old Town, just a half-block from Duval Street.

The Banyan Resort (323 Whitehead Street, 33040; 305–296–7786 or 800–225–0639) consists of six historic Conch homes now converted into 38 luxury suites. Each comes decorated in soothing neutral shades, with comfortable couches and lots of natural wicker, and all have fully equipped kitchens. One reader described it as having "the flavor of Old Key West, with a laid-back atmosphere and comfortable clean accommodations," but we need more recent feedback. Similarly, we need current reports on the **Island City House** (411 William Street, 33040; 305–294–5702 or 800–634–8230), made up of three guest houses sharing a private tropical garden. The mansion house was built in the 1880's as the private home of a wealthy Charleston family; the more casually decorated Arch House dates from the same period and was originally built as a carriage house; the Cigar House is modern, built of natural cypress, and takes its architectural style from a cigar factory that once occupied this site; the well-equipped rooms have contemporary decor.

Curry Mansion Inn 👫   *Tel:* 305–294–5349
511 Caroline Street, 33040   800–253–3466

Newly opened as a B&B in 1989, the Curry Mansion has been owned since 1975 by Edith and Albert Amsterdam, and has long been a Key West tourist attraction. Listed on the National Register of Historic Places, the lavishly detailed house includes original woodwork, stained and bevelled glass, and heirloom antiques from the Amsterdam family.

"The main house is a fully restored and period decorated 1899 mansion built by Florida's first millionaire. By day, the mansion is also run as a tourist attraction, with self-guided tours, but if you stay overnight you have the run of the place. Or you can sleep out back in the newly built units surrounding a small courtyard with swimming pool. We tried and liked both, but found the courtyard units to be quieter. The owners hold a complimentary happy hour every night in the courtyard, and offer a continental breakfast buffet in the same place at 8:30 A.M. of juice, cereal, muffins, and rolls.

"Our room was bright, airy, and clean, with contemporary wicker furnishings and pastel coloring; the king-size bed and air-conditioning made for a good night's rest. The atmosphere is very cordial, with guests exchanging restaurant tips and the Amsterdam's always helpful with any questions. Great blueberry muffins." *(B. Lang)* More comments?

Open All year.
Rooms 2 suites, 13 doubles—all with private bath and/or shower, telephone, radio, TV, desk, air-conditioning, fan, wet bar. All with sun deck or balcony. 4 rooms in original mansion, 11 in guest wing.
Facilities Full access to historic Curry Mansion with parlors, dining room, library, billiard room. Heated swimming pool, off-street parking. Guest privileges at Pier House Beach Club, with beach, restaurants, bar. Tennis, golf nearby.

Location Old Town Key West. 130 m S of Miami. From Duval St. turn right on Caroline St. to inn.
Restrictions No smoking. Street noise in some rooms.
Credit cards Amex, MC, Visa.
Rates B&B, $140–225 suite, $125–185 double. Extra person, $25. Children under 10 free in parents' room. 2–night weekend/holiday minimum.
Extras Wheelchair access. Crib, babysitting. French, German, Italian spoken.

Duval House
815 Duval Street, 33040

Tel: 305–294–1666

Choosing just the right spot for relaxing may be the most difficult part of your stay at Duval House. Will it be poolside or under the century-old banyan tree? In the lounge or on the balcony to watch the rest of Key West stroll by? This inn, formed by a cluster of Victorian homes, has been renovated in accordance with historic preservation requirements, and features a comfortable mix of wicker and antiques. Hibiscus flowers, picked daily, freshen each guest room, while Bahamian fans whirl lazily overhead. The inn has been owned by Richard Kamradt since 1989, and is managed by Jeff Murphy.

"Our room, while small, was spotlessly clean and well-maintained. The pool is located in a tropical garden surrounded by a deck, with enough chairs for all the guests. Breakfast includes cereal, muffins, bagels, coffee cake, donuts, and juice; coffee is served continuously throughout the day. The staff is helpful in recommending restaurants." *(Michael A. Miller)*

Open All year.
Rooms 3 suites, 26 doubles—3 with a maximum of 3 sharing bath. All with air-conditioning, fan, deck. Some with desk.
Facilities Lounge with TV, books, games; breakfast room. Swimming pool. Golf nearby. Snorkeling, swimming nearby.
Location Historic district. 120 m S of Miami, 90 m N of Havana, Cuba. Bus. Rte. #1 to Duval St., right on Duval.
Restrictions Light sleepers could be affected by traffic noise in two rooms. No children under 15.
Credit cards Amex, MC, Visa.
Rates B&B, $108–170 suite, $60–145 double, single. Extra person, $15. 2-night holiday minimum.

La Terraza de Marti ✗
1125 Duval Street, 33040

Tel: 305–294–8435
800–476–5283

Better known as the La-te-da (say it fast), La Terraza de Marti was named for José Marti, a Cuban patriot exiled to Key West. Long owned by Lawrence Formica, the La-te-da is a complex of seven Conch-style buildings linked by verandas, bridges, decks, and stairways, and festooned with flowers and palm trees. A bi-weekly event is the Wednesday and Sunday tea dance (one straight, one gay), a favorite with locals and tourist alike. "Divine dinners; guest rooms in the tradition of the fine food they serve." *(Nancy Peycke)*

Open All year.
Rooms 25 suites and doubles in 7 buildings—most with private bath and/or shower. All with air-conditioning. Some with kitchenette, double whirlpool tub, wet bar, stereo.

Facilities Restaurant, bar with dancing on Wed., Sun. afternoons; decks, porches. Swimming pool.
Location Historic district.
Restrictions No children.
Credit cards Amex, MC, Visa.
Rates Room only, $53–188.

Marquesa Hotel ✗   *Tel:* 305–292–1919
600 Fleming Street, 33040   800–UNWIND–1

Listed on the National Register of Historic Places, the Marquesa is a 1880s boarding house rescued from near destruction by hard work, good taste and nearly $2,000,000. A concierge tends to your every whim, and your senses will be soothed by bedtime Godiva chocolates, fresh flowers, and Caswell Massey toiletries. The hotel restaurant, the Cafe Marquesa, offers a creative menu, with such dishes as lobster ravioli with seafood sauce; sesame seed encrusted rack of lamb; and Brazilian-style pork.

"An exceptional small hotel built as a residence over 100 years ago. Once a decayed boarding house, it has been converted into a delightful, luxurious inn by Carole and Erik deBoer. The rooms are bright, cheerful and most have porches overlooking the pool. Each is complete with a spacious bath, quality reproduction furniture, and a slow-moving fan. Each morning the *New York Times* was delivered to our door and when we went out to dinner, the bed was turned down, the towels changed and waste baskets emptied. The staff remained unobtrusively in the background but were instantly available to offer service." *(Sheila & Joe Schmidt)* "Making a return visit, we were glad to see that the inn's original standards have been meticulously maintained, with impeccable housekeeping and an efficient, helpful staff. Sitting on our porch in the balmy tropical night was fabulous." *(JS)*

Open All year.
Rooms 15 suites and doubles—all with private bath and/or shower, telephone, TV, air-conditioning, stocked wet bar. 7 with deck.
Facilities Lobby, restaurant, terraces, decks. Heated swimming pool. Off-street parking.
Location Historic district, corner Fleming and Simonton Sts. 4 blocks from Gulf, 11 blocks from Atlantic, 5 blocks to center.
Credit cards Amex, MC, Visa.
Rates Room only, $175–275 suite, $105–175 double. Extra person, $15. 2-night holiday minimum. Alc dinner $40; early-bird special.
Extras Babysitting.

The Mermaid & the Alligator   *Tel:* 305–294–1894
729 Truman Avenue, 33040

So many inns take their names from historical figures that it signals a refreshing change when one takes a lighter approach. This B&B was named for two statues (a mermaid kissing an alligator) located behind the inn's octagonal-shaped jacuzzi pool. A Queen Anne Victorian built in 1904, the Mermaid & the Alligator has been owned by Michael and Ursula Keating since 1987. Each guest room has a different decor: Art Deco, Queen Anne, Southwest, and so on. Breakfasts include juice, coffee,

FLORIDA

fresh tropical fruit—perhaps mango and papaya, a cheese platter, boiled eggs, and a variety of breads and breakfast cakes made by Ursula. "A peaceful and tranquil escape. The Garden Room is our favorite with its private access to the pool. Owners Michael and Ursula are gracious and superb at tending to our needs, yet respect our privacy. Ursula's coffee is heavenly, too!" *(Kathleen & Patrick Whelan)*

Open All year.
Rooms 5 doubles—all with private shower and/or bath, air-conditioning. 1 with porch.
Facilities Common room, jacuzzi pool, large sun deck, gardens. Off-street parking.
Location 165 m S of Miami. On beach-side of Old Town.
Restrictions No children under 16. No pets permitted.
Credit cards Amex, MC, Visa.
Rates B&B, $49–145 double.
Extras German spoken.

Pier House ✗
1 Duval Street, 33040

Tel: 305–296–4600
In U.S.: 800–327–8340
In FL: 800–432–3414

Once the only sizable hotel of distinction in Key West, recent chain hotel construction was putting a bit of pressure on the Pier House. A multi-million dollar renovation and expansion have brought its guest rooms and landscaped grounds up to snuff; its location on a private beach at the foot of Duval Street has always been first rate. Most recently built are the Caribbean spa rooms, many with double whirlpool tubs, steam saunas, terrycloth robes, and a few with gas fireplaces.

"A small beachfront hotel in the center of downtown Key West, the guest rooms are nicely furnished and comfortable, although a bit small for the price. There is a small but excellent beach with full facilities, although it does face the 'wrong way' for the best sun. Topless swimming for women and G-strings for both sexes can be seen on the beach, but this is Key West. There are several restaurants and a fine wine bar in the hotel, and dozens of places to eat or shop within walking distance in town. The staff is helpful and pleasant. You do not need a car if you stay here." *(Willis Frick, also Truman Talley)* Your comments appreciated.

Open All year.
Rooms 13 suites, 144 guest rooms—all with full private bath, telephone, radio, TV, air-conditioning, fan. Some with whirlpool bath, steam sauna, fireplace.
Facilities Restaurant, bar, decks. Swimming pool, beach, off-street parking.
Location Historic district.
Credit cards Amex, MC, Visa.
Rates Room only, $225–725 suite, $135–350 double. Extra person, $35.

Popular House/Key West B&B
415 William Street, 33040

Tel: 305–296–7274

Jody Carlson has lived in Key West since 1975, and has owned the Popular House since 1987. She is pleased to share her in-depth knowledge of restaurants, sights, local history, and water sports with her guests. The

Popular House is a turn-of-the-century Victorian, built by shipbuilders. Listed on the National Register of Historic Places, it has 13-foot-high ceilings, hardwood floors, natural wood paneling on the walls, and white moldings. Rooms are decorated in Caribbean style, with overstuffed couches and bright contemporary paintings.

"Jody Carlson greeted us graciously and showed us to our large airy room. Breakfast included fresh fruit, fresh-squeezed orange juice, home-made muffins and pastries, and delicious Cuban coffee for the stout-hearted (regular also available)." *(Mary Fournier)* "Jody has two golden retrievers, who love to be petted and beg for food. The inn's atmosphere is warm and casual." *(Laura Prizzi)*

Open All year.
Rooms 6 doubles, 1 single—2 with private bath, 5 with a maximum of 5 people sharing bath. All with air-conditioning, fan.
Facilities Living room, kitchen, porches, sun decks. Hot tub, sauna. 5 blocks to beach.
Location 90 m S of Miami. Historic district. 3 blocks from Duval St.
Restrictions No children.
Credit cards Amex, Encore, Visa.
Rates B&B, $69–135 double, $49–89 single. Extra person, $10. 5% senior, AAA discount. 3-night weekend minimum. 5-night holiday minimum.
Extras French, German spoken.

The Watson House   *Tel:* 305–294–6712
525 Simonton Street, 33040

Dating back to 1860, the Watson House was purchased by an Ohio family named Baron during the middle of the Civil War. Key West was then a Union stronghold, and the Barons must have been quite confident of the eventual outcome of the war to make the purchase. The Watson House has been owned Ed Czaplicki and Joe Beres since 1984. They've furnished their inn eclectically with Art Deco, white wicker, Haitian art, and 19th century period reproductions used to individually decorate each room. Rates include a continental breakfast.

" From the street you see a lovely old Bahamas-style home, surrounded by a wrought-iron fence. Entering through the backyard gate, you dis-cover a swimming pool, Jacuzzi, and patio. There are two suites for rent on the second floor, plus the cabana suite off the pool. Each has its own distinct style, but all are done with the finest materials and the best in furniture. We stayed in the apartment and slept in pine four-poster beds and cooked our meals in the all-white new kitchen, and spent our evenings in the living room with the two French doors open to the back porch and pool area. Privacy prevails. We felt as though we had slipped away to our own little resort in the heart of Key West. Cat lovers will enjoy the resident cat, Princess." *(Kathleen Novak & Michael Niedenfuehr, also DLG)* More comments please.

Open All year.
Rooms 2 suites, 1 double—all with private bath and/or shower, telephone, radio, TV, desk, air-conditioning, ceiling fan. Suites have full kitchen.
Facilities Patio, deck, swimming pool, hot tub.

Location Center of Historic Preservation District. At corner of Simonton and Southard Sts. 1 block E of Duval.
Restrictions No children. No pets.
Credit cards Amex, MC, Visa.
Rates B&B, $115–295 suite, $85–195 double, $85–105 single. Extra person, $15. 2-night minimum stay.
Extras Ground-floor cabana wheelchair accessible; equipped for the disabled.

LAKE WALES

Reader tip: "Take time to see the Bok Tower Gardens, off Alternate Route 27 of Tower Boulevard. The tower is striking (pink Georgia marble with tile work at top), the carillon is worth hearing, and the gardens are pleasant. The coffee shop is surprisingly good and you can eat outside. Visitors are encouraged to buy food for the carp and squirrels, which kept the kids busy while we enjoyed the grounds. What a change from Disney World."*(Diane Wolf, also LG)* "The old railroad depot with its interesting memorabilia is also worth a look." *(HB)*

Chalet Suzanne ♠ ✕   *Tel: 813–676–6011*
U.S. Highway 27 and 17A North,   800–288–6011
P.O. Drawer AC, 33853

In the most unlikely setting, amid the orange groves and alligators of central Florida, yet not far from "Theme Park USA"—a.k.a. Orlando—is the Chalet Suzanne. Set on beautiful green lawns and bordering a lake, it is about as far as you can get from Florida's standard motel accommodations.

Over fifty years ago Bertha Hinshaw turned her home into an inn and restaurant, to support the family after her husband died and the stock market crashed. The inn soon gained a reputation for good food and lodging and was included in Duncan Hines's first *Guide to Good Eating*. During World War II the main building, including the kitchen and many dining rooms, burned down completely. No building materials were available because of the war, so the stables, rabbit hutches, and chicken coops were added to existing structures. Additional rooms have been built since then, and the result is an unlikely hodgepodge of munchkin-size towers, turrets, and gables that ramble in all directions on fourteen levels. You might think that the Good Witch of the North had it specially delivered from the Land of Oz. In fact, its uniqueness has given it a place on the National Register of Historic Places

Bertha Hinshaw made eighteen trips around the world, bringing back glass, china, tiles, and stained glass windows; the chalet's Swiss, Scandinavian, French, Oriental, Spanish, and Turkish architecture was inspired by what she saw. Not surprisingly, rooms vary dramatically in size and decor, although most are spacious, with cozy seating areas and inviting thirties-era decor; bathrooms are dated but functional, many decorated with stunning hand-painted tiles.

After Carl Hinshaw, Bertha's son, returned from World War II, he and his wife Vita gradually took over the management of the inn and continue to operate it today, with the help of their children, Tina and Eric. Carl also developed the Chalet Suzanne line of gourmet canned soups, based on his mother's original recipes.

Although very expensive, the restaurant is one of the best in Florida: "Service is excellent—attentive but totally unobtrusive, professional yet completely relaxed and friendly. The menu never changes: you start with their signature broiled grapefruit with chicken liver—you have to eat it to believe how good it tastes—followed by the peppery romaine soup—the ingredients are secret but lettuce is not among them—a seasonal salad—ours included zucchini and artichoke, seasoned with dill, served with their tiny but addictive potato rolls. The choice and originality of the main courses is limited, but they are prepared to perfection, and portions are extremely generous." (SWS, also Lillie Galvin)

"Bertha Hinshaw's first instruction to the men she hired was to throw away their plumb bobs and measuring tapes. The results are delightful. The inn's interior is compatible with the exterior, which is to say that the floors are not always level and you may find a step or two between bedrooms, bath, and sitting areas. The restaurant is composed of several dining rooms, adjoining at odd levels and angles, of course, with no uniformity in furniture or place settings, which are, for the most part, put together from many old sets of fine china and flatware collected by the Hinshaws during years of European travel." (Jim & Marty Marsden)

"Breakfast, although expensive, was delicious—tiny Swedish pancakes with lingonberry sauce—and served with the same attentiveness that makes the dinners so special. The waitresses were extremely helpful and patient with our children. Our kids really liked the lemon sorbet served between courses at dinner so we asked for that as their dessert (and were given huge portions), while we had an equally delicious one which combined a chocolate filling between thin layers of meringue. Diners who are taken with the Norwegian ashtrays used as soup dishes can buy them at the restaurant gift shop. More ceramics are available at the studio where some of the potters will take special orders, so you can design your own or have an item personalized. The tile work inside and outside of the rooms is incredible. The charm here is the inn's quirkiness—a quality that doesn't necessarily appeal to everyone." (Diane Wolf) "Serene atmosphere, excellent restaurant; rooms comfortable, eclectic, not luxurious." (HB) "I'm not royalty, but I certainly don't mind being treated as though I were. The bell boy, desk staff, and restaurant personnel were extremely cordial, yet never overdid it. In spite of the superb food you have already written about, the service may be the thing I remember the longest. They are masters at being available without being intrusive. My small room was furnished with fresh flowers, a fruit basket with chocolates and hard candy, and a decanter of sherry. It had a small sitting area, two bureaus, two small closets, and a double bed; the bath had a skylight and was beautifully tiled." (Mary Morgan)

Areas for improvement: "We loved our stay, but felt that it's time for some maintenance and refurbishing. The grounds needed tending, the concrete patio outside our room was cracked and flaking, and some of our

FLORIDA

room furnishings were a bit tired." And: "I couldn't find an electrical outlet in the bathroom."

Open All year. Restaurant closed Mon. May through Dec.
Rooms 4 suites, 26 doubles, 1 single—all with private bath and/or shower, telephone, TV, air-conditioning. Some with radio, desk, fan, balcony, courtyard or patio.
Facilities Restaurant, bar, lounge, living room, wine dungeon, library, patio, gift shop, antique shop. Pianist, organist in restaurant and lounge weekends. 70 acres with swimming pool, private lake, badminton, croquet. Private airstrip. Self-tours of soup cannery. Tennis, golf nearby.
Location Central FL; Polk County. 1 hr. SW of Orlando, 40 min. S of Disney World, 4 m N of Lake Wales. From I-4, take Rte. 27 S to Rte. 17A. Go E on Rte. 17A to inn.
Credit cards Amex, CB, Discover, JCB, MC, Visa.
Rates B&B, $95–195 suite, double, single; extra person, $12. MAP, $295 suite. Alc lunch, $27; alc dinner, $51. Prix fixe lunch, $28–40; prix fixe dinner, $59–73. 6% tax and 18% restaurant food service charge additional. MAP packages May–Nov.; honeymoon packages.
Extras Two rooms with wheelchair access. Airport/station pickups. Pets permitted by prior arrangement. Crib, babysitting. German, Yugoslavian spoken.

LITTLE TORCH KEY

Little Palm Island ✗   *Tel:* 305–872–2524
Mile Marker 28.5, Route 4, Box 1036, 33042   800–343–8567

If you'd like to escape to a private tropical island, complete with hand-thatched bungalows, luxurious South Seas–style decor, and gourmet French cuisine—just 120 miles from Miami—read on. Occupying the whole of a five-acre island, Little Palm Island is located at the western end of the Newfound Harbor Keys, where the Newfound Harbor meets the Atlantic. This advantageous location gives it a sand and coral base, not mangrove like most other islands. Originally known as Little Munson Island and long used as a private family retreat and fishing camp, the island was a favorite vacation spot of President Truman. John Kennedy came to watch the filming of *PT 109* in 1962, and because of his visit, the state of Florida supplied the island with telephone and electric service.

In 1988, the island was converted into a resort. The original fishing lodge is now the Great House, home to the restaurant and two suites. Most guests are accommodated in bungalows holding two suites each.

"The spacious suites are decorated with wicker furnishings, vivid prints, and Mexican tile accents. The atmosphere is very quiet and relaxed. Although the island was nearly fully booked during our visit, we often felt as if we were the only ones there. The location is good, isolated yet near Key West with its airport and activities. The entire island is beautifully landscaped, and the pool area is lovely, with comfortable lounge chairs and big plush towels." *(Ken & Karen Gruska)*

"The refrigerator and bar in each room was always kept fully stocked, often replenished twice daily. The mosquito netting over our king-sized

bed, while not functionally necessary, was a very lovely touch. The food
is creatively prepared and attractively presented at a consistently high
standard. LPI is not for everyone, though. Although we found its small
size most appealing, it might be a deterrent to others; there are no tennis
courts or golf courses on the island." *(J. Hatcher Graham)*

"Managing partner Ben Woodson does more than go the extra mile
to make sure his guests are taken care of—along with partner Jack Rice
and the staff, they work hard to make everyone feel welcome and cared
for. The food is good by any standard, but its quality is even more
impressive when you realize that everything has to be shipped down to
the Keys, transported to the island by boat." *(Bob Blitz)* "Very expensive
but worth it. The food is irresistible. We especially enjoyed the chilled
fruit soups. The staff was friendly and exceptionally friendly. Our bungalow had a thatched roof, and a porch for sitting. There were ham-
mocks scattered among the palm trees. The 20-minute boat ride to the
hotel is lovely, revealing beauty you can see only from the water." *(Jane
Mattoon)*

Open All year.
Rooms 30 suites—all with full private bath with whirlpool tub, double sinks, and
outside shower; desk, air-conditioning, fan, deck with hammock, coffee maker, wet
bar.
Facilities Restaurant with live music twice weekly. 5 acres with swimming pool,
beaches, bicycling, fishing, snorkeling, sailing; all equipment provided. Dive shop,
fishing; scuba certification.
Location FL Keys. 120 m S of Miami. At Mile Marker 28.5 (Little Torch Key),
turn into Dolphin Marina and park at shore station (pink building on R) for Little
Palm Island. 30-min. drive from shore station to Key West.
Restrictions No smoking on launch boat. No children under 9.
Credit cards Amex, MC, Visa.
Rates Full board, $430–573 suite for 2 persons; extra person, $126. Room only,
$308–458 suite for 2; extra person, $52. No tipping. 2–3 night weekend/holiday
minimum. Alc breakfast $7, lunch $14, dinner $38. All-inclusive packages.
Extras Wheelchair access. Pickup from Key West airport, $40 per couple. French,
Spanish spoken.

MIAMI

For additional area entries, see **Coconut Grove, Coral Gables, and
Miami Beach.**

Miami River Inn ¢   *Tel:* 305–325–0045
118 S.W. South River Drive, 33130   800–HOTEL–89

Owner Sallye Jude doesn't mince words when describing the guest
rooms at the Miami River Inn. Guests can choose from "cozy quarters,
spacious quarters, or deluxe quarters," all individually decorated with
antiques and period pieces. As part of a revitalization of a neighborhood
known recently as East Little Havana, the inn and neighboring apartments have been created out of nine buildings, some dating back to the

early 1900s, overlooking the vibrant Miami riverfront. Rates include continental breakfast and afternoon tea; John Cowden is the manager.

"An interesting restoration in the oldest area of Miami. Because the property is large, there is a nice sense of privacy and quiet. Sallye has done an excellent job of decorating with quaint old furniture, and curtains which she has made herself. While the breakfast room is small, the adjacent pool area is lovely and perfect for enjoying your meal. The rooms and grounds are spotless, the staff pleasant, and the manager was very helpful in giving directions to locate the inn (it's a bit tricky). The inn is a short walk from downtown, with ample parking within the compound; security seems excellent." *(Sheila & Joe Schmidt)* "Endorse existing entry." *(JS)*

Open All year.
Rooms 40 doubles—all with private bath and/or shower, telephone, TV, air-conditioning, fan. 2 with fireplace, balcony. Guest rooms in 4 buildings.
Facilities Lobby, poolside breakfast room, four common rooms; one with fireplace and books. Off-street parking. Gardens, swimming pool, hot tub, croquet court. Golf, boating, swimming nearby.
Location East Little Havanna. 10 min. walk to downtown.
Restrictions Night-time walks not advised. Noise could disturb light sleepers in some rooms. Smoking restricted.
Credit cards Amex, MC, Visa.
Rates B&B, $60–125 double or single. 10% senior, AAA discount.
Extras Wheelchair access. French, Spanish spoken.

MIAMI BEACH

Known as South Beach or SoBe, the mile-square Art Deco district of south Miami Beach encompasses 800 buildings dating from the 1930's and 1940's. Wander along Ocean Drive between 5th and 9th Streets to see the best of them. Many have been restored as hotels, as noted below. In general, rooms in the Art Deco hotels are smaller than most modern hotel rooms are today.

Don't forget that Miami is a big city, where the twin scourges of crime and drugs can quickly sour the vacation of any traveler who isn't citywise. Consult your hotel staff about which neighborhoods are safe, and which routes to walk.

Reader tip: "Your visit will not be complete without a dinner at **Joe's Stone Crab Restaurant** in Miami Beach. Close to 400,000 diners annually enjoy terrific seafood from mid-October to mid-May; the restaurant closes when crab is out of season."

Information please: Through 1990, there was a clear consensus that the **Cavalier Hotel & Cabana Club** (1320 Ocean Drive, 33139; 305–534–2135 or 800–338–9076) under the management of Don Meginly was the best place to stay in the historic Art Deco district. Unfortunately, financial mismanagement put the hotel's ownership group into receivership, and the bank has hired a local motel management company to run the Cavalier, as well as its sister hotels: the Leslie, the Carlyle, and the Cardozo. A mature example of the Art Deco style, the Cavalier was built in 1936 and restored in 1985. Double rates for its 40 rooms range from $65–175 (depending on size and season) and include continental breakfast. Comments greatly appreciated.

We'd also like reports on some other Art Deco hotels in the historic district: The **Park Central Hotel** (640 Ocean Drive, 33139; 305–538–1611), an Art Deco classic with lavender trim and the obligatory porthole windows, offers rooms done totally in period, and is home to a restaurant, Lucky's, serving first-rate American cuisine. Other possibilities include the **Century** (140 Ocean Drive, 33139; 305–674–8855), a two-story charmer with relaxing atmosphere and a capable staff;**The Clevelander** (1020 Ocean Drive, 33139; 305–531–3485), with 65 rooms and an attractive swimming pool; and the **Waldorf Towers** (860 Ocean Drive 33139; 305–531–7684), with graceful architectural curves highlighted by pink and yellow trim. Rooms are decorated in pastel pinks and greens, and guests can breakfast on the veranda.

For additional area entries, see also **Coconut Grove, Coral Gables, and Miami.**

MICANOPY

Reader tips: "Micanopy is a tiny sleepy Old Florida town about ten to fifteen minutes south of Gainesville, with many enticing antique shops." *(TS)* "While in the area, drive about ten miles east to Cross Creek to visit the Marjorie Kinnan Rawlings Home, and stop for lunch or dinner at the Yearling Inn [904–466–3033] for some of Rawlings' favorite dishes: fried turtle, frog's legs, catfish, or gator tail, accompanied by hush puppies, topped off with a slice of delicious lime pie." *(JS)* "Cross Creek, restored home of Marjorie Kinnan Rawlings is very popular. We stopped there first, to put our name on the waiting list, since tour groups sizes are limited, then had lunch at the Yearling Inn. We'd also recommend making reservations for the Wild Flowers Cafe, just outside town on Hwy 441, open for lunch and dinner. Though casual, the food is very good; our grouper and desserts were exceptional." *(HB)*

Herlong Mansion ¢   *Tel:* 904–466–3322
402 NE Cholokka Boulevard, P.O. Box 667, 32667

Although the Herlong Mansion dates back to 1875, it was completely rebuilt in 1915 in the Colonial Revival style, with a wide veranda supported by four massive Roman-style columns. It sits back from the street, surrounded by old oak and pecan trees. A 1987 restoration (requiring 162 gallons of paint stripper) has returned the mansion to its original splendor, showcasing its leaded glass windows, mahogany, oak, and maple inlaid floors, and "tiger oak" paneling. In 1990 H.C. "Sonny" Howard purchased the mansion and is planning further improvements to both the house and grounds. Rates include a full breakfast on Friday and Saturday, with a continental breakfast offered Sunday through Thursday.

"Sonny was very helpful in directing us to nearby points of interest.

FLORIDA

The mansion is conveniently located in town, near antique shops and a bookstore, housed in original old buildings, giving the village an early 1900s air." *(HB)* "Mr. Howard made us feel like friends who were visiting his home; the furnishings and cleanliness are impeccable; breakfast was excellent, accompanied by delightful background music."*(Patrick Dekle, also Marie Regojo)*

Open All year.
Rooms 2 suites, 4 doubles—all with private bath and/or shower, radio, air-conditioning, fireplace. 5 with balcony.
Facilities Parlor, dining room, living room, library, all with fireplace; veranda. 2 acres with garden.
Location 12 m S of Gainesville, 24 m N of Ocala; take Micanopy exit off I-75 or Rte. 441 to inn in center of town.
Restrictions No smoking.
Credit cards MC, Visa.
Rates B&B, $95–115 suite, $75–95 double. Extra person, $5.
Extras Airport pickups, $25.

MINNEOLA

Lake Minneola Inn ¢   *Tel:* 904–394–2232
508 Main Avenue, P.O. Box 803, 34755

Lake Minneola is one of 13 lakes connected by the cypress-lined canals of north central Florida. This region had been a resort destination for decades before Mickey Mouse was even a gleam in Mr. Disney's eye, as attested by area's many century-old hotels. The Lake Minneola Inn is one of these, recently restored by Stephen and Shari Parrish to highlight its architecture while preserving some of the original fixtures and furnishings. The simple decor features glowing wood floors, antique and reproduction furniture, with pastel colors predominating. Rates include a continental breakfast served in the dining room or on the porch.

"Stephen's mother Nell acts as host and provides information on local activities. Our large room opened to a wide porch furnished with white wicker and baskets of ferns, and we enjoyed the view of the lake over tall glasses of iced tea. While the inn's only been in operation for a short while, they've got what it takes to do well." *(B.J. Hensley)* "Firm beds, lovely linens, warm friendly atmosphere." *(Marianne Vos)*

Open All year.
Rooms 1 suite, 9 doubles—all with private bath and/or shower, air-conditioning.
Facilities Dining room, porch. On lake with beach, dock, swings. Pontoons, canoes. Boat slips, $6/night. Golf nearby.
Location Central FL. 25 m NW of Orlando, 22 m N of Disney. From Florida Turnpike, take Exit 285 6 m S to Main Ave. Bear right to inn on right, on E shore of Lake Minneola.
Restrictions Smoking on porches only. Children over 5 welcome.
Credit cards MC, Visa.
Rates B&B, $80 suite, $45–65 double. Rollaway, $6.

MOUNT DORA

Lakeside Inn 🛉 ✕   *Tel:* 904–383–4101
100 North Alexander Street, 32757   800–556–5016

A historic inn built in the 1880s, the Lakeside was expanded and updated
in the 1920s, when it was a fashionable resort, frequented by F. Scott
Fitzgerald, among others. By the 1980s it was saved from the wrecking
ball by a group of local investors, who spent over $5,000,000 restoring
it. Unfortunately, this proved an overwhelming sum, and the partners filed
for bankruptcy in 1989. We are unclear as to the present financial status
of the inn, but in any case, it doesn't seem to be having a negative effect
on readers' experiences here. "The road from Orlando (Route 441) to Mt.
Dora is an unsavory stew of traffic lights and nudie bars, placing one's
arrival in Mt. Dora in sharp contrast. Now listed on the National Register
of Historic Places, the hotel has a quiet setting, overlooking the swimming
pool and lake beyond. Its extensive porches have plenty of old-fashioned
rockers, perfect for reading or conversation. Although both bodies of
water look equally inviting, the management recommends the former for
swimming because of the resident alligator who occupies the latter. Inside,
the inn is decorated with Laura Ashley fabrics and wall coverings and
period reproduction furnishings; the color scheme is ivory, dusty rose, and
soft blue or green. Most rooms are spacious, but even the smallest have
plenty of room for the basics." *(SWS)* One of our favorite getaways; good
food, comfortable accommodations." *(S. Louis Carpenter)* "Mt. Dora has a
picturesque New England–style main street with some appealing shops."
(Mary Morgan)

Open All year.
Rooms 87 doubles—all with full private bath, telephone, TV, air-conditioning.
Facilities Lobby/library, restaurant, lounge with entertainment. 10 acres with
gardens, croquet, shuffleboard, putting green, swimming pool, 2 lighted tennis
courts; lake beach for sunning, fishing, boating. Golf nearby.
Location Central FL, 25 NW of Orlando. 45 m to Disney World. Downtown
historic district. From I-95 or FL Tpke., take I-4 to Rte. 441. Go N on Rte. 441 to
Mt. Dora.
Credit cards Amex, CB, DC, MC, Optima, Visa.
Rates Room only, $65–135 double. Extra person, $10. Mystery, weekend, golf
packages.

NAPLES

An elegant community of gracious homes and trendy shops and restaurants, Naples' key attraction is its seven miles of white sand beaches, ideal
for sunning, swimming, and shelling. Visitors can choose from a full menu
of water sports, visits to nature sanctuaries, golf, and tennis.
   Reader tip: Although not recommended for overnight accommodation, *Sheila & Joe Schmidt* suggest the **Rod and Gun Club** (P.O. Box G,
Everglades City 33929; 813–695–2101) as a pleasant stop for a drink or

a light meal. "When travelling between Naples and Miami we often visit this remote spot, surrounded by mangrove and swamp. This rustic lodge, once a favorite with presidents from Truman to Nixon, is on the water and the screened porch (the mosquitoes are awesome) has a lovely view, and is a pleasant place for a drink or snack."

Inn by the Sea ¢   813–649–4124
287 11th Avenue South, 33940

Built as a tourist house in 1936, the Inn by the Sea was restored as a B&B in by Elise Orban in 1989, when it was featured as a designer showcase by the South Florida Chapter of the American Society of Interior Design. Many decor elements provided by the showcase have been combined with such "old Florida" touches as heart pine and cypress woodwork, white iron and brass beds, wicker furnishings, and floral fabrics. Surrounded by tropical plantings of coconut palms, bird of paradise, and bougainvillea, the inn is listed on the National Register of Historic Places. Its pink wooden cove siding and pinkish-white roof of galvanized shingles were common during the thirties but are rare today. Guests receive a breakfast of homemade muffins and bread, natural cereal, fruit, and fresh-squeezed orange juice (there's a tree in the back yard).

"Lovely decor, short walk to the beach, and towels and chairs are provided." *(Travis Goss)* "The restoration of the inn was well done. Rooms are bright and cheerful. Housekeeping is very good. The inn is within walking distance of the beach, shops, and downtown." *(JS)*

"A place where you can park your car and not get in it all weekend; bikes are available for longer trips beyond the neighborhood. Breakfast is varied, from scones to muffins, fruit and granola, light enough for the tropial climate yet substantial and plentiful." *(Mr. & Mrs. Robert Maser)* More reports required.

Open All year.
Rooms 1 suite, 5 doubles—4 with private bath, 2 with a maximum of 4 people sharing 1 bath. All with desk, air-conditioning, fan.
Facilities Living room with stereo, TV/VCR; library; dining room; sun room; patio, garden. 2 blocks to beach for swimming, shelling, boating, fishing. Cambier Park nearby for tennis, horseshoes. Several golf courses nearby.
Location Gulf coast. Olde Naples Historic District. 30 m S of Ft. Meyers, 100 m W of Miami. From I-75 or SW Regional Airport, take I-75 S to Exit 16. Bear right to Goodlette Rd. and turn left. Go 4 m to end and turn right on U.S. Rte. 41 and continue to 5th Ave. South (toward beach), then turn left on 3rd Ave. South. Continue to 11th Ave. South to inn at corner.
Restrictions No smoking. No children.
Credit cards Amex, Visa.
Rates B&B, $75–125 suite, $45–110 double.
Extras Local airport/station pickups.

NEW SMYRNA BEACH

Information please: Mott's Indian River Lodge (1210 South Riverside Drive, 32168; 904–428–2491 or 800–541–4529) is a turn-of-the-century resort hotel brought up-to-date with private baths and air-conditioning.

The lodge's restaurant offers buffet specials for both lunch and dinner, but no alcohol is served to comply with the Christian beliefs of its management and many guests. "We stopped by for iced tea and thoroughly enjoyed the river view from the cool, shady porch and the restaurant. The large lobby is equally inviting, with white wicker rockers in comfortable seating clusters. Our waitress told of us of the days when it was a popular place for Al Capone's 'girls'; these days, most guests appeared to be senior citizens." *(Linda N. Todd)* Additional comments?

Riverview Hotel ¢ ✕
Tel: 904–428–5858
103 Flagler Avenue, 32169

For over 100 years the porches of the Riverview Hotel have provided the perfect vantage point for surveying the yacht traffic on the intracoastal waterway. This former bridge tender's home, supplemented by a contemporary restaurant and marina, has been completely restored; the decor provides a tropical flavor with wicker furnishings, louvered wooden shutters, and brightly painted Haitian art. Purchased in 1990 by Jim and Christa Kelsey, these experienced owners of several marinas in the Keys feel that they have found the perfect spot, "just enough rooms to keep us busy and not so many that we can't make every single one very, very special." The restaurant, Riverview Charlie's, features seafood in all its guises—broiled, fried, blackened, steamed, in salads, pastas, and casseroles. Non-fish eaters should not despair—there is also a selection of non-swimming entrées. Rates include a continental breakfast delivered to your door, and evening turndown service with chocolates.

"The Riverview is old-fashioned Florida at its best. My room was simple, with a white and hunter green decor, ceiling fan, and a door to the veranda. After the over-priced gaudiness of some Orlando hotels, it's a breath of fresh air. The beautiful beach is just six blocks away. Dinner in the riverfront restaurant was excellent. " *(Linda N. Todd)*

Open All year
Rooms 3 suites, 15 doubles—all with private bath and/or shower, telephone, radio, TV, air-conditioning, fan, balcony.
Facilities Dining room, restaurant, bar/lounge. Occasional evening entertainment. Fax, copy machine available. Swimming pool. Off-street parking, room service. Tennis, beach, golf nearby.
Location Volusia County. 20 m south of Daytona Beach. In historic downtown area.
Restrictions Light sleepers should request poolside rooms. Children over 10 preferred.
Credit cards Amex, MC, Visa.
Rates B&B, $130–150 suite, $60–90 double. Extra person, $10. 10% senior, AAA discount. 4-night minimum Daytona Race, Power Boat Race weeks. Alc lunch, $10; alc dinner, $25.
Extras Limited wheelchair access. Local airport pickups. Crib, babysitting.

OCALA

The center of Florida's thoroughbred racing industry, many streets in Ocala's historic district are lined with gracious Victorian mansions, shaded

FLORIDA

by moss-draped oak trees. Nearby is the town of Silver Springs, famous for its crystal clear waters. Ocala is located in north central Florida, about 28 miles south of Gainesville, and about 55 miles northwest of Orlando.

Seven Sisters Inn
820 S.E. Fort King Street, 32671

Tel: 904–867–1110

Imagine a century-old Queen Anne Victorian, complete with turret and verandas, surrounded by green lawns and old-fashioned flower beds. Outside of town, thoroughbred horses gallop over rolling hills bordered by white fencing. Quite a vision, you say, but in Florida? In fact, that's very much what you'll find at the Seven Sisters Inn, a gracious, three-story home built in 1888, fully renovated in 1986, and purchased in 1990 by Bonnie and Ken. Such period details as handmade quilts, antique wicker chairs, armoires, and brass and iron and four-poster beds, are highlighted by the light and sunny atmosphere most contemporary travelers prefer.

"Everything in our room coordinated with the basic theme of white and red roses. The armoire was hand-painted with roses to match those in the wallpaper. Although fairly small it had a sitting area with magazines and books, and the bed had reading lights on either side. The bath was immaculate with a claw-foot tub and a shower ring, a pedestal sink and matching wallpaper. There were plenty of fluffy white towels and beautifully trimmed white sheets. Breakfast was a real treat—raspberries in cream, blueberry muffins with coffee and juice, then peach-covered thick-cut French toast stuffed with cheese and served with apricot brandy sauce and baked ham." *(April Burwell)* "We stayed in Lanetta's room, a cozy, little room with a four-poster bed and an antique armoire with hat boxes decorating the top. The front porch with its wicker chairs and tables was a delightful place to sit and read." *(Stephanie Robertson)*

"Bonnie and Ken are delightful and helpful in providing information about the area. The inn itself was beautifully decorated for Christmas. Housekeeping is impeccable right down to the ironed sheets."*(Sheila & Joe Schmidt)* "Our room, Sylvia's was spacious and elegant, done in green and cream, with a gorgeous king-sized bed. Exquisite linens, fresh flowers, fireplace, and an immaculately clean bathroom made it a delight. The friendly helpful staff gave us a tour of all the rooms, and each was charming. The delicious breakfasts included home-baked muffins and a different entrée every day." *(Donna & Robert Jacobson)*

Areas for improvement: "Although exquisitely decorated, the antique white wicker tables in the dining room offered no leg room for my six-foot-tall husband!" And: "When we visited, Lottie's Loft on the top floor did not appear to be walled in or sound-insulated, making it noisy for those sleeping below, and providing minimal privacy for those staying in the loft. Carpeting would help, as would enclosing the loft, or at least the stairwell."

Open All year.
Rooms 5 doubles—all with full private bath, desk, air-conditioning, fan. 1 with fireplace.
Facilities Garden room, club room with TV, games, library, porch. ½ acre with lawn, garden.

90

Location From I-75, take Exit 69 onto Rte. 40 E (Silver Springs Blvd.). Go 3 m, and after passing town sq., turn right on 8th St. or Wenona St., left on SE Fort King St. to inn on right.
Restrictions No smoking. No children under 13.
Credit cards Amex, MC, Visa.
Rates B&B, $85–115 suite or double. 2-night holiday minimum.

ORANGE PARK

Inn at Club Continental ¢ ✕ 🕭   *Tel:* 904–264–6070
2143 Astor Street, P.O. Box 7059, 32073

Set on the St. John's River, the Club Continental was built in 1923 as the private winter estate of Caleb Johnson, founder of the Palmolive Soap company. Johnson's grandson converted the property from private residence to country club, and later added guest housing open to the public. Guest rooms are in the Inn at Winterbourne, an 1870 Victorian frame building on the Club's grounds, while the dining and sitting rooms are in the Spanish-style clubhouse building. Guests at the inn enjoy all the club's facilities, and the club is still owned and run by Johnson's great-grandchildren. "Three of the buildings are listed on the National Register of Historic Places. The gardens are beautiful, the food very good, and the common rooms very handsome."*(Betty Richards)* Rates include a continental breakfast, and the dinner menu includes such entrées as snapper with pesto and sundried tomatoes, or veal with green peppercorns and lemon butter.

"We felt we were living in the 1920s in grand style. Our second-floor rooms, the Mexican Room and the Continental Suite were filled with period pieces and overlooked the water. Brunch was excellent and is usually sold out; make advance reservations." *(Lowell Corbin)*

Open All year. Restaurant closed Sat. and Mon.
Rooms 2 suites, 5 doubles—all with full private bath, radio, TV, desk, air-conditioning, fan.
Facilities Dining room, bar, pub, conference facilities, verandas. 35 acres on river with 3 swimming pools, 2 tennis courts, marina, sailboat charters, weekly children's program.
Location 10 m SE of Jacksonville. 30 m NE of St. Augustine. From I-295 take Rte. 17 to Kingsley Ave. and turn left. Continue to Astor and turn right.
Credit cards Amex.
Rates B&B, $350 suite, $60–75 double, $55–70 single. Alc brunch, $6; alc lunch, $6; alc dinner, $20.

ORLANDO

Reader tip: "For a fun evening, visit Church Street, a historic railroad depot converted into an entertainment center, with a wild-west saloon and 'opera house,' a ballroom and dessert cafe, a seafood bar, and a wine cellar."

For additional area entries, see **Lake Wales, Minneola, and Winter Park.**

Information please: For a home-style B&B, head 35 minutes northeast of Orlando to **Clauser's B&B** (201 East Kicklighter Road, Lake Helen 32744; 904–228–0310). Long-time Florida residents Marge and Tom Clauser invite travelers to their two-guest room B&B, an 1880s Victorian house furnished with family heirlooms, handmade quilts and afghans, and lots of country touches. The $65–85 double rates include a full breakfast—perhaps sautéed cinnamon apples, bran muffins, cheese omelets, and ham. Another possibility about a 30-minute drive south of Disney World is the **Van Rook Inn** (106 South First Street, Haines City 33844; 813–421–2242), a 1920s home offering a tea room for breakfast and lunch and five guest rooms with private bath. Rates range from $60–75.

Courtyard on Lake Lucerne ¢ 👫   *Tel:* 407–648–5188
211 North Lucerne Circle East, 32801   800–444–5289

Like fans of Tinkerbell in the play *Peter Pan*, you have to believe that there is more to Orlando than theme parks and chain hotels. A visit to the Courtyard at Lake Lucerne, will make your wish come true. While this group of three buildings shares a common courtyard, the architecture and decor of each is totally distinct. The Norment-Parry Inn is Orlando's oldest house, dating from 1885, and it offers lavish furnishings of American and English antiques, accented with floral wallcoverings and fabrics. The Wellborn, one of the finest surviving Art Deco buildings in town, was originally an apartment building, and it has been fully restored; all suites are complete with kitchenettes. Furnishings include a zebra-print sofa, bronze sconces, glass block walls, and a pink-and-white exterior. The I.W. Phillips House, a 1916 antebellum-style manor house, has wooden verandas wrapping around three sides, a Tiffany stained glass window, and a ballroom-sized reception hall. Guest rooms have a Belle Epoque atmosphere with ornately carved furniture, marble-topped tables, and brocade fabrics. Rates include a continental breakfast buffet. "The Norment-Parry is stunningly furnished with English antiques, and is neat, clean, with a great location in the heart of the city, just off the expressway." *(PB, also Joe & Sheila Schmidt)*

Open All year.
Rooms 3 suites with double tubs, ceiling fans, verandas in I.W. Phillips House; 12 suites with kitchen in The Wellborn; 6 doubles, 1 suite with fireplace in Norment-Parry—all with private bath and/or shower, telephone, TV, air-conditioning.
Facilities Reception hall with piano, kitchen. Veranda, garden with fountain. Parlor with fireplace in Norment-Parry Inn. Health club, tennis, golf nearby.
Location 20 min from Walt Disney World. From I-4, exit at Gore. Go west on Gore Rd. to Delaney. Turn north and go to N. Lucerne Circle E. Turn left onto road and inn is on right.
Credit cards Amex, MC, Visa.
Rates B&B, $85–150 suite, $65–85 double. Extra person, $10. AARP, AAA discounts.
Extras Wheelchair access to I.W. Phillips House. Crib, babysitting.

PALM BEACH

Plaza Inn ¢   Tel: 407–832–8666
215 Brazilian Avenue, 33480   800–BED–AND–B

The pale pink, Art Deco-style Plaza Inn, built in 1940 as the Hotel Ardma, has been reborn as Palm Beach's only B&B hotel. Situated on a palm tree-lined, residential street, it's just one block from the beach and a short walk to the many shops and restaurants of famous Worth Avenue. Owner and resident manager, Ajit Asrani, notes that the extensive renovations completed in October of 1990, "added some European touches to our bed and breakfast concept, and no two rooms are alike." Wicker, mahogany, pine, brass, or oak furnishings are complemented by green and burgundy draperies, linens, and wallpaper.

"Rooms are pleasant and well-equipped. Bathrooms contain nice touches like straw baskets of soaps and shampoos, and plenty of big towels. The dining room feels snug and appealing with ruffled print curtains and flowered china. English-style breakfasts of juice, fruit, cereal, eggs, meat, and fresh muffins are served. A courteous staff makes a visit to this hotel especially enjoyable." *(Elaine Williams)* "The whole staff went out of their way to be make me feel welcome." *(Mrs. J.L. Livingstone)*

"The inn's location is wonderfully central, yet high hedges and lush landscaping make the pool area lush and private. The outside lighting is particularly well-done and accents flowers, trees, and the entire building beautifully. The renovation was obviously done with great care to retain original architectural details whenever possible. Every member of the staff went out of their way to make me feel special." *(John S. Leach, Jr.)*

Open All year.
Rooms 1 suite, 47 doubles—all with full private bath, telephone, radio, TV, air-conditioning, ceiling fans, refrigerator. Some with desk.
Facilities Lobby, breakfast room, piano bar with entertainment, heated swimming pool, hot tub. Room service. 1 block from public beach. Tennis, golf, fishing, boating nearby.
Location E FL. 60 m N of Miami. 4 blocks from Worth Ave.
Credit cards Amex, MC, Visa.
Rates B&B, $75–150 suite, $47–140 double, single. Extra person, $15. Weekly, monthly rates.
Extras Airport/station pickups, $10. Small pets permitted. Crib; babysitting can be arranged. Spanish spoken.

PALMETTO

Five Oaks Inn ¢   Tel: 813–723–1236
1102 Riverside Drive, 34221

Five Oaks Inn is a Sears, Roebuck catalog house that was delivered, disassembled, to Palmetto at the turn of the century. The inn has been owned by Frank Colorito since 1986; Bette and Chet Kriessler are the innkeepers. Framed by massive oaks and magnolias, and overlooking the Manatee River, rates include a welcoming drink and a hearty southern breakfast. The dark oak woodwork throughout the house is complemented by the period decor; guests especially enjoy relaxing on the wicker rockers of the airy sunporch.

"Our large comfortable room had a sea captain's decor, but my favorite spot was the wraparound downstairs sunporch. Bette and Chet go out of their way to please their guests—their outstanding service is this B&B's best feature. One night, we asked for hot water for bedtime tea. Bette told me that she would bring it up to our room, and within a few moments she brought a tray with hot water in a silver tea pot, special china cups, lovely cloth napkins, deviled eggs, and homemade cookies. The hearty breakfasts were different every day; we were never hungry until late afternoon. There were always plenty of big, fluffy towels, too."*(Imogene C. Tillis)*

Open All year.
Rooms 1 suite, 3 doubles—all with private bath, radio, desk, air-conditioning, fan. Some with telephone, gas fireplace.
Facilities Living room with fireplace, library with fireplace, TV/VCR, books. Bar with stereo. Swimming, boating, fishing nearby.
Location 10 m S of St. Petersburg. 10 m N of Sarasota. 3 blocks from center.
Restrictions No smoking in guest rooms. No children.
Credit cards MC, Visa.
Rates B&B, $100–110 suite, $55–65 double. Extra person, $10. Senior discount. Weekly, monthly rates.
Extras Airport/station pickups. German spoken.

PENSACOLA

Reader tip: "We highly recommend Jamie's French Restaurant (904–432–5047), located in an 1860s Victorian home, elegantly furnished with walnut sideboards, mirrors, and lace curtains. We thought the seafood superb (best snapper we've eaten in Florida), and the desserts wonderful. For dessert we had New Orleans-style bread pudding with whiskey sauce and chocolate cake. It's located on Zaragossa Street, an interesting mix of shops and homes. The restaurant was full on the Monday night we visited, and reservations are advisable for lunch or dinner." *(HB)*

New World Inn 🛉 ✕   *Tel:* 904–432–4111
600 South Palafox Street, 32501

Pensacola has one-upped St. Augustine by having flown five flags during its history: French, Spanish, British, American, and Confederate. Today, principal sights here include the Naval Air Station and aviation museum, and the ruins of a seventeenth-century Spanish fort. Other attractions include the museums and restored houses of the historic district and the gorgeous beaches of the Gulf Islands National Seashore.

The New World Inn reflects Pensacola's international history in its decor, utilizing reproductions of Louis XV, Chippendale, and Queen Anne in its individually decorated guest rooms. Handsome woodwork high-lights the lobby area and stairs to the second floor, giving the inn an older, gracious feeling. Photographs of early Pensacola highlight one of the inn's dining rooms, while the other has beautiful windows overlooking the courtyard; the bar is English in style. Rates include a continental breakfast, and the cuisine at lunch and dinner is continental, emphasizing seafood.

"Large, clean, comfortable rooms. Manager and front desk staff unfail-ingly helpful, considerate, and polite." *(J.R. Norcliffe)* "Fully endorse last year's entry. Rooms beautiful, staff charming and helpful, excellent food in Michael's pub." *(Betty Jayne Hensley)* "We can only affirm the existing praise for this inn. The inn is well located for exploring the downtown area with its recycled buildings, now full of shops, art galleries, and restaurants. Palafox Street is full of great stores for buying and browsing and interesting old architecture." *(HB, also SWS)* "Equally enjoyable on a return visit, with a most helpful staff." *(HB)*

A word to the wise: One guest noted that sounds from the lobby carry to some of the guest rooms; for a quieter stay, request a more distant room. Also: "Planting hedges at the edge of the courtyard would screen the view of the parking lot beyond."

Open All year. Restaurant closed Sun.
Rooms 2 suites, 14 doubles—all with full private bath, telephone, radio, TV, air-conditioning, fan. Most with desk.
Facilities Restaurant, bar/lounge, lobby. Courtyard, fountain, gardens. Bicycles. Swimming, tennis, charter fishing nearby.
Location W FL panhandle, near Alabama border. Follow Rte. 29 to end; becomes Palafox St. Inn in downtown historic harbor area, adjacent to New World Conven-tion Hall.
Credit cards Amex, CB, DC, Discover, MC, Visa.
Rates Room only, $100 suite, $80 double, $70 single. Extra person, $10. Children under 12 free in parents' room. 10% senior discount. Weekend, weekly, corporate discounts. Alc breakfast $6; lunch, $10; dinner, $45.
Extras Airport/station pickups. Wheelchair access. Crib, babysitting. French, Spanish spoken.

PINELAND

Cabbage Key ✕   *Tel:* 813–283–2278
P.O. Box 200, 33945

Bridges and causeways to the mainland have totally transformed the complexion of the Sanibel and Captiva barrier islands. If you'd like a change from the area's typical resort condominiums, consider Cabbage Key, accessible only by boat and changed little in the past 50 years. In 1938, mystery writer Mary Roberts Rinehart built a home here, which was later expanded to include a restaurant and a few guest rooms. Jimmy Buffet immortalized the restaurant's cheeseburgers in a song, although seafood dishes and key lime pie are also specialities. An eccentricity of the decor are the hundreds of signed dollar bills papering the walls of the bar and restaurant. Supposedly, it all started when a fisherman put his name on a bill and pinned it to the wall as insurance that he would always have a buck for a beer and a sandwich if times were tough.

"Once you get here, all you can do is relax and get into the spirit of the island. The inn is not luxurious, but the plain furnishings seem appropriate. The focus is on the famous restaurant and bar which serves up to 300 people a day for lunch—all boaters coming in for the famous cheeseburgers. The staff all live on the island, and are nice and accommodating; they really get to know the guests, spending lots of time sitting, talking, and drinking with them. During the day, the harbormaster, Terry, a great old salt who always has a beer in his hand but never shows the effects, rents you a little skiff to take you cross the sound to Cayo Costa, a state nature preserve with nine miles of unspoiled beach. They packed us a picnic and we had a delightful day. Cabbage Key is a total experience which isn't for everyone, but for those who can hang loose it is a real find." *(Pamela Young)*

And another viewpoint: "Our room needed a thorough cleaning, and the bathroom was long overdue for renovation. We needed more towels, and found the staff to be preoccupied with the boating crowd, many of whom were heavy drinkers. We'd go back, but only to stay in one of the cottages, which have a more private setting, and more modern baths and kitchens."

Open All year.
Rooms 4 cabins with kitchen, private bath; 6 doubles with shared bath.
Facilities Restaurant, bar. Nature trail, docks.
Location SW FL. 20 m NW of Ft. Meyers, 5 m S of Boca Grande. In Pine Island Sound, between Pine Island and Cayo Costa, north of Captiva.
Restrictions Restaurant noise in rooms. Water is sulfurous.
Credit cards MC, Visa.
Rates Room only, $145 cottage, $130 suite, $65 double. Alc dinner, $20.
Extras Tour boat pickups, $25.

ST. AUGUSTINE

St. Augustine, founded in 1565, is the oldest city in North America. With a few interruptions, it was under Spanish rule until 1821, and many of its restored Spanish colonial homes were built in the 1700s. The city's architecture also has a strong Victorian component, dating back to the 1880s, when Henry Flagler did much to popularize St. Augustine as a fashionable resort. St. Augustine is on the northeast Florida coast, 30 miles north of Daytona and south of Jacksonville, and 100 miles northeast of Orlando.

Reader tip: "St. Augustine has become a disconcerting mix of honkytonk and remembered elegance; we'd recommend a visit on your way elsewhere." *(AJH)*

Also recommended: Although on a noisy street, the turn-of-the-century **Old Powderhouse Inn** (38 Cordova Street, 32084; 904–824–4149) is recommended principally for its "central location, a veranda to catch the sea breezes, and delicous breakfasts of a soufflé one morning, waffles the next." *(Andy & Judy Hoffman)*

Information please: In the heart of the historic district is the **Casa de Solana** (21 Aviles Street, 32084; 904–824–3555) a B&B built in 1763 and decorated with the owner's family heirlooms. The inn's four suites have private baths, balconies or fireplaces. Rates include a full breakfast, chocolates, sherry, and bicycles.

We need more feedback on the **Westcott House**, (146 Avenida Menedez, 32084; 904–824–4301) listed in previous editions. Purchased by the Dennison family in 1983, it was rundown and neglected, with virtually no more plumbing or electricity than it had when built in the 1880s. Eleven bathrooms, miles of wiring, and endless gallons of paint and yards of wallpaper later, the Westcott was ready to welcome its first guests. Overlooking Matanzas Bay, this coral-and-white building has many verandas, ideal for relaxing and reading. Guest rooms are individually furnished with period American and European antiques and reproductions, all with either a king-sized bed or two queen-sized beds.

Kenwood Inn
38 Marine Street, 32084

Tel: 904–824–2116

This historic neighborhood was already old when the Kenwood was built between 1865 and 1885; just a few blocks away is the Oldest House, built in the early 1700s, while homes in the restored Spanish Quarter date from the 1750s. This former boardinghouse and hotel was renovated in 1984; Mark, Kerriane, and Caitlin Constant became its owners in 1988. Rooms are decorated in a wide variety of New England styles, from Shaker to country Victorian. The owners describe their inn as having the "charm and informality of a New England country inn, providing an escape from the modern environment for young and old."

"The rooms are furnished with functional antiques, from iron beds to canopied four-posters. The owners make you feel like a welcomed family friend. The self-service continental breakfast includes fresh orange juice, freshly baked goods, and coffee. You can eat at the large dining room table, in front of the living room fireplace, in the light and airy wicker-furnished sun-room, or outside in the courtyard. The innkeepers have menus from the better restaurants in town and will advise you and make your reservations. The common areas are comfortable, homey, and inviting. The whole inn is spotless, and the guest rooms have many touches one would only expect in a private home." *(Ted & Laura Phelps)*

"One of my favorite pastimes is simply sitting on the upper porch, with book, pipe, and libation, watching the horse-drawn carriages pass. Meanwhile, my wife is ensconced in a chair by the pool enjoying the sun and conversation with other guests." *(Mr. & Mrs. Earl Cranston)*

"The owners were most accommodating with our last-minute booking. They graciously allowed us to look at very many of their rooms before we chose our favorite. The lemon-flavored seed cake was out-of-this-world, as was the date-nut bread and four other varieties of cakes and rolls provided." *(Barbara Charlton)*

Some areas for improvement: "Our bed felt soft and lumpy; the bedside reading light seemed inadequate, and the inn could use a little sprucing up."

Open All year.
Rooms 4 suites, 10 doubles—all with private bath and/or shower, clock-radio, air-conditioning, fan; some with desk, TV, fireplace, balcony.
Facilities Sunroom with TV, stereo, books, living room with fireplace, dining room with fireplace, TV/game room. Courtyard, swimming pool. Tennis, golf nearby. 5 m to beaches.
Location St. Johns County. Historic district. 3 blocks S of Bridge of Lions.
Restrictions No smoking. No children under 9. Some street noise in two rooms. On-street parking only; very limited due to narrow streets. Guests can leave bags at inn, then park 1 block away at Avenida Mendez or at private parking lot also 1 block away.
Credit cards Discover, MC, Visa.
Rates B&B, $85–125 suite, $55–85 double, $45 single. Extra person, $10. 2-3 night weekend, holiday minimum. 10% senior, AAA discount.

St. Francis Inn ₵   *Tel:* 904–824–6068
279 St. George Street, 32084

The St. Francis Inn was built in 1791 of *coquina*, a limestone formed of broken shells and coral cemented together. The inn was used as a private residence until 1845, when it became a boardinghouse; a guide to St. Augustine published in 1869 describes it as one of the city's best.

"As the oldest inn in St. Augustine, you really feel its history—the floors creak, the balconies slope." *(Stephanie Robertson)* "Every morning we were greeted with fresh rolls, doughnuts, and coffee. The morning paper awaited us in the sunlit sitting room, where you could sit down and eat, or pick up a tray to take to your room." *(June Harrah)* "The St. Francis Inn is decorated throughout with an eclectic assortment of antiques and Persian rugs, and with a tremendous collection of old and new books. There is a nice (but small) pool in the back courtyard, and a fountain in the front garden." *(Janet Lay)*

"Each room is filled with antiques, blended with modern wicker. Our third-floor apartment was complete with sitting room, kitchen, and king-sized bed. We peeked at the other rooms when going up and down the book-lined staircase, and each had its own personality. " *(Alison Young)* "Our room had an exceptionally comfortable double bed, with a fireplace to take off the evening chill. One evening we smelled popcorn and found a big bowl awaiting us in the downstairs common area." *(Lynn Burdeshaw)* "Although the inn has celebrated its 200th anniversary, the facilities are extremely well maintained and modernized in such a way that does not detract from its historic value. The staff is most accommodating and cleanliness is exceptional. We enjoyed the Sunday evening entertainment—a singer and a story teller." *(Douglas Aurand)* "The innkeepers went out of their way to explain local folklore, make restaurant suggestions, and provide many ideas for local sights to see." *(Christine Woolard)*

Open All year.
Rooms 6 suites, 7 doubles, 1 cottage—all with private bath and/or shower, TV, air-conditioning; some with desk, fireplace, kitchenette. Separate 2-bedroom cottage with kitchen, fireplace, sleeps 4.
Facilities Living/family room with TV, piano, fireplace, books; breakfast room with fireplace, books; balcony. Sunday evening entertainment. Bicycles. Patio, courtyard, swimming pool. Ocean swimming and fishing nearby. On-site parking.

Location Historic district; 3 blocks from restored town.
Restrictions No smoking in guest rooms.
Credit cards MC, Visa.
Rates B&B, $65–80 suite, $47–65 double. Extra person, $8. Weekly, monthly rates available. Rates include admission to Oldest House.
Extras Crib. Spanish spoken.

ST. GEORGE ISLAND

Information Please: Off the coast of neighboring Carrabelle, the **Pelican Inn** (mailing address: P.O. Box 1351, Fairhope, AL 36532; 800–451–5294) is perfect for people looking for complete R&R, since Dog Island, home to the Pelican Inn, has no shops, no TV, no restaurants, no golf, no tennis—nothing but miles of paths, dunes, clean white beaches with beautiful shells, and a tremendous variety of migratory birds in spring and fall. The two-story inn, encircled by verandas on both levels, is home to eight fully equipped suites; each suite is simply decorated in soft blue and beige, with white wicker furniture and two custom-built double beds. The decor is highlighted with sea art and nautical charts of the area.

St. George Inn ¢ ✗   *Tel:* 904–927–2903
Franklin Boulevard and Pine Street, Box 222, 32328

It took a lot of determination for John and Barbara Vail to construct the St. George Inn; twice the causeway was washed away by hurricanes and oyster boats had to be rented to haul in building materials. John feels it has been worth the effort to live and work on an island "the way Florida used to be in the '30s—with pristine beaches and a small population. The pace is slow and relaxed—the nearest movie theater is 65 miles away. Don't come for glitz and glitter but for the beach, the water, and the spectacular sunsets." While the island is the longest of the barrier islands in Florida, it is also among the narrowest. The inn sits right in the middle, yet is just 660 feet from the Gulf of Mexico in one direction and 650 feet from Apalachicola Bay in the other direction. The guest rooms have French doors opening to a wraparound porch and water views. The inn's dining room offers a simple dinner menu, with French onion soup as an appetizer and such entrées as broiled chicken, ribeye steak, and seafood.

"While the building is just five years old, you feel as if you've stepped back in time. Like a Shaker home, the decor is simple. Beyond the beauty of the hotel is the warmth and comfort provided by John and Barbara. How lucky they are to be doing exactly what they want, where they want." *(Susan Santiago)* "The inn is gorgeous and absolutely clean. Owners wonderful, food excellent." *(Julie Emrick)*

Open All year.
Rooms 8 doubles—all with full private bath, TV, air-conditioning, fan, balcony.
Facilities Dining room with fireplace, lounge with TV, piano, books; wraparound porch.
Location 75 m SW of Tallahassee, 60 m E of Panama City, 15 m SE of Apalachicola.

Restrictions Children over 12 preferred.
Credit cards MC, Visa.
Rates Room only, $50–60 double. Extra person, $5. 2-night weekend minimum June–Aug. Alc dinner, $17. $2 causeway fee.
Extras Local airport pickup.

ST. PETERSBURG BEACH

Information please: In a quiet setting close to swimming, sunning, and beachcombing is the **Bayboro House B&B** (1719 Beach Drive S.E., 33701; 813–823–4955). Gordon and Antonia Powers have decorated their Victorian home with furnishings collected over the years, "just because we like them." Rooms are equipped with private bath, color TV, and air-conditioning, and the $50–65 rates include a continental breakfast. Another St. Petersburg possibility is the **Island's End Resort** (1 Pass-A-Grille Way, St. Petersburg Beach 33706; 813–360–5023) with five comfortable, weather-beaten cedar cottages right on the water—quite a contrast to the massive apartment building next door.

The Inn on the Beach ¢ 🏃   *Tel: 813–360–8844*
1401 Gulf Way, 33706

Amidst the high rise hotels, condo complexes, and sometimes shabby rental units, it's difficult to find a place for a beach getaway. It's even harder to find one that has a friendly, helpful staff and freshly renovated rooms. Owner Ron Holehouse began the renovation of this 1920s house in 1989, and added ceramic tile floors, private baths, oak kitchen cabinets, and 1,000 square feet of decks. Individually decorated with brass, wicker, and antique accents, each unit has a fully equipped kitchen and access to barbecue grills. The inn is located on Pass-A-Grille, an auto-accessible island that is 30 blocks long and one block wide. Now a National Historic District, it offers white sandy beaches, with the Gulf Mexico is on one side and Boca Ciega Bay on the other.

"The inn is a cozy, pleasant place to stay, and the staff are friendly. They know who you are and you can find them easily should you need anything. Our room had a king-sized brass bed and glass wall tiles; another room had a huge balcony overlooking the Gulf. The tile floors are a nice touch and practical in a beach location. The inn's bicycles were perfect for riding to the grocery a few blocks away." *(Karen Fixler)*

"I was there over the Easter weekend, and believe it or not, the Easter Bunny visited me! When I left I felt that I had been visiting friends." *(Sandra Chesley)* "Gentle, quiet location perfect for beach lovers. Inviting interiors. Excellent food nearby." *(Ann Dutton)* "Clean rooms, good view, comfortable porches—in short, a find."*(Virginia Morrison and others)*

Minor quibbles: "A hook on the back of the bathroom door would have been a thoughtful touch; one of the bicycles needed repair."

Open All year.
Rooms 12 efficiency apartments—all with private bath, telephone, TV, desk, air-conditioning, fan, refrigerator. Some with radio, fireplace, balcony.

Facilities Center courtyard with deck. Bicycles, beach chairs, fishing poles, barbecue. Tennis, beach, boat rentals nearby.
Location 10 m to downtown St. Petersburg, 30 m to Tampa.
Credit cards None accepted.
Rates Room only, $40–110. Extra person, $7.
Extras Wheelchair access. Airport pickup, $10. Crib.

SANIBEL ISLAND

Information please: The **Island Inn** (Box 659, Sanibel Island 33957-0659; 813–472–1561) offers 57 traditional rooms overlooking the gulf; most rooms have screened porches and the reasonable rates include breakfast and dinner. It's right on the beach and also offers two tennis courts and a heated swimming pool.

Casa Ybel Resort 👬 ✕ 🎾   *Tel:* 813–481–3636
2255 West Gulf Drive, P.O. Box 167, 33957   800–237–8906

Meaning "House of Isabel", the Casa Ybel is built on the site of Sanibel's first resort, and its award-winning restaurant, Truffles at Thistle Lodge, is designed to resemble the home built for this Isabel as a wedding gift by her father, one of the island's first settlers. The individual villas are decorated in pastel colors, with accents of wicker and bamboo. The pool area, complete with water slide and children's pool, offers a very welcoming environment for families. A complete array of activities, from sailboats to shuffleboard, are provided; if you run out of ideas, there's a recreation staff to keep you moving.

"The location is the best on the island, and every villa has an ocean view and no elevator or lobby to contend with on your way to the beach. The pool is big and pretty, and the pool bar is convenient for light lunches." *(Rose Marie Olaechea)*

Areas for improvement: An otherwise pleased respondent noted that their unit needed refurbishing. Comments?

Open All year.
Rooms 114 1- and 2-bedroom villas—all with private bath and/or shower, telephone, radio, TV, kitchen. Some with screened porch, VCR.
Facilities Restaurant, children's program, 6 tennis courts, heated swimming pool, wading pool, hot tub. Rental bicycles, boats.
Location SW FL. 150 m S of Tampa. From I-75, take Exit 21. Follow to Sanibel Island
Credit cards Amex, CB, Discover, MC, Visa.
Rates Room only, $125–295 villas. Extra person, $10. Weekly rates.
Extras Crib.

SEASIDE

Information please: Part of the Seaside resort development, **Josephine's B&B** (101 Seaside Avenue, P.O. Box 4767, 32459; 904–231–1940 or

800–848–1840) is a recently built Greek Revival building, offering seven guest rooms with four-poster beds, settees, balloon curtains, Battenburg lace comforters, marble bathtubs, and a wet bar. The sitting room even has such period touches as beaded tongue-and-groove paneling and heart pine flooring. Rates include full breakfast, and range from $135–165.

Seaside   *Tel:* 904–231–4224
P.O. Box 4717, 32459   800–635–0296

"Though it is a new development, Seaside is a well-designed Victorian-style community, on a beautiful beach in the panhandle of Florida. It is quiet, excellent for both families and couples, with ample opportunities for walking, bicycling, and relaxing at the beach. It has a full range of sports, restaurants, a fine market and deli, shops, and proximity to many other towns. You can choose from four different types of accommodations— Honeymoon Cottages and Dreamland Heights (each adults only), The Motor Court (modern reflection of an early motel), and a selection of private cottages and homes for rent. The entire area has won architectural awards and praise, and continues to attract architects to design more homes and beach pavilions. Even the children's playground in the park has Victorian touches.

"It's all charming and a lot of fun. We stayed in a private cottage which included a kitchen supplied with coffee, croissants, and fancy jams for breakfast, plus bottled water and soft drinks. Despite the fact that all is less than 10 years old, you truly feel that you are in an earlier era as you stroll the brick streets and sand pathways, past all the lovely porches and pastel wood frame homes. The easy availability of various kinds of foods and other pleasures is great." *(Celia McCullough & Gary Kaplan)*

Open All year.
Rooms 53 1-2 bedroom cottages—all with full private bath, telephone, radio, TV, kitchen.
Facilities Restaurants, 2 tennis courts, croquet, shuffleboard, 3 swimming pools, beach for watersports.
Location W FL Panhandle, approx 65 m E of Pensacola. Between Grayton and Seaside Beach. From Pensacola, take Rte. 98 E, & turn towards the Gulf at signs for Grayton Beach. From Panama City, take Rte. 98 W to Rte. 30 A.
Credit cards Amex, MC, Visa.
Rates Room only, $210–1,552 cottage, $95 double in Motor Court.

TALLAHASSEE

Governors Inn 🏃   *Tel:* 904–681–6855
209 South Adams Street, 32301   In FL: 800–342–7717

The capital of Florida, Tallahassee is also home to Florida State University and Florida A&M; other sites of interest include the Tallahassee Junior Museum, a favorite with children, and the Maclay State Gardens, stunning in early spring for their azaleas, camellias, and dogwood.

The Governors Inn opened in 1985 in a century-old building that had once housed a general store. During the renovation, only the roofing, beams, and outside walls were retained; everything else was gutted, to make way for the four-star luxury hotel now in operation. Managed by Charles Orr, the inn features guest rooms each named after a former Florida governor and furnished with four-poster beds, black oak writing desks, and rock maple armoires; the decor is slightly masculine.

"This inn appears to have been created by gutting a giant livery stable and an abutting two-story office building. The architect did an excellent job of meeting the challenge. A post-and-beam construction dominates an atrium-like area in the stable section, with two levels of rooms off each side. Although inviting and attractive, these rooms are small, with no outside windows. Our room was in the office building section, with twelve-foot ceilings and huge windows opening onto a side street. All the staff, from bellman to chambermaid, were warm, outgoing, and obviously dedicated." *(DB)*

"You could not ask for a more dedicated, concerned, manager and staff than at the Governor's Inn. Our room was clean and quiet. Rates included a breakfast of juice, melon, muffins, and croissants, and an afternoon cocktail hour. Terrycloth robes, shoeshine service, and the daily newspaper of your choice were among the other amenities. The valet parking is a great convenience in this downtown area where parking is scarce. We had dinner at Andre's Second Act, just across the street. The food was excellent, although the stairs leading down to the restaurant makes it difficult for the disabled." *(HB)*

Open All year.
Rooms 8 suites, 29 doubles, 3 singles—all with full private bath, telephone, radio, TV, desk, air-conditioning. Some with fan, fireplace, refrigerator or whirlpool bath.
Facilities Breakfast room, patio. Valet parking.
Location W FL panhandle. Center of town. 2 blocks N of Capitol, at corner of Adams and College.
Restrictions Minimal interior soundproofing. No smoking in some guest rooms. No elevator.
Credit cards Amex, DC, Discover, MC, Visa.
Rates B&B, $145–215 suite, $79–135 double, $79–119 single. Extra person, $10. 2-night minimum football/special event weekends. 10% senior, AAA discount.
Extras First-floor rooms with wheelchair access. Free airport/station pickups. Crib, babysitting.

WAKULLA SPRINGS

Wakulla Springs Lodge ¢ 👫 ✗   *Tel:* 904–224–5950
1 Springs Drive, 32305

If you feel your life will not be complete without seeing the place where Johnny Weissmuller filmed *Tarzan of the Apes*, then make a reservation today for the Wakulla Springs Lodge. The lodge was built in 1937 by Ed Ball, a real-estate millionaire and DuPont in-law, who had fallen in love with the natural beauty of this area and managed to preserve and protect the 2,900 acres which now make up Edward Ball Wakulla Springs State Park. The outside of the lodge is Spanish Mission in style, with stuccoed walls and red tiled roofs; the interior is striking for its lavish use of Tennessee marble in everything from the registration desk to the soda fountain, the fireplaces to the bathrooms, and, perhaps most distinctive, the specially designed checkers tables that dot the lobby. Other decorative motifs include the Aztec and Toltec Indian designs painted on the cypress ceiling beams of the lobby, the Spanish tiles framing the doorway, and the Moorish archways and windows.

The lodge restaurant offers a full range of dishes; the specialties are the navy bean soup, pan-fried chicken, and fried or broiled shrimp. Guest rooms are decorated with antiques and thirties-era furnishings, many original to the lodge.

The key focus of attention here is the spring itself. Source of the Wakulla River, the spring produces over 600,000 gallons of water every minute. Its basin reaches a depth of 185 feet, yet the water is so clear you can see all the way to the bottom.

"After a hectic week in Tallahassee, Wakulla Springs made a relaxing escape. My room was old-fashioned but pleasant, and the southern-style cooking tasty and reasonably priced. Best of all was the chance to see a piece of the real Florida on the park's nature trails and boat rides; unlike the jungle cruise at Disney World, this one has real alligators, osprey, and ibis. Buy a copy of the illustrated booklet describing the history, legends, and habitat of the springs." *(Diane Gayles)*

"Three generations of our family came here over Christmas vacation to enjoy the relaxed family-oriented atmosphere. We were warmly received on a frigid night, and a hot dinner was served with the utmost consideration to less than patient youngsters and their tired, testy parents and grandparents. Our evenings were spent chatting with other guests around a log fire, our days were filled hiking the nature paths and observing wildlife. The lake tour gave us a first-hand glimpse of alligators and endless species of birds and plant life. The meals were varied enough to satisfy our assorted demands, and the staff often went beyond the call of duty to supply the little extras that make a vacation special." *(Harriet Soffes)*

"Our room was decorated in 1930s-style furniture, in good condition with a firm mattress. The feeling of being away from everything is great. It's a place for beautiful walks, and a jungle ride with real wildlife to see. The lobby was inviting, and the staff ready to help with bags. The food is reasonably priced and quite good." *(HB)*

And a word to the wise: "I've tried several times to reserve a room, but they're always booked. Call well ahead for peak periods."

Open All year.
Rooms 1 suite, 26 doubles—all with full private bath, telephone, air-conditioning. Some with desk.
Facilities Lobby with TV, fireplace, piano, checkers tables; restaurant, terrace, gift shop, snack bar, conference rooms. 2,888 acres with swimming, river and glass-bottom boat tours, nature trails.
Location W FL panhandle. 15 m S of Tallahassee. Midway between Apalachicola and Perry. From Tallahassee take State Rd. 61 S, then go E on Rte. 267. From E or W, take Rte. 98.
Credit cards MC, Visa.

Rates Room only, $245 suite, $50–80 double, $42–80 single. Extra person, $5. Business, off-season packages. Children's portions.Alc breakfast, $4–6; alc lunch, $6–10; alc dinner, $25.
Extras Wheelchair access. Crib, babysitting available with advance notice.

WINTER PARK

For additional area entries, see **Lake Wales, Minneola, and Orlando.**
   Also recommended: The Fortnightly Inn (377 East Fairbanks Avenue, 32789; 407–654–4440), a renovated 1911 town house not far from the campus of Rollins College, has oak and heart pine floors, and original brass hardware and ceramic shower heads, complemented by period furnishings. While owners Frank and Judi Daley do not live on the premises, an attentive staff takes care of guests' needs; rates include breakfast served between 8A.M. and 9A.M.. Though the inn was well-insulated when restored, light sleepers might want to ask for a room at the back. *(Joe Schmidt)*

Park Plaza Hotel ✗
307 Park Avenue South, 32789

Tel: 407–647–1072
800–228–7220

If you've despaired of finding a hotel in the Orlando area with fewer than 500 rooms you'll be delighted with this small hotel. Built in the heyday of Florida railroading and fully renovated by owners John and Sandra Spang, its antique- and wicker-filled rooms look out onto a plant-filled balcony that runs the length of the second floor. Beds are turned down each night with a Godiva chocolate, and the morning brings a continental breakfast accompanied by the *Wall Street Journal.* The first floor houses the Park Plaza Gardens restaurant, serving seafood and meat dishes in a glass-enclosed patio garden. This downtown area of Winter Park attracts pedestrians who stroll among the shops, restaurants, and galleries. Tree-lined Park Avenue ends nearby at the campus of Rollins College, the oldest in Florida.
   "We spent New Year's weekend here on your recommendation, and had a delightful stay." *(BJ Hensley)*

Open All year.
Rooms 11 suites, 16 doubles—all with full private bath, telephone, TV, desk, air-conditioning, ceiling fan. Some with balcony.
Facilities Restaurant, bar, piano lounge, lobby with fireplace, balcony. Fishing 2 blocks away. Valet parking. Golf nearby.
Location N central FL. 5 min. N of downtown Orlando. From I-4, take Fairbanks Exit E to Park Ave. and go left.
Restrictions No children under 5. Train noise might disturb light sleepers.
Credit cards Amex, CB, DC, MC, Visa.
Rates B&B, $135–150 suite, $75–110 double. 10% senior, AAA, corporate discount. Weekly rates available.
Extras Wheelchair access via elevator. Station pickups. Crib. Spanish, Italian, French spoken.

Georgia

Ballastone Inn, Savannah

There's more to Georgia than peaches and peanuts, Jimmy Carter and Scarlett O'Hara. For urban delights, visit Atlanta, one of the country's most sophisticated cities which successfully combines contemporary culture and "Old South" charm; tour graceful historic homes in Savannah; or time-travel with a peek into Macon's antebellum mansions. In northwestern Georgia, visit New Echota (outside of Calhoun), the former Cherokee capital where Sequoyah developed a written language for his people; then stop by nearby Chatsworth to see the Vann House, a mansion built by a Cherokee chief and noted for its unusually colored interior paint. In northeastern Georgia, tour the mountains, then stop by 1000-foot Tallulah Falls. Want more water? Get your fill by canoeing through the Okefenokee Swamp or visiting posh St. Simons Island.

Information please: Close to the North Carolina border is the **Lake Rabun Hotel**, a rustic and reasonably priced lodge, dating back to 1922 and furnished with handmade rhododendron and mountain laurel furniture (Lake Rabun Road, Route 1, Box 2090, Lakemont 30552; 404–782–4946).

Rates listed do not include 7% Georgia sales tax, plus additional local taxes where applicable.

ATLANTA

Virtually leveled by General Sherman during the Civil War, Atlanta recovered fairly quickly, becoming a major rail hub by the end of the century. Today, Atlanta is a modern city whose population has exploded in the past three decades; its airport is one of the busiest in the country; the traffic jams on its highways rival those of Los Angeles.

Also recommended: When you're in the mood for the best in a big city hotel (551 rooms), the **Ritz-Carlton Buckhead** (3434 Peachtree Road NE, 30326; 404–237–2700) "is well worth the money for an all-around luxurious yet friendly atmosphere. Wonderful rooms done in antique reproductions, and baths with all the extras—thick fluffy towels and robes, full length mirrors, nightly turn-down service. No noise from the street, hall, or other rooms. Two of Atlanta's most exclusive malls are nearby; ask for a room with the Phipps Plaza view—you can see to the horizon. Good food and service in both restaurants too." *(SHW)*.

In the same neighborhood but half the price is the 371-room **Terrace Garden Inn** (3405 Lenox Road N.E., 30326; 404–261–9250 or 800–241–8260). One frequent contributor *(MDS)* describes it as a "lovely inn with an exceptional staff. Large lovely rooms with turndown service and pillow mints. There's a good restaurant, a nice bar, pleasant meeting rooms, and an attractive health club, with indoor pool, racquetball, and tennis. Lots of excellent shopping is nearby in this lovely upscale area of Atlanta."

For an additional Atlanta-area listing, please see **Marietta.**

Ansley Inn	*Tel:* 404–872–9000
253 15th Street N.E., 30309	800–446–5416

Centrally located in a tree-lined neighborhood in midtown Atlanta, the Ansley Inn is a Tudor mansion built in 1907. Built as a private home, it served as an exclusive boarding house for young women for many years. It fell on hard times after World War II, as did many similar mansions. In 1987, three neighbors bought the house, reopening it in 1989 as a luxurious B&B, after extensive renovations. The decor includes marble floors, crystal chandeliers, Oriental rugs, and reproduction furnishings. Guest rooms are individually done, some with brass beds with contemporary furnishings, others with four-poster rice-carved beds with English period decor. Run more as a small hotel than a B&B, it's popular with business travelers during the week, and as a romantic escape on weekends. Rates include continental breakfast and afternoon refreshments.

"We found fresh flowers in our room when we arrived, and breakfast waiting in the morning. We had still-warm muffins, fresh fruit, and coffee. The inn is close to many local attractions, and the subway runs nearby so even more distant places are easy to reach." *(MW)* Comments most welcome.

Open All year.

Rooms 1 suite, 11 doubles—all have full private bath with Jacuzzi, wet bar, telephone, radio, TV, desk, air-conditioning, fan. Some with fireplace.

Facilities Dining room, living room, and conference room with fireplace. 24-hr. room service; laundry service. Health club privileges, pool. Conference facilities, fax and copy service.

Location Ansley Park, midtown arts/business district. From I-75 or 85, exit at 14th St. Go E to Peachtree St. Turn left and go 1 block to 15th St. Bear right to inn ahead on right. Close to theaters, parks, shopping, subway.

GEORGIA

Credit cards Amex, DC, En Route, MC, Visa.
Rates B&B, $156–195 suite, $100–120 double, $80–125 single. Weekly, monthly, corporate rates.
Extras Wheelchair access. Babysitting. Italian spoken.

Shellmont Bed & Breakfast Lodge ¢ ♦♦   *Tel:* 404–872–9290
821 Piedmont Avenue N.E., 30308

Built in 1891, and listed on the National Register of Historic Places, Shellmont is an excellent example of Victorian design. Stained, leaded, and beveled glass abounds, as do intricately carved interior and exterior woodwork, elaborate mantels, mosaic-tiled fireplaces, and accurately re-produced original stenciling. Ed and Debbie McCord, owners since 1984, cater to individuals who appreciate fine craftsmanship, architecture, and turn-of-the-century design.

The Shellmont is located in midtown; some of the city's best restaurants, live theaters, art cinemas, museums, and shopping are within walking distance. Rates include a breakfast of fresh fruit and juice, cereal, dried fruit, and pastries.

"Conveniently located not far from a MARTA stop and trendy Virginia Highland, this Victorian house is filled with antique furniture, and is complete with a front porch and rockers. The McCords are a gold mine of information on old houses, architecture, and interior design. The inn provides a delicate balance between big-city hotel privacy and the casual friendly hospitality of a private home. Except for in-room telephones, all the amenities were there—plenty of towels and soap and hot water, comfortable beds, terry robes, a clock radio, reading materials, fruit, chocolates, and a carafe of wine. Directions to points of interest with maps and suggestions for restaurants were cheerfully provided." *(JS)*

"The setting of the inn is a tree-lined section of Atlanta where many of the beautiful old homes are being lovingly restored. It's an easy drive to downtown shopping, the theater, and the High Museum of Art." *(Carolanne Graham)* "Our family stayed in the carriage house; it was perfect—we enjoyed privacy, plenty of room, a kitchen (ideal when traveling with kids)." *(Jimmy & Kimberly Fike)*

"Debbie McCord dressed in 1880's clothing and served breakfast herself. The food was excellent and our hostess polite and friendly. Exquisite stained glass windows." *(Pat Drake)* "Spotlessly clean. The antique bathtub was a special treat. My 6'4"-tall husband found the bed to be quite comfortable. Guests congregate around the elegantly served breakfast, chatting about places to go and sights to see." *(Cathy Long)*

Open All year.
Rooms 1 suite (in separate carriage house), 4 doubles—all with private bath and/or shower, air-conditioning, radio, TV. Full kitchen in carriage house.
Facilities 3 parlors, library, all with books, magazines, games, fireplaces. Shady garden with fish pond. Free off-street parking. ¼ m to Piedmont Park.
Location Midtown; 1¼ m from city center. Exit I-75/85 N Peachtree to Piedmont; Exit I-75/85 S at North Ave. to Piedmont.
Restrictions Traffic noise in some rooms. Children under 12 in carriage house only.
Credit cards Amex, MC, Visa.

Rates B&B, $80–120 suite, $75–90 double, $65–80 single. Extra person, $15. No tipping. Discount for AARP members. Children under 6 free. 2-night minimum weekend stay.
Extras Electric elevator available for disabled. Crib.

AUGUSTA

Founded in 1737, Augusta became Georgia's first state capital and grew prosperous from the tobacco and cotton crops. In the past century, the city's mild winters have attracted golfers, and the Masters golf tournament draws big crowds each spring. Augusta is located 150 miles east of Atlanta via I-20, at the South Carolina border.

Information please: In the past we've heard good things about the Clairemont Telfair Inns (326 Greene Street, 30901; 404–724–3315 or in GA: 800–282–2405). This collection of 14 beautifully restored Victorian homes and restaurants is now under new ownership and management. Reports please.

Partridge Inn ✕   *Tel:* 404–737–8888
2110 Walton Way, 30904   800–476–6888

The Partridge Inn is a grand old hotel overlooking downtown Augusta. Built in 1890, this historic landmark has been retrofitted with 105 suites complete with bedroom, living room, and fully equipped kitchen. The inn's restaurant offers southern cuisine served in the dining room or outside on the veranda. Rates include a continental buffet breakfast, complimentary cocktail, and hors d'oeuvres.

"The hotel has been completely rehabilitated. We had a large suite for a very reasonable price, and the staff is very accommodating. A fine value, excellent service, and pleasant accommodation. " *(Betty Richards)*

Open All year.
Rooms 105 suites—all with private bath, living room, fully equipped kitchen, telephone, radio, TV, desk, air-conditioning, coffee maker. Many with balcony.
Facilities Restaurant, lobby bar, veranda, swimming pool. Conference rooms.
Location From I-20 take Washington Rd. Exit. Go R on Berckman Rd., then bear L Highland Ave. Take a R on Walton Way. From all other highways take Downtown/Walton Way Exit. Close to business district, shopping, recreational facilities, and airport.
Credit cards Amex, DC, MC, Visa.
Rates B&B, $325 4-bedroom penthouse, $95–105 2-bedroom suite, $70–93 1-bedroom suite. Extra person, $10. Children under 12 free. 10% senior discount. Weekend packages, long term rates available.
Extras Handicap facilities. Free airport/station pickups.

BLAIRSVILLE

Also recommended: Set among the farms, orchards, and mountains that surround Blairsville are the **Misty Mountain Cabins** (Towncreek Road,

Route 7, Box 77886, 30512; 404–745–4786) which provide "more than the basic mountain cabin." Each one- and two-bedroom cabin contains brass or four-poster canopy beds and a fireplace, along with a full bath, kitchen, and covered porch. "Our cabin was as quaint as the home of The Three Bears—new, clean, tiny but well furnished. These cabins make a nice weekend stop in a beautiful part of North Georgia." *(CT)*

Seven Creeks Housekeeping Cabins ¢ ⚷ *Tel:* 404–745–4753
Horseshoe Cove Road, Route 2, Box 2647, 30512

Marvin and Bobbie Hernden have restored one old mountain cabin and have built four new ones over the past fifteen years. All are fully equipped and simply furnished.

"The cabins are snug and comfortable in the winter, cool and breezy in the summer. The facilities are modern, convenient, clean, and well furnished. Bobbie has a fascinating pottery shop and kiln where guests may browse or get more involved. Bobbie, Marvin, and their boys are most helpful, while respecting guest privacy." *(Larry & Joyce Bradfield)*

"The Herndens know no strangers and really have the gift of hospitality. Their special touches include garden-fresh flowers or vegetables on the kitchen table, a lending library, fishing poles, picnic tables, and an outdoor chapel. The well-spaced cabins are set in a beautiful secluded cove with a lovely little spring-fed lake, complete with ducks and fish. We enjoyed hiking in the area, and our toddler loved playing with the dog, goats, pony, and cats." *(Linda & Tom Reeder)*

Open All year.
Rooms 5 1- to 3-bedroom housekeeping cabins, sleep 4 to 8. All with private bath, kitchen, TV, radio, barbecue grill, fireplace.
Facilities 70 acres with hiking trails, private lake for fishing, swimming. Covered picnic area, playground, tether ball, badminton, horseshoes. White-water rafting, horseback riding, canoeing, golf nearby.
Location N GA. 100 m N of Atlanta, approx. 20 m S of NC border. From Blairsville, go S on Rte. 19/129, E on Rte. 180. Seven Creeks is 1 m S of 180 (Wolfstake Rd. W) on Horseshoe Cove Rd.
Credit cards Discover, MC, Visa.
Rates Room only, $40–50 cabin. Extra person, $5. No charge for children under 6. 2-night minimum. Weekly rates. (Linens extra.)

CLARKESVILLE

Information please: In Clarkesville's historic district, and listed on the National Register of Historic Places is the **Burns-Sutton House** (124 South Washington Street, 30523; 404–754–5565). Built in 1901, owners John and Jo Ann Smith have restored its wraparound porches, stained glass windows, and ornate woodwork. Rooms are furnished in period, and the $55–75 rates include a full country breakfast. The Smiths have recently opened a restaurant as well. Another possibility is the 1907 Greek Revival **Charm House Inn** (Highway 441, P.O. Box 392, 30523; 404–754–9347), with four double beds. Reports most welcome.

Glen-Ella Springs Inn ¢ 👤 ✕
Bear Gap Road, Route 3, Box 3304, 30523

Tel: 404–754–7295
800–552–3479

The Glen-Ella Springs Inn has been a country retreat since the early 1900s when Atlanta tourists came to "take the waters" at the inn's spring. After years of decline, the inn was purchased by Barrie and Bobby Aycock in 1986. The buildings had essentially been unaltered since their construction. The Aycocks' restoration involved the addition of indoor plumbing and electricity. Well off the highway on a quiet gravelled road, the inn is surrounded by pine forests and meadows of wildflowers. Rates include continental breakfast; a typical dinner might include corn chowder, salad with lemon dill dressing, trout pecan or Cajun shrimp with pasta, and apple bread pudding with cinnamon ice cream.

"At the turn of the century, Glen-Ella Springs was an oasis for those seeking the healing properties of a nearby mineral spring. The spring is long gone, but the inn is more restorative than ever! To get there, you drive down a series of two-lane North Georgia roads—dotted with less than scenic gas suppliers and rundown stores. The route doesn't become scenic until you turn down the gravel road that leads to Glen-Ella. About a mile ahead is the inn, a delightful red wood lodge with wraparound porches and white rocking chairs. The lobby has a huge floor-to-ceiling fireplace and a variety of chintz-covered sofas, chairs, and loveseats that somehow go together. Our suite was roughly twice the size of our old New York city apartment; it had a parlor with fireplace and TV, a dressing room with shower, and a bedroom with elegant antiques. The dining room is a must, with a fantastic menu and an inventive chef—not the downhome cooking you might expect. But the county council won't allow the inn to have a liquor license, so be sure to bring wine with you from Clarkesville." *(Nancy & John Schultz)*

"Our suite was furnished with antiques, handmade quilts and rugs. The walls, floors, and ceiling were all of pine, yet the bathroom was completely modern. We relaxed on the rocking chairs on the balcony, overlooking the gardens and mineral spring, and sunned ourselves on the deck surrounding the beautiful swimming pool. The delicious food ranges from homemade muffins and local trout to fresh vegetables and heavenly desserts. The Aycocks' hospitality makes you feel especially welcome." *(Anna Culligan)*

"Barrie and Bobby have their guests' peace and comfort always in mind. The dining room is only an amble away from the relaxing guest rooms. The seafood, beef, and veal are all first quality, and the key lime pie is the best." *(Mary Mallard)*

Open All year. Restaurant open Wed.-Sun. from Jan. to June, and Tues.-Sun. from June to Jan.

Rooms 2 suites with fireplace, 14 doubles—all with full private bath, telephone, radio, air-conditioning. Some with TV, desk, fan, balcony.

Facilities Restaurant, living room with fireplace, games, books; terrace. 17 acres with swimming pool, flower and herb gardens, nature trails, mineral spring. Close to Lake Rabun. Tennis, golf nearby.

Location NE GA. 85 m NE of Atlanta. From Atlanta take I-85 N to I-985 to Rte. 441. Continue approx. 8½ m past Clarkesville and turn left at Turnerville Hardware and follow signs to inn.

Restrictions Thin walls make noises audible; restaurant noise in some rooms. Slow service possible in restaurant Saturday nights in season. "Well-behaved children welcome."
Credit cards Amex, MC, Visa.
Rates B&B, $135 suite, $70–90 double. Extra person, $10. 2–3 night weekend minimum stay Oct. and holiday weekends. Full breakfast on weekend, $4. Alc lunch $8–10, alc dinner $30.
Extras Dining room wheelchair access. Crib. Babysitting by prior arrangement.

COMMERCE

The Pittman House ¢   *Tel:* 404–335–3823
103 Homer Street, 30529

The Pittman House is a 1890s four-square Colonial house, owned by Tom and Dot Tomberlin since 1988; they have decorated with period antiques throughout, creating a setting of simple warmth. The guest rooms are spacious and inviting, mostly plain white walls, ruffled white or ivory tie-back curtains, new handmade quilts, and Oriental rugs. Combination ceiling fan/overhead lights ensure good lighting and comfortable temperatures (assisted by central air-conditioning). The generous breakfast varies each day; in addition to juice and fresh fruit, you might be served a sausage cheese casserole, a potato omelet, and blueberry muffins; the next day, apple cinnamon nut pancakes with honey butter syrup, bacon, and a scrambled egg casserole might make up the menu. Guests are welcomed with such treats as brownies, caramel bars, or Amish bread.

Although you may prefer to spend your day lazily rocking on the big old chairs on the wraparound veranda, or curled up with a good book on the wicker-filled sunporch, the Tomberlins can steer you to such local attractions as Lake Lanier, Lake Hartwell, Chateau Elan vineyards and local museums. "The Tomberlins say, 'Make yourselves at home,' and they mean it. A plate of homemade cookies might await in your room, or warm brownies might be just out of the oven down in the kitchen. If you're looking for conversation, you can find always find a friendly gathering of guests and a Tomberlin or two; a cozy spot is always available for privacy and quiet. Guests enjoy day trips to the mountains, the winery, the many outlet malls, or a picnic and a cool summer's slide down satiny boulders in a rushing creek over at Flat Shoals. Early risers are welcome to slip down the stairwell, poke a sleepy head through the kitchen door, and find the Tomberlins preparing breakfast for their guests like Santa's little elves. One of my favorite things is to sit at the round oak table in the center of the kitchen with its crocheted white cloth, indulge in that first cup of fresh coffee, and chat with Tom about his wood carving or local history while Dot studies what'll go into the oven next. By the third cup of coffee, I leave the Tomberlins to put the finishing touches on breakfast, while I wander to a rocking chair on the front porch to watch the sun make its way to day."*(Sunny McMillan, and others)* "Tom and Dot were gracious hosts, eager to satisfy any need or request. Their home is lovely and immaculate. Our room was most comfortable, with lovely linens and plenty of blankets and pillows. Dot is a great cook and left special treats in our rooms every day. The breakfast is bountiful and delicious, with Tom hovering in the background to make certain everything is perfect."*(Alyson Meeks, also Margaret J. Lowers)*

Open All year.
Rooms 4 doubles—2 with maximum of 4 sharing bath. All with air-conditioning. Telephone, radio, TV, desk available.
Facilities Family room with TV/VCR, books; living room with books; enclosed sunporch; wrap-around porch. Tennis, golf nearby. Swimming, boating, fishing nearby.
Location NE GA. 65 m NE of Atlanta. 70 m SW of Greenville, SC. 2 blocks from center. Take Exit 53 on I-85 to US 441 South. Go 3 ½ m to Pittman House on right.
Restrictions Light traffic noise. No smoking. "Well-behaved children welcome."
Credit cards MC, Visa.
Rates B&B, $50 double, $45 single. Extra person, $10. Corporate rates.
Extras Crib.

CUMBERLAND ISLAND

Also recommended: Built in 1870, the **Goodbread House** (209 Osborne Street, St. Marys 31558; 912–882–7490) is within walking distance of the Cumberland Island ferry. Carefully restored, it offers wide pine floors and antique decor; each guest room has a fireplace, ceiling fan, air-conditioning, and a private bath. The $60 rates include afternoon wine and cheese, a continental breakfast, and the morning paper. "The Geismars made us feel right at home; service and food were excellent. The guest rooms are magnificent, extremely clean, well-lighted, and comfortable. The beds, pillows, and linens were of top quality, and the plumbing is modern. It's located on the beautifully landscaped and quiet main street, right across from the post office." *(Imogene Tillis)*

Information Please: The **Riverview Hotel** (105 Osborne Street, St. Mary's 31558; 912–882–3242), which was built in 1916, rests on the banks of the St. Mary's River, near the ferry to Cumberland Island National Seashore. Renovated in 1976, the hotel has been owned by Jerry Brandon since 1984. The inn restaurant, Seagle's, serves three hearty meals daily (no lunch on weekends), and specializes in fresh seafood and steak; fried shrimp with hush puppies and cole slaw is an all-time favorite.

Greyfield Inn ¢ 🏃   *Tel:* 904–261–6408
"Grand Avenue"
4 North Second Street, Chandlery Building
Drawer B, Fernadina Beach, Florida 32034

The natural beauty of most of Georgia's barrier islands has been overwhelmed by massive hotel and condominium projects, along with the requisite tennis courts and golf courses. A welcome exception is Cumberland Island, the largest and southernmost at 17½ miles long. Thomas Carnegie (brother to steel magnate Andrew) bought land on Cumberland

Island in 1881, and built an imposing mansion, Dungeness. Eventually a total of five mansions were built, but most, with the exception of Grey-field, burned down and now lie in ruins. In 1972, much of island was designated as a National Seashore. An imposing four-story white mansion built in 1901, the Greyfield opened as an inn in the 1960s.

Rates include three meals daily. Breakfast consists of fresh-squeezed orange juice and fruit; homemade muffins; bacon or sausage; and eggs, pancakes, or the chef's fancy. Picnic lunches are packed in baskets or knapsacks and are available after breakfast. Dinner is more formal (sports jackets and dresses are suggested), and is served in the dining room with candlelight, fresh flowers, and a beautiful island sunset. The nightly entrée includes fresh seafood, Cornish game hen, lamb or beef tenderloin, home-made breads, fresh vegetables, and home-baked desserts. Hors d'oeuvres are served in the honor system bar before dinner.

"Originally built as a home for a daughter of Thomas Carnegie, this inn is a wonderful and amazing experience, as is the island on which it is located. The Carnegie family once owned the entire island as a plantation for Sea Island cotton, and the ruins of their old mansion plus some of its outbuildings still stand. Carnegie descendants still own the Greyfield and the parts of the island that are not yet part of the National Seashore. Only 300 persons at a time are allowed access (by boat only) to the island, to cause minimum disturbance to the wild horses, deer, wild turkeys, armadil-los, alligators, birds, and other wildlife that quite visibly roam the island. The inn is the only place to stay except the camping area and a house available for weekly rentals. Naturalist-led nature and history jeep tours are provided by the inn. Hiking, birding, shelling, fishing, clam digging, swimming, beach walking, and hunting for fossilized shark's teeth are favorite activities. The house is completely furnished with old family photos, portraits, original furniture, well-worn Oriental rugs, books, and a huge bathtub in the shared bath. There's even graffiti etched into one of the bedroom window panes by a little girl who grew up in the house; she's now in her nineties and lives up the road. Carnegie family members live in the compound and visit the inn, telling guests fascinating stories of past decades on the island. Service is personal, friendly, excellent, elegant. Terrific porch swings." (Celia McCullough & Gary Kaplan)

"This place is not for everyone. The only ways to reach the inn are by advance reservation on one of the ferries, or by private plane to the 'Cow Pasture' landing strip. There is no provision for privately owned boats. Meals are expertly prepared and delicious. We walked for two hours and saw only one human but lots of wildlife. The private beach is the most beautiful I've ever seen." (Lillie Galvin)

And a word to the wise: "Plumbing is inadequate so be prepared." Also: "When the wind blows from the mainland, the occasional smell of a distant paper factory is unpleasant."

Open Sept. 1 thru July 31.
Rooms 2 suites, 7 doubles—1 suite with private bath, rest share 1 bath (tub—no shower). All with ceiling fans. Some with desk. Backyard shower house.
Facilities Dining room with fireplace, living room with fireplace, books; bar, library, balcony, porch with rockers, swings, fans. 1,300 acres with shelling, fishing, clam digging, swimming, 50 m of hiking trails, beachcombing, jeep tours. Bicycle rentals.

Location SE GA, at FL border. 40 m N of Jacksonville, FL. Private ferry from Fernandina Beach, FL (1½ hrs.; Nat'l Park Service ferry from St. Mary's, GA (45 min.). Private airstrip.

Restrictions Smoking in bar only. Advance notice for dietary restrictions required. Emergency radio-phone only; no regular telephone communication. No stores on island; bring along all essentials, including bug repellent, hiking shoes (winter), rubber boots or old sneakers (summer), rain gear.

Credit cards MC, Visa.

Rates Full board, $210–245 suite, $190–210 double, $135–145 single. Children's rates. 17% service. No charge under 2. 2-3 night minimum spring/fall weekends, holidays. Reservations for spring/fall weekends recommended at least 6 months ahead.

Extras Ferry pickups. Playpen.

DAHLONEGA

Nestled in the foothills of the Blue Ridge Mountains, Dahlonega was the site of the first gold rush in the United States. The old saying "There's gold in them thar hills" refers not to California but to Dahlonega! The name of the town is the Cherokee word for precious yellow metal. Area activities include hiking, rafting, canoeing, fishing, and panning for gold. Dahlonega is located in the North Georgia mountains, 65 miles north of Atlanta; from Atlanta, take Route 19/400 from I-285.

Information please: A historic country hotel in Dahlonega is the **Smith House**, with 16 basic guest rooms and a dining room serving traditional southern cooking; rates are very reasonable (202 South Chestatee, 30533; 404–864–3566).

About 25 miles northeast of Dahlonega are the tiny villages of Sautee and Nacoochee. **Grampa's House** (Highway 17, Box 100, Sautee-Nacoochee 30571; 404–878–2364) is a Victorian farm house, built in 1872. Rates for its three guest rooms (all shared baths) are $50–65, including a full southern breakfast with cheese grits. Close by is the **Stovall House** (Highway 255, Route 1, Box 1476, Sautee-Nacoochee 30571; 404–878–3355), an 1837 farmhouse on 26 acres, with five guest rooms, all with private baths. Rooms are furnished with family antiques, hand-stenciling, and handmade curtains. Guests love to relax on the wrap-around porch with beautiful mountain and valley views. Rates range from $65–75 including a continental breakfast; the inn is also home to a well-regarded restaurant.

Nearby is the village of Helen, a once-dying lumber town born-again as an ersatz Bavarian village (only in America!). Nevertheless, everyone seems to enjoy it, and a well-known place to eat and stay is the **Hofbrauhaus Inn** (1 Main Street, Helen 30545; 404–878–2248). Its schnitzels and German tortes are famous, and three guest rooms upstairs are available for recuperation. Reports on any and all of the above most welcome.

Reader tip: "Visiting westerners will need to adjust their concept of what constitutes a 'mountain' when traveling in North Georgia. These are low hills, pretty when the leaves are on the trees, less so in the winter months."

Mountain Top Lodge at Dahlonega ¢   *Tel: 404–864–5257*
Route 7, Box 150, 30533

A gambrel-roofed barn-style home built in 1985 by innkeeper David Middleton, the Mountain Top offers a rural retreat in the North Georgia mountains. Guest rooms are decorated with pine furniture, mountain crafts, antiques, and flea market treasures. Readers continue to report with delight on the Mountain Top: "On a return visit, we found everything just as wonderful as when we first reported on this inn. The lower level has been renovated for both dining, opening up more sitting areas for guests. Of all the inns we've visited, this one has the best, most pampering breakfast." *(Leslie Ellis)*

"Combines the charm of grandma's house with the amenities of a fine hotel. The guest rooms are decorated with beautiful antiques and are immaculately clean. The country breakfast feast is served family style, creating a wonderful opportunity to get to know the other guests and owner David Middleton. A spring or fall visit is especially lovely, when you can wander the woods admiring the dogwoods or foliage." *(Gina Killgore)*

"Our room, #5, had a small sitting nook complete with nicely uphol-stered love seat, duck motifs on the wall, an old pipe stand with pipes (and candy in the humidor), oak furniture, private balcony. There was even a reading lamp on both sides of the bed! Also: lots of reading material, classy magazines, books, antiques here and there, duck prints, nicely appointed (though small) private bath, chairs with crocheted doilies on the back, little plate with a piece of freshly baked pound cake and homemade fudge wrapped and tied with a blue ribbon. The landing at the top of the stairs has a few antiques, books, prints and a carafe of sherry with glasses.

"I was able to peek into the three other rooms on the second floor. Number 8 has a four-poster bed, and a separate little sitting room with bent twig furniture, and leaf and flower motifs. Number 7 has a 'country' motif, with an old-fashioned quilt/bedspread, old-fashioned country clothes on a wall, and baskets. Number 6 has many dolls, even a doll house and cat, and a little area filled with teddy bears, Raggedy Anne dolls, and doll furniture. All the rooms have lots of little extras like an old leather shoe sitting on top of a cabinet, or other interesting conversation pieces.

"Downstairs there is a living room area (called the great room) and a snack room with all sorts of goodies (charge for some), a fridge stocked with soda and juices, cookies, and a microwave oven. Upstairs is a game room with shelves of books, all sorts of board games and a very interest-ing cloth fish with colorful 3-D scales. For breakfast we had excellent ham, sausage, hot fruit compote, cheese, eggs, juice, biscuits. Everyone sat around family-style at several tables and the food just kept coming and coming." *(SC)*

"David is an accomplished artist and has done a beautiful mural in the dining room, and several of his other paintings grace the walls at the lodge. His friendly dogs will greet you on arrival and will keep you company during your visit." *(Sue Murphy)*"Great food: Mexican frittata and cheese biscuits one morning, fresh-baked chocolate chip cookies one afternoon; a plate of banana bread in our room. We took lots of wonderful walks." *(Gene & Helen Curtis)*

Minor niggle: "Our room needed an extra mirror in the bedroom for fixing hair and makeup."

Open All year.
Rooms 2 suites, 11 doubles—all with private bath and/or shower, air-conditioning, fan. Some with desk, fireplace, refrigerator, deck. Radio on request.
Facilities Dining room, common room with stereo, piano, wood-burning stove, books; TV room, guest kitchen/refrigerator, game room, deck, covered porch. 40 acres with hot tub, trails, picnic areas. Rafting, trout fishing, hiking, horseback riding nearby.
Location 60 m N of Atlanta. 5 m from town. From Dahlonega square, go 3 ½ m on GA 52 W. Turn right on Siloam Rd. Go ½ m and turn right on Old Ellijay Rd. Follow to end and turn left into entrance.
Restrictions No children under 12.
Credit cards Amex, MC, Visa.
Rates B&B, $80 suite, $65–125 double, $55–115 single. Extra person, $10. 20% discount for 5-day stays. Mid-week discount.
Extras Ground-level rooms wheelchair access; 1 small step to porch.

Worley Homestead ¢ 🛉　　　　　　　　　*Tel:* 404–864–7002
410 West Main Street, 30533

In 1983, Mick and Mitzi Francis decided to buy and restore the old homestead, built in 1845, that was the home of Mitzi's great-grandparents and their children for sixty years. Today the house is furnished with antiques, and the staff dresses in period costume. The cottage's private parlor, dining nook, kitchen, and canopied bed make this inn a honeymoon favorite.

"The staff of the Worley Homestead are more than willing to sit by the fireplace and sip tea or Coke with you and relate tales of the town and the house, including the resident ghost, Claude. The night we were there another couple claimed to have seen and heard more than one ghost on a previous visit. The Worley offers a Southern-style country breakfast complete with cream gravy, sausage, home-cured ham and bacon, eggs, hot fruit compote, blueberry muffins, grits, and biscuits the way Captain Worley liked them—with cheddar cheese or molasses (jam or jelly is optional!)." *(Leneta Appleby)*

"The inn imparts a real feeling of history, conveyed by the pictures and background information about the carpetbagger family that took over the original homestead. You feel as if they are going to return at any minute and ask you to leave their home. In my bedroom I found what was supposed to be the owners' hairbrush, mirrors, gloves, and shoes, although they really weren't that old. The rooms are small with private baths; some tubs are converted hot water tanks." *(Patricia Drake)*

"Very neat and clean. Lots of antiques and old photos of the original owners. Delicious and filling breakfast—definitely no need to eat until dinner. The owners also own a stable a few miles away where they arrange riding trips in the mountains." *(Deborah Brown)*

Open All year.
Rooms 1 suite, 6 doubles, 1 cottage—all with private bath, radio, TV, desk,

air-conditioning, fan. Some with fireplace. Cottage has two bedrooms, one bath, kitchen.

Facilities Parlor with fireplace, games; dining room with fireplace. 1 acre with gazebo, picnic area, horseback riding. Trout fishing, canoeing, rafting, hiking, gold panning nearby.

Location 50 m N of Atlanta. 2 blocks off Town Square, across from North Georgia College. From Town Square, go West on 52 and 9. Then 2 blocks to inn.

Restrictions No smoking. Traffic noises might disturb light sleepers. "Well-behaved children welcome."

Credit cards Amex, MC, Visa.

Rates B&B, $59–65 in cottage or suite, $49–55 double, $44–50 single. Extra person (over age 12), $10; children under 12 free. Trail riding, mountain touring packages.

Extras Some rooms wheelchair access. Crib; babysitting can be arranged.

GAINESVILLE

Information please: A newly built B&B is the **Whitworth Inn** (6593 McEver Road, Flowery Branch 30542; 404–967–2386), six miles south of Gainesville and just minutes from Lake Lanier. The $55 rate includes a full breakfast.

The Dunlap House   *Tel:* 404–536–0200
635 Green Street, 30501

The Dunlap House was built in 1910 and was extensively renovated in 1985 as a luxury B&B inn; it was purchased by Rita and Jerry Fishman in 1990. After extensive construction, involving new wiring, plumbing, and heating, the inn now offers guest rooms handsomely decorated with quality reproductions, including lots of floral chintzes and custom-made rice and four-poster queen and king-size beds. Guests are supplied with designer linens, oversize towels, and terry robes. The inn's many business guests enjoy the message-waiting telephones, among other amenities. Rates include the morning paper, a continental breakfast of fresh fruit and juice, rolls, and beverage, and afternoon tea.

"Dunlap House had everything I could possibly need or desire in a B&B. The service is attentive but not bothersome, the rooms are exceptionally clean and decorated in impeccable taste. Even though it is an older home converted into a B&B, it was obvious no skimping had occurred in upgrading the inn." *(Marc & Charmaine Lawrence)* "Extra touches extended to a hair dryer and telephone in the bathroom. Our room had a fireplace and several comfortable chairs. The large porch is a wonderful place to relax and enjoy the delicious breakfast of fresh fruit and homemade breads. Parking is ample and convenient." *(Blanche & Alan Williams)*

"Exceptionally helpful, friendly service. Superb breakfast of freshly baked banana nut muffins, and cantaloupe with fresh strawberries. Right down to the cherry flavored butter, everything was superb!" *(Marie G. Hearn, and others)*

Open All year.
Rooms 2 suites, 7 doubles—all with private bath, telephone, TV, air-conditioning. Some with desk, fireplace.
Facilities Common area, reception room, kitchen facilities, dining room with fireplace, porch. Lake Lanier for all water sports.
Location N GA. 60 m N of Atlanta. From I-985, take Exit 6. Go north 2 m on Hwy. 129.
Credit cards Amex, MC, Visa.
Rates B&B, $135–210 suite, $75–105 double, $65–95 single. Extra person, $10. 10% senior discount. Weekly, corporate rates. Packages.
Extras Airport/station pickups. Wheelchair access; 1 guest room has bath equipped for disabled.

GREENSBORO

Early Hill B&B   *Tel: 404–453–7876*
1580 Lickskillet Road, P.O. Box 275, 30642

Travelers who think of B&Bs as specializing in "country cuteness" are in for a delightful surprise at Early Hill. This magnificent Georgian manor house has been decorated with considerable elegance, including crystal chandeliers, Oriental carpets, and carefully swagged draperies. The inn has been owned since 1985 by Leonard Shockley, and is now managed by Robert Thomason; rates include a continental breakfast.

"Built in 1825 by a brother of Georgia governor Peter Early, Early Hill was once the manor house of a plantation of over 10,000 acres, with as many as 100 outbuildings. Despite its diminished acreage, it still retains a country ambience and the flavor of an era where the lifestyle was slower-paced and laced with friendliness and warmth. We were welcomed graciously, and invited to relax, pick the pecans, take walks—in short, to make ourselves at home. Our spacious room had plenty of windows (the original shutters are still in use), overlooking the spacious pecan tree-lined backyard, leading to the woods in back. Our friend's room shared the same view, and had a fireplace and a blue color scheme. We had hoped to catch a glimpse of their supposedly resident ghost, but slept too soundly in the inn's comfortable beds! We enjoyed playing the grand piano in the main parlor, painted effectively in a soft tomato red, and watching TV with Edna in the family room. The staircase is a masterpiece—we took a dozen pictures. There is a fishing lake nearby, and the antebellum homes of Madison are a beautiful 20-minute drive away." *(April Burwell)*

Open All year.
Rooms 1 suite, 5 doubles—4 with private bath, 2 with a maximum of 4 people sharing 1 bath. All with desk, air-conditioning, fan.
Facilities Dining room, living room, library, TV room, veranda. 25 acres with lawns, croquet. Golf, tennis, fishing, boating, hunting nearby.
Location 40 m NE of Macon, 50 E of Atlanta. 2½ m outside town. Take Hwy. 278 W 1½ m to Lickskillet Rd. and turn right; inn on left.
Credit cards Amex, MC, Visa.
Rates B&B, $70 suite or double. Extra person, $5.

JASPER

The Woodbridge Inn ¢ **⋔** ✕   *Tel:* 404–692–6293
411 Chambers Street, 30143

One of North Georgia's best restaurants, the Woodbridge, is housed in an historic inn, dating back to the 1850s; overnight accommodations are found in the adjacent contemporary wood-sided lodge. Rooms are cleanly furnished with motel-style decor, and most provide lovely vistas over-looking the swimming pool to the hills and Blue Ridge Mountains beyond.

Joe and Brenda Rueffert have owned the inn since 1976 and combine southern hospitality with European cuisine. Joe is originally from Bavaria, so it's not surprising to find rainbow trout and Wiener schnitzel on the menu. The keynote here is fresh ingredients; everything is homemade, from the salad dressings to the pies.

"Joe is an excellent chef and is thoughtful as well. One night I had pork with mushroom sauce, the next, pan-fried trout. The view of the mountains is relaxing, and the pool area is especially nice. Rooms are modern and comfortable with very large baths. Jasper is a sleepy little town but here are beautiful state parks in the area." *(Barbara Browning)*

Open All year. Restaurant closed Mon.
Rooms 4 suites, 4 doubles, 4 singles—all with full private bath, telephone, radio, TV, desk, air-conditioning, fan. Most with balcony.
Facilities Restaurant, deck. 2 acres with swimming pool. Tennis, golf, hiking, lake swimming, and fishing nearby.
Location Pickens County, 60 m N of Atlanta. Walking distance to town. From Atlanta, take I-75 N to I-575 N to Rte. 5 N to Rte. 53 E to Jasper; alt. rte., at end of I-575, take Rte. 5A to Jasper.
Credit cards Amex, Discover, MC, Visa.
Rates Room only, $65–75 suite, $45–65 double, $40–45 single. Children under 12 free. 10% senior discount. Alc lunch, $6–10; alc dinner, $25. Dinner served Tues.–Sat.
Extras Wheelchair access. Local airport pickups. Pets permitted. Crib, babysitting. German spoken.

JEKYLL ISLAND

Jekyll Island Club **⋔** ✕ 🎾   *Tel:* 912–635–2600
371 Riverview Drive, 31520   800–333–3333

One hundred years ago, the Rockefellers, Morgans, Goodyears, Astors, Pulitzers, and other American millionaires set up a club to relax and get away from the pressures of excessive wealth. Called the Jekyll Island Club, it accepted only society's "crème de la crème," and served as a winter Newport. The club proved to be a great success, and by the turn of the century, was equipped with the high technology of the day—both electricity and telephone communications. In fact, it was the site of the nation's first transcontinental telephone call, in 1915. Favorite sporting activities included golf, tennis, bicycling, and hunting. The club's era ended in the thirties with the Great Depression and it finally closed at the outset of World War II.

After the war, Jekyll Island was purchased by the state of Georgia and opened for public use; fortunately, most of the island remains a state park, and only a third of it can be developed. The club is isolated from recent development because it faces the Intracoastal Waterway, while modern construction is primarily on the Atlantic beachfront side of this narrow island.

In 1986, an investment group leased the club (listed on the National Register of Historic Places) from the state of Georgia and spent $17 million restoring and refurbishing it. Ornate woodwork and gold leaf have been returned to their original splendor, while the baths have been modernized some with of whirlpool tubs. Rooms have been elegantly furnished with custom-made Queen Anne reproductions.

"Jekyll Island is a very lively resort area, wonderful for bicycling, with over twenty miles of trails. The building is surrounded by verandas, where you can relax on wicker chairs overlooking the river, enjoying the view and the tempting smells of sourdough bread and croissants baking in the hotel deli. Inside, the pillared dining room is especially striking, while the handsome suites are furnished elegantly with dark colors. The suites also have fireplaces, as well as private semicircular porches overlooking the river. (The porches can be glassed-in for continued enjoyment in cooler weather.) The enormous marble baths combine period charm with all modern amenities." *(Marjorie A. Cohen)* More comments needed.

Open All year.

Rooms 18 suites, 118 doubles—all with full private bath, telephone, TV/VCR, radio, desk, air-conditioning. Most suites with porch, fireplace. 24 rooms in San Souci Cottage.

Facilities Dining room, room service, delicatessen, parlors, lounges, verandas. 7 acres with beach club with all water sports, deep-sea fishing, croquet, horseshoes, volleyball, badminton, children's program, swimming pool, marina, 8 outdoor tennis courts (5 lighted), 1 indoor court, 63 holes of golf, gift shops, valet parking.

Location SE GA. 75 m S of Savannah, 65 m N of Jacksonville, FL. Exit I-95 at Brunswick. Take Rte. 25 to Rte. 50 to causeway to island. Club is part of 240-acre national historic district, in central part of island, on inland side.

Restrictions Non-smoking rooms available.

Credit cards Amex, CB, DC, Discover, MC, Visa.

Rates Room only, $99–159 suite, $89–115 double, $69–89 single. Extra person, $20. MAP, full board rates available. Reduced rates for children. Sports, dinner theater, murder mystery, and other packages. Senior discount. Alc lunch, $12; alc dinner, $40.

Extras Rooms equipped for handicapped; elevator. Airport/station pickups. Shuttle service on island. Crib, babysitting, play equipment, games. Spanish, French, Italian spoken.

LOOKOUT MOUNTAIN

Also recommended: While too large at 300 rooms for a full entry, readers may want to take a peek at the **Chattanooga Choo-Choo Holi-**

day Inn (1400 Market Street, Chattanooga TN 37402; 615—266—500 or 800—TRACK—29), located in the depot of that memorable railway. Listed on the National Register of Historic Places, the lobby offers seating beneath the soaring dome of the vestibule. "Most of the rooms are in three different motel sections, but the antique-filled rooms in the old railroad cars are charming, spacious, and romantic. Be sure and ask for one facing the gardens. Had an acceptable dinner at the Station House restaurant and enjoyed the live singing." *(Ruth & Derek Tilsley)*

Information please: About 10 miles southeast of Lookout Mountain is the **Captain's Quarters Inn** (13 Barnhardt Circle, Fort Oglethorpe, 30742; 404—858—0624), built in 1902. The inn has four guest rooms, renting for $50—80; each has a private bath and cable TV. A snack room is available to guests at almost any hour.

The Lookout Inn ¢ 🛉   *Tel:* 404—820—2000
Formerly "Johnson's Scenic Court"
Scenic Highway, 30750

In North Georgia, at the Tennessee border, is the aptly named Lookout Mountain. A frequent correspondent reports that: "This place is not fancy. In fact, it is downright plain, but its spectacular views make it special. It literally perches at the very top of Lookout Mountain and two of the banks of rooms face outward over Chattanooga and the valley. The valley at night is a mass of twinkling lights. We go there to escape, sit, meditate, and simply enjoy the view together." *(Leslie Ellis)*

The lodge was bought by Covenant College in 1988, and considerable upgrading is underway. In 1989 they added a lobby and porch area with large deck and fireplace; in 1991 they redecorated some of the rooms with a simple country look, and redid half the bathrooms. Dan and Becky Maddy are the managers. Rates include a breakfast of coffee, juice, and a sweet roll.

"All the Lookout Mountain attractions are within ten minutes, yet this little inn sits into the mountain in such a fasion that one feels away from it all. I met the innkeeper and found her very warm and pleasant." *(Mary Morgan)*

Open All year.
Rooms 16 doubles—all with private bath, TV, air-conditioning.
Facilities Lobby with fireplace, covered porch, decks, heated swimming pool.
Location NW GA. At TN border, 10 m SW of Chattanooga TN. 2 m above Rock City. Across from Covenant College.
Credit cards MC, Visa. 32 4650, 46,
Rates B&B, $55—65 suite, $32—49 double, $28—39 single. Extra person, $5. AARP discount. Special and off-season rates.
Extras Crib.

MACON

A trading center since its founding, Macon remains a manufacturing center to this day. Much of the downtown business area and the College

Hill residential neighborhood has been designated as a historic district. The city is located in central Georgia, 82 miles southeast of Atlanta.

Information Please: In nearby Perry, the **New Perry Hotel** (800 Main Street, P.O. Box 44, Perry 31069; 912–987–1000) has had a hotel on its site since 1850, when the first stagecoach came through town. In 1924, the Old Perry was razed to make room for the New Perry Hotel. The hotel has been owned for over forty-five years by Yates and Harold Green, who added a modern motel behind the hotel. Rooms are comfortable but basic, adequately furnished, not "decorated."

1842 Inn 👫

Tel: 912–741–1842

353 College Street, 31201

The 1842 Inn consists of an imposing antebellum Greek Revival mansion—which opened in 1984 after a year-long restoration job—and an adjacent Victorian cottage. Owner Aileen Hatcher has furnished the rooms handsomely with Oriental rugs, antiques, and quality reproductions; Fran Rigdon is the manager.

Rates include a light breakfast, brought to your room with the morning paper; shoeshine; evening turndown service; and afternoon coffee or tea. "A beautifully restored southern mansion, with all the comforts of firm new mattresses, up-to-date plumbing, and sound-insulated walls, plus in-room telephone and a TV, discreetly tucked away in the armoire." (MW)

"Helpful, friendly check-in, convenient off-street parking. Beautiful Christmas decoration in the common areas. Our room, 'Nancy Hanks,' had matching wallpaper, bedspreads, and bath towels. Good lighting made reading in bed a pleasure. After dinner, we were invited to take tea by the fireplace, lit especially for us. Although we enjoyed it as a weekend retreat, the ample desk and storage space would make it just as appropriate for business travelers. Breakfast included tea, coffee, juice, croissant, and a delicious baked apple." (April Burwell) "Fully endorse existing entry. Our room had lovely rose-colored walls and coordinating sheets. Though service was slow, we had an excellent prime rib dinner at Bealls, in a restored Greek Revival mansion three doors down from the inn." (Eugene Preaus)

Other points: "Although fine for an overnight, our room lacked adequate closet space for an extended stay." Also: "Although the inn is safe and secure, it is in a rough neighborhood. Evening strolls are advisable only in the inn's garden, which is fenced with camera surveillance."

Open All year.

Rooms 22 doubles—all with full private bath, telephone, radio, TV, desk, air-conditioning. 9 rooms in annex. Some with whirlpool tubs, fireplaces.

Facilities 2 parlors. 1 acre with garden. Off-street parking. Lake, beaches nearby.

Location 1 m from center. Exit 52 off I-75; go W on Georgia St.; left on College to inn.

Restrictions Light sleepers should request a second floor room away from lobby.

Credit cards Amex, MC, Visa.

Rates B&B $70–90 double, $60–80 single. Extra person, $10. Reduced rate for children. 10% AARP discount.

Extras Wheelchair access. Some rooms specially equipped for disabled. Crib.

123

Victorian Village ✗   *Tel: 912–743–3333*
1841 Hardeman Avenue, 31201

Four restored Queen Anne–style Victorian homes dating from 1847 to 1897 and linked to a common courtyard via a latticed walkway make up the Victorian Village. Rooms are furnished with period antiques and reproductions, and rates include continental breakfast, the morning paper, and evening wine or sherry. E.J. Nobles is the innkeeper.

"Beautifully restored inn, with inviting public areas. Most guest rooms have lovely antique beds with down comforters, and fireplaces with elaborate mantels; TVs are concealed in the antique wardrobes. Ice water was brought in a glass pitcher, with glass goblets. Soft terrycloth robes hang in the bathroom, perfect after you've stepped from the huge whirl-pool bath. Sherry is served in public areas each evening, and a lovely breakfast of coffee, juice, fresh fruits, muffins, and pastries is served in the breakfast parlor. The Village Bistro, housed in the inn, offers excellent service and delicious continental cuisine. Our delicious dinner included onion soup, salad, filet mignon, stuffed mushrooms, fresh vegetables, and desserts of mocha torte and chocolate cake." *(Donna Jacobsen)*

Open All year.
Rooms 26 doubles in 4 houses—all with full private bath with whirlpool tub, telephone, radio, TV, air-conditioning, ceiling fan. Some with private cupolas, porches, fireplaces.
Facilities Restaurant, parlor with fireplace and weekend entertainment, courtyard, gift shop.
Location Historic district. 70 m S of Atlanta. Take Exit 52 off I-75 onto Hardeman Ave.
Restrictions No smoking in Main House.
Credit cards Amex, CB, DC, MC, Visa.
Rates B&B, $125 suite, $85 double, $75 single. Extra person, $10. 10% senior, AAA discount. Alc lunch, $6.95; alc dinner, $40.
Extras Wheelchair access. Crib.

MADISON

Brady Inn ¢   *Tel: 404–342–4400*
250 North Second Street, 30650

A welcome stopover on the Charleston–New Orleans stagecoach route, scores of handsome homes were built in Madison before the Civil War. That these homes are still around for us to enjoy today is attributed to the efforts of U.S. senator Joshua Hill, an anti-secessionist and a roommate of Sherman's at West Point. Although much of Georgia burned on Sher-man's infamous March to the Sea, Madison was spared.

"We were in Madison in December, when many of the town's lovely homes are open to tour (they're also open in May). Our bedroom had two double spool beds and adequate bedside lighting. The ample breakfast included delicious cantaloupe, followed by grits, eggs, sausage, and En-glish muffins. The owners were very helpful and provided us with a walking tour map of Madison. The inn was restored by them and it occupies two buildings. We peeked into another room—a Victorian dream." *(April Burwell)*

Open All year.
Rooms 1 suite, 6 doubles—all with full private bath, radio, air-conditioning, fan. 4 rooms in annex.
Facilities Dining room, parlor with TV. Swimming, boating, fishing, golf nearby.
Location 60 m E of Atlanta. 30 m S of Athens. 2 blocks from town square.
Restrictions Nearby trains may disturb light sleepers.
Credit cards None accepted.
Rates B&B, $105 suite, $55 double, $44 single. Alc lunch $8, dinner $15.
Extras Wheelchair access. Bus pickups. Pets OK. Babysitting by pre-arrangement. German spoken.

MARIETTA

Michael and Grace's Guest House ¢   *Tel: 404–427–7841*
1085 Arden Drive, 30060

Michael and Grace Yang have owned their house since 1980, but it was not until 1989 that they opened their home to guests. Located a short way from downtown Atlanta, the Guest House is a southern colonial-style building, offering a full breakfast and very homey accommodations.

"We found the Michael and Grace Guest House behind a horse-shaped drive, partially obscured by trees and shrubs. Four great white pillars supported a Parthenon-shaped entrance sporting white rocking chairs. Michael greeted us at the door and escorted us on a tour. On entering we found an open hall with a wide, curving oak staircase that lead to a balcony entrance to the two bedrooms. To the left was the reception area and beyond lay the breakfast room, overlooking a tree-shaded lawn. To the right was the large kitchen and part-time maid's quarters. Farther on, we entered the great lounge with a grand piano (yes, guests can play it) and a marble fireplace.

"My room contained a four-poster king-size bed, a king-size TV, and a king-sized bathroom with a large tub, two separate vanity units, a shower, and a separate toilet. The other twin room had a separate lounge with TV and library, but its private bathroom was not en suite. The walls were hung with Chinese script scrolls and original water colors. The furniture appeared to be English antique. The rooms have hardwood floors with Oriental rugs. Overall, the effect was of a classical Colonial English home.

"A plentiful breakfast was served daily, with lots of fresh fruit and a wide choice of fare. A well-stocked refrigerator supplied most of our needs in the evenings and weekends, but the most delightful touch was the late supper snack of fresh fruit and biscuits that appeared each evening in the bedroom." *(George Cusdin)* "The owners were very helpful in recommending excellent restaurants nearby, and familiarizing us with local points of historic interest." *(Joanne Averell)*

Open All year.
Rooms 2 doubles—both with full private bath, telephone, clock/radio, TV, air-conditioning, desk.

125

Facilities Lobby/reception area, sun-room, kitchen, living room, room with fireplace and piano, library. Tennis nearby.

Location 12 m NW of Atlanta. Take I-75 N to Exit 112, Loop 120 and continue W 3.5 m. Turn L at Power Springs Rd. Go 2 m and on top of hill turn L on Arden Rd. 5th house on L.

Restrictions Smoking discouraged.

Credit cards None accepted.

Rates B&B, $70–85 suite, $55-65 double. Extra person, $10. Reduced rates for families, longer stays.

Extras Laundry service. Airport/station pickups. Chinese spoken.

MOUNTAIN CITY

Information please: Just a bit further north, The **Moon Valley Resort** is a handful of isolated lakeside cabins, but people are said to come from all over for the gourmet meals prepared by chef/owner Robert Moon (Route 1, Box 680, Rabun Gap 30568; 404–746–2466).

The York House ¢ ♦   *Tel:* 404–746–2068
2210 Old Orchard Drive, P.O. Box 126, 30562

Listed on the National Register of Historic Places, the York House has been in operation for almost 100 years and is the oldest inn in the North Georgia mountains, located in the coolest spot in Rabun County.

"York House is just far enough off the main road to be rural, yet still accessible to several ski areas and numerous other attractions in the forests of northeast Georgia. Owners James and Phyllis Smith have lovingly restored each room with period antiques and have created an atmosphere of calmness." *(Carl R. Brown)*

"Rooms are spotless, with great attention to detail. The hosts were friendly and helpful with suggestions for nearby dining and doing. Breakfast arrived in our room just when we ordered it, and consisted of homemade breads, sweet buns, and the best coffee ever, brought on a huge silver tray." *(Brent Blake)*

"This beautiful inn is set right up against the Georgia mountains, with two stories of wrap-around porches. Our room was clean and comfortable, although the little TV seemed out-of-place, and the walls are very thin—not surprising in an old place. Hiking in the nearby state parks was wonderful; we followed a trail leading from Lake Burton into the mountains, past gorgeous waterfalls." *(BK)*

Open All year.

Rooms 1 suite, 12 doubles—all with private bath, TV, ceiling fans. Some with radio, desk, air-conditioning, balcony, fireplace. Suite with fireplace.

Facilities Double parlor with fireplaces, games, and piano. 5 acres with tree swing, picnic area, spring house. White-water rafting on Chattanooga River, trout fishing in nearby creeks, boating on Lake Burton. Hiking in nearby state parks; horseback riding nearby. 10 m to downhill skiing at Sky Valley and Scaly Mt.

Location NE GA; Rabun County. 120 m NE of Atlanta; 3 m to NC border, 7 m to SC border. Inn located between Mt. City and Dillard, ¼ m off Hwy. 441.

Restrictions Smoking in lobby and on porches only. "Well-behaved children welcome."

Credit cards MC, Visa.
Rates B&B, $70–80 suite, $55–65 double. Extra person, $10. Children under 12, $5. Holiday theme weekends. 2-night holiday weekend minimum. 10% AARP discount.
Extras Ramp from driveway for disabled. Bus station pickups. Crib.

NEWNAN

Parrott-Camp-Soucy Home   *Tel:* 404–253–4846
155 Greenville Street, 30263   584–7386

The Parrott-Camp-Soucy Home is an exceptionally striking house, built in the 1840s in the Greek Revival style. It was sold in 1885 and was then "Victorianized" with the addition of elaborate moldings, woodwork, and French mansard roof. Chuck and Sam Soucy tried to buy the house when they first saw it in the early 1970s but weren't able to do so until 1984. By then, the Soucys' had a lot of experience in house renovation, which the place badly needed. All the wiring and plumbing needed replacement, and the roof had completely deteriorated. Eventually everything was restored, and the B&B opened in mid-1986. A stickler for historic authenticity, Mrs. Soucy was able to duplicate the original colors of the house: five different shades of gray, gray-white trim, and red for the window sashes.

The interior of the house is decorated with period antiques, hand-carved woodwork, and stained glass windows. Rates include a breakfast of fruit, juice, coffee, eggs and sausages, croissants and rolls.

"Newnan is known as the City of Homes, and has several excellent examples of Greek Revival, Federal, and Victorian architecture. The Parrott-Camp-Soucy Home is a Second Empire Victorian that has been faithfully and painstakingly redone and enhanced with period wallpaper and furniture, including a documented sideboard given to Lillie Langtry by Edward VII. The baths are large and beautifully done." *(Leneta Appleby)*

"No detail was overlooked in the restoration, from the push-button light switches and stained glass windows to the plushly appointed rooms and antique doll collection. The well-kept grounds were beautifully landscaped, and the pool and spa are a focal point for the very private backyard. The house was absolutely immaculate, the plumbing perfect, and the lighting well planned." *(Susan McMullen)*

"I learned about this inn through a book, *Daughters of Painted Ladies*, and just had to go. Sam welcomed us and told us about Newnan and its historic areas. When we returned, she spent hours telling us about their house, its restoration, and its furnishings. Her husband Chuck was equally hospitable." *(Kristen Downing, also Donna Jacobson)*

Open All year.
Rooms 3 doubles—1 with full private bath; 2 sharing 1 bath. Air conditioned.
Facilities Dining room, parlor, TV room, billiard room. 2 acres with gazebo, formal gardens, heated swimming pool, hot tub, off-street parking.
Location NW GA, 25 m SW of Atlanta. 4 blocks from Court Square.
Restrictions Smoking restricted. No children.

Credit cards None accepted.
Rates B&B, $70–75 double, $60–65 single.

PINE MOUNTAIN

Also recommended: A major resort complex too large (800 units) for a full writeup here is the **Callaway Gardens** (Pine Mountain 31822-9800; 800–282–8181), "about 70 miles south of Atlanta. The resort has a golf course and large lake with a full complement of water sports. There are five restaurants altogether, but we ate amazingly well from the Plantation Room buffets. A variety of accommodation is available, but we stayed in the very comfortable Mountain Creek Villas." *(SHW)* "Lovely location with woods and a variety of indoor and outdoor gardens. Opportunities for walking, bicycling, seeing wildlife. Nicely appointed cottages—ours had a kitchen. We found an Italian restaurant outside the complex for a tasty dinner. We had a sumptuous breakfast in the Plantation Room overlooking the garden, with interior floral displays. The butterfly house alone makes the trip worthwhile." *(Celia McCullough, also Lynn Fullman)*

Mountain Top Inn ¢ ♔ ✕ 🎋   *Tel:* 404–663–4719
Hwy. 190 at Hines Gap Road, P.O. Box 147, 31822   800–533–6376

For a bit of relief from the summer heat, head up the hill to the top of Pine Mountain, where the 1500-foot elevation of the Mountain Top Inn keeps temperatures about 10° cooler than the valley below. Owned since 1988 by Larry Callaway, and managed by Rick Wambach, accommodation is available in both lodge rooms and in luxurious log chalets and cabins, furnished with country furnishings and some antiques; a few even have whirlpool baths. Rates include a continental breakfast of coffee or tea, juice, and choice of toast or sweet rolls; full breakfast is available by request. The lodge restaurant also serves sandwich lunches, and generous portions of Southern cooking or barbecue at dinner.

"A beautiful area of Georgia, with lots to see and do. This inn is set on a mountain top, barely out of the state park in a very wooded setting. The chalets are set among the trees on the mountainside, and the restaurant is at the top, with beautiful views from the dining room. Pine Mountain trail offers 23 miles of hiking; fishing is nearby, and Callaway Gardens offers something for everyone. Warm Springs is just as close, with the Little White House and antique stores." *(Melanie McKeever)* More comments needed.

Open All year.
Rooms 12 cabins, 20 doubles—all with TV, air-conditioning. Some with radio, desk, fireplace, refrigerator, kitchen, porch, whirlpool tubs.
Facilities Dining/breakfast room, weekend entertainment. 155 acres with swimming pool, tennis, children's play equipment. Hiking trails, fishing lake, golf, nearby.
Location E central GA. Halfway between Warm Springs and Calloway Gardens, bordering Roosevelt State Park. From Rte. 190, go N at 7-mile marker on Hines Gap Rd.

Credit cards Amex, MC, Visa.
Rates B&B, $115 cabin, $45–54 double. Extra person, $8. Senior discount. Reduced rates for families. 2-night weekend minimum. Full breakfast, $7; alc lunch, $6; alc dinner, $12.
Extras Wheelchair access. Airport/station pickups. Crib.

ST. SIMONS ISLAND

Information please: Just across the causeway from St. Simons Island is an alternative base for touring the Golden Isles—the **Brunswick Manor** (825 Egmont Street, 31520; 912–265–6889). Transplanted New Englanders Claudia and Harry Tzucanow, have restored a century-old mansion, decorating it entirely with Victorian antiques and period reproductions, complimenting the original woodwork and stained glass. Eight guest rooms and cottages are available, at rates ranging from $50–100, including full breakfast, afternoon tea, and evening sherry. Reports most appreciated.

Little St. Simons Island 🏃   *Tel:* 912–638–7472
P.O. Box 1078, 31522

To get to Little St. Simons, you leave your car at the locked parking lot on St. Simons Island and take a 20-minute boat ride to this private retreat. Since the maximum capacity of the lodges on this 10,000-acre island is twenty-four people, you'll find as much solitude as you desire. With the variety of habitats on the island, and its location in the path of a number of migratory patterns, the opportunities for bird-watching are outstanding. You can hear the alligators bellowing in late spring, and see the loggerhead sea turtles coming ashore in the summer to lay their eggs. Three resident naturalists are available to answer questions, and readers report that their presence really adds to the experience. Guest speakers also put in appearances from time to time: marsh and wetlands experts, birding authorities, local historians and storytellers, sea kayaking instructors, and astronomy experts.

Rates include three meals a day, evening hors d'oeuvres, wine with dinner, snacks and hot and cold beverages on request, picnic lunches, use of all facilities and equipment, and access to all experts. The food is home-cooked, including southern and creole specialties, such as shrimp creole, smoked ham, cornbread, and pecan pie. Guest rooms are located in several cottages, with the main lodge dating back to 1917; the Honeymoon Cottage was built in 1920 and refurbished in 1986, while the remaining two were constructed in the eighties.

"For those who like peace and quiet, pleasant surroundings, superb service, hiking, shelling, bird-watching, and fishing, along with eating good solid meals in a family setting, and just plain doing nothing. This place is closest to owning one's own secluded camp . . . without having to do any of the work. We found that the naturalists in residence were knowledgeable and went out of their way to see to your needs." *(Percy H. Ballantine)*

129

"One of the country's best-kept secrets. LSSI is a privately owned island, irregularly shaped but roughly five by two miles. The attraction is the island itself. Great for bird-watchers (the number and variety of birds are incredible), animal-watchers (for the armadillos, alligators, deer, an occasional snake), swimmers (six miles of beach for twenty-four guests), horseback riders, surf-fishers, boaters, loafers, honeymooners, and anyone who doesn't want an 18-hole golf course and disco at their resort. Best times are spring and fall. Summer may be hot and a bit buggy. Winter is for the owners and deer-hunters, mostly. We were there in May, which was great." *(Robert Saxon)*

"Swimming in a pool fed with artesian well water was heavenly, and all equipment, including the riding horses, were in good condition. The island itself is a beautiful place, although we felt a bit like a movable feast for the mosquitoes during our late April/early May visit." *(EB)* More comments welcome.

And a cautionary note: Although most of our readers have loved LSSI, it's not a place for everyone. As one respondent put it,"This is not a place for someone who sweats out the arrival of his *New York Times* until late in the day . . ." Dress is very casual, and there is no air-conditioning. The island is an equal-opportunity nature preserve, and mosquitoes, rattle-snakes, and alligators are as welcome as any other species. Although plenty of guests have been tortured by the first category, none have ever been bitten by the last two, so not to worry; in fact, the rattlesnakes are very shy and are rarely seen.

Open March to May & Oct. to mid-Nov.

Rooms 2 bedrooms in main lodge. 2 cabins with 2 bedrooms, 2 cabins with 4 bedrooms—all with private bath and/or shower, fan, screened porches, living rooms.

Facilities Dining room, living rooms with library/bar, fireplace; family room. Swimming pool. Slide shows, games, crafts, stargazing. 8 acres for lodge complex; barrier island is 10,000 undeveloped acres, with 6 m of ocean beach. Swimming, surf-casting, shelling, boating, bird-watching, hiking, horseback riding, canoeing.

Location SE GA, Glynn County. 70 m S of Savannah, 70 m N of Jacksonville, FL. Northernmost of the Golden Isles. Nearest mainland town, Brunswick, GA.

Restrictions No smoking in dining room. No children under 5. Children must have good table manners.

Credit cards MC, Visa.

Rates Full board, $275–375 double, $175–275 single. Extra person, $100. Children's, family rates during summer months. 2-night minimum. Extended-stay discounts. Rates available for meals only, or for day trips.

Extras Airport/station pickups; varying fee. No charge for boat transportation from St. Simons to Little St. Simons.

SAVANNAH

Savannah was founded in the eighteenth century by the English general James Oglethorpe and has been a major port ever since. Today, elegant yachts have replaced the pirate ships and China clippers of the early days, but a surprising number of Savannah's original buildings have survived.

In fact, Savannah now claims to have the largest urban National Landmark District in the U.S., with over 1,000 restored homes in an area 2½ miles square. Some are now museums; many more are inns and restaurants. In fact, it seems to us that Savannah has more B&Bs these days than you can shake a croissant at!

Savannah is located 255 miles southeast of Atlanta, 136 miles north of Jacksonville, Florida, and 106 miles south of Charleston, South Carolina. It's a 16-mile drive to the Atlantic Ocean beaches.

Parking in Savannah's historic district can be a problem. Some inns have a limited number of on-site spaces, while others do not. If you're traveling by car, be sure to ask your hosts for advice.

We suggest starting your exploration of the town at the Visitors Center on West Broad Street. There's an audiovisual program to introduce you to the city, lots of brochures, and a well-informed staff to answer questions.

Reader tips: One reader *(FB)* reported that she was advised by her innkeeper against walking alone at night, after dinner. Unfortunately, although large sections of downtown Savannah have been beautifully restored, some parts are still slums, and there have been problems. Muggings are a definite problem, so ask your innkeeper for advice.

Come early or late or expect a minimum half-hour wait on line, but head for Mrs. Wilkes Boarding House (107 West Jones Street) where enormous Southern-style breakfasts and lunches are served weekdays at penny-pinching prices. There's no menu, but your table will be covered with a dozen (or more) different dishes.

Information please: We'd like comments on the **Mulberry** (601 East Bay Street, 31401; 912—238—1200 or 800—554—5544), a well-known Savannah luxury hotel listed in earlier editions but dropped because of lack of positive feedback. Another inn we'd like to hear more about is the **Olde Harbour Inn** (508 East Factors Walk, 31401; 912—234—4100 or 800—553—6533). Reporting on a recent stay, *Carol Moritz* noted that their suite overlooking the river was decorated with lovely period furnishings, and had a well-equipped kitchen. Rates included a continental breakfast of cereal, rolls, doughnuts, Danish, croissants, and juice, plus afternoon port and cheese, and evening ice cream. The inn has recently changed ownership, so more reports are requested.

Another place we'd like more feedback on is the **Liberty Inn** (128 West Liberty Street, 31401; 912—233—1007 or 800—637—1007) which was built by Savannah's long-time mayor, William Thorne Williams, in 1834. Frank and Janie Harris opened it as the Liberty Inn—one of Savannah's oldest—in 1979, after a 13-month restoration. Rooms are furnished with original fireplaces, exposed beams, antiques, and period pieces.

Also recommended: The **River Street Inn** (115 East River Street, 31401; 912—234—6400 or 800—253—4229) is located in the heart of the Landmark district. The inn overlooks the Savannah River and is near all of the downtown attractions. Rates range from $79—119, and include continental breakfast, morning newspaper, afternoon wine reception, and homemade chocolates before one retires for the evening; families will be glad to note that there is no charge for children under 18. *(EJ)*

Ballastone Inn   *Tel:* 912–236–1484
14 East Oglethorpe Avenue, 31401   800–822–4553

Originally known as the old Anderson House, the Ballastone Inn dates back to 1853. When the inn was restored, the original owners renamed it the Ballastone in recognition of the ballast stones of which much of the city had been built. In the early nineteenth century, English sailing ships dumped their ballast stones at nearby Yamacraw Bluff, to make room for the bales of cotton to be taken to England.

Rates at the Ballastone include a welcoming glass of sherry and bowl of fruit, continental breakfast with fresh flowers and a morning paper, brandy and chocolates at bedtime, overnight polishing of shoes, and terry robes in the bath. Rooms are individually decorated in a variety of styles, with antiques, queen- and king-size beds, and modern baths. Authentic Savannah colors are used throughout, coordinated with Scalamandre fabrics. Late-afternoon tea and cocktails are served in the garden, bar, or in the antique-filled parlor. The inn was purchased by Richard Carlson in 1987. Readers continue to be delighted with this inn: "Located next to the Juliette Low House, the inn was surprisingly warm in feeling, due in large part to the friendly reception we received from the manager and desk clerk. Meal suggestions were wonderful, and menus were available to help in the decision." *(Caroline & Jim Lloyd)* "Best of all is the considerate care of strangers—I was watched going to and from my car, given dining suggestions, and even assisted in meeting locals who could help with my research." *(Joan Severa)*

"There are only five or six rooms on each floor, with spacious halls and sitting rooms on each floor. The doors of unoccupied rooms are left open for guests to sneak a peek; all we saw were spacious and beautifully decorated, with canopy or Charleston rice beds. A bowl of fresh fruit and magazines awaited us. The terry robes were a nice touch, as was the brandy and chocolate, and fresh towels at bedtime. Best was a breakfast of fresh orange juice, fresh strawberries and pineapple, and two different types of muffins, delivered to our room on a silver tray at the appointed hour with the Sunday paper." *(Linda Bamber)*

"Our bed had an excellent mattress and reading lamps on each side of the canopied bed. The bathroom was sparkling white. We enjoyed the small garden off the parlor—a lovely place to sit with a glass of complimentary sherry." *(Amy Peritksy)* "Everything you said and more. Coffee, tea, and sherry were available around the clock; cocktails are available in the cozy bar. A large selection of movies is there for the taking. Breakfast is served when and where guests request it. We were made to feel as though we were the only guests." *(Louise Murphy)*

Open All year.
Rooms 3 suites, 15 doubles—all with private bath and/or shower, telephone, radio, TV/VCR, air-conditioning. Some with whirlpool bath, fireplace.
Facilities Parlor with fireplace, videotape library, breakfast room, bar/lounge, patio. Small garden. Off- and on-street parking.
Location Historic district. 6 blocks from riverfront.
Restrictions No children under 17.
Credit cards Amex, MC, Visa.

Rates B&B, $150–175 suite, $75–145 double. Extra person, $10. Corporate rates Sun.–Thurs.
Extras Limited accessibility for disabled, elevator. Small pets allowed.

Eliza Thompson House 👫

5 West Jones Street, 31401

Tel: 912–236–3620
In GA: 800–447–4667
Outside GA: 800–348–9378

The Eliza Thompson House was built in 1847, in the heart of what is now Savannah's historic district, and was purchased by the Smith family in 1990. Now fully restored, it retains much of the old, with modern conveniences added.

"The Eliza Thompson House is situated on a shady street within walking distance of downtown. We stayed in the St. Julian room, a large, quiet room loaded with antiques—painted cupboards, an enormous four-poster bed (requiring a step stool to climb in), and a carved wooden fireplace. Graciousness and service were again the key here—coffee, everything was served on fine china. In spite of the formality, there is nothing stuffy about one's welcome." *(MFD)* "Exceptional hospitality from the staff, and especially from new owner Lee Smith." *(EDC)* "A lovely hotel with nice furnishings and small rooms. The late afternoon sherry and hors d'oeuvres offered a welcome respite from the heat. Parking presented no problem, and Ermine—a front desk institution, apparently—combined her roles of mother hen and city-insider with aplomb." *(Andrew Jay Hoffman)* "The morning paper was at our door, and a pleasant breakfast of quiche, croissants, muffins, blueberries, raspberries, cereal, cheese cake, and freshly squeezed juice was served in the courtyard. The rooms are spotless, and furnished with antiques—many of which are for sale." *(Bette Cooper)*

Open All year.
Rooms 25 double rooms—all with full private bath, telephone, TV, desk, air-conditioning. Some with fan. 13 rooms in annex.
Facilities Parlor with games, fireplace, magazines. Landscaped courtyard with fountains. Limited parking. Tennis, golf nearby. Swimming, boating, fishing nearby.
Location Chatham County. Historic district. Between Whitaker and Bull Sts.
Restrictions Smoking restricted in some rooms.
Credit cards Amex, MC, Visa.
Rates B&B, $68–108 double, $68–88 single. Extra person, $10. Reduced rates for children in parents' room. AAA discount.
Extras Wheelchair access. Airport/station pickups. Crib, babysitting.

The Foley House Inn

14 West Hull Street, 31401

Tel: 912–232–6622
800–647–3708

Foley House was built in 1896 and restored in 1982. Among the more interesting finds of the renovation was a skeleton lying behind a wall—a knife still stuck in its breastbone! Although there have been no ghost sightings reported, any returning spirit would undoubtedly be impressed with the lovely decor and service here. Rooms are beautifully furnished with four-poster Charleston rice beds, antiques, and Oriental rugs, and baths are modern. Rates include a continental breakfast of croissants, bagels, and Danish pastry with fresh fruit, juices, coffee or tea, served with the morning paper in the room or in the courtyard; afternoon tea; evening sherry, port, wine, and soft drinks; and shoeshine and turndown services.

"An elegantly restored townhouse. We especially enjoyed breakfast on the iron balcony just outside our bedroom." *(Timothy Ladd)* "Excellent service, comfortable bed, large room with attractive decor." *(Dawn Allison)*

Open All year.
Rooms 20 doubles—all with full private bath, telephone, radio, TV, desk, air-conditioning, fireplace. Some with Jacuzzi, VCR, balcony. 4 rooms in annex.
Facilities Parlor with fireplace, videotape library, 2 courtyards with garden, fountain, hot tub. 20 min to ocean.
Location Center of historic district. On Chippewa Sq., between Whitaker and Bull Sts.
Restrictions No off-street parking; staff will feed meters on weekdays (weekends free). Smoking limited to certain rooms.
Credit cards Amex, MC, Visa.
Rates B&B, $85–165 double, $75–165 single. Extra person, $10. 10% AAA, senior discount.
Extras Crib.

The Gastonian   *Tel:* 912–232–2869
220 East Gaston Street, 31401

From California modern to Savannah historical was quite a change in location and life-style for Hugh and Roberta Lineberger. But they were sure enough of their innkeeping plans to invest $2 million in the 1986 restoration of two connecting Savannah mansions, built in 1868 in the Regency Italianate style. The interiors are highlighted with fine woods and hearty pine floors, decorative moldings and brass, and wallpapers in the original Scalamandre Savannah pattern. Depending on the room, the decor ranges from French, Italianate, English, Victorian, or Colonial, but all have authentic antiques, Persian rugs, and rice poster or Charleston canopied beds. Rates include a full breakfast and the morning paper; wine, fresh fruit and flowers to greet your arrival; and afternoon tea and evening sweets and cordials.

"Beautiful decor without being cute or precious. The whirlpool baths are relaxing and a big change from home. Wine and fruit awaits when you check in, and peach liqueur and a praline is placed in your room every night. The Caswell-Massey toiletries are a nice extra, as are the warm terry cloth robes. The Linebergers are very knowledgeable about Savannah, and made terrific restaurant recommendations. Breakfast is served family style in either the kitchen or the lush dining room, depending on the number of guests; the food is good, especially the bacon quiche." *(Rachel Gorlin, also Robert Berrey, and others)* "Southern hospitality with California efficiency." *(Bill Jordan)* "Our first B&B, and we felt like children in fairyland. An extraordinary experience." *(Eugene & Domenica De Lauro, also Pat Borysiewicz)*

"Our large room was beautifully appointed, the bath spotlessly clean. The Linebergers are gracious hosts, and pay careful attention to detail. Off-street parking is provided behind the inn and although it looks small, we had no problems. Two blocks away is Forsyth Park, a real treat when the azaleas are in bloom." *(Lynda Oswald, also Robert Lenz)*

Open All year.
Rooms 3 suites, 10 doubles—all with whirlpool bath, telephone, radio, TV, air-conditioning, fireplace. Some with desk, fan.
Facilities Kitchen/breakfast room, parlor, dining room, courtyard with hot tub, off-street parking.
Location Historic district.
Restrictions No smoking. No children under 12.
Credit cards Amex, MC, Visa.
Rates B&B, $195–225 suite, $98–165 double. Extra person, $25. Midweek discount. Corporate rates.
Extras Wheelchair access; some rooms equipped for the disabled.

The Haslam/Fort House 🏃
417 East Charlton Street, 31401

Tel: 912–233–6380

The Haslam/Fort House combines the privacy of one's own garden apartment with the advantages of a knowledgeable resident innkeeper—host Alan Fort can enthusiastically recommend the best the city has to offer. The apartment is ideal for a family or two couples traveling together. Children are welcome, and Alan notes that "the house dog Humphrey (a most affable host) is always available for company or as a play companion for little ones. An additional attraction is our pet rooster (with a decided speech impediment) and two hens."

"This is a totally private apartment, beautifully decorated with every amenity and comfort anticipated by host Alan Fort. The refrigerator was stocked with store-bought breakfast fixings, plus chilled wine and liqueurs. Appointments were in every way deluxe as concerned the bath, bedrooms, and living room. Maps, brochures, etc., to guide us about town and recommended restaurants were all provided. We came and went on our own and could not have asked for nicer or more complete accommodations, and at a very reasonable price." *(Ann W. BeVier)*

"The location is perfect, just minutes away from the historic riverfront shopping area; Alan directed us to wonderful antique shops." *(Robert J. Sauve)* "Our children enjoyed the toys, especially the little dollhouse and the checkerboard, while the adults were grateful for the extra room and the lovely garden." *(Victoria Smeraski)*

An area for improvement: "We thought the entire apartment needed a thorough spring cleaning."

Open All year.
Rooms 1 2-bedroom suite, with living room, full bath, kitchen, telephone, radio, TV, VCR, desk, air-conditioning, working fireplace, fan, balcony.
Facilities Living room/library with books, games; garden patio. On-site parking. Tennis, golf nearby. Swimming, boating, fishing nearby.
Location Historic district. 15-min. walk to all attractions. 12 mi east of I-95. Between Habersham & Price Sts., adjacent to Troup Square.
Credit cards None accepted.
Rates B&B, $165 for 4, $95 for 2, $65 for 1. Extra person, $35. No charge for children under 7. Family minimum $100 per night. Weekly rates.
Extras Pets permitted, $10 one-time charge. German, Norwegian, Spanish, some

GEORGIA

French spoken. Crib, potty chair, toys, babysitters. Wheelchair access. Airport/station pickups.

Jesse Mount House
209 West Jones Street, 31401

Tel: 912–236–1774

The Jesse Mount House is a Greek Revival building, constructed in the 1850s. Lois Bannerman and Howard Crawford moved here from Connecticut in 1984; they occupy two floors of the house while the guest suites make up the other two floors. Spacious rooms, handsomely decorated with reproduction pieces and antiques, are well lit, with lamps and bed tables on both sides of the bed. Other highlights include the four gilded harps, owned by Lois, a concert harpist, and the Steinway grand piano in the parlor. Rates include a continental breakfast of fresh orange juice, muffins, croissants, and coffee, served in the dining room; candy, sherry, and fresh fruit are left in each suite.

"A lovely house with all the little touches that make the difference—extra towels, a dish of candy, the owners' eagerness to give us information on Savannah." *(GR)* "Their suites are ideal for a longer stay in this historic city." *(CD)* "Fully endorse existing entry. Mrs. Bannerman once played the harp for FDR and has an inscribed photo of him. Many restaurant menus and books about Savannah are available, and a famous restaurant is just a few houses down. Good location for walking the historic district." *(Celia McCullough)*

Open All year.
Rooms 2 3-bedroom suites, each with sitting room, full private bath, telephone, radio, TV, desk, 2 gas-burning fireplaces, air-conditioning, refrigerator, coffee maker. 1 suite with full kitchen
Facilities Dining room, parlor with piano, harp; large deck, walled garden with tables, chairs, fountains. Golf and boating nearby.
Location Historic district.
Credit cards None accepted.
Rates B&B, $90 double; $125 for 3 people; $150 for 4 people; Extra person, $15. No tipping. 2 day minimum on weekends.
Extras 1 suite at ground level, airport/station pickups, $20. Pets by prior arrangement. Crib, babysitting.

Magnolia Place
503 Whitaker Street, 31401

Tel: 912–236–7674
800–238–7674

Framed by greenery, Magnolia Place was built in 1878 in the Victorian style by a wealthy cotton merchant; its sweeping verandas on the first and second floors have tall windows overlooking Forsyth Park. The mansion was eventually divided into apartments, and even served as Civil Air Defense headquarters during World War II. Now owned by Ron and Travis Strahan, Magnolia Place opened as an inn in 1984, after extensive renovation and refurbishing. The original foyer skylight, crown moldings, parquet floors, and elaborate inlaid woodwork, are complemented by 18th- and 19th-century antiques and period reproductions. All guest rooms have custom-made queen- or king-size four-poster beds, many with canopies and side drapes. Rates include a breakfast of fresh fruit and juice, cereal, croissants and coffee served in the parlor, garden, or veranda; afternoon tea and cookies; and evening turndown service with chocolates and cordials.

"Magnolia Place is one of the 'grand houses' with truly impeccable appointments. The scale is large and so is much of the furniture; the more you look at the furnishings, the more you appreciate the eye and taste of whoever was responsible for it." *(William MacGowan)* "A very formal, well-manicured inn with a staff that is always ready to accommodate every need. While we were out to dinner our bath was cleaned, fresh towels placed in the bathroom, our bed was turned down, and cordials and fudge left at the bedside. It's expensive but worth every dollar." *(Shelley Matthews)* Minor niggles from a reader who "loved this inn so much that [she is] not even tempted to try Savannah's other inns": Stronger lights needed for reading in bed; no electrical outlet in her bathroom for a hairdryer. Also, another reader warns that Forsyth Park is lovely during the day, treacherous at night.

Open All year.
Rooms 13 doubles—all with full private bath, telephone, radio, TV/VCR. Some with gas fireplace, Jacuzzi tubs.
Facilities Parlor, videotape library, garden with hot tub.
Location Victorian district, ½ block from historic district. On Whitaker, near corner of Gaston St., overlooking Forsyth Park.
Restrictions No children.
Credit cards Amex, MC, Visa.
Rates B&B, $125–165 suite, $85–115 double. Packages available. Group, corporate rates.

Presidents' Quarters 🏃
255 East President Street, 31401

Tel: 912–233–1600
800–233–1776

Over $1 million was spent to renovate this historic (1850s) building as a B&B inn, which opened in the spring of 1987. Commemorating the fact that twenty U.S. presidents visited Savannah, the inn is decorated with hundreds of pieces of presidential memorabilia—both federal and Confederate. Furnishings include both country white pine and Chippendale reproductions and brass beds, and guest rooms are done in deep muted colors of green and rose. Although the inn is new, innkeeper Muril Broy is an old hand in this field; she was previously the manager of another Savannah inn.

Rates include a continental breakfast of juice and fruit, breads, rolls, Danish, and coffee, tea, or cocoa, plus afternoon tea with fruit breads and tea cakes, and an in-room carafe of Georgia wine. A "jogger's breakfast" and route map are also available.

"Extremely hospitable staff. Our second floor room had a beautiful and comfortable king-sized four-poster bed. The adjacent sitting room had a fireplace and a usable desk. The room was cleaned to perfection as was the large cheerful bathroom. Every last detail had been attended to from the crisp bed linens to the plush towels, soaps, lotions, robes, and more. A tasty breakfast was served on polished silver at our choice of locations—bed, balcony, sitting room, patio, or stair landing (very large with dining table)." *(Perri & Michael Rappel)* "Standard of guest rooms and service is outstanding." *(Michael McNulty)*

"On a return visit, we enjoyed a different, but equally beautiful room. Everything was immaculate, and standards have remained high. We arrived at tea-time and were greeted by an array of delicious baked goods, dips, cheeses, and a selection of Georgia wines. The young man at the desk was friendly and helpful with dinner plans. The pastries at breakfast are homemade and equally delicious. As noted in last year's entry, they are reheated in the microwave, but with the exception of the strudel, the taste was not adversely affected." *(Perri & Mike Rappel)*

Open All year.
Rooms 7 suites, 9 doubles—all with full private bath, telephone, radio, TV/VCR, desk, air-conditioning, fan, refrigerator. Some with balcony, fireplace, Jacuzzi.
Facilities 3 lobby/sitting areas, courtyard, Jacuzzi. Safe-deposit boxes.
Location Historic district. Off-street parking.
Restrictions No smoking in some rooms.
Credit cards Amex, DC, Discover, MC, Visa.
Rates B&B, $107–157 suite, $87–97 double. Extra person, $10. Children under 10 free in parents' room. 10% senior discount. Honeymoon, special occasion packages.
Extras Wheelchair access; some rooms equipped for disabled. Crib, babysitting. German, Italian spoken.

SENOIA

Senoia is located in central Georgia, about 37 miles south of Atlanta. Senoia is 9 miles south of Fayetteville, between Griffin & Newnan, at the intersection of routes 85 and 16.

The Culpepper House ¢   *Tel:* 404–599–8182
35 Broad Street, P.O. Box 462, 30276

Construction on the Culpepper House began in 1871; longtime owner Dr. Wilbur Culpepper remodeled the building a few years later in its present Queen Anne Victorian style, with gingerbread trim and stained glass windows. Mary A. Brown bought the house in 1982 and restored it as a B&B. The inn is in Senoia's historic district, now listed on the National Register of Historic Places, thanks in part to Ms. Brown's efforts.

"Senoia is a small, heart-of-Georgia town—about a ½-hour drive from Atlanta, although it felt like a century of difference. Culpepper House is solid, homey, and full of evidence of the owner's life and family history. Mary Brown was a professional dietitian who retired early to do 'B&B' in a house as similar to her grandfather's as possible. The food was excellent. Take the time for the self-guided walking tour of the town's fifteen or twenty houses of note, built when Senoia was made wealthy through the railroad and agriculture." *(Margaret Miller)* "The rooms are impeccably clean, and Mary Brown is delightful. This place is an 'old-style' B&B, not the fancy decorator version. The decor combines handsome Victorian antiques with typical fifties- and sixties-era furnishings." *(SWS)*

"Mary Brown is a vivacious hostess and makes you feel right at home.

She is well versed in the history of the house and the area in general. The excellent breakfast included homemade preserves and fresh sourdough bread. Our spacious room had a nice view." *(Patricia Earnest)*

Open All year.
Rooms 1 suite, 3 doubles—1 with private bath, 3 with maximum of 4 people sharing bath. All rooms with air-conditioning; 2 with desk. TV, telephone, radio available upon request, or shared in den.
Facilities Dining room, breakfast room/kitchen, living room, TV room/library, wraparound porch. 1 acre with croquet, swings. Golf nearby.
Location 1 block from Hwy. 16.
Restrictions No smoking upstairs. No children over 1 and under 10.
Credit cards None accepted.
Rates B&B, $65 suite, $55–60 double, $50/60 single. 10% senior discount. Family discount upon request. No tipping.
Extras Airport/station pickups by advance request. Crib, babysitting, games available on request.

The Veranda ¢ 🏃 ✕   *Tel:* 404–599–3905
252 Seavy Street, Box 177, 30276

A white clapboard building with Doric columns, The Veranda was built in 1907 and is listed on the National Register of Historic Places. Bobby and Jan Boal purchased the house in 1985, and after extensive remodeling, opened its doors as an inn. Many rooms feature the original tin-covered ceilings and stained-glass windows. Antiques and memorabilia, including Oriental rugs, a player piano, and a bookcase owned by President McKinley, add to the old-fashioned atmosphere. Guestrooms are spacious with high ceilings, armoires, rocking chairs, and hand-made quilts. At night when the beds are turned down, guests often discover a small "pillow treat," such as a homemade fruitcake or a miniature kaleidoscope. For those who enjoy mind-stretching activities, a gift shop downstairs offers an extensive collection of kaleidoscopes and unique games. Rates include a breakfast of sourdough French toast with muscadine syrup, cinnamon rolls, and a three-cheese omelet, or perhaps Belgian waffles, and a fruit cup of strawberries and bananas. Dinners are no less tempting—a recent meal included onion soup, shrimp mousse, chicken-broccoli casserole, green salad, and raspberry layer cake.

"Jan and Bobby are hospitable and attentive innkeepers. Bobby's culinary talents are outstanding, making mealtime a special treat. Rooms are large and comfortable. The many sitting areas come equipped with unusual books and magazines, as well as small games which provide opportunities for conversations with other guests." *(Alice Young)*

Open All year. Dinner by reservation Fri. & Sat.
Rooms 9 doubles with full private bath, air-conditioning. 2 with radio, desk. 1 with fan. 1 with whirlpool tub.
Facilities Dining room, parlor with player piano and pipe organ; veranda, gift shop.
Location In historic district. ½ block from town center.
Restrictions No smoking in public rooms. No alcohol in dining room. No children over 1 or under 10.
Credit cards Amex, MC, Visa.

Rates B&B, $75–110 double, $60 single. Extra person, $15. Prix fixe dinner, $23. Family rates.
Extras Wheelchair access. Crib. Babysitting by prior arrangement. German spoken.

STATESBORO

Information please: About 40 west of Statesboro, via Route 80, is the little town of Swainsboro, home of the **Edenfield House Inn** (358 Church Street, P.O. Box 556, Swainsboro 30401; 912–237–3007). Surrounded by dogwoods, huge pines, and oak trees, the inn was built in 1895, and renovated in 1984. Its nine guest rooms combine traditional decor with such amenities as in-room telephones, television, clock/radios, and marbled private baths. The reasonable rates includes continental breakfast, morning paper, and evening turndown and pillow treat. Reports appreciated.

Statesboro Inn ♦ ✕   *Tel: 912–489–8628*
106 South Main Street, 30458

Listed on the National Register of Historic Places, the Statesboro Inn combines 19th-century charm and furnishings with 20th-century conveniences. Built in 1904 and restored in 1985, innkeepers Bill and Bonnie Frondorf are especially proud of the inn's quality furnishings, homey atmosphere, and impeccable housekeeping.

"We stayed in room number 3 furnished with fine Georgian antiques from England, two queen-sized beds, a working fireplace, and a wonderful bath with whirlpool tub and separate stall shower. We felt like we were staying in a country house hotel in England. The service and hospitality were equally warm. The innkeeper gave us a map and we were able to explore the lovely residential area after dinner as well as visit Georgia Southern University. The front porch was great for sitting and rocking in the late evening. The dinner, prepared by their Belgian chef, was superb. We had escargots à l'ail as a starter and filet mignon grillé as a main course. The wine list was nice, since the county is dry. Breakfast was a country feast. This inn represents restoration work at its finest, worth the trip alone for a preservationist." *(Russell Wynings)* "A fine restoration, including some outstanding wood paneling. Gracious hospitality." *(Sheila & Joe Schmidt)*

As of this writing the inn was for sale; make further inquiries when booking.

Open All year. Restaurant closed Mon. & Sun.
Rooms 1 suite, 8 doubles—all with telephone, TV, desk, air-conditioning, fan. 4 with radio, 2 with whirlpool tub, fireplace, porch.
Facilities Dining room with fireplace, living room, porch, patio. Off-street parking. Golf, tennis, Ogeechee River nearby.
Location 50 m NW of Savannah. Center of town on Hwys 301 and 25.
Restrictions No smoking in dining room.
Credit cards Amex, Carte Blanche, DC, Discover, Enroute, MC, Visa.
Rates B&B, $56–90 double, $49–80 single. Extra person, $7. Kids under 17 free.

THOMASVILLE

Reader tip: "Thomasville has small museums and many beautiful old homes. The Rose Test Gardens are included in the wonderful Chamber of Commerce tour. The gardens are a must for any rose lover. The citizens of Thomasville have great civic pride, and roses are everywhere. The people are friendly and helpful. We enjoyed a plesant lunch at a popular restaurant, Melissa's." *(HB)*

Evans House B&B ¢   *Tel: 912–226–1343*
725 South Hansell Street, 31792   *Tel: 912–226–0654*

Built in 1898, the Evans House is located in an area of late Victorian houses built across from 27-acre Paradise Park, in what was then suburban Thomasville. Unlike most nearby homes, it was built in a transitional style bridging the asymmetry of the Victorian era and the more simple formality of the emerging Neo-classical style. Lee Puskar, who's owned Evans House since 1989, has furnished it with a mixture of turn-of-the century and contemporary pieces, and welcomes guests with brandied coffee and cookies.

Breakfasts vary daily, but might include fresh squeezed orange juice, melon with strawberries, sausage, eggs to order, grits, buttermilk biscuits, and blueberry bran muffins one day; and sparkling cranberry juice, fresh fruit cup, glazed apple pancakes topped with apple glaze, bacon, and nut rolls the next.

"Well-kept home, excellent service, good location, homey ambiance, warm and congenial attitude of owners. Food was terrific, good parking." *(Christopher Steinhoff)* "Friendly owners put me quickly at ease, and I felt I'd known them all my life. With their security system I felt extremely safe at this inn." *(Rita Gable)* "Genuine warmth and welcome; exceptionally comfortable beds. Lee Puskar respected my lactose intolerance while preparing the best blueberry crepes and French toast (with a generous ration of crisp country bacon) I've ever eaten."*(EMJ)*

Open All year.
Rooms 1 suite, 3 doubles—all with private bath and/or shower, radio, desk, air-conditioning, fan.
Facilities Dining room, living room with TV, entrance hall & library with fireplaces, guest kitchen with refrigerator and refreshments. Off-street parking, bicycles.Tennis courts, golf nearby. Park across street.
Location S central GA. 45 min. N of Tallahassee, FL. Park Front Historic District. 1/4 m from downtown.
Restrictions No smoking.
Credit cards None accepted.
Rates B&B, $85 suite, $50–70 double, $45–65 single. Weekly, commercial rates.
Extras Airport/station pickups. Pets with prior arrangement.

Susina Plantation 🐾   *Tel: 912–377–9644*
Meridian Road, Route 3, Box 1010, 31792

"Susina is a Greek Revival residence built in 1841 and listed on the National Register of Historic Places. The high-ceilinged rooms are furnished with carefully chosen antique four-poster beds, chests, and hand-crocheted bedspreads. The parlor is large and comfortable with scrap-books full of historic details. The dining room focuses on a majestic table which seats over 12, but there are smaller tables for those who prefer more private dining. Many guests are en route to or from Florida, come from all over the U.S., and enjoy exchanging conversation and stories." *(Judith Wilkins)*

"We decided to detour off I-10 to see the roses in Thomasville just before the big festival and parade at the end of April. Many large planta-tions are located in this area, though only two are open to the public: Susina, where one can stay and dine well, and nearby Pebble Hill which one can tour. We thoroughly enjoyed our tour of the latter, and only wish we had had time to explore the kennels and stables as well. Susina is surrounded by lawns and woodlands and gives a real feel for plantation living. The grounds are wonderful for walking and admiring the live oaks draped with Spanish moss, magnolias, and flowering bushes. The verandas are great for reading. Long-time owner Anne-Marie Walker serves a wonderful dinner with home-baked rolls and wine. The full breakfast was equally delicious. This Swedish lady provides quality cuisine in a relaxing Southern plantation setting, plus big fluffy towels, firm comfortable beds, and plenty of atmosphere." *(HB)* Other opinions: Two other readers agreed on the lovely setting, but felt that the house needed a bit of sprucing up.

Open All year.
Rooms 8 doubles—all with private bath and/or shower, desk, air-conditioning, balcony.
Facilities Dining room, living room, screened verandas. 115 acres with 2 m jogging trail, stocked fishing pond, swimming pool, tennis court, horseback riding. Golf, hunting nearby.
Location SE GA, just N of FL border. 12 m S of Thomasville, 22 m N of Tallahassee. Follow Susina signs off Rte. 319 to Meridan Road (S.R. 155).
Credit cards None accepted.
Rates MAP, $150 double, $100 single. Prix fixe dinner with wine, $30.

WARM SPRINGS

Hotel Warm Springs ¢ ✕   *Tel:* 404–655–2114
17 Broad Street, P.O. Box 351, Warm Springs 31830;

Best known as the home of Roosevelt's Little White House, Warm Springs now attracts visitors for its historic significance as well as its numerous craft shops. "Lee and Gerrie Thompson believed they were resurrecting history when they began restoring the 80-year-old Hotel Warm Springs in 1988. The town's only hotel in Roosevelt's day, members of the press, secret service, and assorted dignitaries stayed here when Roosevelt was at the Little White House.

"When you step into the tiled lobby, with its antique reception desk, cord switchboard, old typewriter, and original telephone booth, you may also be carried back to the days when members of the press used neither a fax nor a modem to get their stories into the 'Final' edition. Off the lobby, the original drugstore and soda fountain is now a restaurant where Lee is the chef. President Roosevelt and his associates came for here for homemade peach ice cream (you can have a dish too) and Coca-Cola; today it's open for lunch and dinner. The second floor guest parlor, complete with 12-foot ceilings, crystal chandelier, and ornate plaster moldings, is where overnight guests are served a welcoming cocktail and a full Southern breakfast. The room decor varies; the suite has the original English oak furnishings made in Eleanor Roosevelt's Van Kill Furniture Shop in New York state, while another room is decorated with Victorian heirlooms from Gerrie's family. The Thompsons offer gracious hospitality, and love to share the history of their little hotel." *(Lynn Fullman)*

Open All year.
Rooms 2 suites, 9 doubles—all with private bath and/or shower, air-conditioning.
Facilities Lobby, restaurant, guest parlor, gift shop, off-street parking.
Location E central GA. Center of town.
Credit cards Amex, MC, Visa.
Rates B&B, $80–100 suite, $55–65 double. Corporate rates. 10% senior discount.

We Want to Hear from You!

As you know, this book is only effective with your help. We really need to know about your experiences and discoveries. If you stayed at an inn or hotel listed here, we want to know how it was. Did it live up to our description? Exceed it? Was it what you expected? Did you like it? Were you disappointed? Delighted? Have you discovered new establishments that we should add to the next edition?

Tear out one of the report forms at the back of this book (or use your own stationery if you prefer) and write today. *Even if you write only "Fully endorse existing entry" you will have been most helpful.*
Thank You!

Kentucky

Old Louisville Inn, Louisville

Kentucky's history is a rich and complex one—Daniel Boone explored and hunted here, Abraham Lincoln was born here, and Stephen Foster and Harriet Beecher Stowe wrote about Kentucky. In the development of the U.S., Kentucky has served as a bridge state: Linking the north and south, it was a slave state but fought for the Union in the Civil War; from Virginia to Missouri, settlers passed through on their way west.

And there is far more to present-day Kentucky than Churchill Downs, the Derby, and horses. A key common denominator is the dominant limestone strata responsible for the state's bourbon (the water), bluegrass (the color), and dramatic scenery (cliffs, canyons, and caves). At Cumberland Falls State Park visitors can walk out on flat limestone slabs to watch a 125-foot-wide, 68-foot-high swathe of water plunge dramatically to the boulders below. During a full moon, the resulting pervasive mist forms a rare "moonbow" visible only here and at Victoria Falls in Zimbabwe, Africa. If you're not claustrophobic, explore some of the 300 miles of charted limestone passages in Mammoth Cave, including some areas used for human habitation over 4,000 years ago.

Other spots to explore: Shaker Village at Pleasant Hill, with its architecturally distinctive buildings where superb design emphasizes stately simplicity; nearby Harrodsburg's Old Fort Harrod—site of the first permanent English settlement west of the Alleghenies; Hodgenville, where visitors can see Abe Lincoln's birthplace and an enormous sinkhole; and the many TVA lakes scattered throughout the state, which offer limitless recreational opportunities.

Reader tip: If you're traveling on I-64 between Louisville and Frankfort or Lexington, stop in Shelbyville for lunch at the **Science Hill Inn**, a beautifully restored historic complex including some attractive shops, a gallery of English antique furniture and silver, and a restaurant specializing in Kentucky rainbow trout, corn bread, and lemon chess pie (502–633–2825). *(GM)*

Rates do not include 5% state sales tax and 3% lodging tax.

BARDSTOWN

Bardstown is one of Kentucky's oldest towns, with many historic buildings, and it is a center for the growing of tobacco and the distilling of bourbon. Sights of interest include the local historical museum, the Getz Museum of Whiskey History—from colonial days to Prohibition—and My Old Kentucky Home State Park. This park is home to Federal Hill, a mansion that probably inspired Stephen Foster to write "My Old Kentucky Home." From June to early September the "Stephen Foster Story," a musical pageant featuring the composer's melodies, is sung in the park's amphitheater. Bourbon aficionados will want to take the tours of the nearby Jim Beam and Maker's Mark distilleries. Here also is a Trappist abbey that sells a very distinctive (and strong) cheese.

Bardstown is in central Kentucky's Bourbon County, 35 miles south of Louisville.

Information please: Listed in many earlier editions is **The Old Talbott Tavern** (107 West Stephen Foster Avenue, 40004; 502–348–3494), one of Kentucky's most historic inns. Among the tavern's famous visitors were King Louis Philippe of France, Abraham Lincoln, Jesse James, Daniel Boone, Stephen Foster, and James Audubon. Meals include both typical American cuisine—steak, shrimp, chicken—and old Kentucky favorites—rabbit, quail, fried chicken with cream gravy, and catfish with hush puppies. Although worth visiting both for its historical significance and for its downhome cooking, one recent report expressed dissatisfaction with the housekeeping: "We thought the rooms, especially the bathrooms, were inadequately cleaned." Another reader loved the history surrounding the inn and its dining room: "The rabbit and catfish were absolutely delicious, and in keeping with the local spirit the inn's bartender took us through a bourbon taste testing session. But I wouldn't suggest an overnight stay for people who want a firm bed—I think ours was there with Jesse James!" Comments?

Jailer's Inn ¢   *Tel:* 502–348–5551
111 West Stephen Foster Avenue, 40004

After two centuries as a jail, Fran and Challen McCoy bought the old jail and jailer's residence at public auction in 1987, and have converted it into a unusual B&B. Four of the guest rooms have been decorated with antiques and Oriental rugs, but the fifth, the former women's cell, is done in prison black and white, with framed reproductions of cell-wall graffiti hung on the walls.

"We had a cozy and comfortable room, where we could take a shower without disturbing the other guests; the brick walls are so thick, no sound can get through. The next morning we enjoyed a delicious breakfast of orange juice, cereals, muffins, and croissants served at a gleaming mahogany table." *(Rita Langel)* "Beautifully decorated and owned by folks who love the inn and its history. All four of the spacious rooms in the main house have high ceilings. Our favorite room, Number Four, is located on the corner and is decorated in tasteful floral prints. Breakfast treats include sausage bread or sticky buns." *(JR Jupica)*

Open March 1 to Dec. 31.
Rooms 4 doubles, 1 cottage—all with private bath, desk, air-conditioning, fan.
Facilities Breakfast room, TV/VCR room, gazebo, picnic area. Off-street parking. Swimming pool, golf nearby.
Location 35 m S of Louisville. 65 m SW of Lexington. Center of town. Adjacent to Court Square.
Restrictions No smoking in guest rooms.
Credit cards Amex, MC, Visa.
Rates B&B, $65 double, $55 single. Extra person, $5.
Extras Limited wheelchair access. Pets permitted by prior arrangement. Crib, babysitting.

BEREA

Boone Tavern Hotel 👫 ✕ 🛋️   *Tel:* 606–986–9358
Berea College   800–366–9358
Main & Prospect Streets, CPO 2345, 40404

Berea College was founded in 1855 to provide quality education for financially needy but academically gifted Appalachian students. Students pay no tuition, but all are required to work at least 10 hours a week in one of the 120 work programs. Berea is known for having preserved the skills of mountain craftsmen; students operate six different craft shops where furniture, games, weaving, toys, ceramics, brooms, and wrought iron are crafted by traditional methods. Walking tours are provided by students every day but Sunday.

Boone Tavern Hotel was founded in 1909 as a guest house for the college. Although it's been expanded and modernized many times since then, it's still 80% student-operated. Many of the students are majoring in hotel management, and most of the guest-room furniture has been made by students. The Tavern is known for good regional food, particularly the spoonbread and pies.

"The busboys/girls, baggage handlers, cashiers, desk clerks, and dining-room waiters are proficient, courteous, and plain fun. Be sure to try the spoonbread. Note that there's no tipping; the menu reads 'We believe in the dignity of labor.' " *(Jim Lyle)* "Best value we've encountered. Our room was huge with a magnificent king-sized bed which sells for $3200 in the local shops. The bathroom was not up to the same standard—towels were thin. Meals were inexpensive and delicious, and the service everywhere was great. Excellent shopping in immediate area. *(Carol & Nick Mumford)* More comments welcome.

Open All year.
Rooms 57 doubles—all with private bath and/or shower, telephone, radio, TV, desk, air-conditioning.
Facilities Restaurant, gift shop, lounge with TV, parlor, bridge rooms. 140-acre college campus, with tennis courts, running track, heated swimming pool, golf, hiking trails.
Location Central KY; foothills of the Cumberland Mts. In center of town 50 m S of Lexington, 2 hrs. N of Knoxville, TN. Just off I-75.
Restrictions No alcohol. No smoking in restaurant.
Credit cards Amex, DC, Discover, MC, Visa.
Rates Room only, $54–72 double, $46–62 single. Extra person, $7. Rollaway bed & crib, $6. Children under 12 free in parents' room. 10% AARP discount. No tipping. Alc breakfast, $3.50–7.50; alc lunch, $5–12; alc dinner, $10–18.
Extras Wheelchair access; some rooms equipped for the disabled. Pets permitted by prior arrangement. Crib. French, German, Spanish spoken.

COVINGTON

Covington is located in north central Kentucky, on the Ohio River, two miles south of Cincinnati, Ohio, and 90 miles north of Lexington. Of particular interest is the River Center, a mixed-use development project, and home to Covington Landing, a floating entertainment complex with a theater, replica steamboat, and a turn-of-the-century riverfront atmosphere.

Amos Shinkle Townhouse 🚰   *Tel:* 606–431–2118
215 Garrard Street, 41011

Former Covington mayor Bernie Moorman and his partner, Don Nash, bought this 1850s brick town house in 1983 and began its renovation, uncovering some of the original wall murals in the process. Many of the original plaster ceiling medallions and cornices were preserved, and several of the public rooms retain their Rococo Revival chandeliers. Much of the decorating was completed by a group of Cincinnati-area design firms when the house was showcased as a local fund-raiser. In 1987, the carriage house was restored, providing additional rooms; the original horse stalls have been redesigned as sleeping quarters for children.

"Rooms are decorated with gorgeous antiques—my favorite includes a carved four-poster bed. Bernie and Don are the most delightful hosts." (*Jean Alexander Hayes*) "All the rooms are large and well decorated, although those in the main house are especially huge and elegant, with modern, luxurious baths—the one with the whirlpool tub was my favorite. The main house has 16-foot ceilings both upstairs and down, which is quite unusual. The breakfast was delicious, offering a choice of four different entrées, including Cincinnati's answer to scrapple." (*Suzanne Johnson*)

"We stayed in the renovated carriage house. It was sparkling clean, and special touches included various candies, delightful handmade shades for the tiny windows, and the world's fluffiest towels. A special delight is an antique music box which Don demonstrated for us. Breakfast would have tempted the most ardent dieter, and was served elegantly on Noritake china. The joy of this B&B is its proximity to a plethora of activities, from waterfront shops to the culinary delights of Cincinnati's top restaurant, La Maisonette." *(Zita Knific)*

Open All year.
Rooms 7 doubles, all with full private bath, radio, TV, air conditioning. 3 in main house, 4 in carriage house. 1 with whirlpool tub; 2 with desk; 4 with telephone.
Facilities Dining room, parlor with grand piano, pump organ; porches.
Location 1 1/2 blocks from river, in Riverside Historic District; across the Roebling Suspension Bridge from Riverfront Stadium.
Credit cards DC, MC, Visa.
Rates B&B, $65–105. Extra adult, $10. No charge for children under 15. No tipping. Senior discount.
Extras Airport/station pickups, $5. French, German spoken. Ticket service for greater Cincinnati area.

Sandford House ¢ 🏃   Tel: 606–291–9133
1026 Russell Street, 41011

Built in 1820 as a private home by Thomas Sandford, northern Kentucky's first U.S. Congressman, Sandford House was acquired by a Baptist theological seminary. In the 1890s, it became an exclusive finishing school for young ladies; more recently it served as a parish house for the priests of a local parish. Although the original design was Federal, the building was remodeled in the Victorian Second Empire style (with a mansard roof) after a fire in the 1880s. Owned by Linda and Dan Carter since 1988, it opened as a B&B in 1990. Rates include a full breakfast of fresh fruit and juice, with French toast, waffles, or perhaps an egg and cheese casserole, served in the garden gazebo in good weather.

"Linda showed us through the newly renovated house; Don, a retired chemist-turned-railroad buff was off 'riding the rails.' Our room was small but lovely; its pastel walls accented the high corniced ceilings and plush carpeting, providing a feeling of elegance. The counter for the bathroom sink was originally part of an altar, recycled from one of the house's earlier uses. Breakfast was served on fine china in the beautiful dining room. A dog complete with wagging tail finished the setting." *(Zita Knific, also Jackie VanDemark)* "A safe and secure setting, with great warmth and hospitality. The best part of the Sandford House is having breakfast with Linda and Dan Carter. It's like visiting newly discovered relatives who serve your favorite food!" *(Rebecca Saybrook)*

Open All year.
Rooms 1 apartment, 1 suite, 1 double—all with full private bath, radio, TV, air-conditioning. Suite with whirlpool tub, patio, refrigerator. Apartment with desk, refrigerator, washer/dryer.
Facilities Dining room, living room with fireplace, family room with TV/VCR, pool table. Laundry facilities. 1 acre with gardens, hot tub, patio, gazebo.
Location Old Seminary Square Historic District. 10 min. from downtown Cincinnati, 5 min. from Covington Landing, 2 blocks from Basilica. Exit I-75 at 12th St. & go E. Turn left on Russell St. to inn between 11th St., & Robbins.
Restrictions Train noise might disturb light sleepers. Smoking in living room only.

Credit cards MC, Visa.
Rates B&B $85–95 suite, $55 double, $50–90 single. Extra person, $10. No charge for children under 12.
Extras Airport/station pickups.

HARDIN

Kenlake Lodge ¢ 👫 ✕ 🏹
Route 1, Box 522, 42048

Tel: 502–474–2211
800–325–0143

A resort owned and run by the State of Kentucky, Kenlake Lodge is located on the western shore of Kentucky Lake, one of many man-made reservoirs created by the Tennessee Valley Authority. The dining room in the lodge serves three meals daily.

"We've stayed at Kenlake twice; once in the motel-type rooms in the main lodge and once in the housekeeping cabins, scattered about the property in small clusters. The rooms and cabins are not fancy but are very clean and comfortable. The real attraction here is the peaceful lakeside setting. Although there's a full range of sports available, Kenlake is a great place to relax and do as much or as little as you like. Just across the lake from the lodge (via a bridge) is the TVA's Land Between Lakes, a large nature preserve with a variety of additional recreational opportunities including interpretive programs, hiking trails, horseback riding, and demonstration farms." *(James & Janice Utt)*

Open All year. Closed Christmas week.
Rooms 48 doubles in hotel, 21 1-bedroom cottages, 8 2-bedroom cottages, 1 3-bedroom cottage, 4 efficiency cottages—all with full private bath, telephone, radio, TV, desk, air-conditioning, fan.
Facilities Dining room, game room with TV. 1800 acres with indoor/outdoor tennis, beach, swimming, fishing, marina, boat rentals, hiking trails, horseback riding, golf, playground equipment, children's activity program.
Location W KY. 100 m NW of Nashville, TN. 15 M SE of Paducah.
Restrictions No alcoholic beverages sold.
Credit cards Amex, CB, MC, Visa.
Rates Room only, $56–72 suite, $46–66 double, $34–51 single. Extra person, $5.50. No charge for children under 16. 15% senior discount. Alc breakfast $3, lunch $5, dinner $10.
Extras Wheelchair access. Crib.

HARRODSBURG

The Harrodsburg area is home to two of Kentucky's finest inns. If your time in the state is limited, this town, oldest in the state, is probably the one to visit. Sights of interest include Old Fort Harrod State Park, with its historic buildings and amphitheater, featuring dramatizations of the stories of Daniel Boone and Abraham Lincoln; Morgan Row; and Shakertown at Pleasant Hill (see page 123).

Harrodsburg is located in central Kentucky's Bluegrass Region, 32 miles southwest of Lexington.

A worthwhile side trip from Harrodsburg is the **Elmwood Inn** (606–322–2271) in Perryville, 10 miles to the southwest on Route 68. Open for lunch and dinner, this 1840 Greek Revival building is "set on the banks of a small river. The food is mostly southern cooking, with hot homemade breads and very gracious service. The owners, Mrs. Bradshaw and her son, are always around, making sure everything is OK. The dining rooms are light, airy, and full of antiques. Nearby Perryville Battlefield State Shrine commemorates a major Civil War battle." *(Al Meade)*

Reader tip: "Mercer County is dry, so come prepared. If you'd like to enjoy a glass of wine with dinner, phone the restaurant in advance to see if it's OK."

Information please: Ms. Jesta Bell's (367 North Main Street, Harrodsburg 49339; 606–734–7834) is a recently opened B&B, named for the former owner of this brick home, built in the 1850s. Its five guest rooms share three baths, and the $65 rates include a breakfast of fresh fruit salad and home-baked treats. Reports?

Beaumont Inn ♦ ✗

638 Beaumont Drive, 40330

Tel: 606–734–3381

Listed on the National Register of Historic Places, the Beaumont dates back to 1845. Formerly a school for girls, it was first known as the Greenville Institute, then Daughter's College, and finally as Beaumont College. Annie Bell Goddard, a graduate of Daughter's College and a teacher at Beaumont, bought the property with her husband in 1917 and converted it into an inn. Ownership and management passed to her daughter, Mrs. Pauline Dedman; four generations later, Chuck and Helen Dedman continue the family tradition. The inn's rooms are spread out over a number of buildings, including the original main building of the school, a brick building with Greek Revival–style Doric columns, as well as several other buildings and cottages of varying sizes. Restaurant specialties include the inn's own Kentucky-cured ham, fried chicken, corn pudding, and orange-lemon cake.

"The Beaumont Inn is situated well off the main highway (but clearly marked) on a peaceful knoll. The sitting room is gracious—large mirrors, lace curtains, floral wallpapers, and velvet-covered furniture. The furniture in our cheerful, high-ceilinged room was Victorian; our private bath was rather small and plain, but clean." *(MFD)*

"The Beaumont is a majestic-looking building, with lots of lovely trees on the grounds. Our suite was located just across a little street from the main building. Our bedroom was comfortably furnished with antique beds, one a regular-size cherry spindle bed, and the other a single spindle bed, ideal for a child. Extra blankets and pillows were stashed in a closet and in bureau drawers. There was an antique bureau, bedside table and several chairs, one a comfortable rocking chair. The balcony was heavenly, with old-fashioned gliders. Our living room had good reading lamps, a hide-a-bed sofa, several comfortable lounging chairs, and a great secretary desk.

"The meals were very good; even though we had booked the latest dinner possible (7:30), we had a short wait until the people from the earlier seating had cleared out and we could be seated. Our set dinner included a great cauliflower soup, a cucumber and tomato salad, ham, mock oyster casserole, lima beans, delicious homemade biscuits, ice cream, and coffee. The other desserts looked exceptional, but we were too full. Breakfast is an enormous array of hot and cold cereal, pancakes, eggs, grits, hot breads, fruit, and more. The Beaumont is a very busy place. Families might be best off staying in the buildings away from the main inn; the elegant dining experience is best suited for children of school age and up." *(Joyce Whittington)* "Superb meal, beautifully served by friendly waitresses; seconds are encouraged. The country ham was perfection." *(MDS)*

"The main building is an elegant brick structure with Corinthian columns; the other buildings are a cottage behind the inn, a frame building across the street, and a stone building about a block away. The two rooms I saw in the main building were large, decorated in original heavy Victorian decor, with floral wallpaper and cabbage rose carpets; bathrooms are basic, but clean and functional. The furnishings are posh, the effect uncluttered—but the result is comfortable, like a visit to the home of your wealthy grandmother. In the front entry hall, Mr. Dedman has a collection of floor-to-ceiling Civil War memorabilia." *(SHW)*

Open Mid-March–mid-Dec.
Rooms 1 cottage, 29 doubles—all with private bath and/or shower, telephone, TV, air-conditioning. Rooms in total of 4 buildings—main building, Bell Cottage, Goddard Hall, Greystone House.
Facilities Restaurant, parlors, lounge, library. 30 acres with 2 tennis courts, swimming pool, gift shop. Fishing, boating, golf nearby.
Location Central KY, Bluegrass Region. 32 m SW of Lexington.
Credit cards Amex, MC, Visa.
Rates Room only, $68–90 double, $48–75 single. Extra child, $10; adult, $15. Full breakfast, $6; alc lunch, $6–10; alc dinner, $11–16. Weekly rates. Mid-week packages.
Extras Airport/station pickups for additional fee. Crib.

Shaker Village of Pleasant Hill ¢ 🛉 ✕   *Tel: 606–734–5411*
3500 Lexington Road, 40330

Shaker Village preserves 27 original 19th-century buildings, accurately restored and adapted. Visitors (day and overnight) take self-guided tours of the buildings where interpreters and craftsmen explain the Shaker approach to life and religion. Shaker music programs are also offered on many weekends.

Shakertown at Pleasant Hill is a nonprofit educational corporation; it is listed on the National Register of Historic Places and has been declared a National Landmark. It is the only such restoration with all services in original buildings, and the only historic village offering all overnight accommodation in original buildings.

Don't be confused by references to both the Shaker Village of Pleasant Hill and to Shakertown at Pleasant Hill; both are mentioned in their literature and both names refer to the same place. It's also helpful to note that although their mailing address is in Harrodsburg, Pleasant Hill is actually seven miles away. Advance reservations are strongly recommended for both rooms and meals. *John Blewer* speaks for most readers when he notes that "Shaker Hill is a wonderful experience that shouldn't be missed, excellent for families and history buffs."

"Each room is furnished with reproductions of Shaker pieces seen in the museum rooms in the surrounding buildings; a complete house (a bit apart from the village) has also been restored for family reunions. The serene mood that settles over the village in the evening after all the day visitors have gone home is my lasting memory of my stays here." *(Mrs. Perry Noe)* "The trundle beds mean that four of you can share one large room, each with a comfortable bed. Meals are served in the Trustees' House, which has one of the most spectacular twin spiral staircases I've ever seen." *(Ann Delugach)*

"Our room in the Trustees' House was large, clean, comfortable with twin beds, rockers, desk, and chair. Some noise drifted upstairs from the dining rooms. We preferred our smaller room above the broommaker's shop on our last visit because it was more quiet and remote." *(KLH)* "Our authentic Shaker room—with chairs up on pegs—was in the Wash House; the bathroom was new and modern. The food was wonderful, with freshly picked vegetables right from the garden outside the back door. After dinner, drive ten minutes to see the outdoor dramatization of the life of Daniel Boone or take a ride on a river ferry boat." *(Susie Preston)*

"I stayed in the Old Stone House and loved the clean, uncluttered simplicity of the design and authentic furnishings of this 1811 building, with its beautiful views of the bluegrass country. My room had a comfy bed with soft pillows and linens and a handsome Shaker spread. The staff was friendly and helpful, and all took seriously the Shaker admonition that there is no dirt in heaven. Superb country breakfast buffet—scrambled eggs, bacon, sausage, assorted fruits, juices, grits, gravy, cereal, light bite-sized biscuits, and pumpkin muffins. Delightful costumed guides gave fascinating information about the Shakers and how they built things to last. " *(Carol Moritz, also Robert Montgomery)*

Minor niggles: "I would have preferred not having TVs. The neighbors had theirs on really loud and it just didn't fit the mood." Also: "The adults were charmed, but our kids were bored after a couple hours in the 90° heat with no swimming pool."

Open All year. Closed Christmas Eve and Day.
Rooms 72 doubles with private bath and shower, telephone, TV, desk, air-conditioning. Accommodations in 14 restored buildings.
Facilities Sitting rooms, restaurant. 2,200 acres. Paddlewheel riverboat rides on Kentucky River. Craft shops and demonstrations.
Location Central KY, Bluegrass Region. 80 m SE of Louisville, 25 m SW of Lexington, 7 m NE of Harrodsburg, on US Rte. 68.
Restrictions No alcoholic beverages in dining room (dry county). Traffic noise in North Lot dwelling.
Credit cards MC, Visa.
Rates Room only, $50–90 double, $40–70 single, plus 8% tax. No charge for children under 18 in parents' room. Extra adults, $6. Country buffet breakfast, $5.25; alc lunch, $6–9; prix fixe dinner, $11–16. Children's menu. No tipping. Winter package rates, excluding holidays, $90–130 per person, including 2 nights' lodging and 5 meals. Tours and programs available. Summer harvest weekend events.
Extras Crib.

LEXINGTON

A city wealthy from the tobacco industry, Lexington is home to the University of Kentucky, Transylvania University, and many beautiful antebellum and Victorian buildings, a number of which are now open to the public as museums. But the real attraction here is thoroughbred horses. Head for the Kentucky Horse Park, for 1,000 acres of bluegrass, where you can learn everything you ever wanted to know (and more) about equines, then sign up for a tour of the area's best horse farms.

Lexington is located in central Kentucky, 101 miles south of Cincinnati, Ohio, and 78 miles east of Louisville.

Information please: We're also curious about the **Butler's Inn** (2575 Danville Road, Nicholasville 40356; 606–885–3555), a B&B 16 miles south of Lexington on Route 27. Listed on the National Register of Historic Places, it served as a stagecoach stop and later as a hospital during the Civil War. Rates include a full breakfast with fresh baked pecan rolls, and the air-conditioned rooms have TVs and private baths. Reports?

Another possibility is the **Sills Inn** (279 Montgomery Avenue, Versailles 40383; 606–873–4478 or 800–526–9801) just 15 minutes west of Lexington. Built in 1911, this three-story Victorian-style home offers five guest rooms with private baths, and is decorated with family heirloom Kentucky antiques. Rates range from $45–75, and include a full breakfast, served in the formal dining room, and access to the fully stocked guest kitchen.

Gratz Park Inn 👫 ✕
120 West Second Street, 40507

Tel: 606–231–6666
Outside KY: 800–227–4362

Although Lexington is well supplied with chain hotels and motels, there was no small hotel here until the Gratz Park Inn opened in July of 1987. Located downtown in the historic Gratz Park area, it is a small luxury hotel with a comfortable but elegant atmosphere. Housed in a 1916 Georgian Revival–style building; the interior was gutted as part of the renovation process. Unfortunately, the total renovation costs exceeded $9 million, and the hotel was unable to generate enough income to cover the mortgage costs. In January 1990 a foreclosure sale took place, and the hotel was bought by HFC Commercial Realty Inc. and is affiliated with Clarion Carriage House luxury hotel chain; occupancy rates are up, and things are looking up for the hotel after a rocky period.

"Lovely, unlike anything else in Lexington; helpful staff. The attractive lobby is decorated with antiques, area rugs, hardwood floors, gilt mirrors, and brass sconces, and it has a freestanding fireplace set between two support pillars. The hotel elevator is gorgeous. It's paneled in mahogany, with green suede cloth insets and a brass ceiling. The bar lounge also features paneling, brass fixtures, hunt prints, a fireplace, and dark blue upholstery. Each room is decorated differently, but all have antique reproduction furniture, four-poster beds, and armoires that conceal TVs. The baths are huge, with marble sinks and vanities, plenty of shelf space, and good lighting. Our dinner was very good and the service was attentive

153

without being obtrusive. Classical music plays softly in all public areas. The ambiance is wonderful—quiet and elegant in a well-partitioned room with overstuffed semi-circular banquettes and French doors to a brick patio." *(SHW)* Additional reports needed.

Open All year.
Rooms 6 suites, 38 doubles, all with full private bath, telephone, radio, TV, desk, air-conditioning.
Facilities Lobby, restaurant, bar/lounge with entertainment Wed.–Sat., conference rooms. Concierge service; 24-hour room service. Off-street parking.
Location Downtown. Historic Gratz Park area.
Credit cards Amex, CB, DC, MC, Visa.
Rates Room only, $129–249 suite, $99–114 double. Extra person, $10. Senior, corporate, group discounts. Alc lunch, $10; alc dinner, $36.
Extras Equipped for the disabled. Airport/station pickups. Crib, babysitting.

Rokeby Hall ₵
318 South Mill Street, 40508

Tel: 606–252–2368

An 1880s Queen Anne-style town house, Rokeby Hall was restored in 1985; Brenda Cornett is the resident manager.

"This pleasant B&B is the last house in the Mill Street block overlooking downtown. It was originally the rear wing of the 'Great House on the Hill,' which burned many years ago. The location is convenient; Mill Street is a narrow road, somewhat busy during the day but very quiet at night. Hardwood floors, an Oriental rug, silver on the Queen Anne sideboard, and morning sunlight pouring in the tall windows enhanced the hearty breakfasts, different every day. We had ham and eggs the first day, and French toast the second, served on lovely china and silver at the antique Queen Anne table; we were told that special requests were no problem.

"Guest rooms consist of the original parlor, converted into a medium-sized guest room with a queen-sized four-poster bed, and a tiny bath tucked into a former closet. Upstairs at the front of the house is the master bedroom suite with a small sitting room, a queen-sized canopied bed and lavish bathroom, done completely in white tile, with a huge claw foot tub and a large corner glass-doored shower. A second upstairs room has both a double and a twin four-poster beds, while the last room is the smallest, with just enough room for two twin beds and a dresser, although its bathroom is ample. All the furnishings are antique or reproduction, with carpeting on the hardwood floors." *(SHW)*

Minor quibbles: "Our room needed better lights for reading in bed." Also: "For an inn so lovely, we were a little disappointed by the small bars of Ivory soap in the bathroom."

Open All year.
Rooms 1 suite, 3 doubles—all with private bath and/or shower, telephone, radio, TV. 3 with fireplace.
Facilities Dining room with fireplace, entry hall. Garden, off-street parking.
Location South Hill Historic District, at corner of S. Mill and High Sts. 2 blocks E of Civic Center, 3 blocks S of Court House, Festival Marketplace, Victorian Square.
Restrictions Traffic noise in front rooms.

Credit cards Amex, MC, Visa.
Rates B&B, $75–90 suite or double. Extra person, $15. Corporate rates, weekly rates.

LOUISVILLE

Louisville is known best for the Kentucky Derby (the most famous two minutes in sports), and as the state's cultural center year-round, with great jazz clubs, superb live theater, and several truly gracious residential areas where homes date from the 1870s. Louisville is located in the north central part of the state, on the Ohio River, across from Indiana.

Also recommended: For an additional area entry, see our listing for the **The Kintner House Inn** in Corydon, Indiana, 20 miles to the west.

Information please: Probably the two best-known places to stay in Louisville are the **Brown** (4th & Broadway, 40202; 502–583–1234 or 800–HILTONS) and the **Seelbach** (500 4th Avenue, 40202; 502–585–3200 or 800–626–2032), two historic hotels that have been lavishly restored to their original turn-of-the-century splendor. Both have excellent restaurants, rooms furnished in period, and an elegant atmosphere, but at 300 rooms each, they are a bit beyond the scope of this guide; reader reports invited!

Another possibility 45 miles south of Louisville is the **Olde Bethlehem Academy Inn** (7051 St. John Road, Elizabethtown 42701; 502–862–9003). For 130 years a prominent Catholic girls boarding school, this historic landmark is now run as a four-guest-room B&B, with an eclectic decor ranging from Queen Anne to rice beds to country and crafts. Future plans of owners Mike and Jane Dooley include a restaurant, craft shop, and swimming pool. Nearby is **Petticoat Junction B&B** (223 High Street, Glendale 42740; 502–369–8604), a 1870s farmhouse furnished with antiques, vintage linens, and a blend of country and Victorian decor. Glendale is a 150-year-old village with three good restaurants and plenty of antique shops.

Listed in previous editions is another nearby inn, the **Doe Run Inn** (500 Coleman Lane, Brandenburg 40108; 502–422–2042). Dating to 1816, it was built as a fieldstone mill, set by a stream feeding into the Ohio River, and is well-known for its weekend smorgasbords, including frogs' legs, fried catfish, Swedish meatballs, and baked ham. Closed during much of 1991 for renovations, we need more reports before re-instituting it for a full write-up. Reports?

Old Louisville Inn ¢ 🏃   *Tel:* 502–635–1574
1359 South Third Street, 40208

Most people spend 20 years in the corporate world before finding their avocation in innkeeping; Marianne Lesher found her calling a lot sooner. After graduating from college, she set out to explore the U.S. and ended up in Martha's Vineyard for seven years, managing an inn. Her next stop was Lake Tahoe, California, where she ran a B&B. Coming back home to Louisville, she found that the city's rebirth made it just the right time to open Louisville's first bed and breakfast inn; judging from the reactions of her guests, Marianne made the right choice. Built in the Second Empire style as a private residence in 1901, the Old Louisville has a striking lobby, complete with massive columns, and twelve-foot ceilings adorned with murals.

"Innkeeper Marianne Lesher opened this magnificently restored Victorian mansion in August of 1990. The guest rooms are all appointed in appropriate period furnishing with special touches such as the handmade quilts and lace canopies on the cherry pencil-post beds. The bathrooms complement the original fixtures with adequate electrical outlets and great water pressure for the showers. Our breakfast of fresh fruit, yogurt, granola, fresh-baked muffins, and a marvelous cheese and spinach strata, accompanied by fresh-squeezed orange juice and outstanding just-brewed coffee." *(Tim & Caroline Heine)*

"Excellent location in a residential area close to downtown, with beautiful tree-lined street and stunning architecture. Restaurants, the theater, and Shakespeare in the Park are all within walking distance. Homey touches for each room include fresh flowers, potpourri, and a 'rent-a-cat' program. Breakfast is impossible to pass up, even for confirmed non-breakfast eaters." *(Arthur Edwards)* "A bottle of chilled champagne and a plate of fresh fruit awaited our arrival in the Honeymoon Suite on the third floor, converted from the original ball room. It has a queen-size lace canopied bed, glass-enclosed cases filled with antique wedding memorabilia, a chaise longue, and a table for two. I had a chance to look at all the rooms, and can report that each one is charming and unique, although the least expensive shared-bath rooms are more modest in decor." *(Thea Reis)*

Open All year.
Rooms 3 suites, 8 doubles—7 with private bath and/or shower, 3 with a maximum of 6 sharing bath. All with radio, desk, air-conditioning. Honeymoon suite with whirlpool bath.
Facilities Breakfast room, living room with stereo, game room with TV/VCR, library, laundry, porch. Courtyard, picnic area. Tennis, golf nearby.
Location Old Louisville. Downtown between Ormsby & Magnolia.
Restrictions No smoking in breakfast room, kitchen.
Credit cards MC, Visa.
Rates B&B, $90–150 suite, $65–75 double, $50–65 single. Extra person, $10. Children under 10, free. Romance package.
Extras Airport/station pickup. Crib, babysitting.

MIDDLESBOROUGH

The RidgeRunner ¢   *Tel: 606–248–4299*
208 Arthur Heights, 40965

B&B's are a new concept in Middlesborough, Susan Richards found out when she decided to buy a big house, make it her home, and open it to the public. "Being from Pennsylvania, I was familiar with the concept," Ms. Richards said, and through her perseverance the RidgeRunner became the first B&B in Bell County in the spring of 1989. A 20-room Victorian built in 1894 for the first mayor of Middlesborough, J.M. Brooks, and located on the street commemorating the city founder, Alexander Arthur, the house has a massive, 57-foot brick porch across its front, ornate wood paneling, and stained glass windows. The name is derived from the way the house "rides" the ridge overlooking the town, with views of the Cumberland Mountains.

A typical breakfast might include pancakes with homemade blueberry sauce, baked eggs with ham and cheese, scrambled eggs with sausage gravy and biscuits, or homemade yogurt with fruit, bran muffins and juice, served with homemade jams and jellies, and fresh fruit. "People seem to appreciate homegrown food, and we grow our own raspberries, blackberries, strawberries, and raise our own meat, milk, and eggs," notes Susan.

A short drive to the southeast is the Cumberland Gap National Historical Park, commemorating the famous Appalachian pass through which Daniel Boone and most of the early pioneers passed on their way west. Over 50 miles of hiking trails are available, and Pinnacle Overlook, offering views of three states, can be reached by car.

"Warm and interesting hosts; tasty and plentiful food; comfortable furnishings; quiet neighborhood with ample off-street parking." *(Nadine & Charles Prentice)* Additional comments helpful.

Open All year.
Rooms 5 doubles—2 with private bath and/or shower, 3 with a maximum of 6 people sharing bath. All with radio, desk, fan.
Facilities Dining room, living room with piano, books; library, porch, picnic area. Golf nearby. Cumberland Gap National Park, Pine Mountain State Park, Cudjo Caverns nearby.
Location SE KY, near TN and VA border. 80 m N of Knoxville, TN. 2 m from center of town. From town, go on Cumberland Ave. to 20th St. and turn left. At Edgewood Rd. turn left and bear right around the hill to Birnamwood, then to Arthur Heights. Inn is the 2nd house on ridge on the left at the "T".
Restrictions No smoking. No children under 16.
Credit cards MC, Visa.
Rates B&B, $45 double, $40 single. Extra person, $15.
Extras Airport($25)/station pickup.

We Want to Hear from You!

As you know, this book is only effective with your help. We really need to know about your experiences and discoveries. If you stayed at an inn or hotel listed here, we want to know how it was. Did it live up to our description? Exceed it? Was it what you expected? Did you like it? Were you disappointed? Delighted? Have you discovered new establishments that we should add to the next edition?

Tear out one of the report forms at the back of this book (or use your own stationery if you prefer) and write today. *Even if you write only "Fully endorse existing entry" you will have been most helpful.*
Thank You!

Louisiana

Barrow House, St. Francisville

Everybody goes to New Orleans sooner or later, and although it's a big city, you can get a good taste of its delicious food, distinctive architecture, and famous jazz in just a few days' visit. Beyond New Orleans, the state offers a potpourri of cultures and landscapes. North of the city, across Lake Pontchartrain Causeway, horse farms and dense pine forests provide a peaceful contrast to New Orleans' famous excesses. To the south, scenic Route 90 leads to Houma, the heart of Cajun country. Rent a boat here to explore and fish in Louisiana's legendary bayous, swamps and marshes. Continue west on Route 90, then detour to Avery Island, the home of McIlhenny Tabasco sauce. Up the road, visit the restored antebellum plantation homes in New Iberia.

Note: You'll frequently hear the words *Cajun* and *Creole* used in Louisiana. The former refers to the French settlers of Acadia (present-day Nova Scotia), who were expelled from Canada by the British in the 1750s and settled in Louisiana, which was then French territory. (The word *Cajun* is derived from the word *Acadian*.) The latter describes the descendants of the early French and Spanish settlers of this region. Although time has produced some overlapping, their heritage and traditions are quite different.

Information please: If you're heading up the River Road from New Orleans, consider overnighting at **Oak Alley**, a columned Greek Revival mansion prefaced by a magnificent double row of 250-year-old live oaks (Route 2, Box 10, Vacherie 70090; 504–265–2151).

We'd like to alert readers to the recent feedback on **Tezcuco Plantation** (Burnside, 3138 Highway 44, 70725; 504–562–3929), an antebellum raised cottage with 15 cabins (former slave quarters) converted for B&B

accommodation. The location is convenient, just an hour from New Orleans, and the plantation's grounds are lovely, with mature live oaks and magnolias. The plantation has been for sale for some time, and basic upkeep and maintenance has been neglected. We had reports from two independent readers who visited the same night. One reported that her "cottage was quaint but very rustic. Breakfast was delivered to the door on a silver tray, and the tour of the plantation mansion was especially enjoyable." The other agreed that the breakfast was excellent and the staff friendly, but noted that their "cottage was dirty; only one burner of the stove worked, roaches were everywhere, and lights were burnt out." It is hoped that a change of ownership will bring Tezcuco the investment it needs to bring it back up to par.

About 75 miles west of New Orleans is **Madewood Plantation House** (4250 Highway 308, Napoleonville 70390; 504–369–7151), a 21-room Greek Revival mansion listed on the National Register of Historic Places. This white-painted mansion and surrounding cottages contain an extensive collection of period antiques including canopy or half-tester beds, marble fireplace mantels, hand-carved woodwork, and fanned windows. Rates include a candlelit dinner and full breakfast in the dining room, as well as a tour of the grounds. Madewood has been listed in many previous editions of this guide. Although some guests continue to convey their satisfaction with the food, accommodations, and hospitality offered, several well-traveled readers wrote in to express their disappointment with the exact same things; part of the problem may stem from the fact that the owners live in New Orleans, and are not always available at the plantation.

Natchitoches, the oldest permanent settlement in the Louisiana Purchase, is worth exploring. Those wishing to overnight in this pretty, lakeside town may enjoy the **Fleur-de-Lis Inn**, an inviting B&B in the historic district (336 Second Street, 71457; 318–352–6621).

Rates listed do not include Louisiana sales tax of 7 1/2%, plus local taxes where applicable.

JACKSON

Although a number of historic buildings await restoration, for now Jackson consists of a few commercial buildings at the junction of Routes 10 and 68. About 100 miles northwest of New Orleans, Jackson is reached by taking I-10 to Baton Rouge, then Route 61 north to Route 68 into Jackson. From Natchez, Mississippi, go south on Route 61, then east 11 miles to Jackson.

Information please: We'd like to hear more about **Asphodel Village** (Highway 68, Route 2, Box 89, 70748; 504–654–6868), a complex consisting of the main house, a full-service restaurant, a gift shop, and a collection of buildings providing overnight accommodation for B&B guests. The main house dates back to 1820 and is built in the Greek Revival cottage style; it is open for tours weekdays from 10 A.M. to 4 P.M.

"The rooms in a recently completed building were attractively deco-

159

rated in reproduction 'country decor'; others in an older building seemed adequate, but undistinguished. A tour group was having lunch when we stopped by, and the mood was not very inn-like." *(SWS)* Reports please.

Milbank House ¢   *Tel:* 504–634–5901
102 Bank Street, P.O. Box 1000, 70748

Although this was originally a bank, you'd never know it from Milbank's classic antebellum architecture (circa 1836), furnished with museum-quality antiques. Rates include a full breakfast and a house tour. Milbank is owned by Mr. and Mrs. Leroy Harvey and managed by Dale and Mary Booty.

"Though quite close to the road, Milbank is an imposing structure, furnished entirely in period with Mallard tester and hand-carved oak beds, huge old armoires, crystal chandeliers, and much more. A night spent here would really carry one back to an earlier era, although central air-conditioning and modern plumbing ensure that the experience wouldn't be overly authentic. Unlike most plantation homes, where common rooms are out-of-bounds except on the tour, the entire house is available to guests. It would be perfect for a small family reunion or two or three couples travelling together, since you would have the entire place for your group. On the other hand, there is no resident innkeeper, so a single traveler or even a couple would feel uncomfortable overnighting alone. The Bootys also run the Bear Corners Restaurant a few doors away. The main dining room is attractive, highlighted by a huge hollowed out cypress log canoe, now used as a buffet for the Sunday buffet. It was a good value at $9.95 including dessert and coffee, with pork tenderloin, chicken pot pie, fried plantains, fried okra, cole slaw, and salad, with bread pudding served for dessert. The food was tasty and more than ample, but much heavier than we usually eat." *(SWS)* And another opinion: "Our mattress was soft, and we were told not to use the staircase handrail, as it was not in stable condition." Additional reports appreciated.

Open All year.
Rooms 4 doubles—1 with private bath, 3 with maximum of 6 sharing bath. All with air-conditioning.
Facilities Dining room, living room with piano, kitchen, balcony.
Location In town. From Baton Rouge, take I-110 North to La. 61. Go north on La. 61 12 m to La. 68. Turn right and travel on La. 68 for 11.5 m. Turn left onto La. 10 and travel 2 m into Jackson. From Natchez, travel south on La. 61 to La. 10. Turn left onto La. 10 and travel 11 m into Jackson.
Restrictions No smoking.
Credit cards None accepted.
Rates B&B, $65–75 double.

LAFAYETTE

Located in south central Louisiana, Lafayette is the capital of Cajun Country; many Acadians settled here after being driven out of Nova Scotia by the British in 1755. Of particular interest is Vermillionville, a recreation of the original 18th-century Cajun and Creole village; the Live Oak Gardens, especially beautiful when both azaleas and tulips are in bloom; the Acadian village, a folk museum celebrating 19th-century Acadian life; nearby plantations, and a variety of celebrations and festivals year-round. Lafayette is 131 miles west of New Orleans.

Information please: Built in 1806, **Mouton Manor** (310 Sidney Martin Road, 70507; 318–237–6996) has two guest rooms, furnished with primitive Cajun and country Acadian pieces. Another possibility in Washington, 25 miles north of Lafayette is **Camellia Cove** (205 West Hill Street, Washington 70589; 318–828–7362). Listed on the National Register of Historic Places, this B&B offers Cajun hospitality; built in 1825, its rooms are furnished with Louisiana antiques, and the reasonable rates include a breakfast of homemade biscuits, fig preserves, and local honey.

Bois des Chênes 🏃   *Tel:* 318–233–7816
338 North Sterling Street, 70501

Listed on the National Register of Historic Places, this Acadian-style plantation home has been restored to its original 1820 configuration, and furnished with Louisiana French period antiques, highlighted by Coerte and Marjorie Voorhies' collections of pottery, antique weapons, and textiles. Part of the Charles Mouton Plantation, the B&B is housed in an 1890 carriage house at the rear of the plantation house. It was recently decorated with antique furnishings, brass fixtures, and immaculate bathrooms. Each guest room has a different decor: Country Acadian, Louisiana Empire, and Victorian. Rates include a full breakfast, a welcome bottle of wine, and a house tour.

"Best of all was the Voorhies' kindness. They provided a splendid antique brass child's bed, complete with teddy bear, for our toddler, and even entertained him during breakfast, a delicious meal of coffee, freshly squeezed orange juice, bacon, fresh fruit, boudin (sausage), and pain perdue (French toast). Afterwards, we got a history and tour of the plantation house, and a slide show of the before pictures." *(Barbara Mast James)* "We cruised through Atchafalaya Swamp with Mr. Voorhies, and enjoyed his knowledge and love of the area. We were charmed by their house as well." *(Ruth & Derek Tilsley)*

Open All year. Closed Christmas Eve & Day.
Rooms 1 suite, 3 doubles—all with private bath, radio, TV, air-conditioning, fan, refrigerator.
Facilities Breakfast room, solarium, porch. 2 acres with patio, aviary. Atchafalaya Swamp, hunting, fishing tours.
Location Historic district. From I-10 take exit 103A S to Evangeline Thruway. Go 3 lights to Mudd Ave. Turn left and go 3 blocks to intersection with N Sterling. Inn is on SE corner. Continue on Mudd past inn and enter circular driveway on right at "35 MPH" sign.
Restrictions No smoking.
Credit cards Amex, MC, Visa.
Rates B&B, $105 suite, $85 double, $55–85 single. Extra person, $20. Children under 12 free in parents' room. Crib, $10. 10% senior, AAA discount.
Extras Wheelchair access. Airport/station pickups. Pets by prior arrangement. Crib, babysitting. French spoken.

Ti Frere's ¢   *Tel:* 318–984–9347
1905 Verot School Road,   800–484–1068
Highway 339, 70508   ext. 5658

Begun in 1880 by Ti Frère (Little Brother) Comeaux, this brick and cedar house was restored in 1985 by Peggy and Charles Mosely.

"The Moselys were warm and inviting hosts, knowledgeable about local activities and eager to share their enthusiasm. Our canopy bed had plump pillows and a lace coverlet. After a relaxing morning chat over coffee and juice, breakfast was served in the dining room: crawfish casserole, bacon, grits, fresh biscuits, strawberries and cream. When I told Peggy that I'm not a seafood lover, she was happy to whip up an omelet for me." *(Nancy Barker)*

"From the moment we sat down with Peggy to sip our mint juleps, a truly enjoyable weekend began. Peggy shared some of the local history with us, then Charlie showed us his Audubon prints. In the morning, Peggy gave us a silver tray to take pre-breakfast coffee back to our rooms. Long terrycloth bathrobes and ample towels were provided for our use. The whirlpool tub in our bathroom was relaxing after a long day. Our bedroom had a full tester bed with a down comforter and an abundance of pillows. Peggy had a whole list of different places to eat, and was very helpful in steering us away from the tourist traps. Breakfasts were delicious and different each day, including broccoli and ham quiche and our first taste of black-eyed peas." *(Chrys Bolk)* "Sparkling clean, beautifully furnished, and catering to the guest—not the almighty dollar. We arrived on a chilly evening to a warm fire, and were greeted with drinks and appetizers. Our room had attractive antiques and a carved fireplace. We were charmed by Peggy's stories and the beauty and comfort of her intriguing home. Another plus was the plentiful breakfast served at our convenience." *(Sherrie Beal)*

Open All year. Closed Christmas week.
Rooms 1 suite, 3 doubles—all with private shower and/or bath, TV, air-conditioning. 2 with clock/radio. 1 with whirlpool tub and working fireplace.
Facilities Parlor, dining room, kitchen garden room, porches. 1 acre with garden, croquet, gazebo. Swimming nearby.
Location 2 m from town.
Restrictions No smoking. No children.
Credit cards MC, Visa.
Rates B&B, $100 suite, $60 double, $50 single. Extra person, $15. No tipping. 10% senior discount.
Extras Station pickups.

NEW ORLEANS

Cognoscenti inform us that the city under discussion here is called *Nu-Awluns*, never *New Orleens*.

The French Quarter is roughly rectangular in shape, bordered by Canal Street to the west, Rampart Street to the north, Esplanade to the east, and the river to the south. Canal Street forms a border between the French

Quarter and the financial district, with the Convention Center at Canal and the river. The big chain hotels—the Sheraton, Marriott, Westin, etc. are all in this area. Bourbon and Royal Streets run east/west, and are very noisy; the quietest section of the quarter is the beautiful residential area to the east, just north of the French Market.

Rates here are generally lowest from mid-June to Labor Day and highest during Mardi Gras, Sugar Bowl, Super Bowl, and other peak festival times. (Mardi Gras rates are not listed here.) Advance reservations are also recommended during the city's famous Jazz and Heritage Festival, usually held during late April and early May; be prepared to pay the top rate *in advance.* State and local sales taxes are 11% and are not included in the rates. Parking can be a problem; if traveling by car, be sure to ask for information when reserving your room. A few hotels provide on-site parking; most have arrangements with nearby garages. One reader complained that the garage she used closed very early, making it difficult to get the car in or out at night.

Hotel rooms in the French Quarter tend to be small, with a bed and not much in the way of easy chairs or usable desk space. If you plan to do anything other than sleep in your room, ask about the availability of larger doubles; if finances permit, book a suite. Although most bed & breakfast inns have attractive balconies and courtyards, very few offer parlors or even dining rooms for guests to gather inside. If you'll be visiting when it's either too hot or too chilly to enjoy being outdoors for long, make an effort to book a room in one of the establishments that does provide interior common space.

People come to New Orleans for many reasons, but peace and quiet are not usually among them. It is a noisy city, and light sleepers should request the quietest possible rooms, or bring along some ear plugs! Visitors should also be alert to the problem of street crime, a real problem at night in parts of the French Quarter and in the Garden District. If the streets are crowded, there's generally no problem; if they're empty, get a cab right away or call one from the hotel or restaurant, and wait *inside* until it comes.

Reader tips: "Be sure to allow plenty of time for just hanging out in front of the Cathedral in Jackson Square, where music is always playing and there's always something going on. After you've made the obligatory visits to the French Market for souvenirs and the Café du Monde for *beignets* (benyay) and *café au lait* (lay), be sure to visit the nearby Jean Lafitte Visitor Center where you can sign up for terrific free walking tours of the French Quarter and Garden District. We thought Arnaud's restaurant was good but over-rated, but had a fabulous lunch at the Commander's Palace in the Garden District after our walking tour." *(RSS)* "Café Maspero, on Decatur, across form the Jackson Brewery has fabulous Mufalettas, and their pastrami sandwiches are equally renowned. Abita Beer, a local brew, is great in all its varieties. For breakfast, Croissant d'Or on Rue Ursuline, has wonderful pastries and coffee, served in a traditional coffee house atmosphere." *(Steve Holman)*

Also recommended: Received too late for a full write-up was *Chrys Bolk's* report on **Jensen's B&B** (1631 7th Street, 70115; 504–897–1895). "This large Victorian home had a combination of old and modern furnishings, with ceiling fans to supplement the air-conditioning. Ample literature about the city was available, along with a helpful guide to the Garden District. Baths are shared, but there were enough so that we didn't have to wait. One was decorated with Mardi Gras masks and another had a huge claw foot tub. Our children were welcomed, and played with the Jensen's kids. Breakfasts were simple but good—bran muffins and fresh strawberries, and the location was convenient, a block from the trolley and walking distance to the Garden District. It's comfortable and homey, yet we never felt like we were intruding." Rates are very reasonable, ranging from $45–65. Another late recommendation was received for the **Chimes Cottages** (1146 Constantinople Street, 70115; 504–899–2621), three guest cottages set behind an 1876 Uptown home. Just three blocks from St. Charles Avenue, the cottages are enhanced by stained and leaded glass windows, French doors, cypress staircase and a brick courtyard. Each cottage has a telephone, refrigerator, coffee pot, TV, stereo, queen and twin beds, and laundry facilities. Rates are reasonable and children are welcome.

Although far too big at 600 rooms for a full entry *Artmesia Spargo* recommends the location, housekeeping, service, and package rates at the **Monteleone Hotel** (214 Royal Street, 70140; 504–523–3341). Even more intriguing in the too-big-but-still-wonderful category is the **Windsor Court Hotel** (300 Gravier Street, 70140; 504–523–6000 or 800–262–2662) with 325 suites and doubles. As the city's first and only 5-diamond hotel, *Alex & Beryl Williams* describe it as "a civilized haven of peace and quiet. Easily the best hotel we've ever visited. On arrival we were invited to sit down to register and were escorted to our room. We had a beautifully furnished junior suite with a small balcony. The restaurant is most attractive and the food is excellent. In the parlor areas they serve English tea, accompanied by a quartet."

Information please: An interesting possibility on the streetcar line, about halfway between the French Quarter and the university area is **The Columns** (3811 St. Charles Avenue, 70115; 504–899–9308). This Italianate Victorian mansion was built in 1883, and offers guest rooms decorated with period antiques (B&B, $75 double), a wonderful Victorian-style bar, and an elegant dining room serving New Orleans food at lunch and dinner. In the university area is the **Park View Guest House** (7004 Saint Charles Avenue, 70118; 504–861–7564), a Queen Anne Victorian home built in 1884, and located next to Audubon Park. The inn offers antique-furnished rooms, stained-glass windows, and unusual architectural detailing. Listed in earlier editions, ownership changes and renovations make more reports a good idea. Another intriguing option at the edge of the French Quarter is the newly restored Victorian mansion, **Melrose** (937 Esplanade at Burgundy, 70116; 504–944–2255). For rates of $200–250 double, you get an antique-filled room, a full Creole breakfast, evening cocktails, heated swimming pool, and even airport transportation in the inn's limo.

Less than 30 minutes from the French Quarter is **Seven Oaks**, a new home built in the style of an antebellum cottage. Much of the building material came from the original Seven Oaks, a Greek Revival mansion demolished in the 1970s. The decor combines antiques, collectibles, and contemporary furnishings in just the right balance and the surrounding gardens invite guests for a relaxing stroll (2600 Gay Lynn Drive, Kenner 70065; 504–888–8649).

Listed in earlier editions but dropped for lack of reader feedback is the century-old **Sully Mansion** (2631 Prytania Street; 504–891–0457), still featuring some of the original stained glass, the 12-foot coved ceilings and ornate medallions, the 10-foot cypress doors and heart-of-pine floors. The inn is located in the heart of the Garden District, just 1½ blocks from the famous Commander's Palace restaurant. Rates include a continental breakfast of pastry, juice, coffee or tea.

Dauphine Orleans Hotel   *Tel:* 504–586–1800
415 Dauphine Street, 70112   800–521–7111

A restoration of an 18th-century townhouse design, the Dauphine offers the hospitable atmosphere of a small hotel. New Orleans-style *lagniappes* include a continental breakfast, morning paper, turndown service, welcome cocktail, hors d'oeuvres, and the opportunity to take home unfinished books from the guest library.

"The rooms are nice, though not extravagant, and are decorated with a mixture of period reproductions and generic hotel furnishings. Request one on the courtyard, or overlooking the swimming pool for a little more elbow room. The upstairs rooms are very quiet. We spent our days walking everywhere in the Quarter and felt safe. In the sunny kitchen a buffet breakfast of juice, cereals, fresh fruit, toast, English muffins, and sweet rolls was offered each morning. The staff was exceedingly friendly and helpful. An added plus is the hotel jitney, a 1950s open-air jeep with tasseled awnings and a terrific repertoire of horn-honking music; it provokes envious looks from all pedestrians. We like the pool, the little library, and the hors d'oeuvres at happy hour—and our kids were welcome to nibble too." *(Stephanie Reeves, also James Johnson)*

Open All year.
Rooms 9 suites, 100 doubles—all with private bath, telephone, radio, TV, desk, air-conditioning. Some with balcony. 18 in annex.
Facilities Breakfast room, library, bar/lounge, exercise room. Valet parking, swimming pool, hot tub.
Location Latin Quarter between Conti & St. Louis Sts.
Restrictions Some non-smoking guest rooms. Some street noise in front rooms.
Credit cards Most major cards accepted.
Rates B&B, $120–225 suite, $75–150 double. Extra person, $10. Senior, AAA discount.
Extras Jitney transportation (8 A.M.-8 P.M.) in Latin Quarter, business district. Pets welcome. Crib, babysitting. French, Italian, Spanish spoken.

French Quarter Maisonnettes ¢   *Tel:* 504–524–9918
1130 Chartres Street, 70116

Built in 1825 by the Soniat-Duffossat family, this house has maintained much of its original architecture, including the flagstone carriage drive and inner courtyard. Rates include the morning paper and a copy of the owner's helpful folder on restaurants and sights of interest.

"Mrs. Junius Underwood has owned the Maisonnettes for over 30 years. Guests receive their own keys to let themselves into the hotel through the huge wrought-iron gates. There is no parlor for meeting other guests, although the courtyard is an inviting place to sit. (It even has a cat-size spiral staircase for the resident felines!) Rooms are comfortably furnished with big leather sofas and chairs (which fold out into beds), and bookshelves well supplied with vacation reading." *(Caroline Weintz)*

"Great location on a quiet street, in a lovely neighborhood at the east end of the Quarter. Mrs. Underwood is a very classy lady, delighted to help her guests relax and enjoy New Orleans, while Jesse, major domo of the Maisonnettes for the past 30 years is always around to help and advise. The spacious rooms have usable kitchenettes and adequate bath-rooms. Although one room we saw had handsome four-poster beds, most of the furnishings can most charitably be described as utilitarian—clean, comfortable, sixties-era motel stuff—but at these prices, who's complaining? Without question the best buy in New Orleans, and usually booked way in advance for that reason. For breakfast, get fresh-baked croissants at the Croissant D'Or bakery, or head over to the Cafe du Monde (about the same distance in the opposite direction) for coffee and doughnuts New Orleans style." *(SWS)* More comments welcome.

Open Aug. 1–June 30.
Rooms 7 1-bedroom suites with private shower, TV, desk, air-conditioning, fan, fireplace, refrigerator, balcony.
Facilities Courtyard with fountain, patio. Parking in garage 1½ blocks away, $5 nightly.
Location French Quarter, near Esplanade St.
Restrictions No children under 12.
Credit cards None accepted.
Rates Room only, $45–55 suite. Extra person, $10.
Extras Limited wheelchair access. Well-behaved pets by prior arrangement.

Grenoble House 🏃   *Tel:* 504–522–1331
329 Dauphine Street, 70112

Those planning a week-long stay in New Orleans may want to stop reading after this listing. The Grenoble House is an all-suite inn in a restored 19th-century home right in the French Quarter. Rooms combine antiques, flowered fabrics, and coordinating contemporary pieces with kitchens fully equipped with everything from dishes to microwave ovens and icemakers. The rates, especially reasonable for a week's stay, include a breakfast of croissants and coffee; maid service is provided twice weekly. *(TM)*

"Central location in the business area of the French Quarter. It's a busy section, so be sure to ask for a room away from the street. Our suite was extremely spacious, with modern and antique reproduction furniture. The patio area is very large, with a lovely pool, although some landscaping work remains to be done. The weekly rate is a terrific value, and is worth it even if you are only staying for four days." *(SHW)* "We were delighted with our spacious and well-equipped suite." *(Gina Leone)*

Open All year.
Rooms 21 1- and 2-bedroom suites, all with full private bath, telephone, radio, TV, air-conditioning, kitchenette. Some with balcony, fireplace.

Facilities Patio areas with garden, swimming pool, hot tub, covered barbecue area. Fishing nearby.
Location French Quarter. 3 blocks from Canal St. Take exit 235 A from I-10.
Restrictions Traffic noise in front rooms.
Credit cards Amex, Enroute, MC, Visa.
Rates B&B, $65–195 suite. Weekly rates, $560–910. Extra person, $10.
Extras Pets permitted with prior arrangement. Crib, babysitting.

Hotel Maison de Ville ✗

727 Rue Toulouse, 70130

Tel: 504–561–5858
800–634–1600

The Maison de Ville dates back to the 18th century. It was built for a pharmacist named Peychaud, whose claim to fame may have been the invention of the cocktail; his drink was bourbon and bitters—the Sazerac. This hotel was sold late in 1985 to the Lancaster Hotel Group and is now managed by Lloyd Francis. A number of room renovations (some of them a bit overdue) were completed in 1988.

The hotel consists of eight buildings, including the Audubon Cottages, about a block and a half away. The Bistro Maison de Ville opened in 1986, and features Provençal and Mediterranean dishes, such as eggplant caviar, grilled shrimp with coriander, breast of duck in mint jelly glaze, fettucini with oysters and mussels, and sour-cream chocolate cake and lemon tart. "Probably our best meal in New Orleans. We would have returned but reservations are needed weeks ahead. Prices are reasonable for fine dining in New Orleans." *(SHW)*

"A favorite, situated in the heart of the French Quarter. The reception area is small but opens into a lovely sitting room, facing an inner court-yard. Our room was directly off the patio. It was a simple paneled affair, furnished with rustic antiques, a fireplace, TV, and spacious bath. The main door is locked in the evening so people don't wander in off the street." *(MFD, also Dane Wells)*

"Rooms in the main house feature high ceilings, four-poster beds, European antiques, and marble sinks. Thanks to the thick stucco walls, even those facing the bustle of Toulouse Street are cool and quiet. Like most of the older homes downtown, the main house opens onto an inner courtyard, this one of brick, flower-lined and with a three-tiered fountain and café tables where guests may take their continental breakfast and cocktails.

"Old slave quarters, now turned into guest rooms, line one side of the courtyard. The smallest has only a single bed and writer's desk, another is drapery-lined and dwarfed by its king-size bed, a perfect love nest. The continental breakfast consists of a croissant and jam, fresh-squeezed orange juice, and strong chicory coffee, served with the *Times-Picayune* and a red rose. I left my beat-up cowboy boots outside my door one night and recovered them in the morning spit-polished and looking like new. After-noon cocktails are served compliments of the house." *(Tony Gentry)* "My double room in the main building, overlooking Toulouse, was tiny. I was able to climb out on the roof, where there were some patio chairs, and sit, listen to music, and people watch. The service was excellent and the staff very capable and friendly. Exceptional breakfast croissants were served promptly in the garden." *(Risa Gordon)*

And another opinion: "Nice, but overrated and expensive. Some rooms are noisy and/or small, others are in need of sprucing up." Also: "We stayed in one of the famous Audubon Cottages, and found it to be totally unacceptable—dirty, shabby, and poorly maintained." More comments please.

Open All year. Restaurant closed Christmas, Thanksgiving, Mardi Gras.
Rooms 2 suites, 16 doubles, and 5 separate cottages, all with private bath and/or shower, telephone, radio, TV, air-conditioning, minibar. Cottages with kitchenettes. Some rooms with desk, refrigerators, fireplaces.
Facilities Restaurant, parlor, courtyard with fountain. Valet parking, $12 daily. Unheated swimming pool at the Audubon Cottages for all hotel guests.
Location French Quarter.
Restrictions Noise of location will disturb light sleepers. No children under 13.
Credit cards Airplus, Amex, CB, DC, Discover, MC, Visa.
Rates B&B, $205 suite, $125–175 double, $85–165 single, and up. Cottages, $305–385. 10% senior discount. 2-4 night minimum for weekends/special events. Alc lunch, $20; alc dinner, $40.
Extras French, German, Italian, Spanish spoken.

Hotel Provival 🏃 ✗
1024 Chartres Street, 70116

Tel: 504–581–4995
In LA: 800–621–5295
Outside LA: 800–535–7922

Several 19th-century buildings—a town house, an ice house, a general store, and a stable—were linked and renovated to create the Hotel Provincial, long-owned by the Dupepe family. The hotel has five landscaped interior courtyards and patios, one with a swimming pool. The charming high-ceilinged guest rooms are decorated with Creole antiques, French furnishings, floral fabrics, and modern appointments. Kids will enjoy a swim in the hotel's small but refreshing pool, and all will appreciate its convenient but quiet location. The hotel restaurant/coffee shop, Honfleur, serves three meals daily, offering standard American coffee shop food along with Creole cuisine. *(Carolyn Boyd, also A. Johnson)*

Open All year.
Rooms 97 suites and doubles—all with private bath, telephone, radio, TV, air-conditioning. Some with refrigerator.
Facilities Restaurant, meeting room, balconies, courtyard with fountain, patios, swimming pool. Free on-site parking.
Location East end of French Quarter. 1 block from Royal St., 2 blocks from Jackson Square and French Market.
Credit cards Amex, CB, Discover, MC, Visa.
Rates Room only, $110–130 suite, $70–105 double, $65–100 single. Extra person, $10. No charge for children under 18 in parents' room. AAA, Senior discount. Family, weekly, corporate rates.
Extras Crib (free).

Hotel Villa Convento ¢
616 Ursulines Street, 70116

Tel: 504–522–1793

Since Larry and Lela Campo bought the Villa Convento in 1982, they have been continuously improving and upgrading this 1848 building, a single-family dwelling until the 1940s. The Campo family is very much involved with the day-to-day running of the hotel, and are anxious to see that their guests enjoy their stay in New Orleans.

"The hotel was formerly a convent dormitory and there is a real family feeling among the staff and guests. The rooms facing Ursulines have traditional wrought iron balconies, while the others overlook the court-yard. Our room was small but had a cozy feel and was a welcome sight after a long day of sightseeing. A breakfast of croissants and coffee is served in the courtyard; They come fresh and hot from the Croissant D'Or bakery directly across the street. The staff made wonderful suggestions on what to see and do during our visit. The hotel has a little elevator which is convenient because the stairs are narrow. The building is very secure and we felt comfortable coming and going at all hours. What impressed me most about the hotel was the friendliness of the staff and guests. The many international visitors made it feel like a European pension." *(Christine Pflug)*

A word to the wise from another delighted guest: "Your readers should be aware that breakfast is served in the small courtyard, partly covered by green plastic roofing. While that's fine in good weather, it's less appealing if it's cold or rainy."

Open All year.
Rooms 2 suites, 22 doubles—all with full private bath, telephone, TV, air-conditioning. 20 with fan, 18 with radio. Some with balcony.
Facilities Courtyard with fountain. Parking garage 2 blocks away, $7 per night.
Location French Quarter.
Restrictions Light sleepers should request rooms away from street. No alcoholic beverages allowed. No children under 9.
Credit cards Amex, MC, Visa.
Rates B&B, $95–165 suite, $54–95 double. Extra person, $10. 2-night weekend, holiday minimum.
Extras Spanish spoken.

The Josephine   *Tel:* 504–524–6361
1450 Josephine Street, 70130

Built in 1870 in the Italianate style, the Josephine is furnished with French antiques, gilt mirrors, and silver sideboards. Guest rooms open onto galleries overlooking the surrounding lawns or courtyard garden.

"Dan Fusilier and his wife Mary Ann Weilbacher are New Orleans natives—Dan from a colorful Cajun heritage, Mary Ann slightly more 'uptown.' Both offer as close as a visitor can get to New Orleans' legend-ary hospitality. It's just one block from the St. Charles streetcar, so you can reach the French Quarter inexpensively, without the hassle of parking or the noise of staying in the Quarter. Dan knows the city's restaurants and can always give guests a reliable recommendation. The rooms are large and beautiful with wonderful antiques and delightful common rooms. The king-bedded room has a wonderful bed from the Hapsburgs and the bathroom has both a shower and a claw-footed tub. Breakfast is thick Louisiana chicory coffee or tea, homemade biscuits with marmalade, and fresh-squeezed orange juice, served on Wedgwood china with ster-ling flatware." *(Tatiana Maxwell)*

A word to the wise: "More variety at breakfast would be appreciated, and larger appetites might want something heartier." Also: "Although not surprising in an old house, the hot water was rather slow to make an appearance one morning. When we checked out, Mary Ann was too rushed to chat or even give us our bill, so she sent us a copy of our Visa charge slip a week later."

Open All year.
Rooms 1 suite, 3 doubles, 2 singles—all with private bath and/or shower, telephone, TV, desk.
Facilities Living room, balconies, courtyard, lawn.
Location Lower Garden District, at corner of Prytania St. 1 block from St. Charles streetcar & Pontchartrain Hotel.
Credit cards Amex, MC, Visa.
Rates B&B, $75–135 double, plus 15% service. Family, senior, off-season discounts. 5-night minimum during special events.

Lamothe House 🚶
621 Esplanade Avenue, 70116

Tel: 504–947–1161
800–367–5858

Lamothe House was built in 1830 by Jean Lamothe, a wealthy sugar planter from the West Indies. The hotel's courtyard still has the original flagstones, which were imported as ships' ballast. The original double townhouse had a porte cochere leading to the courtyard, but in 1860 this was converted to twin stairways, and the hand-carved Corinthian columns were added. In 1989, the Lamothe House was purchased by a local company that owns several other New Orleans guest houses. Rates include a breakfast of croissants, juice, tea, and coffee, evening coffee, morning newspaper, and bathroom toiletries.

"The entire inn is done in genuine Victorian furnishings, authentic to the period and of very good quality. First-floor suites are huge, gorgeous double parlors. The third-floor suites are somewhat smaller, but are lovely. The peaceful courtyard has lots of greenery, and the free on-site parking is a real plus. The inn sits on a pretty, quiet, boulevard, at the eastern edge of the French Quarter. If you really like Victorian furniture and antiques, it's the best place to stay in New Orleans." *(SHW)*

"Breakfast is served on elegant china and silver, but the best part is exchanging restaurant and sightseeing recommendations with the other guests." *(AD)* "The very existence of the dining room (off the front desk, so no one can miss it) tells you that you are in a home, not a hotel. It makes a surprising difference." *(Caroline Weintz)* "The inn is near the Mint Museum and the French Market. Breakfast was good, the service attentive, and the innkeepers were very nice." *(Laurie & Bruce Ford)*

A few minor negatives: "Our lovely suite was over the garage, and the noise of the garage door opening was bothersome." And: "The regular doubles here are very tight, with small baths. Although the three-way bulbs are a help, some rooms have rather dark furnishings and wall treatments—accentuated, perhaps, by the dark rainy weather during our visit." Comments required.

Open All year.
Rooms 9 suites, 11 doubles, all with private bath and/or shower, telephone, radio, TV, air-conditioning. All suites with desk. 2 suites, 4 doubles in annex.
Facilities Dining room, small courtyard, free on-site parking.
Location Eastern boundary of French Quarter, between Royal and Chartres Sts. 7 blocks from Jackson Square. Take I-10 to Esplanade exit.

Restrictions No smoking in common rooms.
Credit cards Amex, MC, Visa.
Rates B&B, $125–225 suite, $85–105 double or single. Summer rates, $99 suite, $69 double. Extra person, $15.
Extras Cribs, babysitting.

Le Richelieu Hotel 👫 ✗

1234 Chartres Street, 70116

Tel: 504–529–2492
800–535–9653

Several restored buildings, including a 19th-century Greek Revival row house and a macaroni factory now make up Le Richelieu. Longtime owner Frank Rochefort describes his hotel as having an intimate, elegant European atmosphere. He lives on the hotel property and tries to make sure his staff "do their best for guests," which is probably why the hotel has such a high rate of both occupancy and returning guests. Another plus is its "self-service" parking lot, avoiding the inevitable delays (and extra tips) of valet parking.

"Although we chose this place for its easily accessible parking and toll-free reservations number, we were tremendously pleased with our choice. The location was central, and the lobby attractive. When we complained to one of the desk clerks about the pretentiousness of some of the well-known restaurants, she recommended a couple of places that she enjoyed, and they suited us to a T." *(Steve Holman)* "Especially clean rooms, beautifully furnished. Charming staff give you a feeling of warmth and caring; they are happy to make arrangements for tours and entertainment." *(James & Lovera Dudman, also Lowell Corbin)*

"Our spacious room overlooked the courtyard and swimming pool. It had ample room for a king-sized bed, armoire for both the TV and drawers for clothing, easy chairs, and a workable desk. Furnishings were quality reproductions, with coordinating drapes and bedspread. The bed was firm and comfortable, with extremely soft sheets. The bathroom was basic, but had lots of storage space, and ample towels. We had a good breakfast of omelets and biscuits in the small dining area between the bar and the swimming pool. Our waiter was efficient and friendly, although I wish they didn't use those little hermetically sealed packets of jam and cream. We loved the quiet location, just a block or two from the French Market, where we loaded up on tie-dyed tee-shirts for the kids, and Cajun spices for us. Although other New Orleans hotels offer a more authentic 19th century atmosphere, Le Richelieu provides an unbeatable combination— exceptionally livable rooms, a swimming pool, and easy parking—all in all a remarkable value." *(SWS)* "Fully endorse existing entry. Though our room looked out on a side street, it was quiet." *(Glenn & Lynette Roehrig)* "Just as good on a return visit as it was the first time." *(SH)*

Open All year.
Rooms 17 suites, 70 doubles, all with full private bath, telephone, radio, TV, desk, air-conditioning, ceiling fan, refrigerator. Some with balconies.
Facilities Lobby, café, bar/lounge. Courtyard, swimming pool, free private self-park-and-lock lot. Room service.
Location French Quarter. On Chartres St. in between Gov. Nicholls and Barracks Sts.
Credit cards Amex, DC, Discover, En Route, Eurocard, JCB, MC, Visa.

Rates Room only, $125–425 suite, $90–110 double, $80–100 single. Extra person, $10. Packages available. Alc breakfast, $5–6; alc lunch or supper, $7–10.
Extras Limited wheelchair access. Crib, babysitting. French, Spanish spoken.

Maison Dupuy Hotel ✗
1001 Toulouse Street, 70112

Tel: 504–586–8000
800–535–9177
In LA: 800–854–4581

Seven French Quarter town houses were restored to create the Dupuy House, owned by Delta Queen Steamboat Company. Some rooms overlook the street, while other have French doors opening onto balconies overlooking the lushly planted courtyard and the swimming pool. The furnishings are reproduction French Provincial, and many rooms have been recently redone in soft pink or aqua tones. The hotel restaurant, Le Bon Creole, serves three meals a day; lunch-time favorites are the Po-Boy sandwiches and the soup and salad bar.

"On the northern edge of the French Quarter, this was the last hotel built in the Quarter before zoning kept new construction out. Parking is available in the hotel's own garage, and the location away from Bourbon Street is quiet. The swimming pool is located in a beautiful interior courtyard and is a delightful place to sip a strawberry daiquiri after a day of sightseeing. The rooms are spacious, well appointed, and modern." *(Tatiana Maxwell)* More reports welcome.

Open All year.
Rooms 194 suites and doubles—all with full private bath, telephone, radio, TV, air-conditioning. 10 with refrigerator.
Facilities Bar, restaurant, heated swimming pool, exercise room, courtyard with fountain, pay valet parking.
Location N central edge of French Quarter. Between Burgundy and N. Rampart Sts., near Louis Armstrong Park.
Credit cards Amex, CB, Discover, MC, Visa.
Rates Room only, $130–150 suite, $115 double. Extra person, $15.

Olivier House Hotel 👫
828 Toulouse Street, 70112

Tel: 504–525–8456

The Olivier Hotel was built as a townhouse in 1836 by Madame Olivier, a wealthy plantation owner. It was purchased by James and Kathryn Danner in 1970, and renovated as a hotel. Rooms have either modern or antique decor, and some have a split-level layout.

"If you like to be in the thick of the action, yet still be able to sleep in a city that doesn't, you'll love the location of the Olivier House. It's just a few doors down from Bourbon Street, in the center of the Quarter, yet the courtyard rooms are amazingly quiet. The tiny swimming pool is fine for a refreshing dunk, and the courtyards are green with lush plantings. Coffee and tea are always available, and you can enjoy a cup before the fire in the comfortable living room, or in the courtyard at one of the many wrought iron tables." *(SWS)*

"Most of the rooms are not romantically decorated, but they are very clean and provide the necessary amenities. The rates are reasonable and the location is prime. The staff is always friendly and we met long-time owner Kathryn Danner on a recent visit." *(SD)* More reports appreciated.

Open All year.
Rooms 4 suites, 36 doubles—all with private bath and/or shower, telephone, radio, TV, air-conditioning. Some with desk, fireplace, balcony, kitchenette.
Facilities Parlor with fireplace and books, 3 courtyards (1 with small swimming pool). Off-street parking.
Location French Quarter. At corner of Toulouse and Dauphine Sts. From I-10, take Vieux Carre exit, follow Basin St. to Toulouse St.
Restrictions Light sleepers should request rooms away from street.
Credit cards Amex, CB, DC, MC, Visa.
Rates Room only, $95–175 suite, $55–115 double. Extra person, $10. No charge for small children in June, July, Aug. Senior discount. Minimum stay during Mardi Gras.
Extras Some pets by prior arrangement. Airport pickup, $7 per person. Crib, babysitting. Spanish, French, Portuguese spoken.

Pontchartrain Hotel 👫 ✕

2031 St. Charles Avenue, 70140

Tel: 504–524–0581
800–777–6193

Small and elegant, the Pontchartrain was built in 1927, and was *the* place to stay in New Orleans for many years. The hotel was becoming shabby but was extensively restored and refurbished in 1989.

"Each floor has nine rooms, and the suites are unusually large with living room, dining area, study, large bathroom and dressing area, and bedroom. The decor in the suites varies from library paneling and English antiques, to chintz and wall-to-wall carpeting, to a bathroom of brown marble, with a copper sink and a bidet. Most of the regular rooms have tole flower paintings on the doors, with dressers and headboards to match. The small doubles face the rear for an unattractive view; suites overlook St. Charles Avenue and the streetcar. Our room had such luxuries as triple-sheeted king-size beds, Neutrogena bathroom amenities, overnight shoe shines, turndown service with petit fours left on the pillow, and three morning papers. Our room was very quiet, even though it was right next to the elevator. The personnel were friendly and attentive—most knew our names and the elevator men knew our floor immediately. Everyone was so accommodating and caring. The hotel was both luxurious yet comfortable and homey. We hated to leave." *(Susan Waller Schwemm, also SWS)*

"The hotel restaurant, the Caribbean Room, effectively combines Cajun and Creole cuisine with the Provençal recipes of their French chef." *(Paul & Elizabeth Lasley)* "The Caribbean Room was rather expensive for breakfast, so we ate across the street in the Versailles Hotel's café, where breakfast was very good and reasonably priced." *(SHW)*

An area for improvement: One reader noted that a few rooms still await renovation; specify your requirements when booking.

Open All year.
Rooms 31 suites, 40 doubles—all with private bath and/or shower, telephone, radio, TV, desk, air-conditioning. Some with refrigerator.
Facilities Restaurants, bar, courtyard. Evening entertainment.
Location Garden District. 5 min. from French Quarter, business district.
Credit cards All major.
Rates Room only, $150–700 suite, $100–200 double. Extra person, $25. No

charge for children under 16. Summer family rate, packages. Senior, AAA discount.
Alc breakfast $10, alc lunch $12; alc dinner $40.
Extras Wheelchair access. Spanish, French, German spoken. Crib, babysitting.
Airport pickup; complimentary limo service to downtown, university, and medical
center areas. Colony Resort.

Saint Charles Inn ¢ 🏃 ✕
3636 St. Charles Avenue

Tel: 504–899–8888

"This hotel has no outstanding features historically, architecturally, or in
its furnishings. The rates include the morning paper and a breakfast
consisting of coffee and a pre-packaged square thing they called a cinnamon roll. But there are two important reasons that we've stayed here three
separate times—location and room size. The hotel is located on the best
part of St. Charles Avenue, and the streetcar stops right in front 24 hours
a day. We leave our car here, and can be in the French Quarter in 10
minutes. The rooms are huge and quiet. On our last visit we had a room
with two queen beds and they looked lost in the room. The management
is helpful but not intrusive." *(James Johnson)*

Open All year.
Rooms 40 doubles—all with private bath, TV, air-conditioning.
Facilities Restaurant/lounge, off-street parking (fee).
Location Garden District. Next door to St. Charles General Hospital, near Louisi-
ana Ave. 10 min. from French Quarter, Superdome; 5 min. to university area.
Credit cards Amex, CB, DC, MC, Visa
Rates Room only, $60–70 double, $55 single. Senior discount. Children under 10
free in parents' room. Extra person, $10.
Extras Crib free. French, Spanish spoken.

Soniat House 🏃
1133 Chartres Street, 70116

Tel: 504–522–0570
800–544–8808

Rodney Smith created the Soniat House in 1983 from two adjoining town
houses that date back to 1829 and 1840, and has furnished it luxuriously
with antiques, hand-carved beds, Oriental rugs, as well as paintings and
sculptures by contemporary New Orleans artists.

"The inn's location in the French Quarter is ideal—just far enough off
the beaten path to stay quiet even during the busiest hours yet still within
walking distance of almost everything in the Quarter. Each room is
furnished differently, but most surround a magnificent brick courtyard,
complete with a fountain and caged lovebirds. There is also an honor bar,
where guests may enjoy wine or cocktails. The bathrooms have imported
soaps, thick towels, and a telephone. The friendly staff is always full of
good suggestions about restaurants, shopping, and sightseeing, and are
great at getting dinner reservations at the busiest restaurants." *(Sue Munt-
ner)*

"Our room was quiet and had a large sitting area with two dropleaf
tables, chest, coffee table, sofa, two armchairs, and a stool. The bedroom
alcove in our petite suite had a queen-sized bed with two reading lights.
The furniture was an eclectic antique mixture, although the paintings were
abstract modern. Our medium-sized marble bath had a Jacuzzi and great
shower pressure with instant hot water and Crabtree & Evelyn toiletries.

174

Beds were luxuriously triple sheeted with nightly turndown service. Rodney Smith was pleasant, proud of his inn, and a bit formal in manner. Breakfast was brought to our room promptly on a silver tray (it's also served in the courtyard), and included fresh-squeezed orange juice, delicious strawberry jam, chicory coffee, and excellent biscuits." *(SHW)*
"Lovely courtyard, elegant rooms. Two of the doubles are a bit on small side, with little in the way of comfortable seating, but furnishings are very stylish." *(SWS)*

"Located in the section of the French Quarter where locals actually live. Staying here is very close to staying at someone's lovely New Orleans home. The rooms are beautifully decorated, and the ones on the street have fabulous natural light; some of the interior rooms have almost no natural light or windows but open onto a handsome indoor/outdoor great hall. Lamps are positioned and fitted with ample wattage for reading. Our suite had several comfortable chairs, a couch, and a day bed." *(TM)*
"Charming with an outstanding staff." *(Ruth & Derek Tilsey)*

"Our room (#22) was handsomely decorated, but the lighting was inadequate in both the bedroom and the bathroom. The staff was friendly, and the chambermaids efficient, but the owner was unhelpful with restaurant reservations, and we waited 45 minutes for breakfast."

Open All year.
Rooms 9 suites, 13 doubles, 2 singles, all with private bath and/or shower, telephone, radio, TV, desk, air-conditioning. Jacuzzi in suites.
Facilities Parlor with honor bar, large courtyard with fountain. Valet parking, $10 (25-min. advance notice).
Location French Quarter. Between Ursuline and Gov. Nicholls Sts.
Restrictions "Travelers with children should inquire."
Credit cards Amex, MC, Visa.
Rates B&B, $185–250 suite, $115–165 double, $100–145 single. Extra person, $25. 2-day weekend minimum.
Extras Wheelchair access. Airport pickup, $25. Cribs, babysitting. French, Spanish spoken.

SAINT FRANCISVILLE

Settled by the English, St. Francisville is in the heart of Plantation Country, an area much favored by Audubon when he worked in this area during the 1820s, living at Oakley Plantation. "Unlike most of the plantation settings we saw, St. Francisville is a truly lovely little town, with quiet streets set off the main highway. Listed on the National Register of Historic Places, the handsome restored historic buildings, lovely gardens, and antique shops make Royal Street well worth exploring. Make it your base to visit the six area plantations (less commercial than those closer to New Orleans, two hours away); particular favorites are Rosedown (the showiest), Greenwood, Oakley, and Catalpa (the homiest), where the owner may show you around herself." *(SWS)*

Reader tips: "We had a good dinner at the St. Francis Hotel (junction of Rtes. 61 and 10; 504–635–3821), but the real highlight here is the well-designed Audubon Gallery, which has an original print of each of Audubon's fabulous drawings. Everyone who visits St. Francisville should stop by to see this superb (permanent) exhibit." *(SC)* "Visiting plantations is not my husband's idea of a fun vacation, so he took off for The Bluff's, St. Francisville's 18-hole Arnold Palmer golf course, and we both were happy." *(MW)*

St. Francisville is set on the Mississippi River, 25 miles north of Baton Rouge and 60 miles south of Natchez, MS, via Highway 61.

Information please: We'd like your comments on **The Myrtles** (Highway 62, P.O. Box 1100, St. Francisville 70775; 504–635–6277), a plantation dating back to 1796 when the general who led the Whiskey Rebellion, David Bradford, fled George Washington's army for the safety of French territory. The original parlors and dining room were further enhanced in 1834 by a subsequent owner, Scotsman Ruffin Stirling, to create a showplace for lavish parties and balls. Five of the guest rooms are in the main house, while four are in a motel wing. It has recently undergone a much-needed restoration, but is for sale again for the second time in as many years.

If you want to feel as though you've stepped back a century or more, a night or two at the **Cottage Plantation** (Route 5, Box 425, on U.S. Highway 61, 70775; 504–635–3674), may be in order. The Brown family has been taking in paying guests for over 35 years, and a restaurant occupies the restored house that originally belonged to the plantation cook, Mattie; specialties include crawfish and a variety of shrimp and chicken dishes. The grounds are highlighted by huge live oak trees (planted in 1812) dripping with Spanish moss. Guests can tour the 1795 plantation home, but are not allowed to gather in its common rooms because of insurance risks; the porch is the only common area for guests to gather. Breakfast is served in the dining room, and includes juice, eggs, bacon, grits, and cornbread muffins. Guest rooms on the ground floor are sunny and pleasant, but lack privacy; some on the second floor are rather dark. The best room is called Brown's Room, a corner room on the second floor with windows on both sides. Double rates are $75. *Note:* Although the Cottage Plantation has been listed in previous editions of this guide, for the past two years they've declined to provide us with updated information, and have requested that their entry be dropped.

Under new ownership is the **St. Francisville Inn** (118 North Commerce, Box 1369; 504–635–6502), listed in earlier editions but dropped for lack of positive feedback. The inn is on a busy commercial street, although it's set well back from the road, and consists of an 1880 carpenter gothic Victorian home, with a wing for guest rooms and a swimming pool in back. Reports (as always) welcome.

Take the ferry across to the "French" side of the river and the many historic plantations of Point Coupée Parish. The **Pointe Coupée B&B** (605 East Main Street, P.O. Box 386, New Roads 70760; 504–638–6254) provides reasonably priced accommodation in three historic cottages.

Barrow House ¢   *Tel:* 504–635–4791
524 Royal Street, P.O. Box 1461, 70775

Built in the saltbox style in 1809 with a Greek Revival wing added in the 1850s, Barrow House is listed on the National Register of Historic Places and is furnished in 1860s antiques. Rates include a continental breakfast;

a choice of four New Orleans' breakfasts are available for $5 extra. Readers continue to tell us of their delight with this B&B:

"Charming owners, handsome decor with many lovely antiques, including Mallard tester beds and coordinating armoires. We relaxed with a complimentary drink (wine, beer, iced tea, or soda) on the screened porch to the sound of the splashing fountain, and had a chance to get to know the Dittloffs. Although St. Francisville has much to offer the traveler, it's worth a trip to Barrow House for the food alone—it's as good or better than any we had in New Orleans. Our dinner, served elegantly by candlelight with fine china, silver, and crystal, included a meat-stuffed pastry, salad with two dressings, and delectable shrimp in mustard cream sauce. Desserts included a choice of a dense chocolate cream, praline parfait, or strawberry crepe. Take a long walk before breakfast the next morning if you're planning to feast on Shirley's full breakfast—poached eggs with beans and rice or grits, accompanied by well-spiced southern or Cajun sausage, called *andouille*." *(SWS)*

"In the morning, after a delicious continental breakfast of juice, fresh fruit compote, homemade muffins, and coffee, we set out to tour this little town. Shirley armed us with a map and cassette player and walking tour tape, and we spent a wonderful morning seeing (and hearing about) the sights—from the historic bank with its stained-glass windows to the fascinating graveyard of the Grace Episcopal Church." *(Beverly Simmons)*

"We appreciated the trusting attitude of our hosts: the freedom to turn on the coffeepot for an early cup of coffee, the help with luggage, their interest and involvement in the community, the easy conversation." *(Harry & Lorene Zimmerman)* "Barrow House is beautifully restored with shining plank floors and beautiful fresh flowers. It is very clean and well maintained. We greatly enjoyed sleeping on the 1860 Mallard bed with its Spanish moss mattress." *(Norman & Catherine Ronneberg, also Sue Doss)* "My mother and I shared the upstairs suite and found it very charming and relaxing. We made Barrow House our base for visiting area plantations. Shirley kept us well-supplied with information on the area, and Lyle iced down our cooler with beer and soft drinks for our day trips." *(Kay & Kitty McKinney)* "We stayed in the first floor room, off the porch where guests gather. We can't wait to return, but will ask for a second floor room, for a bit more privacy." *(MW)*

"The food was exceptional, and the Dittloffs are warm, wonderful hosts. Shirley gave me good local tips and was a big help." *(Shelly McDonald, also Lowell Corbin)* "Fully endorse existing entry." *(Judy & Marty Schwartz)*

Open All year. Closed Dec. 22–25.
Rooms 1 suite, 4 doubles—3 with private bath and/or shower, 2 with maximum of 4 people sharing bath. All with TV, air-conditioning; 2 with desk.
Facilities Dining room, living room, screened porch. 1 acre with camellia collection. Golf nearby.
Location In town, behind the courthouse.
Restrictions "Well-behaved children welcome."
Credit cards None accepted.
Rates B&B, $85 suite, $75 double. Extra person, $15. Full breakfast, $5 extra. Prix fixe dinner, $18–25. "Special Occasions" package.
Extras Port-a-crib.

ST. MARTINVILLE

Settled by Acadians in the mid-1700s, St. Martinville prospered with the arrival of aristocrats fleeing the French revolution. Immortalized in Long-fellow's poem, "Evangeline," the town is where the parted Acadian lovers are said to have met; the centuries-old oak that marks the spot is allegedly the most photographed tree in America. Worth a visit are the Acadian House Museum in the Longfellow Evangeline State Commemorative Area, the St. Martin de Tours Catholic Church, and several other restored buildings and museums.

Reader tips: "St. Martinville is a fine town, the location of the original Acadian settlement in Louisiana. It's also convenient to most other desti-nations in Cajun Louisiana, including Avery Island (home of Tabasco), and the Shadows-on-the-Teche plantation in New Iberia. The food and hospi-tality of the people of this area are unsurpassed." *(R.H. Mitchell)* "Truly the most "authentic" Cajun town." *(Sidney Flynn)*

The Old Castillo Hotel ¢ ✕   *Tel:* 318–394–4010
La Place d'Evangeline
220 Evangeline Boulevard, P.O. Box 172, 70582

"An excellent small hotel set on the Bayou Teche, right at the Evangeline Oak. Built in the early 1800s as a hotel, the Castillo served as a Catholic girls' school until it was bought by Gerald and Peggy Hulin in 1987. We stayed in room #1, which was spacious and lovely, with a view of the bayou, antique furnishings, and a wood floor. We ordered champagne from the bar downstairs, and sat down to relax. The casual restaurant serves excellent Cajun food and the staff is friendly and helpful." *(R.H. Mitchell)* "Delicious food at both lunch and dinner." *(Sidney & Mary Flynn)*

Rates include a full breakfast; favorites on the bilingual English/French menu include such appetizers as alligator boulettes, popcorn shrimp, or seafood gumbo, and seasonal entrées such as crawfish étouffée, catfish, and broiled frogs' legs.

Open All year. Closed Christmas, New Year's Day.
Rooms 2 suites, 3 doubles—all with private bath and/or shower, air-condition-ing. 2 with desk.
Facilities Restaurant, bar/lounge, laundry facilities. Gazebo, picnic area.
Location S LA, 10 m S of Lafayette; 60 m W of Baton Rouge. From I-10, take Exit 109 S on Rte. 31. Go 15 m to St. Martinville, turn right on Evangeline Blvd. to inn on right.
Credit cards Amex, MC, Visa.
Rates B&B, $35–75 double.
Extras French spoken.

SHREVEPORT

Set in northwest Louisiana, near the Texas border, Shreveport owes its development to its location on the Old Texas Trail. In fact, the city is a mixture of both states, with many streets named after early Texas heroes. Sights of interest include the Louisiana Downs racetrack and the Louisiana Hayride in neighboring Bossier City, the famous paintings and sculptures of Russell and Remington at the Norton Art Gallery, and the American Rose Society Gardens, a stunning sight from April through November, plus numerous other gardens and historic places of interest.

Information please: The Columns on Jordan (615 Jordan Street, 71101; 318–222–5912) is a plantation-type house with the look of the Old South, including a handsome columned portico. The house is elegantly decorated with antiques and, more unusually, with vintage clothing displayed on the walls and on manikins. Comments please.

Fairfield Place   *Tel:* 318–222–0048
2221 Fairfield Avenue, 71104

After years at a job that required a lot of travel—and many nights at boring, impersonal hotels—Janie Lipscomb decided it was time to open her own, very personal B&B. After extensive renovation and restoration work, she opened Fairfield Place in 1983, furnishing it with antiques, fine china and crystal, as well as books and paintings by Louisiana writers and artists. Beds are kept cozy by European featherbeds.

"Fairfield Place is located in the Highland area of Shreveport, making it very convenient to downtown, good restaurants, the LSU Medical Center, and Louisiana Downs. The rooms are spacious, and most have king-size beds. Breakfast was delicious, with Cajun coffee, fresh fruit and juice, an unusual egg, spinach, and bacon casserole, marmalade muffins, fresh-baked French pastries, and strawberry butter. The B&B is impeccably clean, and the service is warm and friendly. Janie is a perfect hostess and makes every guest feel right at home." *(Chris Mott, also Shirley Dittloff)*

Open All year.
Rooms 6 doubles with private bath and/or shower, telephone, radio, TV, desk, central air-conditioning, fan and refrigerator.
Facilities Parlor, balcony, porch, courtyard, garden. Boating, fishing, horse racing nearby.
Location NW LA, 319 m from New Orleans. Highland Historical Restoration district, 2 m from downtown. From I-20 W, exit at Fairfield, go left 8 blocks. From I-20 E, exit at Line Ave. S, go right on Jordan, left at Fairfield 6 blocks to inn.
Restrictions No smoking. No children under 12.
Credit cards Amex, Visa.
Rates B&B, $79–105 double, $65–75 single. Extra person, $10.

WHITE CASTLE

Information please: About 35 miles southeast along the Old River Road from White Castle is Vacherie, home of **Oak Alley Plantation** (Route 18, RR 2, Box 10; 504–265–2151 or 504–523–4351 in New Orleans). Named for the lane framed by the 28 immense live oaks planted in the early 1700s, the plantation house was built in the 1830s and rescued from collapse a century later. Overnight accommodations are available in six renovated cottages, at rates of $75–100, including a continental breakfast served in the plantation restaurant; Oak Alley is open for tours daily from 9 A.M. to 5 P.M.. Your comments welcomed.

Nottoway Plantation ♠ ✕   *Tel:* 504–545–2730
Mississippi River Road, P.O. Box 160, 70788

John Hampden Randolph was indeed successful in his desire to have the largest and finest home in the South. Constructed from 1849 to 1859, this Italianate and Greek Revival mansion boasts a total area of over 53,000 square feet and is supported by 22 massive cypress columns. No expense was spared in the building and finishing of the mansion, which was saved from Civil War destruction by a Union gunboat officer. The Randolph Hall, the plantation restaurant, serves delicious Cajun cuisine, with the Cajun Two-Step—"a levee of turkey and sausage jambalaya surrounded by a river of shrimp étouffée"—among its specialties. Rates include a bottle of champagne, flowers, plantation tour, wake-up breakfast, plus a full plantation breakfast.

"The grande dame of plantations, with 64 rooms in all. Although Nottoway is less personal than the smaller plantation homes we visited, it was an enjoyable experience nonetheless." *(Caroline & Jim Lloyd)* "Our room in the garçonniere was beautifully furnished with canopy bed and lovely draperies to match. A small crystal chandelier hanging over the skirted table in the corner cast a romantic glow over two chilled half bottles of champagne. Dinner was elegantly presented, with an abundant selection of Cajun-style entrées and well-prepared Creole desserts. The dining-room chairs are hand-carved mahogany in a style appropriate to the antebellum period. Throughout the inn, great care has been taken to make sure that all the furniture in the rooms is in period.

"In the morning, freshly squeezed juice and warm sweet potato biscuits were delivered on a silver tray promptly at the time requested (after a gentle wake-up call from the front desk). It was hard to imagine needing a full plantation breakfast after this, but we went to the veranda for an excellent meal of eggs or French toast with grits and country sausage. We toured the mansion both in the evening and again early in the morning— before the tour buses arrive. Although the guest rooms in the main house are more elegant (and more expensive), all were appealing." *(Nancy Barker)*

"Nottoway is located across the river road from a Mississippi River levee, although the river can be seen only from the upper-floor rooms. Rooms on the tour are available *only* after 5 P.M. and before 9 A.M.—no exceptions. It may be worth the inconvenience, though, to stay in the Randolph Suite, which has a large wicker morning room, a four-poster Mallard bed, clawfoot tub, pedestal sink—all original—and a huge wrap-around porch overlooking the river. Otherwise, I'd stay away from the crowds of daytrippers in one of the upstairs rooms in the Overseer's Cottage, at the rear of the grounds, near the lily pond and the ducks. These have private terraces, cool breezes, and comfortable furnishings." *(SHW)*

"We had a first-floor room in the cottage; it was nicely furnished with a view of the fountain and pond. The beds were very firm. While large, the staff was attentive—there was someone to carry bags, and the wake-up breakfast arrived exactly when requested. The restaurant menu goes beyond Cajun dishes; a request for non-Cajun fish produced fine results, and the salads were excellent. The swimming pool was well cared for." *(HB)* "We stopped for a house tour and lunch. Gracious greeting, thoughtful and intelligent tour, and a simple meal well prepared and served in lovely surroundings. Excellent staff was friendly and competent." *(Ruth Tilsley)*

Open All year. Closed Christmas Day.
Rooms 3 suites, 10 doubles—all with private bath and/or shower, telephone, TV, desk, air-conditioning. 1 suite with wet bar, Jacuzzi, private courtyard with small swimming pool. 4 rooms in cottage.
Facilities Restaurant with entertainment on weekends. Breakfast room, sitting room, bar/lounge, verandas. 37 acres with reflecting pond, swimming pool.
Location 20 m S of Baton Rouge, 70 m NW of New Orleans. From Baton Rouge, take I-10 W to Plaquemine exit. Follow LA 1 18 m S to plantation. From New Orleans, take I-10 W and exit at LA 22. Go left on LA 70. Follow signs across Sunshine Bridge. Go 14 miles N through Donaldsonville on Hwy. 1 to Nottoway.
Restrictions No smoking. Traffic noise in some rooms.
Credit cards Amex, Discover, MC, Visa.
Rates B&B, $200–250 suite, $125–175 double, $95–175 single. Children under 12 free in parents' room. Alc lunch, $8–12; alc dinner, $24–26. Children's menu.
Extras Wheelchair access.

Mississippi

The Burn, Natchez

Andrew Jackson was one of Mississippi's first heroes. After he defeated the Creek Indian nation and won the Battle of New Orleans, the state's capital was named for him. The Civil War played a major role in Mississippi's history; in addition to the famous siege of Vicksburg, innumerable battles took place across the state, leaving tremendous destruction in their wake.

Today history buffs visit Natchez and Vicksburg in search of antebellum ambience, while beach buffs head south to the Gulf Coast, particularly Ocean Springs, an artists' colony. Plan to spend some time (spring and fall are best) exploring the Natchez Trace Parkway, a 400-mile parkway administered by the National Parks Service. Extending from Natchez nearly to Nashville, Tennessee, it follows the historic trail (or trace) that was one of the region's most frequented roads at the beginning of the 1800s.

Important note: If you're booking a room in an antebellum mansion that can also be visited by the public, remember that rooms on a tour will rarely be available for occupancy before 5 P.M., and must typically be vacated by 9 A.M. Rooms in adjacent buildings may not be quite as fancy, but have more liberal check-out policies.

Information please: Oxford, home of the University of Mississippi and birthplace of William Faulkner, offers the **Oliver-Britt House** (512 Van Buren, Oxford 39655; 601–234–8043), a turn-of-the-century Greek Revival B&B and tea room. About 20 miles north of Oxford is **Hamilton Place** (105 East Mason Avenue, Holly Springs 38635; 601–252–4368), a 150-year-old home furnished with antiques in a historic town filled with nineteenth-century homes. About halfway between Oxford and Memphis, Tennessee is **Hamilton Place** (105 East Mason, Holly Springs 38635; 601–252–4368), built in 1836 and listed on the National Register. Each of its antique-filled four guest rooms have a private bath, and the $65 double rate includes breakfast served in the formal dining room, on the veranda, or in the garden gazebo. Guests may borrow one of the inn's bicycles to tour the historic district, returning to relax in the hot tub or swimming pool.

Down on Mississippi's Gulf Coast, 30 miles west of Biloxi is the **Red Creek Colonial Inn** (7416 Red Creek Road, Long Beach, 39560; 601–452–3080 or 800–729–9670). This three-story raised French cottage has been owned by Dr. & Mrs. Karl Mertz since 1971, and was opened as a B&B in 1988. Rates include a continental breakfast of juice, strudel or muffins, grapefruit with berries or cantaloupe with kiwi, and coffee. Reports on these and any other discoveries, please!

CORINTH

General's Quarters ¢ ✕   *Tel:* 601–286–3325
924 Fillmore Street, P.O. Box 1505, 38834

The General's Quarters is a Victorian home owned by J.L. Aldridge. The guest rooms are simply furnished, some with antique half-tester beds, while the dining room on the first floor has an eclectic decor mixing contemporary seating with antique wooden tables. Rates include a hearty Southern breakfast; dinners are served to the public six nights a week.

"While this Victorian home was nicely furnished, the real highlight of this B&B is its owner. Upon our arrival in 'downtown' Corinth, we called for directions to the inn. J.L., who answered our call, said, 'Wait just a minute. I'll hop in my pick-up truck and come lead you in.' As soon as we arrived, he offered us a swig of his home-brewed 'white lightin'.' Dinner was just then being served, and I tried J.L.'s special recipe whole catfish. It was so good that I ate four! When I asked J.L. if he knew where I might purchase an authentic Civil War sword, he immediately got on the phone to his friends, and tracked down a fine sword at a super price." *(Elliott Kagen)*

Open All year. Restaurant closed Sun.
Rooms 5 doubles—all with private bath, telephone, TV, coffee maker.
Facilities Restaurant, upstairs sitting area, porch.
Location NE MS. 2 m S of TN border, 24 m E of AL border. Near intersection of Hwys. 72 & 45. 22 m from Shiloh National Military Park. Take Business Hwy. 45 N into Corinth; becomes Fillmore St. Inn is at corner of Fillmore & Linden.
Credit cards Amex, MC, Visa.
Rates B&B, $75 double, $50 corporate.

JACKSON

Millsaps Buie House   *Tel:* 601–352–0221
628 North State Street, 39202

Jackson is the capital of Mississippi and its largest city, with a population of 400,000. Back in the 1880s, the city's social elite built mansions along State Street and gathered in each other's homes for dinner parties, tea dances, and croquet. The Millsaps Buie House dates from this period and is listed on the National Register of Historic Places. Its renovation as a bed & breakfast inn began in 1985; the house survived a near disastrous fire and opened fully restored and decorated with beautiful period antiques late in 1987. Rates include a breakfast of fresh fruit and juice, grits, homebaked pastries, sausages and biscuits, and pre-dinner refreshments and hors d'oeuvres.

"Jackson's only bed & breakfast inn offers beautiful decor and gracious southern hospitality, combined with spotless housekeeping and professional service. Rooms on the first and second floors are furnished with period antiques; those on the third floor have a more contemporary decor but are still lovely. Baths are very modern. TVs are discreetly tucked into cabinets, and the touch-tone phones even have a plug for your computer modem!" *(Jean Rawitt)* "Exactly as described. The house is spectacular. Our room on the first floor was beautifully appointed with a king-size bed, good lighting, and excellent shower. Nick's Restaurant, a 10-minute drive, was upscale, quiet, and worth a visit." *(John Blewer)*

Open All year.
Rooms 1 suite, 10 doubles with private bath, telephone with computer dataport, radio, TV, air-conditioning. Some with desk.
Facilities Breakfast room, dining room, parlor with grand piano. 1½ acres with patio, off-street parking.
Location Central MS. 5 blocks from Capitol. From Hwy. 80, go N on State St. to inn at corner of High St.
Restrictions No smoking in public rooms. No children under 12.
Credit cards Amex, DC, Discover, MC, Visa.
Rates B&B, $125–137 suite, $75–130 double. Extra person, $12.
Extras Wheelchair access.

LORMAN

Rosswood Plantation 🏃   *Tel:* 601–437–4215
Route 552, 39096   800–533–5889

Built in 1857 by famous antebellum architect David Shroder, Rosswood has gone from a working cotton plantation of more than 1,200 acres to a completely restored, antique-filled Greek Revival home offering B&B accommodations; the crop has changed from cotton to Christmas trees. Long-time owners Walt and Jean Hylander collected many of the furnishings during the years when his career with U.S. Army Corps of Engineers took them around the globe, and these treasures fit well within the grand style that the original owner, Dr. Walter Wade, envisioned when he built Rosswood for his bride. Dr. Wade also kept a journal of his life before and during the Civil War, which makes great reading for today's visitors. Guest rooms have handmade lace pillows and crocheted bedspreads on the canopy beds. Wake-up coffee or tea is brought to your room each morning a half hour before breakfast, which typically includes fresh fruit and juice; scrambled eggs in cream with ham, bacon, or sausage; garlic cheese grits; and biscuits with Rosswood Muscadine grape jelly or other preserves.

"The Hylanders are a charming and welcoming couple who meet your needs while respecting your privacy. The guest rooms were spacious, quiet, and furnished with beautiful antiques." *(Priscilla Merrill)* "On arrival, we were greeted with a glass of wine. Breakfast was accompanied by fresh flowers, coffee served in silver, and the table was accented with crystal and embroidered linen napkins." *(Donna Mumfrey)* "We felt free to roam the house and grounds, and enjoyed the quiet, country atmosphere." *(Mr. & Mrs. Richard Byerley)*

"Well furnished with many pieces from the Civil War period. Our room had an overhead fan that made it comfortable even on warm nights, so we chose not to use the air-conditioning. The bathroom and plumbing are modern and spotless; parking is under large shade trees. Breakfasts were prepared by Larry and another long-time area resident, Mary, both of whom were delightful and gracious. Every afternoon at 5 P.M., Larry (the chef) served us mint juleps on the porch, and on one occasion provided his own homemade cake as a treat. On another evening, after a particularly long day of touring, we found an assortment of liqueurs waiting for us as a nightcap." *(Joseph Savino)*

Open March 1 to Nov. 15.
Rooms 4 doubles—all with private bath, telephone, radio, TV, desk, air-conditioning, fan, fireplace.
Facilities Dining room, living room with piano, library; all with fireplace. Guest refrigerator, screened/unscreened porches. 100 acres with heated swimming pool, whirlpool spa, stocked lake, play equipment.
Location SW MS, midway between Natchez & Vicksburg. From Natchez take Rte. 61 north approx. 30 m to Lorman. Turn right on Rte. 552, go W approx. 2 m to inn on left.
Credit cards MC, Visa.
Rates B&B, $95 double, $75 single. Extra person, $25.
Extras Limited wheelchair access. Station pickup. Crib, babysitting.

NATCHEZ

Natchez was founded in 1716. Since then the flags of six nations have flown over the city—France, England, Spain, the sovereign state of Mississippi, the Confederacy, and the U.S., Natchez's greatest wealth and prosperity came in the early 1800s with the introduction of cotton and the coming of the steamboat. Extraordinary mansions were built during this period, which ended with the Civil War. Unlike Vicksburg to the north,

Natchez was not of military importance, so although little property was destroyed during the war, further development ceased. As a result, over 500 antebellum mansions survive.

About a dozen mansions, including some of the most important, such as the palatial Stanton Hall, are open to visitors year-round. Most, however, are open only during festivals, called Pilgrimages, which are held for two weeks from early to mid-October and for a month in the spring, from early March to early April. If you plan to visit during one of the Pilgrimages, make your reservations six weeks to three months in advance. Alternative bed & breakfast lodging, as well as tickets for the house tours, can be arranged by calling Pilgrimage Tours at 800–647–6742.

Natchez is in southwest Mississippi, on the Mississippi River, 114 miles southwest of Jackson. Try to travel here via the Natchez Trace, once an Indian footpath, now a two-lane parkway run by the National Park Service between Natchez and Nashville, passing centuries of American history en route. Call the Natchez Trace Parkway Visitors Center for more information (601–842–1572).

Reader tips: "Natchez may not have Vicksburg's Civil War history, but it is small and manageable. The people are friendly and there are lots of antique shops to explore. The Pilgrimage attracts crowds, but it is well-established and organized, with two evening entertainments: *Southern Exposure*, a comedy play, and the *Confederate Pageant.* Some inns and hotels raise their rates slightly during Pilgrimage." *(SHW)* "While in Natchez, be sure to explore Natchez-Under-the-Hill, an area wedged in beneath the Mississippi River bluffs that was once home to gamblers, riverboat hustlers and other ne'er-do-wells." *(SC)* "We learned from a local realtor that several grand mansions are up for sale, so be sure to inquire for details when reserving rooms."

Also recommended: We were unable to get enough information for a full write-up, but received an enthusiastic report from *Lynn Fullman* on **Texada** (222 South Wall Street, 39120; 601–445–4283). "Dr. and Mrs. George Moss, on-site owners, cared enough about restoring this late 1700s building that they had each of the battered exterior bricks turned around. It's that very caring that shows in this home, once a tavern. The many antiques they bought because they like them and want to enjoy them. There are guest rooms in the main house and in a little cottage out back where the Mosses lived while they restored their home. Kids and pets are OK in this cottage, which isn't always the case in a historic B&B. The Mosses are as gracious as you could hope to find, and have added the necessary creature comforts to their rooms, including private, modern baths, a concession to the demands of today's traveler."

Information please: We'd like to request reports on the **Natchez Eola Hotel** (110 North Pearl Street, 39120; 601–445–6000 or 800–888–9140). Built in 1927 and listed on the National Register of Historic Places, this centrally located establishment combines the atmosphere of the Old South with the conveniences of a small modern luxury hotel at double rates of only $60. Be sure to stop by for lunch at the casual Juleps Restaurant that serves a great-tasting buffet at bargain prices. Close by in the historic district is **The Guest House** (201 North Pearl Street, 39120; 601–442–1054), an 1840s brick town house built in the Greek Revival style. Its eighteen guest rooms (with private and shared baths) are furnished with antiques and reproductions, and rates include a continental breakfast in the glass-enclosed Garden Room, an evening beverage served on one of its spacious porches, and nightly turn-down service (with chocolate on your pillow). If you'd like to try a B&B in Natchez-Under-the-Hill, the **Silver Street Inn** (1 Silver Street, P.O. Box 1244, 39120; 601–442–4221) was built as a "bawdy house" in 1840, and is now a four-guest-room B&B.

Although **Dunleith** (84 Homochitto; 601–446–8500 or outside MS: 800–433–2445) claims to be one of the most frequently photographed houses in America, it's certainly not the most written about—by our readers anyway! Listed on the National Register of Historic Places, Dunleith was built in 1855 and was fully restored in 1976 by its current owner, William F. Heins III. In addition to a full southern breakfast, rates include a tour of the house and a welcoming refreshment. More reports needed if you think it merits a full entry.

Rates quoted do not include a 9% lodging tax.

The Briars Inn
31 Irving Lane, P.O. Box 1245, 39120

Tel: 601–446–9654
800–634–1818

Set on a hill overlooking the Mississippi River, The Briars is a plantation-style mansion built in the early 1800s, that was the site of Jefferson Davis' marriage to Varina Howell in 1845. Interior designers and antique dealers Robert Cannon and Newton Wilds purchased the Briars in 1975, and for a number of years opened it to the public for tours and dining. Recently opened as a B&B, the Briars offers guests the pleasure of staying in a genuinely historic setting with "free run" of the house; most other Natchez B&B's limit access to common rooms to supervised tours. Guests are served a complimentary cocktail on arrival. Rates include a full breakfast (menus vary daily) served on fine porcelain and silver. Although the owners live in Houston, the live-in staff is on 24-hour duty; Nancy Diehl and Christine James are the managers.

"In addition to The Briar's historic charm, it is comfortable, and beautifully furnished in exquisite taste. Nancy, our hostess, was charming and very hospitable. The food was delicious, interesting, and cordially served in the dining pavilion. Fortunately, the Briars is not 'on the tour,' so we did not need to rush out of our room, and stay away for the day. Though our expectations were great, the Briars exceeded them." *(Robert Carey)* "Our room and bath on the first floor was very spacious, and was filled with precious antiques. Breakfast was accompanied by an unforgettable view of the Mississippi River." *(Rita Langel)* "Fully endorse existing entry." *(Judy & Marty Schwartz)*

Open All year.
Rooms 1 suite, 12 doubles—all with private bath and/or shower, telephone, radio, TV, desk, air-conditioning, fan, fireplace, deck. 6 rooms in annex.
Facilities Dining room, parlor with fireplace, game room, foyer, porches. 20 acres overlooking Mississippi River, with lawns, gardens, heated swimming pool, gazebo, horseshoes. Boating facilities nearby.
Location ½ m from town. From Route 65-84 By-Pass (John R. Junkin Drive), turn S at the Ramada Inn Hilltop. Continue to inn.

Restrictions No smoking in guest rooms. Children over 12 preferred.
Credit cards Amex, MC, Visa.
Rates B&B, $325 suite, $120 double. Extra person, $50.
Extras Some rooms have wheelchair access; equipped for the disabled. Airport pickup, nominal charge.

The Burn
712 North Union Street, 39120

Tel: 601–442–1344
800–654–8859

The Burn was built in 1835 in the Greek Revival style, with a front portico supported by large Doric columns. It survived the Civil War first as the headquarters for Union troops and later as a Union hospital. Restored in 1978, it is owned by Tony and Loveta Byrne, long-time Natchez residents. The interior features a beautiful semi-spiral flying staircase and rooms decorated with elaborately carved beds and handsome Belgian fabrics. Most of the guest rooms are in the original attached dependency or Garçonnière. Rates include a full southern breakfast, served in the dining room, and house tour.

Fans of the Burn—and they are many—will want to eat at the Pompous Palate, the elegant restaurant recently opened by Mrs. Byrne. Located in a pillared, turn-of-the-century building in downtown Natchez, the menu is eclectic, ranging from escargots to stuffed eggplant to pecan brandy pie.

"The Burn's location is good; although its acreage is limited, the gardens are lovely. The resident owners live on the third floor, and the highlight of our stay was visiting with them. The music room has an operating Regina music box. Overlooking the rear garden is a porch with ornate blue and cream wicker furniture. Two guest rooms are rented in the main house: The Pink Room on the main floor is very large with a four-poster tester bed swagged in pink satin, while the blue room is cool and spacious with a fascinating carved tester bed. Most rooms in the Garçonnière have four-poster beds, although the staircase leading up to them might be a bit tricky for older folks." *(SHW)*

"We stayed in the Garçonnière, in a lovely room with tester beds. Later we enjoyed wine and boiled peanuts by the fire with the Byrnes. In the morning we had a wonderful plantation breakfast with cheese grits, then a tour of the beautifully maintained yet comfortable main house." *(Caroline & Jim Lloyd)* "The Byrne family was a joy, newly discovered dear old friends." *(Yvonne Miller, also Barry Gardner)*

"Tony was the perfect host and helped us plan our stay in a very personal way. The staff was also excellent, keeping us well-supplied with mint juleps and wine, and we enjoyed the cordial informality in the evening. The baked catfish with grapefruit and fennel sauce highlighted our excellent meal at the Pompous Palate. Housekeeping was excellent." *(Elliott Kagen)*

Minor niggles: "Our room in the Garçonnière was on the dark side and we couldn't get the drapes open to get adequate daylight. The facecloths in our bathroom were worn and ready for replacement." Also: "Natchez is extremely busy during the Pilgrimages, and there may not be as much opportunity for personal contact with the Byrnes at these times. The cottage rooms are rarely rented unless the inn is fully booked, as they are not as well furnished."

Open All year.
Rooms 2 suites, 8 doubles—all with private bath and/or shower, TV, air-conditioning, fan. 4 rooms in annex, 4 rooms in cottages.
Facilities Dining room with fireplace, foyer, porch. 4 1/2 acres, swimming pool, patio, camellia gardens. Off-street parking.
Location 7 blocks from Main St. On N. Union St. between Oak and Bee Sts.
Restrictions No smoking in common rooms. No children under 6.
Credit cards Amex, DC, Discover, MC, Visa.
Rates B&B, $100–125 suite, $70–80 double, $60–70 single. Extra person, $15–20.
Extras Station pickup.

Linden   *Tel: 601–445–5472*
1 Linden Place, 39120

Dating back to 1792, most of the present house was constructed between 1818 and 1849, when Linden was bought by ancestors of the current owners. Nearly all furnishings are original to the house, and Linden is especially noted for its outstanding collection of Federal furniture, including many Hepplewhite, Sheraton, and Chippendale pieces.

"At Linden, you are really 'at home' with Jeanette Feltus, in the home that her family has occupied for six generations. Now a widow, Jeanette lives here and is constantly on hand with two maids and cook, seeing to her guests' every need. Being with Jeanette and living with her family's antiques make this place special. The setting is lovely, surrounded by gardens, well off the main roads with no traffic noise, yet is only two turns from the boulevard that leads to downtown.

"Breakfast was served on the porch at 8:30 A.M. *sharp,* and with grits, sausages, scrambled eggs, and curried peaches one day, then ham, steamed eggs, and apricots the next, with lots of homemade biscuits, orange juice, and coffee. The guest rooms open to the porch on one side and lawns on the other, so cross ventilation through the large windows makes the rooms exceptionally light and airy. Rooms in the garçonnière are a bit smaller, but all are handsome with four-poster beds. The rates are very reasonable, considering the size of the rooms and their decor. The brief tour included in the rates is interesting and fun, highlighting such features as an enormous lyre-shaped cypress punkah fan above the dining room table, originally pulled by slaves to cool the guests during dinner." *(SHW)*
"We loved this antebellum mansion. It was fully booked when we were there and it was very pleasant gathering on the gallery for good conversation. Mrs. Feltus is a lovely hostess, and Lily prepares an outstanding Southern breakfast." *(BJ Hensley)*

Minor niggles: Replacing worn towels, sprucing up the gardens, and providing a little more flexibility in the serving of breakfast.

We understand that maintenance burdens at Linden are such that Mrs. Feltus has placed it on the market; we'd suggest inquiring further when calling for reservations.

Open All year.
Rooms 7 doubles with private bath.
Facilities Dining room, parlor with piano, porch, galleries. 3 acres with courtyard, gardens.
Location Take U.S. Rte. 61/84 to Melrose Ave.

Restrictions No children under 10.
Credit Cards None accepted.
Rates B&B, $90 double, $75 single.

Monmouth Plantation ✕   *Tel:* 601–442–5852
Corner of Melrose and Quitman Parkway   800–828–4531
P.O. Box 1736, 39121

Monmouth, a Greek Revival mansion listed on the National Register of Historic Places, was built in 1818 and was purchased in 1826 by John Quitman, who later became governor of Mississippi and a U.S. congressman. Monmouth stayed in the Quitman family until 1905; its restoration began in 1978, when it was purchased by Ron Riches. Period antiques, including many of the plantation's original furnishings, fill the rooms. In 1991, Ron began offering five-course dinners, served by waiters clad in black tie apparel, in the candlelit dining room.

"Owner Ron Riches is a Los Angeles native, but spends about 35 percent of his time at Monmouth, and lives in the house when he is in residence. The cocktail hour begins every day at 5 P.M., with complimentary hors d'oeuvres and an honor bar. The plantation breakfast is different every day and is served on the ground floor of a brick wing of the mansion, followed by a tour of the mansion. The guest rooms in the main house are huge, with elaborate fabrics and furnishings, and such amenities as leather folders of stationery and postcards, bathrobes, and complimentary toiletries. The public rooms are equally fabulous. The parlor has a rare sterling and crystal 'parlor fountain' which works with gravity, similar to an hourglass, while the dining room has a Duncan Phyfe sideboard with reeded cylindrical drum sides. The whole place defines antebellum excess. It is not like being at home, in any sense of the word, but is the most luxurious setting in Natchez." *(WHS)*

"The staff went out of their way to please us. Our third-floor suite was lovely and cozy; thick terrycloth robes were provided. The complimentary hors d'oeuvres consisted of lightly toasted English muffins topped with spiced mushrooms and melted cheese. An honor bar is located in the courtyard, and you can help yourself to anything. The tasty breakfast consisted of grits, biscuits, jam, sausage, eggs, stewed apricots, and poppy seed bread. The grounds are very well maintained, with garden gazebos and benches pleasant for playing cards, reading a book, and just relaxing." *(Darrel & Renate Kurtz)*

"We stayed in the owner's suite, which has beautiful antiques and tasteful decor. We enjoyed attentive service and good food at dinner, and had fun being the only Americans at breakfast, surrounded by a French tour group." *(BH)*

"After touring homes all day, it's a treat to actually sit at one of these formal dinner tables, lights dimmed, and imagine for a moment that you actually live in another time—and in such opulence. The rooms built on the site of the former slave quarters and carriage house are private and elegantly furnished, including a welcome basket of wine, spring water, and pecans. Although they don't have the historic feel of the in-house rooms, but it's not a bad trade-off." *(Lynn Fullman)* "Rooms in the mansion really evoke another era, but you have to be out early to accommodate the tours; the garden cottages are more private, but less historic, having been built just ten years ago. Almost all rooms have views of the lovely grounds."

And another opinion: "Somewhat lacking in warmth; the atmosphere is rather businesslike."

Open All year. Dinner served Tues.–Sat.
Rooms 7 suites, 12 doubles—all with private bath and/or shower, telephone, radio, TV, desk, air-conditioning. Most with fireplace. 6 rooms in mansion, 4 in original kitchen building, 4 in former slave quarters, 4 rooms in annex.
Facilities Parlors, study, patio, gift shop. 26 acres with formal, informal gardens, gazebo, fish pond.
Location 1 m from downtown. At corner of Quitman Pkwy. and Melrose.
Restrictions No smoking in main house. No children under 14.
Credit cards Amex, Discover, MC, Visa.
Rates B&B, $160 suite, $90–135 double. Extra person, $35. Prix fixe dinner, $35 per person.
Extras Limited wheelchair access.

Weymouth Hall ¢   Tel: 601–445–2304
One Cemetery Road, P.O. Box 1091, 39120

"This Greek Revival mansion, built in 1855, is set high on a bluff above the Mississippi River with a fine view. When it was bought by Gene Weber and Durrell Armstrong in 1975, the house had deteriorated to a shell and was on the verge of sliding down the hill into the river. An engineer was hired to assist in reconstructing the bluff and the building was saved. The inn is a total restoration; the ground floor was originally made of concrete finished to look like marble; before rebuilding, it had crumbled back to dirt. Gene Weber has a scrapbook of photos and articles chronicling the restoration. He lives on the third floor and is always available to guests.

"Rooms are furnished with the owners' collection of Victoriana of the Rococo period, 1840s to 1860s—ornate with carving. European and Chinese porcelains abound, and two rooms have river views. The public rooms upstairs include a center entry hall, with the ladies' parlor at the rear and the gentlemen's parlor at the front, both available to guests at any time. The airy guest rooms are average in size with plenty of room for a couple of chairs and a reading table. They have tester, four-poster or canopied beds, and one room has a river view. Baths are modern with fiberglass tubs and linoleum floors, with full-size bars of quality soaps." *(SHW)*

"Breathtaking view and sunset over the river. Very comfortable room with dazzling early Victorian antiques. Gene Weber was most hospitable, and the tasty southern breakfast kept us full for the day. Across the street is an interesting old cemetery where many Confederate soldiers are buried." *(Victor Thorne)* "The hospitality of Gene and his sister Nancy, made it seem as though we were visiting friends rather than paying guests. They joined us for breakfast and took us on a tour of the house." *(Glenn & Lynette Roehrig)*

Open Feb. through Dec.
Rooms 5 doubles—all with full private bath, radio, air-conditioning. 4 with desk.

MISSISSIPPI

Facilities Dining room, sitting room with TV, 2 parlors. 13 acres with gardens.
Location ½ m from town. From post office, go N on Broadway or Canal to
Linton Ave. to Old Cemetery Rd. Inn on left, overlooking river.
Restrictions No smoking. No children under 14.
Credit cards MC, Visa.
Rates B&B, $75 double. Individual house tours, $4.

SUMRALL

Little Lake Farms ¢ 🛉   *Tel: 601–758–3364*
Route 1, Box 554, 39482

Originally purchased as a weekend escape from their Louisiana restaurant,
the wooded acres of Little Lake Farms are the retirement home of Bill and
Tanya Ditto. They added an Acadian-style cottage for B&B guests, and
dug three lakes to accommodate the wildlife; their waterfowl refuge is
now home to Royal Mute and black Australian swans and their cygnets,
and such varieties of wild ducks as Mandarin, teal, and the shy wood duck.
The lakes are stocked with large-mouth bass and blue gill brim, and paths
along the water are convenient for fishing, hiking, and picnicking. Those
born to shop can visit the antique and collectible shops of the small town
of Sumrall (population 1,197).

   Guest rooms are furnished with contemporary and reproduction pieces,
with simple window treatments and floral wallpaper borders. The Dittos'
cooking expertise shows in their menus: recent breakfasts included strawberry compote; scrambled eggs or blueberry pancakes with sausage and
bacon; and homemade sourdough bread, cheese grits, biscuits, or croissants. Special Cajun- or country-style dinners might feature speckled trout
with crawfish etouffeé, quail in gravy, or chicken and dumplings; shrimp
remoulade, turnip greens, fried eggplant, and seafood gumbo are among
the side dishes; and desserts of caramel custard, bread pudding with
brandy sauce, or peach pie will satisfy any sweet tooth.

   "We stayed in the Hibiscus room with its king-size bed, and a view of
the ponds from our window. We breakfasted on heart-shaped waffles with
bacon and fresh fruit; snacks were available later. Tanya and Bill sat on the
back porch and chatted with us during the afternoon. The grounds were
perfect for walking and birding. " *(Joe & Karen Bearden)* "Tanya and Bill
are wonderful hosts as well as cooks. Everything was delicious, from the
fried alligator tail to the jambalaya and home-baked bread." *(Mrs. Larry
Boone)* "The cottage was immaculate in all respects and Tanya made us feel
very much at home. One night, when we mentioned we might come back
late, we found a pot of homemade vegetable soup waiting for us." *(Lois
Frost)*

Open All year.
Rooms 3 doubles—all with private bath and shower, telephone, TV, air-conditioning, ceiling fan. All rooms in guest cottage.
Facilities Great room with fireplace, TV/VCR, stereo, books; guest kitchen/
laundry, porch. 70 acres with swings, gazebo, picnic area, lake, 2 stocked ponds,
paddle boat, fishing, hiking trail.

Location SE MS, 17 m NW of Hattiesburg. From I-59, take Exit 678 to Rte. 49. Go NW 6 m to Rte. 42/44, turn left. Go W 6½ m, turn right on unmarked blacktop road. Go 1½ m to farm on right.
Restrictions No smoking.
Credit cards MC, Visa.
Rates B&B, $45–55. Extra adult, $15; extra child under 12, $5. Weekly rate. 15% senior discount. Box lunch, $5. Dinner by advance reservation, $20 ($50 minimum).
Extras Limited wheelchair access. Crib.

VICKSBURG

When folks talk about "The War" in Vicksburg, it's the Civil War they're referring to, not any of more recent vintage. Because of the town's controlling position, high on the Mississippi River bluffs, Union forces felt Vicksburg's surrender was essential to victory. Repulsed in repeated attempts both from land and water, the town surrendered to General U.S. Grant only after a 47-day siege of continuous mortar and cannon bombardment.

Must-see sights in Vicksburg include the National Military Park and Cemetery and the nearby Cairo Museum, with numerous exhibits and audiovisual programs that bring the history of the battle and the period to life. Amazingly enough, many of Vicksburg's antebellum mansions survived the siege and can be visited today. Check with the Vicksburg Tourist Commission for Pilgrimage dates: 800–221–3536. For a lighter taste of history, stop at the Biedenharn Candy Company Museum to see where Coca-Cola was first bottled in 1894.

Vicksburg is located in southwest Mississippi, 44 miles east of Jackson, via I-20.

Also recommended: While we were unable to get enough information for a full write-up, we received an enthusiastic recommendation for **Grey Oaks** (4142 Rifle Range Road, 39180; 601–638–4424). "Extensive grounds, a wild and beautiful garden, and walking trails winding throughout make Grey Oaks a pleasant spot. The house, also open daily for tours, was reconstructed in the 1940s from the salvageable parts of an 1830s Federal-style mansion in Port Gibson. Owners Dr. and Mrs. Donald Hall are resident owners, and only three guest rooms are available; reservations must be made months ahead. The first floor bedroom has a Hepplewhite canopy bed draped with satin and lace and the pillows are covered in fabric from several old wedding gowns. Rates of $100 per night include a welcoming beverage, a tour of the mansion and grounds, and a continental breakfast of fresh fruit, croissants, preserves, and coffee." *(SHW)*

Reader tips: "The **Delta Point** restaurant is recommended for its magnificent views of the Mississippi. Delicious food and attentive service; make advance reservations for Saturday night." *(HB)* "Unfortunately, the kitchen at the Delta Point was not up to the aspirations of its menu." *(LC)*

"Although Vicksburg is well worth visiting, much of the downtown is depressingly poverty-stricken, and many handsome mansions [including a number of our entries] are set amongst dilapidated shacks. While security is not a problem and all are very happy to see tourists, plan on using your car to get around, and don't plan on any extended strolls. Although a great many antebellum mansions are open for B&B in Vicksburg, relatively few are owner-operated; most have a resident manager and the owners live elsewhere, which inevitably results in a more commercial— but sometimes more private—atmosphere." *(SHW, also LF)*

Information please: Of possible interest' is **Tomil Manor** (2430 Drummond Street, 39180; 601–638–8893), famous for its 32 stained glass windows. Bedrooms are furnished with tester beds, and rates include breakfast and a mansion tour.

Sixty miles north, up the Great River Road, is **Mount Holly Plantation** (Box 140, Chatham 38731; 601–827–2652 or 800–748–9039), a brick Italianate-style mansion built in 1856 and listed on the National Register of Historic Places. Guests can have breakfast on the porch overlooking Lake Washington or in the keeping room; the inn has five guest rooms with private bath. The lake is available for fishing, sailing, and swimming.

Anchuca	*Tel:* 601–636–4931
1010 First East, 39180	800–262–4822

Vicksburg's first B&B, Anchuca was built in 1830 in the Greek Revival style and is listed on the National Register of Historic Places. The mansion is elegantly and elaborately decorated with antiques, complete with the original gas-burning chandeliers and half-tester and canopy beds. Manager Kathy Tanner welcomes "any visitor who wants a historic atmosphere and a relaxing, friendly place to stay."

"Rooms in the former slave quarters have large bathrooms with marble countertops, thick towels, and a selection of bath soaps and shampoo. The one guest room in the main house (on the street side), is large and lovely, with antique French rug, four-poster tester bed, ornate fabrics, Victorian furniture with marble tops, and a silver dresser accessories. There is a fabulous pier mirror above its marble fireplace and a crystal chandelier to add sparkle." *(SHW)* "New since our last visit is an outside bar in the rear, with prices posted; guests help themselves on the honor system. The tasty breakfast was the same: cheese grits, bacon, eggs, sweet muffins, juice, and coffee or tea, followed by a tour of the home. Around 5:00 P.M., spiced or iced tea is served, and one can examine the menus of local restaurants. Though it must be vacated by 9 A.M., we enjoyed the room in the main house, with its high antique beds. The innkeepers were most helpful, and assisted with luggage on request." *(HB, also Dr. & Mrs. Harry Renken)* "The innkeepers welcomed us with a cup of spicy tea, and made dinner reservations for us. Our little room in the slave quarters had an authentic historic feel. Breakfast was served on a gleaming mahogany table, with lace placemats and napkins, silver and crystal, reminiscent of a vanished way of life." *(Rita Langel)*

Open All year.
Rooms 9 doubles—all with private bath, telephone, TV, air-conditioning. Some with desk, fireplace. 4 rooms in former slave quarter, 4 in cottage.
Facilities Breakfast room, library with piano. 1 acre, courtyard, garden, swimming pool, hot tub.

Location Historic district. Take Exit 4B off I-20 to 9th light. Go right on Cherry Street 5 blocks; then right on First East to inn on right.
Restrictions Smoking restricted to some guest rooms.
Credit cards Most major.
Rates B&B, $75–115 double, $70–110 single. Extra person, $15. 10% senior, AAA discount.
Extras Small pets permitted by prior arrangement. Crib. Member, Clarion Carriage House hotels.

Belle of the Bends ¢   *Tel:* 601–634–0737
508 Klein Street, 39180   800–844–2308

High on a bluff overlooking the river is the brick Italianate-style home of Wally and Jo Pratt. This 1876 vintage mansion is furnished with period antiques and steamboating memorabilia, and is named for the finest steamboat ever owned by Jo's grandfather, Captain Tom Morrissey. Fully restored in 1991, guests receive a tour of the house (also open to the public daily from 10 A.M. to 5 P.M.), a history of the Morrissey Line, and breakfast.

"The Pratts have added private bathrooms to the rooms without disturbing the architecture of the old house. The first floor rooms are done in peach and mauve, and are very spacious and comfortable. The upstairs rooms are also done in light colors, an appealing contrast to the dark decor of many other mansions. Jo and Wally joined us for a breakfast of juice, ham with pineapple, cheese grits, and eggs in ramekin with cream, cheese, and bacon slivers. Biscuits and two kinds of homemade muffins were served along with plenty of hot coffee." *(Judy & Marty Schwartz)*

"The restoration has been accomplished by using absolutely top quality materials and workmanship, providing an appropriate setting for a generous selection of antiques and the best of Victorian taste. The linens and soaps were the best quality. The Pratts provided me with a warm and enthusiastic welcome, doing everything they could to make me feel at home."*(Stephen Holman, also Gerald Lambert)*

Open All year.
Rooms 4 doubles—all with private bath, telephone, radio, TV, air-conditioning. 1 with whirlpool bath, desk; 2 with balcony.
Facilities Dining room, living room with piano, books; guest kitchen/laundry. 1 acre, garden. On Mississippi, Yazoo River for water sports.
Location ½ m from center, 1½ blocks E of Washington St., 1 block from the Klein's Landing historic district.
Restrictions No smoking. Prefer children over 8.
Credit cards MC, Visa.
Rates B&B, $75–95 double. Extra person, $20.

Cedar Grove Estate   *Tel:* 601–636–2800
2300 Washington Street, 39180   Outside MS: 800–862–1300
                              In MS: 800–448–2820

One of Vicksburg's finest antebellum mansions, Cedar Grove was built in 1840 and is listed on the National Register of Historic Places. It's been owned by Ted and Estelle Mackey—who live in Natchez—since 1983. Despite the Union cannonball still lodged in the parlor wall, it survived the Civil War with most of the antiques and architecture intact. Guest rooms are available in the mansion, in the poolside guest cottage, and in Little Tara, a smaller mansion on the grounds with eight suites. Rates include a welcoming drink and a full Southern breakfast.

"A substantial part of the furniture is original to the house. Most rooms in the main house have four-poster beds, including a huge one in the master bedroom. The carriage house rooms have beautiful brocade fabrics, with private patios in the rear. The suites have a mixture of antique and contemporary furnishings." *(SWS)* "The accommodating manager greeted us with a complimentary drink which we enjoyed in the back parlor with piano music. The third floor terrace provided a stunning view of the Mississippi River, gardens, and croquet lawn." *(Lynn Fullman)*

"My room had superb antiques, immaculate linens, and a river view. Elegant, ample breakfast." *(Polly Noe)*

Open All year.
Rooms 9 suites, 9 doubles—all with private bath and/or shower, telephone, TV. 8 rooms in annex.
Facilities Dining room, sun parlor, roof terrace. 4 acres, gazebo, fountains, gardens, heated swimming pool, hot tub. Mississippi River nearby.
Location $1/2$m from town center.
Restrictions Smoking restricted. No children under 5.
Credit cards MC, Visa.
Rates B&B, $75–115 suite, double.

The Corners ¢ **♀♂**　　　　　　　　　　*Tel:* 601–636–7421
601 Klein Street, 39180　　　　　　　　　　　800–444–7421

Resident owners Cliff and Bettye Whitney will greet you on arrival at the Corners with a complimentary beverage, and you may well want to sit right down and enjoy it in a lazy rocking chair on the wide gallery as you watch the sun set. Built in 1873, The Corners is listed on the National Register of Historic Places and was built in a style combining Greek Revival and Victorian features. John A. Klein, of Cedar Grove, had the Corners constructed as a wedding present for his daughter Susan. The floors are original heart-of-pine boards 20 feet long and the support walls are three bricks thick. Rooms are elegantly furnished with period antiques, while baths are modern.

"In my experience, the Corners provides the most consistently warm, comfortable experience of all the B&Bs in Vicksburg, perhaps because the Whitneys actually live there full-time and because they treat their guests like family. The Corners has rooms that are beautifully and comfortably appointed, and hosts who leave no stone unturned to please and entertain you. It's charmingly restored, and filled with personal treasures." *(Janet Howe)*

"Bettye made dinner reservations for us at the Delta Point, and ordered them to take good care of us. We had a window table with a fine view of the Mississippi Bridge in the lovely dining room, and returned there again the next night. Breakfast is served in the formal dining room. The Whitneys waited until everyone had gathered in the parlor for coffee before inviting us all to the table. We stayed in the Master Suite, with two

12-foot windows facing the Mississippi River. The rug in this room took two ladies 2½ years to hand hook. The bed is a massive half-tester, and there is plenty of room for an armoire, straight and overstuffed chairs, a tea table, and a dresser. The bath was supplied with very thick towels, and imported toiletries; the bathtub was heavily draped with lace and curtains, which made using it a bit tricky." *(SHW)*

"Upon arrival, we were served coffee and tea in the parlor while listening to soft-playing music. Returning to the inn after dinner, Mr. Whitney lit the parlor fireplace, and we sat there reading through their many interesting books on the area and its history. Mrs. Whitney treated our children, ages six and seven, like young adults, and took an interest in their comfort as well. The Old Court House Museum was fascinating and set the stage for our stay in Vicksburg." *(Darel & Renata Kurtz)*

"I traveled alone and felt very comfortable with the Whitneys. My room was meticulously clean and I slept like an angel on the full tester bed." *(Priscilla Merrill)* "As last-minute arrivals, the Whitneys put us up in the cottage across the street, which was comfortable although not as luxurious as the mansion rooms. For breakfast, all the guests gathered in the dining room and feasted on pecan banana pancakes, bacon and eggs, and homemade biscuits. Seconds were offered and eagerly accepted." *(Judy & Marty Schwartz)*

Open All year.
Rooms 1 2-bedroom cottage, 1 suite, 5 doubles—all with private bath and/or shower, TV, air-conditioning. Some with telephone, desk, fan, fireplace. 1 with radio, refrigerator. 2 rooms in former servant quarters.
Facilities Dining room; parlor with 2 fireplaces, piano, library; country kitchen, veranda. 1½ acres with parterre gardens, croquet. Boating, golf nearby.
Location 1 m from center. From I-20, take exit 1A. Go N on Washington St., left on Klein St. to inn at corner of Klein and Oak Sts.
Restrictions No smoking. Train noise might disturb light sleepers; some noise in Gentlemen's Parlor due to location.
Credit cards Amex, MC, Visa.
Rates B&B, $140–150 2-bedroom suite, $75–95 double, $70–90 single. Extra adult, $20; child under age 6, $10–15; infant, free. House tours, $4.
Extras Limited wheelchair access. Pets permitted by prior arrangement.

Duff Green Mansion ♦♦
1114 First East Street, P.O. Box 75, 39180

Tel: 601–636–6968
800–992–0037

Duff Green, a prosperous Vicksburg merchant, built this 12,000-square-foot Paladian mansion in 1856 as a wedding gift for his bride, Mary Lake Green; her parents had provided the land as a wedding gift. Once the scene of many parties, the mansion was converted into a hospital during the Civil War (Union soldiers on the third floor, Confederates on the second). Mary Green gave birth to a son during the siege of Vicksburg, while taking shelter in a nearby cave, and named him Siege Green. The recent restoration of the mansion combines antiques and period reproductions with exceptionally luxurious appointments; rates include a welcoming drink and a full southern breakfast.

"An immense mansion, filled with truly historic romance, and gorgeously restored. A Florida millionaire, Harry Sharp, and his wife, Alicia,

197

moved to Vicksburg recently and transformed Duff Green into a show-piece, adding a swimming pool and landscaped courtyard. The hospitality is first-rate, the food fine and southern. Each bedroom is gorgeously appointed and peaceful." (Janet Howe)

"Probably the most luxurious B&B in Vicksburg, the Duff Green has more the feel of an elegant hotel than a cozy homestay. It is not a museum, and the whole house is open to guests. The pine floors are original, as are the 14½-foot ceilings and 12-foot windows. The house's relatively high elevation protects it from the noise and less attractive elements of the street below. The French chandelier in the ballroom dates from 1860, while the one in the dining room is of Waterford crystal. The location is quiet, and although the grounds are limited, they are well designed and private, with brick terraces everywhere. Likable owner Harry Sharp lives elsewhere in Vicksburg, but acts as the daytime innkeeper; Marilyn Klages is the night manager. Guest rooms are individually furnished and good sized; the Duff Green suite is massive, covering one-half the third floor." (SHW)

A note of caution: Receptions and parties are often held in the ballroom on the main floor; when making reservations, check to be sure one won't conflict with your visit. Additional reports welcome.

Open All year.
Rooms 3 suites, 4 doubles—all with full private bath, air-conditioning, fireplace. 5 with desk, 1 with kitchenette.
Facilities Dining room, parlor, library, porches, rooftop sun-deck. 1 acre with swimming pool, brick patio with fountain.
Location Historic District. From Hwy. 61, go E on First East St. to inn between Adams and Locust.
Restrictions Smoking discouraged.
Credit cards Amex, MC, Visa.
Rates B&B, $95–150 suite, $55–100 double. Extra adult, $15; children age 6-12, $7.50; under 6, free. Crib or cot, $10.
Extras Wheelchair access in ground-floor rooms. Airport/station pickup, $65. Crib. Spanish spoken.

We Want to Hear from You!

As you know, this book is only effective with your help. We really need to know about your experiences and discoveries. If you stayed at an inn or hotel listed here, we want to know how it was. Did it live up to our description? Exceed it? Was it what you expected? Did you like it? Were you disappointed? Delighted? Have you discovered new establishments that we should add to the next edition?

Tear out one of the report forms at the back of this book (or use your own stationery if you prefer) and write today. *Even if you write only "Fully endorse existing entry" you will have been most helpful.*
Thank You!

North Carolina

Mast Farm Inn, Valle Crucis

Few states offer as much to the traveler as North Carolina—beautiful beaches, long barrier islands, and historic towns in the east, and breathtaking mountain scenery in the west. Mt. Mitchell, at 6,684 feet the highest point east of the Mississippi, lies in the High Country, in the northwestern part of the state. The center of the state, called the Piedmont, is rich in industry, agriculture, and has some of the state's most beautiful golf courses.

The Blue Ridge mountains in the west are home to artisans who create fine Appalachian crafts while traditional "jugtown" potteries line the roads near Seagrove, south of Greensboro. For an introduction to the region's original residents, visit Cherokee in the southwestern corner of the state. Here you can wander through Oconaluftee Village, a reconstructed 1750 Cherokee town, or purchase top-notch tribal arts at the Qualla gallery.

In North Carolina, liquor is sold only through state-owned "A.B.C." stores, although beer and wine are sold in grocery stores in most counties. Some inns provide setups if you bring your own beverage; others prefer that drinks not be consumed in public. Some counties are completely dry, so be prepared! State law prohibits pets in commercial accommodations. Rates do not include 5% state sales tax; some areas charge additional local tax.

Information please: We'd love to have any suggestions for the relatively undeveloped beaches of Brunswick County, between the historic city charms of Wilmington and the South Carolina border at Myrtle Beach. The golf courses and beaches are lovely, and the seafood is to die for (try one of the waterfront shacks in Calabash, "Seafood Capital of the World"). Most people stay in modest motels or rental units, but the big

Victorian homes of Southport might shelter a welcoming B&B or two. Reports?

ASHEVILLE

Asheville is in western North Carolina, at the juncture of interstates 26 and 40, 106 miles southeast of Knoxville, Tennessee; it's just an hour's drive to the Great Smoky Mountains National Park. Asheville is surrounded by more than a million acres of national forest, and is known for its cool mountain summers. Golf, rafting, horseback riding, and hiking are all available nearby. It's also the home of the Biltmore House and Gardens, the Vance Birthplace, the Thomas Wolfe Memorial, and many craft shops and galleries. The Biltmore House is probably its best-known attraction; George W. Vanderbilt (of the railroad/steamship Vanderbilts) was so enamored of the area that he bought 125,000 acres and built this 255-room castle, completed in 1895. Several inns sell reduced-rate tickets to the castle.

Reader tip: "We had a superb dinner at "5 Boston Way," offering huge portions of creative cuisine at reasonable prices. Standouts included the baked Brie with almonds, the chicken stuffed with ham and grits in peanut sauce, and tortellini Carbonara." *(John Blewer)*

Information please: The Lion & The Rose (276 Montford Avenue, 28801; 704–255–ROSE) is a Queen Anne–style B&B eclectically furnished with golden oak, stained glass, period antiques, white wicker, some contemporary California touches, and modern baths. Rates include a full breakfast and afternoon tea; scones, clotted cream, and raspberry jam or lemon cream cake are among the favorites. Reports?

Aberdeen Inn ¢   *Tel:* 704–254–9336
64 Linden Avenue, 28801

Ross and Linda Willard encourage guests to "consider our home as their own." In the summer, you can relax on the wicker rockers and enjoy the view from the twelve-pillar porch of this 1909 house; in the chill of winter, snuggle up by the fire, in a guest room simply furnished with antiques, wicker, and collectibles. A full buffet breakfast and afternoon tea are served on the porch or in the breakfast room.

"Friendly Canadian hosts, Ross and Linda, run this pleasant B&B on a hill in a residential area of Asheville. They have menus for many restaurants, and serve breakfast, weather permitting, on their large, attractive, wraparound porch; cereals plus homemade specialties are the order of the day." *(Celia McCullough)*

Open All year.
Rooms 9 doubles—all with private bath and/or shower, TV, fan. Some with fireplace, desk. 1 room in carriage house with kitchenette.
Facilities Parlor with fireplace, books; family room with games; breakfast room, library, porch. 1/2 hr. from rivers.
Location 6 blocks from downtown. From I-26 or I-40 take I-240 to Rte. 25-N exit. Go N on Merrimon about ¾ mile. Turn right at 5th traffic onto Murdock. Drive

behind "The Hop Ice Cream" and "Boston Pizza" and turn right on Robindale. Turn left on Linden, then immediate right to inn up hill.
Restrictions No smoking. No children under 13.
Credit cards MC, Visa.
Rates B&B, $65–75 double. Extra person, $15. Reduced rates for families. 2-night weekend minimum Oct., Dec.
Extras Airport, bus station pickup, $10.

Applewood Manor
62 Cumberland Circle, 28801

Tel: 704–254–2244

"A lovely turn-of-the-century Colonial Revival set at the top of a wooded hill, the Applewood makes you feel as if you are in the country. The front door opens onto a large foyer with a large parlor and living room to the left and dining room to the right. All rooms are divided by pocket doors and are furnished with handsome period antiques and Oriental carpets. Jim and Linda both do the cooking and care taking, and they are the icing on this already lovely cake of a place. A young couple, the LoPrestis bought the inn after relocating from the New York City area. Jim is an aspiring writer with a dry sense of humor. The inn is very clean, quiet, and convenient, with hot water in abundance." *(Susan McMullen)*

The LoPrestis really enjoy cooking. Their ever-changing breakfast menu might include Belgian waffles with fresh raspberry sauce one day, and Havarti omelets with lemon poppy seed bread and peach jam the next. Favorite afternoon refreshments are peach spice tea with chocolate almond cookies or hot apple cider with spinach-cheese squares. "Breakfast is served on the porch in good weather, surrounded by lilacs and rhodo-dendrons; in cold weather you eat in the dining room, before a cozy fire. Conversation is lively at the four tables, punctuated by Jim and Linda's wit and good humor. The LoPrestis assist with plans and reservations, and invite all to be back in time for afternoon refreshments, which might include tea, sherry, mozzarella and dried tomato puffs, and butter lemon bars. The atmosphere is warm and homelike, with furnishings selected for maximum comfort." *(Bill & Doris Hames)*

"What sets this place apart are owners Jim and Linda. They are not only delightful, warm, and witty themselves, but they elicit these qualities in their guests—even though their ages and backgrounds vary greatly." *(Anne Nicastro)* "When we left it was like leaving old friends. Lots of laughter, great breakfasts and afternoon snacks, and many thoughtful touches. The neighborhood is up-and-coming, with lots of redos and a few rough spots."*(Carole Vesely)*

Open All year.
Rooms 4 doubles—all with private bath and/or shower, radio, air-conditioning, fan. 3 with fireplace.
Facilities Dining room with fireplace, parlor with fireplace, library, porches. 2 acres with flower gardens, swings, croquet, volleyball, badminton, bikes. Tennis nearby.
Location 1 m from downtown. Off-street parking. From Rte. 240 W take Exit 4C/Civic Center/Haywood St. Go right on Haywood, then turn right on Mont-ford Ave. Turn right again on Soco and go to stop sign at Cumberland Ave. Cross to Cumberland Circle to inn.

NORTH CAROLINA

Restrictions No smoking. No children under 12.
Credit cards MC, Visa.
Rates B&B, $70–110 double, $65–90 single. Extra person, $20. 20% senior discount in Sept. 2-night minimum holiday weekends. Murder Mystery weekend, Jan.–March.
Extras Italian, American Sign Language spoken.

Cairn Brae ¢   *Tel:* 704–252–9219
217 Patten Mountain Road, 28804

Meaning "rocky hillside" in Scottish, Cairn Brae is tucked in the Great Craggy Mountains above Asheville. Millie and Ed Adams's contemporary home has a secluded setting, with great views and walking trails, yet is close to downtown. Guest rooms are individually decorated, some with lively floral wallpapers and wicker accents, and others with mellow pine walls and furniture. A breakfast of homemade muffins, cereal, fruit, and coffee is served in the dining room at an octagonal, glass-topped table.

"Our suite afforded a panoramic view through tall windows; it was well-furnished with a comfortable king-size bed and a separate dressing room." *(Barb & Al Easton)* "Coffee by the fireplace every morning was a special treat, as was the sherry and chocolate by our bed at night. The breakfasts included homemade granola and fresh fruit, with excellent baked goods— pumpkin bread, coffee cake, and cranberry bread." *(Martha Ann Mobley)* "Exquisite linens, immaculately clean. Friendly, gracious innkeepers knew the area and helped us plan our tours. Fine scenery." *(Norman Talner)* "Mountain-lodge style architecture combines with warm decor for a sense of tranquility and comfort. Millie and Ed provide congenial, relaxed hospitality. Daily attentions include fresh towels and bedtime sherry, and such breakfast treats as a grits and sausage casserole. The nature trail and stone patio, with its afternoon tea table, swing, and hammock offer views of distant ridges and the fresh scents of rhododendron and laurel." *(Richard & Cindy Lacy)*

Open April through Nov.
Rooms 1 suite, 3 doubles—all with private bath and/or shower. Some rooms with radio, fan.
Facilities Dining room, living room with fireplace, TV, games, phone; deck. 3 acres with walking trails. Swimming, tennis, golf nearby. Close to river for fishing, boating, canoeing.
Location 12 min. from downtown Asheville. Exit I-240 at Charlotte St. (turn left onto Charlotte St.) Go 2 lights to College St. turn left. At the next light, turn left onto Town Mountain Rd. Turn left onto Patten Mountain Rd.
Restrictions No smoking. No children under 6.
Credit cards MC, Visa.
Rates B&B, $85–110 suite, $70 double, $60 single. Extra person, $15. No tipping. 2-day minimum during October.
Extras Airport/station pickup, $20. Babysitting.

Carolina B&B ¢   *Tel:* 704–254–3608
177 Cumberland Avenue, 28801

Built around the turn of the century by Richard Sharp Smith, supervising architect for the Biltmore Estate, this home has a stucco exterior, graced by front and rear porches and two pairs of chimneys. Restored in 1989 by innkeepers Sam and Karin Fain, the warm pine floors shine again in spacious, high-ceilinged rooms. The guest rooms, with large windows and ruffled, organdy curtains, have walnut and brass beds; some have antique dressing tables. The Fains are happy to accommodate dietary restrictions for breakfast; some recent menus included pumpkin-ginger bread, spiced apple rings, and cinnamon French toast; or pineapple-kiwi-banana compote, spinach and cheese casserole, and blueberry muffins; poached pears, eggs Benedict, and cranberry bread with honey butter; accompanied by a choice of juice, coffee, tea, and cereals.

"Sam and Karin Fain and their daughter Regina took off from Washington, D.C., for the slower pace of Asheville. The location is convenient, and this pleasant house has a Prairie-style feel to it. Karin is as good a host as one could wish, and is well informed about area activities. Sam has added a great back deck with an arbor, and has laid out some lovely gardens. Karin's breakfasts are great, and she was kind enough to share a favorite recipe." *(Ripley Hotch)* "The beautifully wooded grounds (flowering dogwoods, rhododendrons, and azaleas) set the mood for a walk to the botanical gardens not far away." *(BAB)*

Open All year.
Rooms 5 doubles, 1 cottage—all with private bath and/or shower, air-conditioning, fan, fireplace.
Facilities Parlor with stereo, books, games, dining room, porches, deck. Off-street parking.
Location Montford Historic District. 1/2 m from center of town. From I-240, take Montford Avenue exit. Turn right onto Montford Avenue then turn right at Chestnut Street. Go one block, turn left onto Cumberland and go 1 1/2 blocks to inn, located on right.
Restrictions No smoking. Children under 12 not permitted.
Credit cards MC, Visa.
Rates B&B, $95 cottage, $75 double, $65 single. Extra person, $20.
Extras Airport/station pickups.

Cedar Crest Victorian Inn
Tel: 704–252–1389
674 Biltmore Avenue, 28803

Cedar Crest was built in 1891 by William E. Breese, one of Asheville's leading citizens. Listed on the National Register of Historic Places, this Queen Anne–style Victorian has a captain's walk, projecting turrets, and verandas at different levels. The interior features original oak woodwork, with stained and beveled glass windows. Innkeepers Jack and Barbara McEwan have owned the Cedar Crest since 1984, and the rates include breakfast, afternoon iced tea or lemonade on the veranda in the summer, wassail in the parlor in the winter, and evening tea or hot chocolate. Additional accommodations are available in the guest cottage, a 1910 bungalow, decorated partially in the Arts & Crafts style.

"The McEwans are really knowledgeable about the history of the area and have lots of books on the subject. The house is as handsome as described; the woodwork was done by the same artisans who worked on the Vanderbilt estate. The entrance to the Biltmore House is within walking distance, as is Vanderbilt Village, which has several good restaurants." *(Maria Schmidt)*

"Our third-floor room had a shared bath, placed conveniently next to our room, and the twin beds were comfortable. We enjoyed the generous breakfast of fresh fruits and juices, cereals, hot drinks, and breakfast breads. We had a delicious dinner at McGuffy's, on the east side of town." *(April Burwell)* "Our room in the cottage was attractive, with vaguely art nouveau decor. Nice evening hot chocolate, tasty breakfast, friendly and informative hosts." *(Celia McCullough)*

"Our room was large, elegant, with a tented ceiling and private bath. The interior decor is exquisite." *(Deborah Reese)* "If your taste runs Victorian, this place is heaven. Breakfast is lovely, with tantalizing hot breads and pastries." *(John Blewer)*

Areas for improvement: "Lighting in our room was very dim; we expected better for $95 nightly."

Open All year.
Rooms 2 suites, 10 doubles—8 with private bath and/or shower, 4 with maximum of 4 people sharing bath. All rooms with telephone, desk, air-conditioning. 3 rooms in separate cottage with parlor, fireplace, sitting room, kitchenette.
Facilities Parlor, dining room, study, grand foyer, large veranda, sitting areas with TV, fireplaces, table games. 4 acres with sitting areas, rose and perennial gardens, croquet pitch. Swimming, fishing, white-water rafting, 10 to 30 min. Cross-country and downhill skiing, 35 min.
Location 1 1/2 m from downtown, 1/4 m N of Biltmore House. Take Exit 50 or 50B off I-40; stay right to Biltmore Ave.
Restrictions Smoking in study only. No children under 12. Traffic/train noise in some rooms.
Credit cards Amex, Discover, MC, Visa.
Rates B&B, $90–160 suite, $70–120 double, $65–115 single. Extra person, $15. No tipping. 2-night minimum, some weekends, holidays.

Corner Oak Manor ¢

Tel: 704–253–3525

53 Saint Dunstans Road, 28803

Handstitchery and handcrafts are a special focus at the Corner Oak Manor, an English Tudor-style home with a curved roof reminiscent of a thatched cottage. Owners Karen and Andy Spradley have created a casual but elegant decor by combing the work of local artisans, with family pieces made by Karen and her sister, Kathie. The house is furnished in soft tones of ivory, rose, blue, and green, and guest rooms have antique or reproduction brass or iron beds. Skill with a needle is only one of Karen's accomplishments; breakfasts are definitely another, and she reports, "I'm always trying new recipes. We only use real cream and real maple syrup, too." Breakfast always includes two homemade breads (maybe apple streusel muffins and cranberry lemon bread); fresh or poached fruit; and an entrée—savory baked eggs with cheddar, dill, chives, and mustard; or pumpkin pancakes with apple cider syrup and sausage.

"Andy and Karen are wonderful hosts who are able to suggest great activities and restaurants in the area. Karen's breakfasts include fresh herbs, vegetables, and berries from her own garden. Fresh juice, fruit dishes, and herbal teas are also included. Extra touches in my room included fresh flowers and candy, bath salts, interesting books, and handmade quilts and afghans." *(PD)* "A very warm and welcoming place. Food is a real highlight, with a wonderful location close to Biltmore House. Enjoyed Karen's chocolate chip cookies as an afternoon snack. Very clean, too." *(Dianne Crawford)*

Open All year.
Rooms 3 doubles, 1 cottage—all with private shower and/or tub, fan. Cottage with radio, air-conditioning, refrigerator.
Facilities Living room with fireplace, piano, stereo; reading/game room; dining room. Deck with hot tub.
Location 2 m from downtown. From I-40, take exit 50 or 50B. Stay in the right lane until Biltmore Ave., then move left and turn left on St. Dunstans Rd. Follow St. Dunstans Rd. two blocks to Grindstaff to inn on right.
Restrictions No smoking. Children under 12 in cottage only.
Credit cards Amex, MC, Visa.
Rates B&B, $90–100 cottage, $80–85 double, $60–65 single. Extra person, $20. Children under 5 free. 2-night holiday weekend minimum. Mystery weekend packages.
Extras Cottage has wheelchair access.

Cornerstone Inn ⊄   *Tel:* 704–253–5644
230 Pearson Drive, 28801

Gary and Nancy Gaither relocated from Denver to Asheville, and in 1990, bought the Cornerstone Inn, a lovely 1924 Dutch Tudor long listed in this guide. They have furnished it with antiques handed down by their parents and grandparents. Gary reports that "it is our hope that our guests will leave feeling refreshed and nurtured."

"Gary and Nancy treat you like their dearest relative in this spacious, immaculate house." *(Adrian Triplett)* "Plumbing, parking, lighting, and location were all good. Nancy and Gary did not hesitate to tailor the evening snack and breakfast to whatever I requested. And you never left the table hungry." *(Leigh Ann Baker)* "In six days, I never had the same breakfast twice. I enjoyed sitting in a rocker on the side porch watching birds and squirrels, and exploring this historic district, even visiting the cemetery where Tom Wolfe and O. Henry are buried." *(Julie Hardy)* "The innkeepers are happy to tell you the history of their many antiques. Nancy's father is a woodworker, and there are fascinating wood games and bowls on display. There was hot coffee and cookies out at all times and a welcoming cold drink when we arrived. The hot cheese, ham, and egg dish we had for Sunday breakfast was delicious." *(Doug & Mariel Peck)*

Minor niggle: "My room had a private bath across the hall; providing bathrobes would be a thoughtful touch."

Open All year.
Rooms 4 doubles—all with full private bath, radio, air-conditioning. Some with TV, telephone, desk, fireplace.
Facilities Living room with fireplace, dining room, sitting room, porch, terrace, library with TV, VCR, stereo, books, games. Walking distance to downtown or to botanical gardens of UNC/Asheville. Tennis, golf nearby. Rafting, boating, swimming nearby. Off-street parking.
Location Montford Historic District, 1 m to center. Take Montford Exit off I-240 W to Montford Ave. Turn left at Watauga, left again at Pearson. From I-240 E, take Business District Exit, go right off ramp, right on Montford, then as above.
Restrictions No smoking. No children under 10.

Credit cards MC, Visa, Amex.
Rates B&B, $65–85 double, $50–80 single. Extra person, $10. No tipping. 2-night weekend minimum, May–Oct. Weekly rates.
Extras Airport/station pickup, $5–10.

Flint Street Inns ¢   *Tel:* 704–253–6723
100 and 116 Flint Street, 28801

Lynne and Rick Vogel restored their circa-1915 home in 1981 and opened it as Asheville's first bed and breakfast. When the English Tudor next door came on the market in 1985, Rick's mother, Marion, took over as inn-keeper there.

"The inn is only a two-block walk from downtown, and a short drive from the Biltmore House and Folk Art Center. The bedrooms are ex-tremely comfortable and are furnished in a manner that reminds one of an earlier age—of fans and silk hats, horse-drawn carriages and gracious living. The living room, with its easy chairs and couch, its cut-glass windows and shelves of period bric-a-brac, is a particular favorite.

"What keeps us coming back is the Vogels' hospitality. If we arrive on a cold, drizzly day we know there will be a fire in the fireplace and hot cider waiting. If we return to the inn on a warm afternoon, they will offer us a glass of chilled white wine while we sit on the porch. They spend enough time with each guest to get to know their tastes and preferences, directing one to the best discount stores, another to the local craftsmen, and still another to the best hiking trails. They are masters of conversa-tion, yet know when to keep a discreet distance." *(Norman & Katherine Kowal)*

"We stayed in the Garden Room, which has a sitting area, stenciling on the stairway, vintage magazines to read, and a large front porch for sitting and relaxing. Rick and Lynne serve a full breakfast of ham, bacon, or sausage, with eggs, biscuits, fresh fruit or spiced apple compote, orange juice, coffee or tea. In the evening they offer wine, hot spiced apple cider (in winter), or lemonade (in summer), accompanied by delicious brownies or cookies." *(Marianne & Ronald Cohn)* "Breakfasts are perfect down to the dishes made by local potters." *(Mary Gregory)*

"Our hosts were happy to engage in pleasant, friendly, and lively conversations, which become infectious and cause the inn's guests to linger in the living room for the evening. Rick and Lynne are almost walking travel guides to the area; there is hardly any reasonable question about the Asheville area that they cannot answer in a flash." *(Torin & Teresa Togut)* "Our twin-bedded room was lovely. The understated decor provides a relaxed atmosphere. We'd go back anytime we were in the area." *(BJ Hensley)*

Another reader noted that the inn and its owners were great, but that their neighborhood, although historic, was still very much "in transition."

Open All year.
Rooms 8 doubles—all with full private bath, radio, air-conditioning, fan. 2 with desk. Inn occupies 2 adjacent buildings.
Facilities Dining rooms, 2 parlors. 1 acre with flower gardens, fish ponds. Off-street parking.

Location Montford Historic District. 3 blocks from Civic Center.
Restrictions No children under 12. No smoking in dining room.
Credit cards Amex, Discover, MC, Visa.
Rates B&B, $80 double, $65 single, plus tax. Extra person, $20. 2-night minimum peak weekends.

Haywood Park Hotel 🏃 ✗

One Battery Park Avenue, 28801

Tel: 704–252–2522
800–873–2392

Asheville's once decaying downtown area is experiencing a renaissance, as its lovely art deco buildings are slowly restored or refurbished. The Haywood Park, built as a department store, has been completely renovated, and is now connected to a sunlit atrium, with a variety of shops and restaurants. Guest rooms are exceptionally spacious, elegantly decorated in shades of pearl gray and soft mauve, and supplied with enough amenities to earn the hotel a three-diamond rating from AAA. The hotel's restaurant offers a limited choice of appealing entrées—perhaps pecan chicken, red snapper with lemon caper butter sauce, and a pasta of the day. Rates include a continental breakfast delivered to your room.

"Our room was huge with built-in television, wet bar, refrigerator, shelves, and drawers. Our spacious bathroom was gorgeous, done in Spanish marble, with a huge bathtub and a separate glass shower stall with two wonderful shower heads at different levels—and even a TV and telephone. Among the ample amenities were soothing oatmeal soap, toothpaste, toothbrushes, and shampoo. There was a second sink in a dressing area outside of the bathroom, and loads of soft, fluffy towels. The management was unusually friendly and helpful, and service was great. An arcade of shops connected with the hotel has a bakery-café called Fat Bruce's, which makes scrumptious cinnamon rolls." *(Frannye Eisner)* More comments appreciated.

Open All year.
Rooms 33 suites—all with full private bath and/or shower, telephone, radio, TV, desk, air-conditioning, wet bar, computer hook-ups. Some with whirlpool tub.
Facilities Restaurant, bar, lobby with classical music weekly, atrium with shops. Sauna, exercise room. Parking garage. Limousine service.
Location Downtown. Take I-240 to Exit 4C. Continue on Haywood St. to Battery Park Ave. on right.
Restrictions No smoking on some guest floors.
Credit cards Amex, DC, MC, Visa.
Rates B&B, $110–250 suite (for 2), $90–200 single. Extra person, $15. Children under 12 free in parents' room. 10% AARP discount. Alc lunch, $5; alc dinner, $25.
Extras Wheelchair access; some rooms equipped for disabled. Airport/station pickup. Crib, babysitting. Member, Treadway Classic Inns.

Old Reynolds Mansion ¢

100 Reynolds Heights, 28804

Tel: 704–254–0496

When Helen and Fred Faber first moved into the Old Reynolds Mansion in 1981, it was half hidden with underbrush, most of the porch rails had rotted off, and the house was virtually impossible to heat. Working seven days a week, the Fabers spent over two years restoring this antebellum house to its present glory. Now listed on the National Register of Historic Places, the house is furnished with a variety of period antiques.

"Our moderately priced room was clean and comfortable, with a private bath. The continental breakfast was most ample, with unlimited supplies of fresh fruit, orange juice, coffee cake, and beverages. We received the most gratifying personal attention from both Helen and Fred, and I wish we could have stayed longer." *(William Schultz)*

"The inn is roomy, clean, charming, and quiet. We enjoyed breakfast and afternoon refreshments on the large veranda, a wonderful place to sit and relax. The Fabers are attentive hosts and interesting people." *(Peggy Cox)*

Open March to Dec. Open weekends only, Dec. to March.
Rooms 10 doubles—8 with private bath and/or shower, 2 with maximum of 4 people sharing bath. All with desk, fan. Many with fireplaces.
Facilities Parlor with fireplace, wide hallways with seating, 2-story porches. 4 acres with swimming pool.
Location 4 m N of center. Take Merrimon Ave./Rte. 25 N past Beaver Lake. Turn right just past traffic light onto Beaver Dr.; turn left up gravel lane.
Restrictions No cigar smoking. No children under 6.
Credit cards None accepted.
Rates B&B, $40–80 double, $36–65 single. No tipping. $10. 2-night weekend minimum.

Richmond Hill Inn ✗
87 Richmond Hill Drive, 28806

Tel: 704–252–7313
800–545–9238

Considering the broken windows, peeling paint, and collapsing porches of Richmond Hill in the 1970s, even a starry-eyed visionary would have been hard put to imagine the extraordinary restoration of this historic mansion. The road to preservation was a long and bumpy one, both literally and figuratively—involving major fundraising efforts by the Asheville Preservation Society and moving the 1½-million-pound building 600 feet. A happy ending—or perhaps a new beginning—began in 1987, when the Education Center of Greensboro bought Richmond Hill, and began its renovation as an inn and conference center. Completed in 1991 were five neo-Victorian cottages housing nine guest rooms. Named for North Carolina trees, they overlook the croquet court and feature large bathrooms, pencil-post beds with down comforters, and fireplaces.

This grand Queen Anne–style mansion overlooks the French Broad River from its hilltop location. Built in 1899 by former congressman and ambassador Richmond Pearson, the guest rooms are named for family members or other prominent figures and authors of Asheville history. The inn's library contains books that belonged to the original Pearson estate, as well as books about western North Carolina, and works by local authors. Much of the inn's original woodwork was saved, including the native oak of the entrance hall, the cherry-paneled dining room, and the fireplaces with neo-classical revival mantels. Guest rooms are decorated with draped canopy beds or four-posters, Victorian antiques, and Oriental rugs, and rates include a full breakfast.

The inn's restaurant, Gabrielle's, was named for Pearson's wife, and it occupies the formal dining room and the enclosed sun porch. Open for both lunch and dinner, the menu is appealing and creative. Budget travelers should stop by for lunch to have a look at this exceptional inn;

mountain trout with shallots, lemon, and hazelnut butter, served with vegetables and rice costs less than $10. Dinner entrées include grilled shrimp with shallots and garlic, served on a bed of tomato coulis and wilted spinach; or duck with two sauces—braised with sherry butter sauce and grilled atop port butter sauce.

"Our room had excellent views and plenty of windows. Everything was extremely clean and in good working order." *(Patricia Gage)* "Our suite was elegant and comfortable. The staff was professional but friendly, and the maid service was exceptional." *(Neil & Polly Graham)* "Dinner and breakfast on the glassed-in porch of Gabrielle's was both delicious and beautifully presented, with a pleasing variety of choices. The views were spectacular both night and day. The setting of the inn high above the river provides lovely vistas toward Asheville and the surrounding ridges." *(Carol & Donald Purcell)* "Our room was large, with feather pillows, cut flowers, and antiques everywhere. The staff was helpful and friendly; the food was especially good." *(Doloris Holladay, also David Joseph)*

Open All year.
Rooms 1 suite, 16 doubles—all with private bath and/or shower, telephone, radio, TV, air-conditioning. Suite with fireplace, wet bar, whirlpool tub. 8 rooms with fireplace.
Facilities Restaurant, lobby with fireplace, piano entertainment occasionally; drawing room with fireplace, 2 parlors with fireplace, ballroom, porch. Meeting facilities. 47 acres with hiking trails.
Location 3 m from center. From I-240, take North Weaverville exit at Rtes. 19/23. Continue on Rtes. 19/23 to Exit 251/UNC-Asheville. At bottom of ramp, turn left. At 1st stoplight, turn left on Riverside Dr., then turn right on Pearson Bridge Rd. and cross the bridge. At the sharp curve, turn right on Richmond Hill Dr. to inn at top of hill.
Restrictions No smoking in guest rooms.
Credit cards Amex, MC, Visa.
Rates B&B, $200 suite, $95–160 double. Extra person, $15. Alc lunch, $7–12; alc dinner, $25–35.
Extras First floor only wheelchair access, equipped for disabled. Airport/station pickup. Crib.

BANNER ELK

Information please: Built in 1912, the recently renovated **Banner Elk Inn** (Route 194, P.O. Box 1953, 28604; 704–898–6223) offers four guest rooms accented with antiques, tapestries, and original artwork. The reasonable rates include a breakfast of homemade whole wheat bread, fruit breads, and an egg dish or special casserole.

Archers Inn ¢ ✕   *Tel:* 704–898–9004
Beech Mountain Parkway, Route 2, Box 56A, 28604

The Archers is a rustic contemporary lodge, owned and operated by Joe and Bonny Archer since 1984. Most guest rooms are paneled in pine; many are exceptionally spacious with ample room for two double beds, a love seat facing the fieldstone fireplace, and table and chairs. Each has a slightly different decor, some with four-poster beds, others with brass and iron headboards; some with fluffy comforters, others with quilted bedspreads. Guests enjoy relaxing on the old-fashioned porch rockers, with lovely views of the mountains beyond, or in the comfortable living room with beautiful mountain views.

Rates include a full breakfast, with family-style dinners served nightly at 6:30 P.M.. The Archers' downhome meals always start with homemade soup and biscuits and conclude with a home-baked dessert—in between you might dig into southern fried chicken, barbecued spare ribs, rice and gravy, string beans, and corn; another time it might be country ham, chicken and dumplings, turnip greens, and spiced tomatoes.

"Pleasant atmosphere and surroundings. My rooms in the annex were extremely large, comfortable, and clean. The meals are tasty and good. The owners are a nice friendly couple, who will do anything to please their guests." *(Ben Ridgely)* "The view from the rooms is breathtaking. The suites are spacious, and cozy with cedar wood-beamed ceiling and large stone fireplace, kitchen and dining area." *(PS)*

Open All year. Restaurant open for dinner 6/15–10/31; for breakfast all year.
Rooms 1 suite, 13 doubles—all with private bath and/or shower, radio, fireplace. 9 with TV, 8 with fan. Some with soaking tub.
Facilities Dining room, living room with TV, porches, decks. 2.5 acres with basketball hoop. 4.5 m to Wildcat Lake for swimming, boating. 2–3 m to downhill, cross-country skiing.
Location NW NC. 123 m NW of Charlotte, 22 m NW of Boone, NC.
Restrictions No smoking in dining room. "Well-mannered children welcome."
Credit cards MC, Visa.
Rates B&B, $55–80 suite, $45–95 double or single. Extra person, $8. 2-night weekend minimum during ski season. Prix fixe dinner, $12.95. Spring packages, with carriage ride.
Extras Crib.

BEAUFORT

Information please: At the **Captains' Quarters** (315 Ann Street, 28516; 919–728–7711) guests toast the sunset with wine or juice, and welcome the morning with a complete English-style breakfast. Built at the turn-of-the-century, this B&B offers three guest rooms with private baths; rates range from $50–100, depending on the room and the season. **The Shotgun House** (406 Ann Street, P.O. Box 833, 28516; 919–728–6248) is named for its straight-line architectural style. Built in 1854, it offers antique decor, designer sheets, and down comforters; freshly squeezed orange juice, eggs and muffins, and homemade apple butter will start your day off right. We'd like to hear more about the **Beaufort Inn**, a 41-room inn right on the water, with its own docking facilities; B&B rates from $40–90 (101 Ann Street; 919–728–2600).

Inlet Motor Inn   *Tel:* 919–728–3600
601 Front Street, 28516

The original Inlet Inn provided seaside accommodations to 19th century visitors; the contemporary Inlet, built on a nearby site, serves the same function. Designed in character with the town's historic architecture, most guest rooms have seating areas and porches with rocking chairs overlooking Beaufort Harbor and Cape Lookout. Rates include a breakfast of coffee, tea, juice, and pastries, as well as afternoon wine and cheese, served in the rooftop Widow's Walk Lounge.

"Comfortably furnished and immaculately clean. There is a good seafood restaurant close by and another nearby restaurant with barbecued ribs to die for." *(Jeanne Smith)* More comments requested.

Open All year.
Rooms 37 doubles—all with full private bath, telephone, radio, TV, air-conditioning, ceiling fan, bar with refrigerator/ice maker. Some with fireplace, porch.
Facilities Lounge, courtyard garden, boat slips. Rental bicycles.
Location Historic district, on Intracoastal Waterway.
Credit cards Amex, MC, Visa.
Rates B&B, $45–100 double. Extra person, $10. 2-night minimum weekends, high season.

Langdon House   *Tel:* 919–728–5499
135 Craven Street, 28516

In 1983 Jimm Prest restored and opened the Langdon House in one of Beaufort's oldest homes. He prides himself on meeting the individual needs of his guests, and will be pleased to arrange anything from a home-baked birthday cake to a sailboat charter. As he puts it: "We are full of information, want to steer you in the right direction, and help things to go smoothly. This is my home, so we're here to fix you a cup of tea to accompany an evening rock on the porch or supply an antacid if those wonderful hushpuppies from dinner are still barking in the middle of the night."

"Langdon House was built in 1733, and has been beautifully restored. We were so pleased with the accommodations that we made it our headquarters for four days of sightseeing within a 75-mile radius." *(William A. Toombs, Jr.)* "The Langdon House itself is a beautiful example of the kind of careful restoration that's currently going on in Beaufort. It's at once period-authentic and modern-convenient. The proprietor, Jimm Prest, did the work himself, and showed me the original attic frame, the addition line of the floorboards, the eighteenth-century stone chimney, and the many knickknacks that make the ambiance genuine." *(Jonathan Mudd)*

"Brandy on the mantel, beds turned down, hot coffee in the morning, followed by fresh OJ, gingerbread waffles, and country ham. When I wanted a rowboat to get to Carrot Island, there it was. It's just a short walk to the working waterfront . . . the restoration of old sailboats, salty dogs living upon the water, and many shops are fun to watch and visit. Guests are served breakfast at their requested time. A beautiful display of fruit breads, fresh fruits, pastries, cheeses, and coffee is served in the sunny parlor." *(Sally Thomas Kutz)*

"Jimm Prest is absolutely charming and gracious, but we found the rooms a bit noisy because of all the wooden floors, and thought the price was slightly high relative to the size of the rooms." *(BG)* More reports needed.

Open All year.
Rooms 4 doubles—all with queen-size beds, private bath and/or shower, radio, air-conditioning.
Facilities Dining room; parlor for reading, games, breakfast; porch; gardens. Bicycles, fishing rods, beach baskets, beach towels, small coolers. 1 block to boardwalk, shops, restaurants. Cape Lookout National Seashore nearby. 5 m to ocean.
Location S coastal NC. 45 m S of New Bern, 100 m N of Wilmington, 150 m SE of Raleigh. Historic district, corner Craven & Ann Sts. From Hwy. 70, turn at light onto Turner St., then left on Ann St. 1 block to inn at corner.
Restrictions No smoking. No children under 12.
Credit cards None accepted.
Rates Room only (midweek), $69–79 double. B&B, $79–115 double, $73–115 single. Extra person, $15. 10% discount for 6-day stays or equivalent. 2-night weekend minimum. Packages available.
Extras Airport/station pickup.

BELHAVEN

River Forest Manor ¢ ✕
600 East Main Street, 27810

Tel: 919–943–2151
In NC: 800–346–2151

Construction of River Forest Manor was started in 1899 by John Aaron Wilkinson, a local lumber and railroad magnate. It took five years to complete the mansion, with its hand-carved ceilings, oak mantels for the eleven fireplaces, sparkling cut glass leaded into the windows, crystal chandeliers, and dining room tapestries. In 1947 it was purchased by Axson Smith, whose widow and sons still operate the hotel today. In 1991 an addition, using the same detailing as found in the original home, was built to house the bar and lounge. Guest rooms are decorated with Victorian furnishings. The 65-dish buffet smorgasbord is available daily from 6 to 9 P.M., with brunch served on Sundays from 10 A.M. to 2 P.M.

"River Forest Manor is a beautiful Georgian-style mansion. It is located on the intercoastal waterway, and therefore has a great many transient boaters either staying in the inn or on their boats moored at adjacent docks. The hotel also has an all-you-can-eat buffet with local vegetable and seafood favorites each night. Both locals and guests eat there; it is a 'must' for any waterway traffic. The owners and staff are friendly, helpful, and gracious. All in all, both the food and the accommodations were a great experience." *(Leneta Appleby)* "Our room had an elaborate carved headboard, a marble-topped table and dresser, and a Victorian settee, along with such modern touches as a telephone and TV." *(Maureen Bennett)* Additional comments required.

Open All year. Restaurant closed Jan. 15 to March 15.
Rooms 3 suites, 7 doubles, 1 cottage—all with private bath and/or shower, telephone, TV, desk, air-conditioning, fan.
Facilities Restaurant, bar/lounge, game room with pool table. 4½ acres with hot tub, tennis court, marina, dock service, nautical supplies, groceries, laundromat. On Pungo River, Inland Waterway.
Location N coastal NC. Beaufort County, 100 m S of Norfolk, VA, 30 m W of Washington, 50 m W of Greenville.

Credit cards MC, Visa.
Rates Room only, $60–75 double in inn, $45–75 double in annex. Extra person, $10. Full breakfast served, extra charge. Buffet dinner, $13; ½ price for children under 12.
Extras Crib.

BLACK MOUNTAIN

The Red Rocker Inn ¢ ✗   *Tel:* 704–669–5991
136 North Dougherty Street, 28711

"The Red Rocker Inn is located in a small, friendly mountain town. The innkeepers, Fred and Pat Eshleman, are warm, very efficient, and hospitable. The inn is an old-fashioned, three-story beige house with wraparound porch, all sizes of red rockers, and a red swing. The walkway is lined with red and white impatiens and geraniums. Each guest room has a name reflecting its decor—the Music Room has old musical instruments and wallpaper with a musical theme; the Preacher's Room has a stained glass window and a prayer bench. You are welcomed as you are seated for dinner, then the innkeeper blesses the meal, served by the courteous and youthful staff. All rooms and grounds are fresh and clean, the lighting and parking ample." *(Ruth Fox & Alice Johnson)*

"The red and white decor, with lace tablecloths, flowers, and beautiful cut-glass stem ware, sets the mood. Servings are generous, and the fried chicken, steak and gravy, country ham, and trout are irresistible. Making your selection of dessert may be the most difficult decision you face all day: Pea-pickin' cake, blackberry cobbler with homemade ice cream, or southern chocolate pecan pie." *(Mrs. J. Lloyd Lanier)* More comments needed.

Open May 1 to Oct. 31.
Rooms 18 doubles—all with private bath and/or shower, fan. 1 with fireplace.
Facilities Restaurant, game room with piano; living room with library, fireplace; sun room with games, puzzles, cards. 1½ acres with flower garden, swings. Swimming pool, tennis, golf, fishing, hiking nearby.
Location W NC, 17 m E of Asheville. 2 blocks from center. Take Exit 64 off I-40 to center of town, turn left and go 2 blocks, then right on Dougherty St. to inn on top of hill.
Restrictions No smoking, no alcohol in public rooms. Parking limited. Children must be well supervised.
Credit cards None accepted.
Rates Room only, $40–70 double, $35–65 single, plus 8% room tax and 17% service tax. Extra person, $10. Full breakfast, $7.50. Alc lunch, $8; alc dinner, $16. Children's menu ½ price.
Extras Limited wheelchair access.

BLOWING ROCK

Blowing Rock is a resort town along the Blue Ridge Parkway, named for a unique rock formation, where air currents from the Johns River Gorge

213

return light objects thrown toward the rock. The town has many attractive craft shops. It's located in northwestern North Carolina's High Country, approximately 7 miles south of Boone, and 110 miles northwest of Charlotte. Blowing Rock is known as the "ski capital of the south." With an elevation of almost 4,000 feet, it also offers cool summers and beautiful fall foliage; one reader warned that summer fog and mist can result in days when you never see the mountain peaks.

Information please: We'd like to hear more about **Grandma Jean's B&B** (209 Meadowview Drive, Boone 28607; 704–262–3670) in nearby Boone, about 7 miles north. This renovated 1920s cottage offers homey rooms in an intimate homestay setting, where "you can relax on the front porch and have another cup of coffee with Grandma." Rates are very reasonable and include a continental breakfast.

We'd especially like reports on the **Ragged Garden Inn** (Sunset Drive, Box 1927, 28605; 704–295–9703) listed in many previous editions of this guide, and owned by Joyce and Joe Villani. Our most recent report noted that the food is as excellent as ever ("the dining room is the best part of the inn"), but we'd like more feedback on the rooms. Comments?

Another long-time entry is the **Eseeola Lodge** (Linville 28646; 704–733–4311), under the same ownership for nearly fifty years. The Eseeola is an old-time mountain resort, open for the summer season, with a restaurant, swimming pool, riding and hiking trails, golf course, and children's program. It's located about 15 miles further south down the Blue Ridge Parkway from Blowing Rock.

Gideon Ridge Inn   *Tel:* 704–295–3644
6148 Gideon Ridge Road, P.O. Box 1929, 28605

The Gideon Ridge Inn was built in 1939 as an elegant yet rustic stone mansion, and it offers beautiful views of the Blue Ridge Mountains. In 1983 Cobb and Jane Milner converted this house to an inn, and have furnished the rooms with many antiques. Jane says that "most of our guests are couples who come to enjoy a break from their routines, or to celebrate special occasions. They do not come to be entertained, but to enjoy our beautiful, restful atmosphere. They leaf through our art books and listen to Mozart and Bach at breakfast; they hike, play bridge, shop for crafts and antiques."

"Located at the end of a quiet street, the inn is set on a high ridge with spectacular mountain views. The easy charm of Cobb and Jane Milner combined with their immaculate and beautifully maintained inn creates a perfect backdrop for a relaxing vacation. The bedrooms are spacious, comfortable; the baths are thoughtfully provided with ample storage space for cosmetics. You always feel at home and well cared for, whether you are being served one of Jane's special breakfasts with homemade scones in the garden room, or you are curling up on the sofa, reading in front of the fire in the large living room, after a day of hiking." *(Elizabeth Rupp)*

"Guests' needs are always well provided for, with big thick towels, cozy comforters, and quiet advice and assistance with dinner reservations given when requested. The stone terrace that wraps around the inn is a

BREVARD

perfect place to watch the moon rise over the mountains, serenaded by the frogs, crickets, and owls. A full breakfast is prepared and served by the Milners; Jane ideally balances the textures, colors, and tastes in her presentation of the meal." *(Jane & Luther Manners)* "The whole area of Blowing Rock is stunning, even in winter. We were told that it gets quite crowded in summer; in January it was deserted and charming. For dinner, the owners sent us to the Speckled Trout, where we enjoyed the best trout and oysters I've ever had. The inn's grounds are perfect for strolling and the view is outstanding." *(BLK)*

"We stayed in the Carriage Room, the newest guest room, which was large, squeaky clean, and furnished with American antiques, including a four-poster bed. Breakfast included Carolina specialties like Smithfield ham sausage." *(Deborah Reese)* "Just as described in your last edition, only better." *(E. Nepomechie)*

Minor niggle: "A low-cal, low cholesterol breakfast alternative would be welcome."

Open All year.
Rooms 8 doubles—all with private bath and/or shower, desk, fan; some with fireplaces.
Facilities Dining room, living room, library with TV, fireplace, terrace. 5 1/2 acres with herb garden, wooded paths. 5 m to downhill skiing.
Location 1 1/2 m to town, 1/4 m W of Rte. 321.
Restrictions No smoking in guest rooms, living or dining room. No children under 12.
Credit cards Amex, MC, Visa.
Rates B&B, $80–120 double, $70–110 single. 2-night weekend minimum during summer, fall months.

BREVARD

The Red House Inn ¢   *Tel:* 704–884–9349
412 West Probart Street, 28712

Built in 1851 as a trading post, The Red House survived attempts to destroy it during the Civil War and many subsequent years of neglect. As the area developed, the building was used in turn as the railroad station, the courthouse, a school, and finally, in 1984, a B&B restored by Lynne Ong. Rooms are decorated with turn-of-the-century antiques, and rates include a full breakfast of eggs, homemade biscuits and muffins, jams, and bacon or sausage, with plenty of coffee and tea. Area attractions include the Brevard Music Center, Flat Rock Playhouse, and numerous hiking trails and waterfalls.

"We had one of the two rooms at the front, which meant we had use of the second-floor veranda. Our room had twin beds and was furnished with Victorian antiques, as was the rest of the house. We loved our hostess, Lynne—she was a great conversationalist and well informed about the area. We enjoyed her cheerful voice singing in the kitchen in the morning, and her friendly smile when serving the delicious French toast for breakfast. The location was great and we had the most beautiful

215

view traveling between Brevard and Waynesville—the Pisgah National Forest and many waterfalls set against the fall foliage. We spent our second day at the Waynesville craft fair, and felt like we were coming home when we returned to the inn at night. The ambiance was wonderful, our hostess delightful, and the combination of Victoriana and modern-day comfort most pleasing." *(April Burwell)*

Little quibbles: "Because there were only three tables, there were two seatings for breakfast; everyone tried to be the first downstairs to make the first seating, which was a bit awkward. Also, low-fat milk is not my choice for a great cup of tea." Your comments welcome.

Open May through Dec.
Rooms 1 suite, 5 doubles—1 with full private bath, 5 with maximum of 4 people sharing bath. All with desk; some with porches.
Facilities Dining room, living room, den, sun porch.
Location W NC. Blue Ridge Mountains, 30 m S of Asheville. 1 block N of Main St., 4 blocks from center.
Restrictions No smoking. No children under 7.
Credit cards None accepted.
Rates B&B, $47–60 suite or double. No tipping. 7th night free.
Extras Airport/station pickup. Babysitting. Spanish spoken.

BRYSON CITY

Located just two miles from the entrance to the Great Smoky Mountains National Park, Bryson City is a center for visitors coming to enjoy hiking, rafting, canoeing, fishing, swimming, horseback riding, and skiing in the Smokies. It's 60 miles west of Asheville, in western North Carolina.

Report from a British contributor about the area: "As you drift down the wonderful Blue Ridge Parkway you tend to assume that the Smokey Mountains, the highest part of the range will be the most beautiful part of all, which is indeed true of the mountain and the road itself. *But*, at either end of the road, and impossible to avoid, are Gatlinburg [Tennessee] and Cherokee. Gatlinburg is merely unbridled development. Cherokee, on the other hand, is truly dreadful. Uncontrolled shabby ribbon development is patrolled by Indians in hopelessly unauthentic dress, waiting to be humiliated by tourists with their cameras at the ready." *(Richard Gollin)* To minimize such, we'd suggest seeking out two valid experiences, the Oconaluftee Indian Village, and "Unto these Hills," a dramatic presentation of Cherokee history.

Folkestone Inn ¢   *Tel: 704–488–2730*
767 West Deep Creek Road, 28713

Owners Norma and Peter Joyce note that "our inn attracts people who love the outdoors, mountains, streams, rivers, and waterfalls; people who like hiking, white water rafting, fishing, and wildlife. Our guests are mainly from larger cities who want to get away to the tranquility of mountain living." The country atmosphere is enhanced by the inn itself; a farmhouse built in the 1920s and renovated in 1988, with stone floors and pressed tin ceilings in the ground floor guest rooms, a mix of antiques

216

throughout the house, and a claw foot tub in every bathroom. Porches on both levels of the house provide a quiet spot for relaxing. Rates include a full English/southern breakfast of meat, eggs, freshly baked breads, and fruit.

"Norma Joyce is from Chattanooga, and Peter is from England; one of their daughters, sometimes home on a working vacation, is a graduate of the Cordon Bleu cooking school in London. We enjoyed a delicious tea with fresh baked scones, and then toured the inn. My favorites were the delightfully cool rooms built into the stone foundation with tin ceilings. A babbling brook meanders just below the inn at the edge of the Great Smoky Mountains National Park." *(Jonathan Douglas)*

"From the moment we arrived and shared a glass of wine, until the last cup of coffee on the day we left, we felt like weekend guests at a friend's country home. Different areas of the inn evoke varying moods, from English pub with cobblestone floors, to Victorian, to country. The mix works well, and there are lots of books, magazines, and rockers on the front porch. The location is delightful, within walking distance of the park entrance, and 15 minutes to Nantahala River rafting." *(Susan Boehlke)*

"The Joyces went out of their way to make us comfortable—Norma agreeably prepared low cholesterol breakfasts for my husband. Our bed was turned down at night and a bit of brandy and a rose was left on the nightstand." *(Donna Sites)* "The inn is away from traffic and busy parts of the city and the view is splendid. The food is definitely something to brag about—always different and always delicious." *(Denise Gelinas, also Carol & Jim Schneider)* "A real home with wonderful advice on local trips, outstanding breakfasts, a chorus of bird songs around you, and total quiet at night." *(Gerhard Bedding)*

Open All year.
Rooms 1 suite, 8 doubles—all with private bath with hand-held shower, fan. 3 with private balcony.
Facilities Dining room, living room with woodstove, piano, stereo; library with books, porch. 3½ acres with croquet, Ping-Pong. Children's play equipment available. Fishing, tubing, white water rafting, boating, swimming nearby.
Location Swain County. 60 m W of Asheville. 150 m NE of Atlanta. 2 m from center of town.
Restrictions No smoking. "Well-behaved children welcome."
Credit cards None accepted.
Rates B&B, $67–79 suite, $50–74 double, $45–73 single. Extra adult, $20; extra child, $10. 2-night weekend minimum April–Nov. and holidays; 3-night minimum Thanksgiving.
Extras Airport pickup, $25.

Fryemont Inn ¢ 🏃 ✕

Tel: 704–488–2159

Fryemont Road, P.O. Box 459, 28713

Listed on the National Register of Historic Places, the Fryemont was built in 1923 by timber baron Amos Frye, who used the region's finest chest-nut, oak, and maple. Long-time owners are Sue and George Brown, and their son and daughter-in-law George Brown IV and Monica.

With open rafters and huge stone fireplaces, the inn's public rooms are rustically handsome, while the chestnut-paneled guest rooms are furnished with a mixture of antiques and ordinary motel-type furnishings. Recent changes include the conversion of what was originally an adjacent cottage into four two-level air-conditioned suites with fireplaces and loft bedrooms. The dinner menu includes both country mountain cooking and continental specialties. Trout rolled in cornmeal and deep fried, southern fried chicken, and country ham with red-eye gravy are favorites in the first category; trout sautéed with mushrooms and white wine, and garlic shrimp in the latter.

"Very quaint, quiet hideaway close to the Smoky Mountains. Excellent meals cooked by owners Sue and George Brown. Nice lobby and porch for relaxing." *(Wendy F. Leader)* "This old favorite has stood the test of time well. Service throughout is charming and efficient, and the rooms large, clean, and comfortable. The food is very good, the dining room rustic but elegant. Common areas inviting, with lots of room for relaxing." *(Melanie McKeever)* "Just as described in your book. Friendly and helpful staff made our stay enjoyable." *(E. Nepomechie)*

Minor quibble: "Brighter lighting in the bedroom."

Open April through Oct. Cottage rooms available all year.
Rooms 10 suites, 30 doubles—all with full private bath and/or shower, desk. Cottage suites with fireplace, TV, wet bar.
Facilities Restaurant; lobby with fireplace, games, TV; library; laundry room; porch. 7 acres with basketball, shuffleboard, swimming pool, tennis court.
Location 1 block to town. From Rte. 74 (Great Smoky Mt. Expressway), turn right (N) into town; right again on Fryemont Rd. to inn on right.
Restrictions No children in cottages.
Credit cards MC, Visa.
Rates MAP, $120–160 suite, $80–105 double, $60–73 single. Extra person, $10–30; children age 2–10, $18. 2-night weekend minimum. Picnic lunch, $3–7; prix fixe dinner, $12–16; reduced prices for children. Senior discount.
Extras Crib, babysitting.

Hemlock Inn ¢ ♏ ✕   *Tel:* 704–488–2885
P.O. Drawer EE, Galbreath Creek Road, 28713

Once a mountain farm, the Hemlock Inn opened in 1952, and has been owned and operated by John and Ella Jo Shell since 1969. In 1988, their daughter Elaine and her husband, Morris White, joined them as innkeepers.

High, cool, quiet, and restful, with an informal family atmosphere, the Hemlock Inn is situated on top of a small mountain (elevation 2300 feet) on the edge of the Great Smoky Mountains National Park. Rooms and cabins are furnished in country antiques and pieces made by mountain craftspeople. Guests enjoy rafting, tubing, and hiking in the surrounding mountains, or just admiring the mountain views from a porch rocker. Breakfast is served promptly at 8:30 A.M., with dinner at 6:00 P.M.; but no other activities are scheduled. Heaping platters of country ham, fried chicken, or other traditional favorites, homemade biscuits or yeast rolls with mountain honey, just-picked corn, or apple and pumpkin chips are brought to the lazy Susans in the middle of each large round table in the dining room.

We applaud the inn's exceptional fee structure; tipping is not permitted, and no service charge is applied. Bravo!

"The owners work hard to keep improving the inn by updating bathrooms, adding new carpets, wallpaper, and more. Reading and dressing lights are good, with plenty of windows overlooking the lovely mountains. We enjoy hiking the short trails on the inn's property, and the beautiful views from the swings and easy chairs on the inn's covered terrace. The friendly concern of the owners and staff, combined with the friendships formed at the big round tables makes for happy vacations. The honest-to-goodness home-cooked food is just wonderful, with meals prepared from special recipes, and an ample choice of entrées, farm-fresh vegetables, homemade preserves, breads, and desserts. Many guests return year after year to the Hemlock." *(Doris & A.R. Tyson)*

"The Shells and the Whites are warm, caring people who sincerely welcome you. Guests of all ages are here, and it is delightful to see children having a terrific time without television. After John says the blessing, we sit down to enjoy a meal of regional foods, and adventures are shared and new friends are made." *(Cheri & Larry Brown)*

Open Late April through Oct.
Rooms 3 cabins, 23 doubles—all with private bath and/or shower, fan. Most with desk, fireplace. Some with porch or deck.
Facilities Dining room with fireplace, library and sun room with books. 64 acres with hiking. 3 m to Deep Creek for tubing, fishing.
Location 3 m N of town. Go N on Hwy. 19 for 2 m, then turn left at Hemlock Inn sign. Go 1 m to driveway on left.
Restrictions No alcohol in public rooms. No smoking in dining room.
Credit cards None accepted.
Rates MAP, $120–157 cabin (for two people), $115–157 double, $95–130 single. Extra adult, $40; extra child age 2-15, $20. No tipping. Crib, $1 per night; roll-away bed, $3 per night. Box lunch, $3; prix fixe dinner, $11.50. 1-2 week minimum stay in cabins; 2-3 day holiday weekend minimum in main house.
Extras Wheelchair access. Crib.

Randolph House ¢
Fryemont Road, P.O. Box 816, 28713

Tel: 704–488–3472
Off-season: 404–938–2268

Set on a mountain shelf overlooking Bryson City, the Randolph House was built in 1895, and is today owned by Ruth and Bill Adams. The inn is furnished with period antiques, some dating back to the 1850s, and many are original to the inn. Although Ruth is a descendant of Amos Frye, who built this mountain mansion, she is best known today for her talents in the kitchen. Rates include a full country breakfast and dinner; favorite entrées include veal Marsala, shrimp scampi, Cornish game hen, local mountain trout, and oven fried chicken, with homemade fruit cobblers, apple or Key lime pie among the dessert specialties.

"Next door to the Fryemont Inn, this charming inn offers a more intimate alternative. It is impeccably maintained and, having tracked down Mrs. Adams in her kitchen, I can attest to the fact that it is sparklingly clean." *(Jonathan Douglas)* More reports welcome.

Open April–Oct.
Rooms 6 doubles—3 with private bath, 3 with shared bath. All with fan. Some with telephone, TV, air-conditioning.

Facilities Dining room, living room with fireplace, porch, books, TV, stereo. Garden with lily pond.
Location At intersection of Rtes. 19 and 74, just W of Bryson City.
Restrictions No smoking in guest rooms. Young children discouraged.
Credit cards Amex, MC, Visa.
Rates MAP, $100–130 double. B&B, $65–75 double. Extra person, $35–55. 10% senior, AAA, travel agent discount. Reduced rates for families.
Extras One room has wheelchair access. Crib.

CASHIERS

Also recommended: Perched on the edge of the Chattooga River Valley is the **Millstone Inn** (Highway 64 West, P.O. Box 949, 28717; 704–743–2737). Built in the 1930s for the community's first physician, the Millstone has cedar-beamed ceilings, pine-paneled walls, rock maple floors, and a decor incorporating quilts, Oriental rugs, and antique paintings and prints. Guest rooms have private baths, mountain or garden views, and some have a kitchen. Breakfast is served in the glass-enclosed porch facing Whiteside Mountain. *(Louise & Richard Weithas)*

High Hampton Inn 👫 ✕ 🎾
Highway 107 South, P.O. Box 338, 28717

Tel: 704–743–2411
800–334–2551
In NC: 800–222–6954

At an elevation of 3,600 feet, High Hampton was built as the private summer home of the Hamptons of South Carolina. It was purchased by the McKee family in 1922, who have retained its traditional atmosphere. Accommodations are plain and rustic, with walls of sawmill-finished pine and sturdy, mountain-crafted furniture. The food is good, plain country cooking, with homemade breads and pastries and home-grown vegetables. Coats and ties are required at dinner. Recent reports confirm the continued validity of these comments:

"We have been going to High Hampton frequently since 1946 and think it is a delightful place. William D. McKee, Jr., has been assisting his father and is well-trained to continue the High Hampton's traditional hospitality. Many of the guests are also the third generation to enjoy High Hampton; we feel that its popularity is due to the personal attention guests receive from the owners. The food and accommodations are excellent, the scenery beautiful, and the activities numerous. They have a marvelous children's program, supervised by an excellent staff. *(Mr. & Mrs. Charles Rawls)*

"I have stayed at High Hampton for 25 years, and find it unique. It has beauty, charm, friendliness, good food, and excellent management. A person traveling alone would find it very informal and friendly. Cashiers is a lovely little village with lots of gift shops." *(Mrs. Theodore Palmer)*

"The cottages and rooms are rustic, basic, comfortable but not elaborate. The lodge is charming, with a huge 4-sided fireplace, where guests gather to play games and to visit. The food is home-cooked Southern. The grounds are magnificent, with a huge dahlia garden where guests are invited to cut a bouquet for their room." *(Betty Sadler, also Louise and Richard Weithas)*

Open April through Nov.
Rooms 7 suites, 123 doubles—all with private bath, desk, fan, deck. Some with fireplace. Some cottages available. 98 rooms in annex.
Facilities Dining rooms, living/game/TV room, piano/organ entertainment in lounge. 1,200 acres with gardens, lake, tennis, 18-hole golf course, archery, canoeing, fishing, hiking, waterfalls, teen center, children's program.
Location SW NC, 60 m SW of Asheville, 155 m N of Atlanta, GA. 2 m S of Cashiers on Hwy. 107.
Credit cards Amex, MC, Visa.
Rates Full board, $65–84 per person, double; $76–88 single. Extra person, $46–53. No tipping, no service charge. Reduced rates for children. Tennis, golf packages available. Extra charges for facilities use, excluding packages. Weekly, monthly discounts.
Extras Some rooms have wheelchair access. Airport/station pickup, $35–50. Kennel for pets. Crib, babysitting, play equipment, games.

CHAPEL HILL

Located in central North Carolina, Chapel Hill is best known as the home of the main campus of the University of North Carolina.

Information please: Though it doesn't have the Carolina Inn's location, for luxury hotel amenities (and a four-diamond AAA rating), including marble-lined baths, health spa, and limousine service, topped off with a continental breakfast, try **The Siena** (1505 East Franklin Street, P.O. Box 2561, 27515; 919–929–4000 or 800–223–7379). Inspired by its Italian namesake, the 80-room hotel has a decor of stone and stucco, columns and arches, with contemporary Italian designer fabrics and furniture. Its restaurant, Il Palio, named for Sienna's famous festival, has gained an excellent reputation for Northern Italian cuisine. Double rates are $100–130; inquire about corporate and AAA discounts.Comments?

Also recommended: For an additional Chapel Hill–area entry, see Pittsboro, for a description of **Fearrington House**.

Carolina Inn ¢ 👫 ✗
Corner of Cameron and Columbia
P.O. Box 1110, 27514

Tel: 919–933–2001
800–962–8519

Built in 1924 in the Colonial Revival style and donated to the University of North Carolina, the Carolina Inn projects a image of the genteel, formal Old South in its handsome lobby and traditional guest rooms. There was some talk of the inn closing, but it appears that money is being invested toward refurbishing the property instead. "The food is adequate and predictable, the service and cleanliness acceptable. The guest rooms and baths are small, typical of the period, but have been redecorated recently. Its key advantage is its position on the UNC campus." *(Ann Baxter)*

"Pleasant and attractive place to stay, with pleasant dining room and a cafeteria." *(Bette Cooper)* "Our room was very small but clean; the cafeteria-style breakfast was good and reasonably priced." *(Pat Torpie)* "For persons doing business on the university campus (where parking is at an extreme premium), its convenient location is second to none." *(James Utt)*

Open All year.
Rooms 140 suites & doubles—all with private bath and/or shower, telephone, TV. Some with radio.
Facilities Lobby, restaurant, cafeteria, off-street parking.
Location 1 block from Franklin St.; across st. from Ackland Museum of Art. ½ m S of Rte. 86.
Credit cards Amex, CB, Discover, MC, Visa.
Rates Room only, $90–125 suite, $55–80 double, $45–75 single. Extra person, $10. No charge for children under 16. Rollaway bed, $10.
Extras Airport/station pickup.

The Inn at Bingham School ¢   *Tel:* 919–563–5583
Mebane-Oaks Road, P.O. Box 267, 27515

A combination of Greek Revival and Federalist styles, The Inn at Bingham School provides elegant accommodation in rooms in the main house, as well as in a log cabin dating back to 1791.

"Although the Bingham School, operating between 1845 and 1865 as a preparatory school for the University of North Carolina, no longer stands, Jane and Bob Kelly did a truly first-class restoration of the head-master's home. They have created a warm inn, rich in architectural detail and southern hospitality, set in the rolling farmland of central North Carolina. The southern breakfast is a treat of the highest order, with homemade heart-shaped biscuits, grits, fresh country eggs, baked apples, sausage or bacon, and a variety of fruit. Jane Kelly's fresh muffins with strawberry butter are not to be missed. During football season, she prepares an egg casserole second to none, to prepare her guests for the afternoon at Keenan Stadium, home of the Tarheels. Gracious proprietors, outstanding architecture, period antique furnishings in comfortable set-tings, the Carolina countryside, and Jane Kelly's cooking and baking all combine to make our stays memorable." *(Nancy Harrison & Nelson Ormsby)*

"A sign near the door says 'The Outer World,' and that's how we felt. Though convenient to Carrboro and Chapel Hill, this inn is an oasis of calm. The Kellys are excellent advisors on restaurants; they have a good collection of menus, and had even printed up maps to the various places." *(Celia McCullough & Gary Kaplan)*

Open All year. Closed Dec. 15 to Jan. 1.
Rooms 1 suite, 5 doubles—all with private bath and/or shower, radio, TV, desk, air-conditioning. 2 with whirlpool tubs, fan. 4 with fireplace.
Facilities Common room with fireplace, game table; dining room, sun-room. 10 acres with croquet. Golf, tennis nearby.
Location 11 m W of Carrboro/Chapel Hill, about 10 m S of I-85.
Restrictions No children under 12.

Credit cards None accepted.
Rates B&B, $110 suite, $85 double, $75 single. Extra person, $15. 2-night minimum peak weekends.
Extras Airport pickup.

CHARLOTTE

Located in the southwestern part of the state, Charlotte is one of North Carolina's largest cities, as well as a major textile-producing center, with hundreds of factories in the surrounding area. The city is home to a number of museums and parks of interest, as well as the University of North Carolina at Charlotte.

Reader tip: "It is very difficult to find restaurants open on Sundays in Charlotte, so it is important to call in advance. Waxhaw, not too far south of the city, is a town of antique shops with excellent prices." *(Judilynn Niedercorn)*

Information please: We'd like to hear more about **The Morehead Inn** (1122 East Morehead Street, 28204; 704–376–3357), listed in previous editions and now owned by the Dunhill Development Company (see below). Located in a tree-lined residential neighborhood it is convenient to downtown Charlotte and to the nearby medical complex; the Morehead is popular with business travelers during the week, and with other travelers on the weekends.

The Dunhill Hotel ✕
237 North Tryon Street, 28202

Tel: 704–332–4141
800–252–4666

Charlotte's only Historic Landmark hotel, the ten-story Dunhill was built in 1929 as the first "all steel frame" highrise in town. Totally renovated in 1988, it has reclaimed its position as a luxury hotel, with attention given to the 18th century-style architectural detail and furnishings. Guest rooms are individually decorated, some with reproduction four-poster beds, and rates include the morning newspaper, and a breakfast of cereal, freshly baked bread and Danish, juice and coffee; complimentary wine and cheese is served in the piano bar.

"Exquisitely furnished, with a staff that is accommodating and top-notch. We had a marvelous view of Charlotte, in the center of the delightful 'Uptown' area. The food in the restaurant, the 'Thistle,' is good and priced well, and dinner was an elegant experience. Local nightlife includes jazz and nouvelle American cuisine at Jonathan's a few doors away, the Prism Bistro for Sunday brunch with a jazz combo, equidistant in the opposite direction. Not far away is the Cajun Queen with delicious authentic food. " *(Judilynn Niedercorn)*

An area for improvement: "Both the food and service at breakfast was not up to the high standards we enjoyed at dinner."

Open All year.
Rooms 60 doubles—all with private bath and/or shower, telephone, radio, TV, air-conditioning, refrigerator. 15 with whirlpool tub. Some with VCR.
Facilities Restaurant, piano bar. Nightly entertainment. Meeting and banquet facilities. Membership privileges at nearby fitness center. Parking garage.

223

Location Uptown.
Credit cards Amex, DC, Discover, MC, Visa.
Rates B&B, $75–85 double, $200 suite. Extra person, $10. Corporate, group, weekend rates. Special packages available.
Extras Wheelchair access; some rooms equipped for disabled. Airport shuttle service.

The Homeplace ¢   *Tel:* 704–365–1936
5901 Sardis Road, 28270

Peggy and Frank Dearien had never stayed in a B&B, let alone run one, when they decided to buy The Homeplace in 1984. A turn-of-the-century Victorian, the inn has been completely renovated, from the foundation to the widow's walk. Windows, insulation, wiring, plumbing, heating and air-conditioning—even the roof was redone, while the house's original hand-crafted staircase, ten-foot-high ceilings, and heart-of-pine floors were preserved. Peggy Dearien has decorated the house with Victorian and country-style furnishings; the guest rooms are done in shades of blue and rose, and many are highlighted by the primitive paintings done by Peggy's father.

"The Homeplace has airy porches, plenty of rocking chairs, and cross-stitchings everywhere. Combine that with the fact that I was greeted at the door with a pitcher of lemonade, and I felt like I was visiting Grandma." *(John Hill)* "My room was spotless, as was the entire home. Hospitality was the next best thing to going home to see your folks after a long time away. Food was superb, graciously served with an option of serving times which made it convenient to schedule personal plans. A bonus was a plate of cheese, crackers, and fresh fruit in the evening, along with homemade cookies. The grounds were lovely, the front porch inviting, the bath immaculate, the warmth pervasive." *(Lynn Grisard Fullman, also Lynn Edge)*

"Although it's located on the corner of a busy intersection, once you're in the driveway of the Homeplace, it's easy to feel as though the city is miles away. The lot is nicely wooded, and the Dearien's have landscaped it beautifully. A gazebo and the rocking chairs on the wraparound porch contribute to this home's charms. We stayed in the downstairs bedroom, which has a private entrance off the porch. The room is full of charming antiques and country touches, and the comfortable mattress and quality sheets on our Victorian highback bed made for a wonderful night's sleep. Soft drinks and fresh fruit were available in the room. Peggy began breakfast with baked apples, followed by scrambled eggs flavored with dill and wrapped in a crepe, asparagus spears, and bagels with parmesan cheese. Frank kept our water, juice, and coffee cups filled to the brim. Our most difficult decision was whether to relax in our bedroom, in the parlor, or in the hammock outside." *(Tawnya & Henry Fabian)*

"The bathrooms are well stocked, with plenty of towels, shampoos, lotions, razors, and such. Lots of extra hangers in the closet, and a firm mattress on the bed. The tantalizing smells coming from the kitchen made this truly a home away from home." *(Dianne Crawford)*

Open All year.
Room 3 doubles—all with full private bath, TV, desk, air-conditioning. Some with fan.

Facilities Dining room, living room, wraparound porch, study with TV, books, stereo. $2\frac{1}{2}$ acres with gazebo, hammock, gardens.
Location Mecklenburg County. 2 m from Rte. 74. 15 min. from center. SE Charlotte at corner of Sardis and Rama Rds. 15 min from I-77 and I-85.
Restrictions No smoking. No children under 10.
Credit cards Amex, MC, Visa.
Rates B&B, $83 double, $73 single. Extra person, $15. 2-night holiday weekend minimum.

The Inn on Providence ¢
6700 Providence Road, 28226

Tel: 704–366–6700

Shaded by tall cedars, this gracious Federal-style brick colonial, with white trim and black shutters, has been owned by Dan and Darlene McNeill since 1985. Decorating with Darlene's collection of 19th century furniture, antique quilts, and family heirlooms, they've transformed a handsome home into an exceptional B&B. According to one of our most critical contributors: "The atmosphere is both elegant and homey, with owner Darlene McNeill making it all look so effortless. The inn is clean and beautiful, quiet and restful. Our breakfast, served in the lovely dining room, was delicious—Swedish fruit soup, orange juice, puffed blueberry pancakes, and ruffled ham. The McNeills understand the importance of down pillows, percale sheets, firm mattresses, and big bath towels." *(Elizabeth L. Church)*

As we went to press, we learned that the inn was for sale; inquire further when making reservations.

Open All year.
Rooms 2 suites, 3 doubles—3 with private bath and/or shower, 2 with a maximum of 4 people sharing bath. All with radio, desk, air-conditioning, fan; 1 suite with fireplace.
Facilities Dining room, library, living room with TV, stereo, and fireplace, screened porch. 2 acres with swimming pool, flower gardens, patio. Tennis, golf nearby.
Location 10 m SE of city. On Hwy. 16 (Providence Rd.) approx. 1 m N of Hwy. 51.
Restrictions No smoking. No children under 12.
Credit cards MC, Visa.
Rates B&B, $65–80 suite, $59–79 double. 2-night holiday weekend minimum.

Still Waters ¢ 🏃
6221 Amos Smith Road, 28214

Tel: 704–399–6299

This cozy log home right on Lake Wiley has been owned by Rob and Janet Dyer since 1989. Guests can bring their own boat, and use the inn's boat ramp and dock, or just sit and enjoy the wooded surroundings, just minutes from the bustle of Charlotte. The family room has contemporary and country-style oak furniture; a wall of windows provides views of the lake through the trees. Breakfast includes orange juice, mixed fruits, sweet rolls, and breakfast steaks, buttermilk pancakes, or herbal omelets.

"Rob and Janet are friendly and accommodating, making you feel like part of the family. The food is excellent and plentiful, with a variety of just-baked goodies and homemade dishes." *(Patrick & Birgitta Dines)* "Very attentive, yet flexible hosts. Good place for children, as the Dyers have a young child." *(Martin Novom)* "It's hard to imagine that such a pretty, wooded, and quiet place could be just ten minutes from the airport. Comfortable bed, clean rooms." *(Greg Stromberg)*

Open All year.
Rooms One suite, two doubles—all with private bath and/or shower, radio, air-conditioning, refrigerator. Some with telephone, TV, desk, deck.
Facilities Living room with TV/VCR, fireplace. Family room, sun porch, deck. 2 acres with sport court. Dock, boat ramp. Golf nearby.
Location 3 m W of town. From I-85, take Sam Wilson Rd. Southbound exit. Cross Wilkinson Blvd. and turn right on Old Dowd Rd. Take 1st left onto Amos Smith Rd. Go 2 m to inn. From Airport or Billy Graham Parkway, take Old Dowd Rd. W past airport entrance. Turn left at Little Rock Rd. to stay on Old Dowd. Pass Sam Wilson Rd. and turn left on Amos Smith Rd. and go 2 m to inn.
Restrictions No smoking.
Credit cards MC, Visa.
Rates B&B, $75–95 suite, $50–75 double. Extra person, $5. 2-night weekend minimum during peak season. Reduced rates for children.
Extras Airport pickup. Crib.

CLYDE

Windsong: A Mountain Inn 🏃
120 Ferguson Ridge, 28721

Tel: 704–627–8059

Gale and Donna Livengood built their "dream inn" in 1988; they had planned to escape Chicago for a warm sunny island, but were entranced by the mountains of western North Carolina. The rooms are large, bright and airy, with cathedral-beamed ceilings, light pine logs, and Mexican Saltillo tiled floors throughout; large windows and skylights let in the mountain and woodland views. Although the inn is new, it escapes that bare look that often plagues newer inns; the Livengoods have artfully decorated the rooms with their collection of Native American art, artifacts, and rugs, and have highlighted the guest rooms with different themes: African safari, country, Alaska, and Santa Fe. "Their love of animals has extended to include a small herd of llamas which they plan to breed.

Rates include a breakfast of fruit and juice, homemade breads and muffins, and a hot entrée, perhaps buckwheat banana pancakes or egg-sausage-mushroom strata. Wine and cheese is often offered in the afternoon, and coffee and dessert after guests return from dinner.

"Donna and Gale meet you on arrival and you know instantly that they are glad you have come to visit their home. The welcome is genuine and the warmth lasts through the goodbyes at the end of your stay. The house is lovely, and rooms are large and comfortable with gorgeous views. The breakfasts are bountiful, delicious, and beautifully presented. Weather permitting, one may swim, play tennis, hike up a mountain, or stroll in the woods; on rainy days, one may curl up with a good book, listen to music, or select a movie from the large video library. *(Donah Burgess)* "Every amenity you could think of and some you might not; fabulous variety of classic movie and opera videotapes, huge tub and fireplace. Genial, generous hosts."*(Stephen Friedlander)*

Open All year.
Rooms 5 doubles—all with full private bath (shower & double soaking tub), fan, fireplace, patio or deck. Telephone, TV/VCR available by request.
Facilities Dining room, common room with wet bar, TV/VCR, tape library, pool table, books, games, piano. 25 acres with heated swimming pool, tennis court, hiking trails. 20 min. to downhill skiing. 30 min to Great Smoky Mts. National Park. 40 min. to whitewater rafting. Golf nearby.
Location W NC, Great Smoky Mts. region. 30 m W of Asheville. From I-40 take Exit 24. Go N on Rte. 209 for 2 1/2 m and turn left on Riverside Dr. Go 2 m and turn right on Ferguson Cove Loop. Stay to the left and go 1 m to inn.
Restrictions No smoking. No children under 12.
Credit cards MC, Visa.
Rates B&B, $80–85 double, $72–77 single. Extra person, $20. 10% discount for 7-night stay.

DILLSBORO

Squire Watkins Inn ¢   *Tel:* 704–586–5644
Haywood Road, P.O. Box 430, 28725

J.C. and Flora Watkins were among Dillsboro's first settlers when they built their home in the 1880s. Unfortunately, J.C. died quite young, leaving Flora with a heavily mortgaged house and business, and a large family to raise. The sheriff arrived with foreclosure papers and the house was to be sold at auction. Flora and her son wrote letters to 150 Masonic Lodges, explaining the situation, and enough money arrived to hold off the sale and save the family home. Flora opened the house to boarders, but when she found some of them drinking and gambling up on the widow's walk, she had the railing (and the boarders) removed. The inn stayed in the Watkins family until it was purchased and restored (including the railing) in 1983 by the Wertenberger family.

"The location is very convenient, just off the highway leading to Cherokee; the national park is less than an hour away. Dillsboro itself is crammed with good-quality arts and crafts shops, unlike the over-commercialized town of Cherokee. Tom and Emma Wertenberger are easy people to talk with, and adept at including everyone in the conversation. My room was a delight—quiet, sunny, lovely furnishings, and sparkling clean, just like the rest of the inn." *(Patricia Harrington)*

"The house is beautifully decorated throughout, and Emma and Tom are the most charming of hosts. Both go out of their way to make your stay memorable, and full of suggested activities." *(Nancy Pruitt)* "We felt like royalty sitting down to breakfast at a table arranged with china, silver, and fresh flowers. The tantalizing aromas and tastes of Emma's homemade casseroles and breads served with fresh fruit, juice, and cereals were complemented by Tom's wonderful service. After a day of adventure, how nice to return to share the excitement over cups of hot tea or coffee. Then off to bed to find our covers turned down and a wonderful surprise on our nightstand." *(Linda Rueff)*

"The inn is restored to its 1880s charm and its beauty is enhanced by tasteful antiques. Our pleasant room was large, bright, and comfortable."

(Tom & Mary Minges) "A lovely and welcoming old house, beautifully furnished. An old pub just opposite does fine meals. " *(Richard Gollin)*

Open All year.
Rooms 2 suites, 3 doubles—all with private bath and/or shower, desk. 3 cottages—all with private bath, kitchen or kitchenette, fireplace.
Facilities Parlor; game room; living room with piano, books; sun porch with books, magazines, games; gift shop. 3½ acres with gardens, pond. Stream, lake fishing, horseback riding, white-water rafting, canoeing nearby.
Location W NC, 50 m W of Asheville. 2 blocks from town. At intersection of U.S. 441 and Haywood Rd.
Restrictions No children under 12 in inn; any age in cottages.
Credit cards None accepted.
Rates Room only, $60–75 cottage. B&B, $73 suite, $68 double, $58 single. Extra person (inn), $12.50, (cottage), $7. Weekly rates available for cottages.
Extras Crib for cottages only. Airport/station pickup.

DUCK

Information please: In neighboring Kill Devil Hills is **Ye Olde Cherokee Inn**, with six reasonably priced guest rooms just 600 feet from the beach (500 North Virginia Dare Trail, Kill Devil Hills 27948; 919–441–6127 or 800–832–0622).

Sanderling Inn 🛏 ✕ 🎋   *Tel:* 919–261–4111
1461 Duck Road, 27949

As much as we love historic old inns, we are equally delighted when readers enthuse about contemporary inns built with style and distinction. The Sanderling is just such a place. Traditional beach front architecture is combined with a modern sense of space, and the decor combines natural oak with wicker, soft pastel fabrics, and Audubon prints. In an adjacent building is the inn's restaurant, housed in a restored turn-of-the-century lifesaving station; shrimp is a particular specialty, but other local favorites include pan-fried chicken with apple fritters, Carolina duckling with black cherry sauce, sweet-potato muffins, and homemade ice cream. A continental breakfast is provided for guests, in addition to afternoon wine and hors d'oeuvres, and a welcoming wine and fruit basket.

"The Sanderling is located on the Outer Banks of North Carolina, north of the shopping strip and tourist area. The inn is near the town of Duck, which has good shops for browsing. The restaurant adjacent to the inn serves extensive breakfasts, lunches, and gourmet dinners." *(Carolyn Myles)*

"Beautifully decorated with bird models and prints. Fortunately, the restaurant is very good, since there are few alternatives nearby." *(Michael Crick)* "Luxurious common rooms with working fireplaces, current magazines and best sellers. Every room has an outstanding view of either ocean or Currituck Sound. The recent opening of the health club gave us a way to fill the time during the occasional rainy day." *(Lana Alukonis)*

"In a relatively unspoiled part of the Outer Banks, the inn overlooks a beautiful, vast private beach. Superbly outfitted rooms, tastefully decorated." *(JM)* "We felt pampered from the minute we walked into the lobby. Our room was huge and spotless. Awaiting us when walked into our room was a wine, cheese, and fruit basket and a handwritten note from the management. We spent relaxing days going from the private beach to the pool to the private deck off our room to the rocking chairs on the front porch to the whirlpool. Sigh. . ." *(Rebecca Anderson)*

Open All year.
Rooms 4 suites, 56 doubles—all with full private bath, telephone, TV, radio, desk, air-conditioning, fan, kitchenette or wet bar, porch. 28 rooms in main inn; all others in 2 separate buildings.
Facilities Restaurant; bar with rooftop deck; library with fireplace; living room with TV/VCR, games; meeting facilities; gallery. Health club with indoor racquet ball, hot tub, private beach, swimming pool, tennis courts. Golf, jogging trails nearby.
Location NE NC, Outer Banks. 80 m SE of Norfolk, VA. 5 m N of Duck. Take Rte. 158 or 64 onto Outer Banks. From Kitty Hawk, go N approx. 12 m to Sanderling.
Restrictions No cigar or pipe smoking in restaurant.
Credit cards Amex, MC, Visa.
Rates B&B, $200–250 suite, $90–200 double. Extra person, $15–30. 2-night weekend minimum. 10% discount 7-night stay or 5-night Sun.–Fri. Corporate rates. New Year's Eve, July 3 Birthday packages. Alc breakfast, $5–9; alc lunch, $8–11; alc dinner, $25–30. 15% service in restaurant.
Extras Wheelchair access; some rooms equipped for disabled. Station pickup, fee charged. Crib, $10; babysitting. Spanish spoken.

DURHAM

Arrowhead Inn   *Tel:* 919–477–8430
106 Mason Road, 27712

The Arrowhead dates from 1775, when it was a large slave-holding property. Owners Jerry and Barbara Ryan have preserved the inn's colonial architecture, and have decorated the rooms in a homey and comfortable style, ranging from colonial through Victorian. A five-foot stone arrowhead stands by the door; erected sixty years ago, it once marked the Great Trading Path to the Smokies, which carried Indians, and then white settlers, to the West. Rates include afternoon refreshments and a full country breakfast.

"Our room had a complimentary bowl of fruit and a clean, quiet room with a fireplace and a door onto the back patio. This home has been carefully restored and charmingly furnished in period. The bathrooms that have been added are modern and spotless. The Ryans provided us with maps, brochures, and discount coupons for area attractions." *(John & Kris Driessen)*

"We stayed in one of the new rooms in the carriage house, with beautiful country-style antique furnishings and primitive quilts." *(Rachel Gorlin)* "The Ryans are personable hosts, ready for conversation when guests wish, but otherwise busy behind the scenes. Clean comfortable room, firm beds, attractive grounds." *(James & Janice Utt)*

"A gracious home, attentive innkeepers. We had left a jacket behind, and discovered it after one hour's drive; when we called it had already been mailed at the post office. Our room had a beautiful quilt and comfortable brass bed. A different breakfast was served each day, and there were delicious cookies for snacking. Now that our son has been accepted at Duke, we can't wait for a return visit." *(Ann Wichman)* "Jerry and his daughter Kathy are great people. They booked us a table at Durham's best restaurant, Magnolia." *(Dr. Levent Cakmur)*

Open All year.
Rooms 2 suites, 7 doubles—5 with full private bath, 4 with maximum of 4 people sharing bath. All with air-conditioning, radio, desk, refrigerator. Some with telephone, TV, fireplace. 3 rooms in carriage house.
Facilities Dining room, family room with TV/VCR, games, stereo, fireplace, books; living room with fireplace, guest refrigerator. 4 acres with gardens, picnic area, swings, fish pond, children's play equipment. Tennis, golf, boating, fishing nearby.
Location Central NC. 8 m N of Durham. 7 m N of I-85. Take Rte. 501 (Duke St./Roxboro Rd.) N; look for West Point on the Eno Park. Go 3 m further N to stone arrowhead at intersection of Rte. 501 and Mason/Snow Hill Rd. to inn on left.
Restrictions No smoking in guest rooms.
Credit cards Amex, MC, Visa, Diners.
Rates B&B, $100–135 suite, $55–95 double, $50–85 single. Extra person, $10. Family discount for extended stays. Winter & summer historic house tour weekend packages.
Extras Cottage has wheelchair access. Crib, babysitting. French spoken.

EDENTON

Edenton is filled with tree-lined streets of 18th- and 19th-century houses. It's located in northern coastal North Carolina on the Albemarle Sound, 90 miles south of Norfolk, 125 miles south of Richmond, VA, and 150 miles east of Raleigh.

Reader tip: "Edenton is a lovely town off the beaten track. The oldest courthouse in the nation is there, and I would particularly recommend a visit to the charming St. Paul's Episcopal Church (1736)." *(Harrison Gardner)*

Information please: Each of the nine guest rooms at the **Granville Queen Inn** (108 South Granville Street, 27932; 919–482–5296) is a "Queen," from the Queen of Egypt with imported bronze sphinxes and tented seating area, to the Peaches and Queen with its ornate Victorian furniture and lacy accents. This turn-of-the-century building features elaborate, and sometimes unusual accessories in all rooms, including the private baths. A five-course breakfast is served, which includes homemade muffins, a choice of entrées, such as grilled chicken or filet mignon, accompanied by an omelet seasoned with tomato and basil, and a "dessert" of a soufflé-like Southern pancake with lemon butter sauce and toasted almonds; each evening is a wine tasting.

The Trestle House Inn (Route 32A, Route 4, Box 370, 27932; 919–482–2282) was built in 1972, and takes its name from the wood that went into its construction. The California redwood timbers were part of a railroad trestle used by the Southern Railroad Company and are believed to be over 450 years old. Comments?

The Lords Proprietors' Inn
300 North Broad Street, 27932

Tel: 919–482–3641

Since they first opened The Lords Proprietors' Inn in 1981, Arch and Jane Edwards have renovated three adjacent Victorian buildings: the White-Bond House, the Satterfield House, and the Pack House. Rooms are furnished with antiques, and beds have been specially constructed by local cabinetmakers.

"Accommodations of the highest quality; staff extremely warm and helpful, personifying Southern hospitality." *(Eugene Preaus, also Laura Lapins)* "I enjoyed canoeing in a nearby mill pond, exploring the world of cypress swamps and beaver dams under a canopy of Spanish moss, then returning at the end of the day to a room in the Pack House. Simple rag rugs from North Carolina's mountains contrast with handsome antiques and fit perfectly with the wide floor boards. The rooms are wonderfully spacious, with high ceilings, skylights, and original windows; the bathroom was a pleasure, with a large shower and a separate bathtub." *(Rick Larson)*

"A lovely old inn, tastefully decorated with quality period antiques, supplemented by overstuffed reading chairs in the parlors. Early risers will find the parlors an inviting place for reading or quiet musings on the events of the day." *(John Blewer, also Lowell Corbin)* "Breakfast was delicious—French toast with blueberry sauce." *(Deborah Farrington)* "We were warmly greeted upon arrival, and shown to our inviting room. The owner directed us on a historic walking tour; upon our return, we found cool iced tea waiting at our door. We breakfasted in a separate one-story dining house, where we enjoyed fresh fruit, orange juice, coffee, eggs, and excellent service." *(Bruce Campbell)* "Everything was spotless, and we had access to a small kitchen; modern conveniences such as TV and VCR did not affect the period atmosphere. Jane and Arch Edwards do everything to get to know their guests and make them feel special, without intruding." *(Denley & Ann Coughman)*

Open All year.
Rooms 20 doubles—all with full private bath, telephone, TV, air-conditioning. Most with desk, 4 with fireplace, fan. Inn occupies 3 adjacent restored homes.
Facilities 4 parlors—3 with fireplace, 1 dining/meeting room, patios, 2 guest kitchens. 1.5 acres with swimming pool. Docks, marinas, golf, tennis, river for fishing, swimming nearby. 1 hr. to Outer Banks beaches.
Location Center of historic district. Follow Hwy. 17 until it becomes Broad St. Inn is 6 blocks N of waterfront at corner of Albemarle and Broad Sts.
Restrictions No smoking in dining room or guest rooms. "Well-behaved children welcome."
Credit cards None accepted.
Rates B&B, $80 double, $55 single. Extra person, $15. Winter weekend program Nov. through March includes Saturday historic home tour and reception, 2 nights B&B, candlelight dinner: $300 for 2.
Extras 1 room has wheelchair access and equipped for disabled. Airport/station pickup. Portable crib, babysitting.

GLENDALE SPRINGS

Glendale Springs Inn ¢ ✕   *Tel:* 919–982–2102
P.O. Box 100, 28629

"An extremely attractive Victorian wayside inn, built in the 1890s. Owner Gayle Winston grew up within two miles of Glendale Springs, and remembers thinking, as a child, that the inn was the most beautiful building she'd ever seen. The guest rooms are lovingly furnished with hooked rugs, beautiful country quilts, and period decor, along with modern conveniences such as electric heat and blankets. The bed was the first inn bed we've yet found that was firm enough to suit. Our room was reputed to have its own ghost, whom we were not privileged to meet. The dinner menu changes nightly, and offers a very unusual choice of appetizers, entrées, and desserts for this diminutive community. One might begin with smoked tuna and salmon salad, continue with chicken with prosciutto and leeks, and conclude with bittersweet chocolate terrine.

"The inn is listed on the National Register of Historic Places, and served as the headquarters for the WPA when the Blue Ridge Parkway was constructed in the mid-thirties. Gardener David Bare has done an intriguing job with flowers, herbs, and shrubs. Glendale Springs also has a most attractive gift and antiques center, and is home to the Holy Trinity Church of Frescoes." *(David & Cheri Kendall)*

"Wake-up coffee is brought to your room between 7 and 8 A.M.; breakfast is served from 8 to 9 A.M.. We enjoyed freshly squeezed orange juice, a plate of attractively served fresh fruit, coffee cake, scrambled eggs (plain or fancy) or omelets, bacon, and coffee or tea. Lunches are delightful and the French-style dinners are marvelous. Lamentably, Ashe County is dry, but one can take one's own libations for the inn to cool and serve. Gayle and her staff are warm, friendly, relaxed, and unpretentious. We stayed across the road in the guest house that had a king-size bed, Jacuzzi, and a front porch for rocking. The Blue Ridge Parkway is our favorite highway, offering innumerable opportunities for sightseeing, picnicking, and sports. We have used it as a focus for vacations from one end to the other." *(Mrs. Joan Reid)*

"Write-up accurately reflects this rambling old mansion. Our room was large, freshly painted, well furnished, and had sufficient lamps and chairs to allow for comfortable reading. The dinner menu was nouvelle French, with garden-grown herbs providing elusive flavors to the pork loin with plum sauce and breast of chicken with garlic cream sauce. Vegetables were exceptional, especially the spinach. The gift shop adjoining the inn has a huge inventory of high quality items—books, textiles, crafts, and all sorts of goodies unexpected in this remote location." *(John Blewer)*

Open April through December.
Rooms 2 suites, 7 doubles—all with private bath. 2 in guest house with fireplace, whirlpool bath, ceiling fan.
Facilities Restaurant, sitting room, library, porches. Hiking, bicycling, golf, canoeing, fishing, swimming, tubing nearby.
Location NW NC, Blue Ridge Mts. Just off Blue Ridge Pkwy., at mile marker 259, near junction with Rte. 16.

Restrictions Traffic noise in front rooms. No children under 10.
Credit cards Amex, MC, Visa.
Rates B&B, $95 suite; $75 double. Extra person, $15. Alc lunch, $4–8; alc dinner, $30.
Extras Wheelchair access.

GLENVILLE

Innisfree Inn   *Tel:* 704–743–2946
P.O. Box 469, 28736   800–782–1290

Innkeepers Dottie and Henry Hoche opened their neo-Victorian home as a B&B in 1989 after realizing that they enjoyed hosting guests; travelers had been knocking on their door from the day the house was finished, so it seemed only natural to make a business out of it. Not content with its dramatic location on a wooded hillside overlooking Lake Glenville, Henry reports that "this place is still evolving. We'll be landscaping for a long time, though we've made a start with a vegetable garden, fruit trees, and grassy lanes meandering over the hill." Breakfast—offered in the tower or on the veranda—includes a selection of cereals, juices, teas, fruit, special breads, homemade jellies, warm pastry or waffles with maple syrup, and coffee; afternoon wine, evening Irish coffee and cordials are served by the fire, and Godiva chocolates are placed at each bedside.

"An exquisite Victorian-replica three-story mansion that fits perfectly in any dream of a secluded hideaway holiday, complete with stained glass dining room tower and great room with full wraparound veranda. Each guest room has different charms, from the flowered wallpaper, brass bed, and mirrored armoire of The Cambridge to the king-size bed and mountain views of Victoria's Suite. The great room with cathedral ceiling and cozy fireplace was perfect for wine or tea in the afternoon, and evening sweet and nightcap. Dottie and Henry are the warmest of innkeepers, and homemade oatmeal raisin cookies were always available for snacks. We sipped coffee on the veranda after breakfast, watching the birds at the numerous feeders." *(Elizabeth Bryant, also Louise & Richard Weithas)*

"From the moment we entered the stained glass front door, we felt the charming, quiet, elegant atmosphere. The view from the living room and wraparound porch was breathtaking. The ambience is conducive to relaxation and healthful living. Every need was anticipated and cared for, and our hosts made us felt welcome in this modern Victorian." *(Mr. & Mrs. David Lashner)*

Open All year.
Rooms 3 cottages, 1 suite, 3 doubles—all with private bath and/or shower, telephone, ceiling fan. 1 with Jacuzzi, 1 with patio. 1 2-bedroom cottage with kitchen, fireplace, veranda.
Facilities Great room with fireplace, dining room with 25-foot tower, observatory room with TV, games; veranda. 10 acres with gardens, walking trails. On lake for water sports; boat rentals, fishing. Tennis, golf nearby. 15 min. to downhill skiing.
Location W NC. 6 m N of Cashiers on Hwy. 107.
Restrictions No smoking. No children under 18 in inn; all children allowed in cottages.

Credit cards Amex, Discover, MC, Visa.
Rates B&B, $149 suite, $79–89 double. Extra person, $20. 10% for stays of 4 or more nights. 2-night weekend minimum during high season.

HENDERSONVILLE

Nestled between the Great Smoky and Blue Ridge Mountains, Hendersonville is both a popular resort and an active farming community. Throughout the nineteenth century, wealthy southerners took refuge from the summer heat in the fresh mountain air, building summer homes and hotels. Today's visitors enjoy hiking in nearby Chimney Rock Park, as well as the town's many summer festivals, highlighted by the North Carolina Apple Festival, a ten-day event held through Labor Day. There's excellent theater in neighboring Flat Rock, and on Monday nights, Hendersonville closes sections of Main Street for two hours of clogging and square dancing. The home of Carl Sandburg, also in Flat Rock, is worth seeing.

Hendersonville is in western North Carolina, 20 miles south of Asheville via I-26.

Claddagh Inn ¢ ♦♦   *Tel:* 704–697–7778
755 North Main Street, 28792   800–225–4700

Claddagh is Gaelic for "love and lasting friendship," and that's just the feeling that Fred and Marie Carberry convey to their guests. The inn was built at the turn of the century, and was purchased by the Carberrys in 1985. Rates include a full country breakfast of eggs, meat, grits, hash browns, fruit, and juice, with a daily special of French toast, waffles, creamed gravy over biscuits, or pancakes.

"Great warm atmosphere, welcoming and relaxed management, artistic room decoration. The rooms are very clean and always smell good. The long porch is well supplied with rockers, hanging ferns, and pleasant company in the cool of the evening." *(Lois Hornbostel)* "Each evening we gathered in the living room and library to compare notes on our day, watch TV, or play games." *(Mrs. R.A. Perrin)* "Our room had a brass bed, maple writing desk, lovely curtains, thick rug, and small sitting room with white wicker and plants. Location is convenient to stores, restaurants. Ample seating in the parlors, and all the rooms are bright and well lit. Sherry is served in the library or on the veranda." *(Ann & Karl Reed)*

Less favorably: "Our room needed new linens and towels; the rug was worn."

Open All year.
Rooms 2 suites, 12 doubles—all with private bath and/or shower, telephone, TV, desk, air-conditioning, fan. Some with radio, fireplace, balcony.
Facilities Dining room, library, parlor with TV, veranda. Bridge games nightly in summer. Tennis, golf, swimming, fishing, boating, rafting nearby.
Location Henderson County. 20 m S of Asheville. 1½ blocks from center. From I-26, take Exit 18B/Rte. 64; go W 2.1 m to Hendersonville. Bear right to inn at corner of N. Main St.

Restrictions Light sleepers should request rooms away from street. No smoking in public rooms.
Credit cards Amex, Discover, MC, Visa.
Rates B&B, $69–89 suite, $42–79 double, $32–52 single. Extra person, $10. Children under 8 free. Weekly rates. Reduced rates for children, families. 2-night holiday minimum.
Extras Airport/station pickup by prior arrangement. Crib.

Waverly Inn ¢ 👫

783 North Main Street, 28792

Tel: 704–693–9193
800–537–8195

Built as a boarding house in 1898, the Waverly Inn is the oldest surviving inn in Hendersonville, and it is listed on the National Register of Historic Places. The inn offers spacious porches—upstairs and down—for rocking, a striking Eastlake staircase in the foyer, and guest rooms comfortably decorated with king- and queen-sized lace-canopied rice beds, spindle beds, and white wicker, along with some dressers from its boarding house days. John and Diane Sheiry bought the inn in 1988, and came to it in an interesting way: both had worked in the hotel and restaurant business on the corporate level, and when John went back to school for his MBA, his thesis was on the operation and marketing of country inns. By the time he graduated, the Sheirys were ready to start a new life as innkeepers.

"John and Diane made every effort to see to our needs: they made dinner reservations, provided special amenities for our room, suggested places to visit, and had our wine chilled and waiting for us at the end of the day. Their improvements to both the plumbing and the decor make the inn a place to remember." *(G. Kemp Liles)* "We were totally satisfied with the attentiveness of our warm and friendly hosts, John and Diane. They have transformed the inn from a sort of sleepy, rundown establishment to a peaceful and restful place to stay. The big country breakfasts are spectacular, especially the whole grain blueberry pancakes; the menu choices are good and enable you to eat like a bird or a beast." *(Charles & Martha Jean Liberto)* "The upstairs sitting room was convenient for telephone calls, ironing, and watching TV. Soft drinks and hot water for tea was available all day, and the innkeepers were helpful with reservations. This homey inn feels like a home with a very personal decorating style." *(Carol Guidi)* "This old house on a tree-lined street has charming rooms decorated in different flower themes. Our room, the Dogwood, had a canopied bed, with wicker chairs out on the porch. Good breakfasts." *(Theresa Boyd)*

Another comment: "Our room was nicely decorated, though the antiques needed a little TLC."

Open All year.
Rooms 2 suites, 14 doubles—all with private bath and shower, radio, desk, fan, air-conditioning. Some with TV, fireplace.
Facilities Dining room with stereo, living room, library with books, 3 TV rooms, porches. 1/3 acre with lawn. Tennis, golf nearby.
Location 20 m S of Asheville. 2 blocks from Historic District. On Main St. between 7th and 8th Aves.
Restrictions No smoking in dining room.
Credit cards Amex, Discover, MC, Visa.

Rates B&B, $90–120 suite, $48–78 double, $48–68 single. Extra person, $10; no charge for children under 12. Senior, AAA discount. Tipping encouraged. Weekend theme packages.

Extras Station pickup. Crib.

HIGHLANDS

Highlands is in western North Carolina, 125 miles north of Atlanta, and 60 miles southwest of Asheville. The town has auction galleries, antique shops, and summer theater, along with hiking, tennis, swimming, horseback riding, fishing, white-water rafting, an 18-hole Arnold Palmer golf course, and skiing. Surrounded by national forest lands, it has little of the commercialism found in other tourist areas. Because of its 4000-foot elevation, the mean temperature is around 75°, making for comfortable days and cool nights.

Reader tip: "One of the prettiest towns of the Blue Ridge Mountains. Highlands is a marvelous place in summer—cool, fresh, and with lots of charming little shops. There are many hiking trails nearby, and the people in the hiking store will advise you on the level of difficulty." *(SN)* "This is waterfall country, and Smoky Mountains National Park is just a one-hour drive away." *(ML)* "We were surprised at the high quality of Highlands' restaurants—for such a small town, they were very good and surprisingly sophisticated." *(MS)* "If you have any connection with Scotland, you'll get an especially warm welcome here. The town has invented a link with the Highlands of Scotland and has a clan center and a better tartan shop than you'll find anywhere outside of Edinburgh." *(Richard Gollin)*

Colonial Pines Inn ¢   *Tel:* 704–526–2060
Hickory Street, Route 1, Box 22B, 28741

Chris and Donna Alley moved from Atlanta in 1984 and renovated this old farmhouse with modern baths and antique and modern country furnishings. Readers continue to rave about Donna and her inn, making advance reservations imperative. (If the Colonial Pines is full, she's very helpful about referring you elsewhere.)

"Colonial Pines is a pretty house, furnished in antiques and period reproductions. Donna is a bright and charming lady; she maintains just the right balance between helping her guests and staying out of the way until needed. We relaxed on the spotless porch swing, gazing out at the mountains, and indulging in peaceful contemplation." *(Antonia Bernstein)* "Donna Alley has done a tremendous job decorating the inn and making it comfortable for guests; her attention to detail makes the difference between adequate and special." *(Sibyl Nestor)*

"The inn is set back from the road on a hillside, offering beautiful mountain views from a three-sided porch. Donna's little extras made our stay delightful—things like an explanation of the specialty breads served at breakfast, the constant aroma of cinnamon and fresh-baked bread, and local directions and advice. The beds are comfortable and the breakfasts—

which include fresh fruits, homemade breads, delicious sausage or ham, eggs, and excellent coffee—are great." *(Mark Lampe, and others)* "There is a nice library of books of local interest, and a grand piano for those inclined." *(Nance Pettit)*

Open All year.
Rooms 2 2-bedroom cottages, 1 suite, 4 doubles, 1 single—all with private bath and/or shower. Suite with TV. 1 cottage with kitchenette, TV, deck; 1 cottage with kitchen, living/dining room with fireplace, TV, telephone, screened porch.
Facilities Dining room, living room with TV, grand piano; porches. 2 acres with picnic table, berry picking.
Location 80 m SW of Asheville, 130 m N of Atlanta. 1/2 m from town. From Main St. take Hwy. 64 E. Go 6 blocks and turn right on Hickory St. to inn at corner.
Restrictions No smoking. "Small children preferred in cottage." Children over 6 in inn.
Credit cards MC, Visa.
Rates B&B, $75–95, guest house, $70–80 suite, $55–65 double, $45–55 single. Extra person, $10. 2-night minimum holidays, peak weekends.

Long House B&B ¢   *Tel: 704–526–4394*
Route 2, Box 638, 28741

The Long House B&B, owned by Lynn and Valerie Long, has natural wood walls, oak floors, antiques, and handmade quilts. "It's a charming 100-year-old log cabin that has been renovated and expanded with careful attention to detail and comfort. The rooms are large and comfortable. Ours had three beds—perfect for our family. The bath adjoining our room was spotless and contained wonderful-smelling soap and shampoo. An added plus was our porch, which gave us a private entrance and a great wooded view. Lynn and Valerie Long couldn't have been more gracious or friendly. Cold drinks were available at all times, and Valerie gave us dinner suggestions and recommended hiking trails." *(Linda Backrack)* "Friendly, helpful hosts, knowledgeable about good walking trails and local sights. All guests ate together and had time to chat over a breakfast of egg casserole, fruit cobbler, meats, and beverages. Nice sitting porch." *(Celia McCullough & Gary Kaplan)*
    "The owners really took the time to get to know every member of our family. Our dormer room had very comfortable beds with lovely quilts and room for four." *(Steve Shipps)* "Breakfast was great with heart-shaped waffles (in honor of our honeymoon), sausage, and fruit. Our room was clean, cool, and comfortable; it opened onto the shaded porch, a pleasant afternoon retreat." *(Teresa Hall)*

Open All year. By reservation only, Jan. through March.
Rooms 4 doubles—all with private bath, ceiling fan.
Facilities Common room with TV/VCR, fireplace; deck with rockers. Fishing, canoeing nearby.
Location 1 1/2 m E of town via Hwy. 64.
Restrictions No smoking.
Credit cards MC, Visa.
Rates B&B, $55–85 double, $45–60 single. Extra person, $15. 2-night weekend minimum, May–Oct. Midweek, off-season discounts. Discount for 4-night stay.
Extras Crib.

Old Edwards Inn & Highlands Inn ¢ ✕   *Tel:* 704–526–5036
Main Street, P.O. Box 1030, 28741   704–526–9380
                                                    Off-season: 912–638–8892

For the past ten years, innkeepers Rip and Pat Benton have kept busy renovating Central House Restaurant, in the original part of the Old Edwards Inn (over 100 years old), then the guest rooms, and most recently the Highlands Inn across the road. The decor throughout is Victorian, with antique furnishings, hand-stenciling, and period wallcoverings in every guest room.

"The staff was exceptionally courteous—assisting us with dinner reservations, giving us helpful tips. Our room had a fresh nosegay of flowers, little candies and a selection of bath amenities; the stenciling on the walls and the ceiling fan added to its charm." *(Leah Fleenor)* "A fabulous restaurant makes this inn superb. Food is delicious and served piping hot. I had baked scallops in dill sauce, and saved room for the inn's justly famous bread pudding in rum sauce. Breakfast is hearty continental, perfect for those who like to rise and eat at their own pace. We enjoyed coffee on the porch as we watched the town wake up." *(Carol Guidi)* "We dined at the Central House and found the service and food to be quite good, especially the locally caught trout." *(Teresa Hall)*

"Highlands is a lovely mix of mountains, rivers, and waterfalls. We had intended to stay one night, but ended up staying for nearly a week. The hotel is right in the middle of this attractive town with its delightful old buildings and upscale shops. It appears that a designer was let loose on the bedrooms of the hotel but the results are excellent for a change. All are beautifully decorated and very welcoming, most with four-poster beds, well-chosen drapes and antique furniture; many have delightful views of the streets of the town. The large sitting room has a huge carved stone fireplace with a roaring log fire. Guests gather for good conversation and delicious snacks, left there to attract those (like me) with no self control. A large moose head stands guard over the fireplace.

"Breakfast is taken across the road at the Highlands Hotel. This excellent buffet offers delicious fresh fruit dishes. The main dining room in the inn has the same welcoming atmosphere, as the rest of the hotel, and the food is freshly cooked and imaginatively prepared. The house trademark is the hush puppy—not, as a Brit might think, an old shoe, but a deep fried doughy bun with a delicious cinnamon taste." *(Richard Gollin)*

An area for improvement: "We wrote twice for information on the inn, but our letters were unanswered."

Open April through Nov.
Rooms 50 suites and doubles—all with private bath. Some with ceiling fan, balcony. Rooms in 2 buildings.
Facilities Restaurant. Golf nearby.
Location In town.
Restrictions Light sleepers should request rooms away from street. No children at Old Edwards; welcome at Highlands.
Credit cards Amex, MC, Visa for payment, not reservations.
Rates B&B, $75–95 suite, $65–95 double. Weekly, monthly rates available.
Extras Highlands Inn with wheelchair access.

HILLSBOROUGH

The Colonial Inn ¢ ✕
153 West King Street, 27278

Tel: 919–732–2461

Although many establishments claim to be the country's oldest inn in continuous operation, The Colonial Inn is clearly a valid contender. The earliest part of the inn dates from 1759; it hosted guests ranging from General Cornwallis to Alexander Hamilton. Since those days, the inn has been expanded and updated considerably. Southern cooking prevails here, with such specialties as pan-fried chicken, country ham, roast beef, fresh seafood, Cornwallis yams, and homemade breakfast and dessert. Hillsborough is a historic town with over 100 eighteenth- and early nineteenth-century buildings.

In 1990, the inn was purchased by Carlton and Sara McKee, who are working hard to establish a welcoming atmosphere and to upgrade 18th-century charm with 20th-century expectations, by adding adequate electrical outlets, reading lamps, and comfortable chairs.

"The food is for those who enjoy delicious home-style southern cooking at a moderate price. I thoroughly enjoyed my Sunday dinner; the Cornwallis yams rate five stars." *(Betty T. Norman)* Additional comments needed.

Open All year. Closed major holidays except Thanksgiving. Restaurant closed Monday.
Rooms 8 doubles—4 with private bath and/or shower, 4 with maximum of 4 people sharing bath. All with radio, desk, air-conditioning.
Facilities Restaurant, lounge, porches.
Location Central NC. 20 m E of Greensboro, 45 m NW of Raleigh. In center of town.
Restrictions Light sleepers should request back rooms.
Credit cards MC, Visa.
Rates B&B, $55–65 double. Extra person, $10. Reduced rates for families. Alc lunch, $5–7; alc dinner, $15.
Extras Port-a-crib.

Hillsborough House Inn
209 East Tryon Street, P.O. Box 880, 27278

Tel: 919–644–1600

The Hillsborough House has been in Bev and Katherine Webb's family for all but one year of the last 138, and it was known as the Webb-Matheson mansion until they restored it as an inn in 1989. Katherine utilized her training as an artist to design a new gallery entryway to keep the splendid front porch free for quiet sitting and rocking; the new space displays contemporary art and treasures salvaged from another family home in town. She constructed the canopy and four-poster beds so that they would conceal trundle beds beneath and draped the frames with coordinating fabrics; the bathroom floors are painted to look like marble or tile. Katherine likes to describe the decor as "comfortable and beautiful, casual and warm, elegant and gracious, eclectic and funky." The Webbs' next

239

project is converting the brick summer kitchen, the oldest building in Hillsborough, into a romantic cottage.

Katherine's creative streak also appears at breakfast, when the menu might include "something absolutely sinful" like puff pastry filled with sweetened cream cheese, citron, raisins, and nuts; a breakfast pizza of a cookie crust topped with custard and fruit; or granola in cookie form with oatmeal, raisins, nuts, carrots, and pumpkins seeds, glazed with peanut butter; accompanied by a fruit cup of mango, kiwi, or other exotic edibles, homemade muffins and breads (maybe molasses oatmeal or an egg braid), a Havarti or farmer's cheese, and a selection of coffees and teas.

"We had taken over the entire home for a family wedding, yet the Webbs were not overwhelmed; their graciousness was superb and constant. The house was large enough for us all to gather on the wonderful front porch (80 feet long) as well as in the living room or den. The younger members could play on the lawn. It was all thoroughly comfortable." *(Allen & Carol Vollen)* "Bev and Katherine are the perfect host and hostess. Katherine's artistic talents add an eclectic air to this old-fashioned home." *(Ada Lea Dew)*

Open All year.
Rooms 5 doubles—all with private bath and/or shower, radio, desk, air-conditioning, fan. 2 with deck.
Facilities Dining room with fireplace, living room with fireplace, den with TV/VCR, library. 7 acres with swimming pool, volleyball, basketball, croquet. Golf nearby.
Location From I-85, take exit 164 (or from I-40, take exit 261) and follow Hillsborough signs. Eventually you will be on Churton St. At the sixth stop light, turn right onto East Tryon St. At the second stop sign, turn left into driveway.
Restrictions No smoking. No children under 10.
Credit cards MC, Visa.
Rates B&B, $95—105 suite or double. Extra person, $25.
Extras Some French spoken.

LAKE LURE

Also recommended: We received a mixed report on the **Esmeralda Inn** (Highway 74, Box 57, Chimney Rock 28720; 7084—625—9105), about five miles west of Lake Lure. "This mountain lodge is quaint and rustic, with a warm and cozy atmosphere. The restaurant is highly recommended, featuring continental cuisine in a relaxed congenial atmosphere. The guest rooms vary greatly; some are decorated in a charming country style with private bath; others can not be recommended until they're renovated. If possible, see the room before booking, or ask for a redone room at the front of the inn, above the lobby."

Information please: About seven miles west of Lake Lure and 14 miles east of Hendersonville is the **Hickory Nut Gap Inn** (Highway 64 East, P.O. Box 246, Bat Cave 28710). Set at the end of a one-mile private road, at an elevation of 2,220 feet, the inn was built as a private retreat in 1950, and offers a screened porch for relaxing, a bowling alley in the basement, and hiking trails for exploring. Constructed of hardwood milled on the property, with six stone fireplaces, the wood-paneled rooms offer comfortable furnishings highlighted by Native American artifacts. Rates are reasonable and include a continental breakfast.

Lodge on Lake Lure   *Tel:* 704–625–2789
Charlotte Drive, Route 1, P.O. Box 529A, 28746

Originally built in 1932 as a refuge for (not from) the North Carolina Highway Patrol, the Lodge at Lake Lure offers rest and relaxation amid spectacular scenery on the shores of this 27-mile-long crystal clear lake. The inn is corporately owned, and is managed by Jack and Robin Stanier. Robing notes that "although our area has the inevitable tourist shops dealing in rubber snakes and tomahawks, we can guide our guests to quality shops filled with mountain crafts and art, weaving, and antiques. In addition to trout fishing in the French Broad River, we can help guests to play at the 12 semi-private golf courses within an easy drive."

"The lodge is a real find in a very scenic area of western North Carolina, set off the main road in a quiet setting with spectacular mountains and lake views from the delightfully cheerful breakfast room. We enjoyed a breakfast of fresh fruit, juice, home-baked breads, preserves, and coffee. The spacious great room has a stone fireplace that can hold eight-foot logs, with a millstone set in the stone chimney. Equally relaxing is the deck at the lake's edge." *(Betty Norman)* More comments please.

Open April 1–Nov. 30.
Rooms 2 suites, 9 doubles—all with private bath and/or shower, fan.
Facilities Living room with fireplace, piano; breakfast room; game room with TV; porch, deck. 3 acres with trails, lake swimming. Rental canoes, boats for fishing. Tennis, golf nearby.
Location Blue Ridge Mts. foothills. 25 m SE of Asheville, 90 m W of Charlotte. From Hwy. 64/74, turn at Lake Lure fire station opposite the golf course. Follow signs to lodge.
Restrictions Smoking restricted to den. No children under 12.
Credit cards Amex, MC, Visa.
Rates B&B, $85–100 suite, $66–90 double. Extra person, $15. 10% AARP discount. 2-3 night weekend, holiday minimum. Discount for 7-night stay. Weekend special package.
Extras Station pickup by prior arrangement. Port-a-crib, rollaway bed. French spoken.

LAKE TOXAWAY

Greystone Inn 🛉 ✕ 🎋   *Tel:* 704–966–4700
Greystone Lane, 28747   800–824–5766

The Greystone is probably the most expensive entry in this chapter, but if you're looking for a truly extravagant mountain getaway, you may find it the perfect choice. Offering luxurious country inn atmosphere in a modern resort setting, the Greystone was established in 1985 by Timothy Lovelace. The inn includes a 1915 Swiss Revival summer mansion, a second building, the Hillmont, a modern structure built to blend in with the style of the original mansion, and the Cottage, a lakeside home adjacent to Hillmont with two suites. The area is being developed for home sites with a private club, and only homeowners and inn guests can use the facilities. Rates include a full breakfast, afternoon tea, and dinner, served in the newly built restaurant, just ten yards from the lake with lovely views from its numerous windows. There's no extra charge for use of any of the sports facilities except for peak season golf; a highlight is the lake cruise which leaves every day at 5 P.M., with a skipper to recount tales of the lake's history.

"We stayed in the Astor Room, an upper-level corner room in the Hillmont, and it would be hard to describe it without using superlatives. The cathedral-ceilinged room was huge, with a sitting area with sofa and chairs in front of a large fireplace, a king-sized bed, an enormous bathroom with Jacuzzi, and a wet bar complete with coffee maker. The furnishings were of excellent quality. French doors opened out onto a spacious covered private deck with wicker furniture, which looks out through the trees onto the lake. Standard-size rooms in the mansion were smaller, although ample." *(Barry Gardner, also DLG)* More reports appreciated.

Open May through Nov.

Rooms 1 2-bedroom cottage, 2 suites, 30 doubles—all with full private bath, telephone, radio, TV, fan. 17 with air-conditioning, 16 with Jacuzzi, fireplace; 13 with wet bar. Some with private entrance, terrace or balcony; 19 rooms in main house, 12 rooms in annex.

Facilities Restaurant with fireplace, lounge with piano entertainment nightly, living room with fireplace, piano; library. 5,000 acres with 640-acre lake, heated swimming pool, 6 tennis courts, 18-hole golf course, croquet, all water sports, children's program, horseback riding.

Location W NC. 50 m SW of Asheville, between Brevard and Cashiers. 2½ hrs. NW of Atlanta, GA. Turn off Rte. 64 onto Greystone La. & go 3.3 m N to inn.

Restrictions Dry county; BYOB.

Credit cards Personal checks for deposit, preferred for payment. Amex, MC, Visa.

Rates MAP, $275–415 suite (for two persons), $218–368 double. Extra child under age 6 in room, $25; age 6–10, 50; age 11 and over, $70. 15% service. 2-night weekend minimum. Discount for 7-night stay. Off-season golf packages.

Extras Airport pickup, $40 round trip. Crib, babysitting.

MANTEO

Also recommended: Budget travelers will be interested in the **Scarborough Inn** (Highway 64/264, P.O. Box 1310, 27954; 919–473–3979), a cozy family-owned B&B with pleasant decor and very reasonable rates of $45–60. All rooms have a private bath and are equipped with a television, a small refrigerator, and a coffeemaker; bicycles are available. "Very comfortable accommodations. The inn is located on a major highway, but with the air-conditioning on we didn't hear any road noises." *(D.J. Farrington)* "We've stayed here several times, always in the same room: it has an outside entrance via the second-floor porch, a high canopied bed as well as another pretty double bed, and a good-sized modern bath; breakfast is a store-bought sweet roll. Across the street is a wonderful Bavarian restaurant called the Weeping Radish. Manteo is a 20-minute ride from the beaches, and prices are much lower than those of the chain hotels along the shore." *(Carol Guidi)*

For families traveling with children, *James Utt* recommends the **Ocean Reef Best Western** (Milepost 8½, 107 Virginia Dare Trail, P.O. Box 1440, Kill Devil Hills 27948; 919–441–1611 or 800–237–5517), eight miles north of Manteo. "The Ocean Reef is an attractive, modest-sized hotel overlooking the ocean. Every room is a suite, with a kitchenette, patio or balcony; it's clean and attractive with plenty of room for a family of four. The pool is nice and access to the beach is steps away. Complimentary coffee and doughnuts are in the lobby each morning. This is a pleasant community to spend a few days. There's some development but it's not over-run—few scattered pieces of tackiness around." Rates range from $50–170, depending on season.

Tranquil House Inn 👫

Queen Elizabeth Street, P.O. Box 2045, 27954

Tel: 919–473–1404
800–458–7069

One of the most intelligent developments in the hospitality industry in the 1980s was the realization that new construction did not preclude individual charm and period decor. The Tranquil House was built in the style of its namesake 19th century inn, yet it is enhanced by the amenities 20th-century travelers expect and enjoy. The spacious rooms are decorated with reproduction lace-canopied, brass and four-poster beds, Oriental or Berber carpets, and handsome wallpapers; the bathrooms are all hand-tiled. Fresh flowers and a bottle of wine greet your arrival. Rates include a breakfast of juice, cereal, muffins or Danish, and coffee or tea. The inn is located right on the waterfront in downtown Manteo, overlooking Shallowbag Bay, and is surrounded by boardwalks and sailboats. Guests enjoy taking the walking tour of Manteo's historic homes; watching the *Lost Colony*, an outdoor drama; visiting the North Carolina aquarium; or just relaxing in a rocker on the inn's ample verandas overlooking the water.

"Absolutely outstanding place to stay. Relaxed atmosphere, beautifully decorated rooms, and friendly staff. Location is ideal for access to the Outer Banks beaches, but close enough to Virginia for an easy trip to the city." *(Steven Lawson)* "The inn is exceptionally clean and fresh, with a relaxing, quiet atmosphere. The staff is polite and helpful." *(Mr. & Mrs. Kenneth Wagner, also Norman Block)*.

Open All year.
Rooms 2 suites, 26 doubles—all with full private bath, telephone, TV, desk, air-conditioning.
Facilities Breakfast room, lobby/living room, library with fireplace, books, lookout room, porches on harbor. Bicycles, barbecue grill, children's play equipment. Tennis, golf, swimming, boating, fishing, windsurfing nearby.
Location NE NC, Outer Banks region, Roanoke Island. 90 m S of Norfolk, VA. Coming from the north, take Rte. 158 to Whalebone Junction in Nags Head. Follow signs to Manteo, bearing right onto Rte. 64/264 W. Turn right at first traffic light on Sir Walter Raleigh St. to inn at harborfront.
Restrictions No smoking in lobby, library, pantry, and certain guest rooms.

Credit cards Amex, DC, MC, Visa.
Rates B&B, $85–125 suite, $55–125 double or single. Extra person, $10. Children under 16 free in parents' room. 10% senior, AAA discount. Special packages. 2-night minimum during summer.
Extras Wheelchair access; some rooms equipped for disabled. Airport pickups. Crib, $10; babysitting.

MARS HILL

Also recommended: We did not have enough information to do a full write-up, but received an enthusiastic report on the **Marshall House** (5 Hill Street, P.O. Box 865, Marshall 28753; 704–649–9205 or 800–562–9258) eight miles west of Mars Hill. "The Marshall House was designed by Richard Sharp Smith, an architect involved with the construction of Biltmore, and sits perched on a steep hillside overlooking the town. It is furnished with eclectic antiques and run with exuberant informality by Ruth Boylan, who has become an expert on the history and culture of the county and its local attractions. Accommodations are comfortable but not plush, and service is tailored to the needs of the guests. Breakfast, usually waffles and pancakes with a variety of local preserves, is served in the dining room or on the porch. The house reflects the quirky charm of the town below it and the county around it. And children and pets are welcome." *(David Wasserman)* Double rates range from $40–60.

Baird House ¢ 🏃   *Tel:* 704–689–5722
121 South Main Street, P.O. Box 749, 28754

Innkeeper Yvette Wessel moved to North Carolina after living for many years in Westchester (New York) and Fairfield (Connecticut) counties. She notes that "aside from parents of Mars Hill College students, winter skiers, and Appalachian Trail hikers, my guests are primarily those who choose these beautiful mountains for a getaway, and who like the rural quality of tiny Mars Hill, with cows and sheep grazing just yards from the house. Many also enjoy the summer repertory theater at Mars Hill College."

The Baird House was built in the early 1900s by Dr. John Baird; at that time it was the grandest house in the area, with servants' quarters, a 225-foot well with the "sweetest water in the world," and two kitchen gardens. The house, a two-story structure, is constructed of brick, with 18-inch-thick interior walls and is furnished with colorful antiques.

"The inn is a fine example of nineteenth-century architecture, combining period with modern convenience. Mrs. Wessel is a warm and gracious hostess, and an interesting, cosmopolitan individual. The atmosphere is homey and comfortable." *(Dr. & Mrs. Robert McKiernan)* "Comfortable beds, good lighting, adequate plumbing and parking. The full breakfasts are delicious and plentiful, and served at a time mutually agreeable to guest and innkeeper." *(Mr. & Mrs. Joseph Lindsay)* "Located in a quiet town, within walking distance of local shops and Mars Hill College. Cordial hospitality and a wonderful variety of breakfasts." *(Mr.& Mrs. John Gatewood)*

Open Jan. through Nov.
Rooms 1 suite, 4 doubles—2 with private bath or shower, 3 with maximum of 6 people sharing bath. 3 with desks, fan; 1 with TV, 1 with fireplace.
Facilities Living room with fireplace, library; dining room with fireplace, porch with rockers. 1/3 acre with patio. Tennis, swimming, fishing nearby. 10 m to downhill skiing.
Location W NC. 18 m N of Asheville. In center of town.
Credit cards Amex.
Rates B&B, $74 suite, $42–53 double. Extra person, $10 (must bring own sleeping bag). No charge for children under 12 in parents' room. Weekly rates.
Extras Port-a-crib. French spoken.

MOUNT AIRY

Pine Ridge Inn ¢ 🛏 ✗ 🏔
2893 West Pine Street, 27030

Tel: 919–789–5034

Pine Ridge is a sprawling mansion built in 1948 and luxuriously decorated with antique and traditional furnishings. Ellen and Manford Haxton bought the inn in 1985; in 1991 they redecorated and repainted some of the rooms. Rates include a southern continental breakfast, and the dinner menu includes such classics as prime rib, chicken Kiev, veal Marsala, and shrimp scampi.

"The Pine Ridge feels like a southern plantation mansion, complete with great white pillars and circular drive. The back of the house looks over a swimming pool and the beautiful North Carolina hills. The entrance foyer is highlighted with a circular stairway, while the main living room has a fireplace and Steinway grand piano; the paneled library beckons with soft velvet-covered couches, and antiques and fresh flowers are everywhere. The Haxtons have updated all the facilities without destroying the house's grandeur. Their attitude toward their guests is one of warmth and charm, openness and pleasantness." *(Mr. & Mrs. Arthur Heitmann)*

"We were immediately made to feel at home. The owners' son greeted us, and gave us a tour of the house—all the rooms are large. Ours had an antique brass bed, polished and inviting, with crisp, fluffy linens and comforter, lots of windows, plenty of space, private bath, sitting chairs, and current issues of great magazines. After checking in, we had a soak in the perfectly clean indoor hot tub. The continental breakfast included fresh juice, freshly baked banana bread, excellent coffee." *(KFR)* "We were warmly greeted, and shown our room before registering. The atmosphere was homey, and the rooms well-decorated and maintained." *(Brenda Bare)*

"Fully support existing description. A nice surprise was the electric blanket on the bed. Baths are huge, with lots of hot water, and the towels were some of the fluffiest I've ever used. We really enjoyed the varied art work throughout the inn." *(Perri & Mike Rappel)*

Minor niggle: "Upgraded soaps rather than little bars of Safeguard would be a treat."

Open All year. Closed week of Christmas. Restaurant open same time.
Rooms 2 suites, 4 doubles—all with private bath and/or shower. All rooms with telephone, radio, TV, air-conditioning. Some with desk.

Facilities Living room with piano, fireplace, library with fireplace, TV, VCR, stereo, books, dining room with fireplace, play room, exercise room. 8 acres with hot tub, swimming pool, tennis court, bike paths. Golf nearby.

Location N central NC. 45 m NW of Winston-Salem, near Virginia border. On Rte. 89; 5 m to town, 2 m from Exit 100 off I-77.

Restrictions Light sleepers should request rooms away from highway. Smoking in library only.

Credit cards Amex, Visa, MC.

Rates B&B, $60–85 double. Extra person, $10. 10% family, senior, AAA discount. Continental breakfast included; full breakfast $6 additional. Alc lunch, $11.50; alc dinner, $18. Weekly rates, weekend packages.

Extras Crib.

MURPHY

Huntington Hall B&B ¢
500 Valley River Avenue, 28906

Tel: 704–837–9567

Those with a sweet tooth, rejoice! Bob Delong, innkeeper of Huntington Hall, is also a trained pastry chef. Guests at this restored 1890s clapboard home can sample his culinary delights, such as crepes with ginger peaches and apricot sauce or French raisin toast with pear sauce for breakfast. Bob and his wife Katie purchased the inn in 1990, and report that "we are most suited for guests wishing to relax and unwind. The house is warm and comfortable, decorated in the tradition of an English country garden home, and the ivy should climb the low stone wall this year! Murphy is a quiet town; there is much to do for outdoor enthusiasts, and a porch for those who would like to kick back and enjoy the mountain breezes. We are avid backpackers and can advise guests on hiking trips in the Great Smoky Mountains. There is plenty to explore for those who take the time to find it."

"You could not ask for more gracious and hospitable hosts than Bob and Katie. The ambiance, decor, comfort, cleanliness, quiet, convenience—parking and location—of the inn are superb. Then there are the extras, like wine before dinner and turned-down beds with luscious, rich chocolate truffles." *(Mel & Gloria Blowers)* "I feel very secure when I visit. There is plenty of personal attention, and it's like visiting friends." *(Mary Lou Faulkenberry)*

Open All year.

Rooms 5 doubles—all with full private bath, TV, desk, air-conditioning, fan.

Facilities Dining room with fireplace, library; living room with TV, breakfast room, screened porch. Swimming pool, tennis, golf nearby. Lakes and rivers nearby for swimming, white water rafting, kayaking, canoeing.

Location W NC. 90 m E of Chattanooga TN, 90 W of Asheville. 2 blocks from downtown. From U.S. 64, take Hwy. 19 to downtown area. Turn onto Peachtree St. Then right onto Valley River Ave. Pass Presbyterian Church and A&P. Inn is on right.

Credit cards Amex, DC, Discover, MC, Visa.

Rates B&B, $45–65 double, $40–49 single. Extra person, $10. Rollaway bed, $10.

Extras Wheelchair access. Airport/station pickups. Crib.

NEW BERN

New Bern is located in mid-coastal North Carolina, 2 hours east of Raleigh, at the confluence of the Trent and Neuse rivers. It's a 45-minute drive to the Atlantic Ocean beaches. The town was founded in 1710 by German and Swiss colonists searching for political and religious freedom. New Bern prospered from the production of tar, pitch, and turpentine. When the royal governor of the Carolinas, William Tryon, saw the need for a permanent capital, New Bern was selected as the site. Tryon Palace, completed in 1770, was the colonial capitol and the first state capitol of North Carolina. New Bern's prosperity continued through much of the nineteenth century, and many of its finest buildings date from the early 1800s. A number of historic buildings have been restored and are open to the public as museums. On a more commercial note, Pepsi-Cola (known originally as "Brad's Drink") was invented here in the 1890s by a local pharmacist, C.D. Bradham.

The Aerie ¢   *Tel: 919–636–5553*
509 Pollock Street, 28560   800–849–5553

The Aerie was built in 1870 and remained in the same family for almost 100 years. Renovated as an inn in 1985, it was purchased by Rick and Lois Cleveland in 1988. Rates include a breakfast of fresh fruit and juice, home-baked muffins or bread, and a choice of such entrées as French toast, Belgian waffles, omelets, buttermilk pancakes, or an egg specialty.

"The Clevelands have redone the inn's interior in Williamsburg colors, Early American furnishings, and wonderful folk art. We stayed in a spacious first-floor bedroom with a new bath. We were offered refreshments upon arrival, and dinner suggestions and reservations were made. The breakfast was wonderful." *(BJ Hensley)*

"Sensitive, polite, and friendly owners; decor reflects a balanced concern for both ambiance and detail." *(Alan & Amy Benedict)* "Located in the historic district, the inn was very quiet and exceptionally clean. The owners were always there to answer questions or lend a hand; food was excellent." *(Tom Coull)* "This is a haven for a woman traveling alone. The breakfasts are terrific—not your 'danish-and-coffee-in-the-lobby' fare." *(MLS, also William MacGowan)*

Open All year.
Rooms 7 doubles—all with private bath and/or shower, telephone, radio, TV, desk, air-conditioning, fan.
Facilities Dining room, sitting room with player piano, games, library, living room with fireplace, patio. Off-street parking.
Location Center of historic district, 1 block from Tryon Palace.
Restrictions No smoking in dining room or guest rooms.
Credit cards Amex, MC, Visa.
Rates B&B, $80 double, $55 single. Extra person, $10. 10% AAA discount.
Extras Airport/station pickups. Babysitting available by arrangement.

NORTH CAROLINA

Harmony House Inn ¢   *Tel:* 919–636–3810
215 Pollock Street, 28560

Built for Benjamin Ellis in the 1850s, Harmony House is a four-room, two-story home with Greek Revival styling. As the Ellis family grew, additions were made, porches were built and then enclosed. Around 1900, two of the builder's sons sawed the house in half and expanded it to enable the addition of another hallway, front door, staircase and four more rooms. Each brother lived in their own half for the next 20 years.

Buzz and Diane Hansen opened the Harmony House in May 1985. They are "delighted that people seem to feel 'at home' in our home!" The inn is furnished with antiques and reproductions, many made by local craftsmen. The Hansens are pleased to offer advice on walking tours and local restaurants, and complimentary soft drinks and juices.

"The warmest, most gracious home away from home you can imagine. Breakfast includes egg/sausage casserole, spiced fruit compote, Diane's own coffee cake, and world-class coffee." *(Lois Cummings)* "Everything about the inn is first-rate, especially the innkeepers. The guest refrigerator, packed with assorted drinks, was an especially thoughtful touch." *(Elizabeth McPhelan)*

"Diane and Buzz Hansen are very proud of their home; it's obvious from Buzz's description and tour when you first register. Rooms are airy and spacious, with high ceilings; our bathroom was large and very clean, with a terrific shower, a rarity in renovated inns. Harmony House is well situated on a street with other inns and within walking distance of many of New Bern's restaurants and historic sites." *(Carolyn Myles)* More comments requested.

Open All year.
Rooms 9 doubles with full private bath, TV, air-conditioning, ceiling fan.
Facilities Dining room, guest parlor with game table. Porch with swings, rockers. Landscaped ½ acre with gardens, lawn furniture. 1 block from 2 rivers, public park, boat ramp, fishing.
Location Center of town, historic district.
Restrictions Smoking in bedrooms only.
Credit cards Amex, MC, Visa.
Rates B&B, $75 double, $55 single. Extra person, $10. No tipping.
Extras Airport/station pickups. Crib. Some Spanish spoken.

New Berne House ¢ 👪   *Tel:* 919–636–2250
709 Broad Street, 28560   800–842–7688

The atmosphere of this Colonial Revival inn encourages guests to slow their pace to that of a less hectic time. Take a nap in an oversized hammock, shaded by magnolia, pecan, and camelia trees; browse through the old books and magazines in the library; or sip afternoon tea on the overstuffed couches in the Rose Parlor. When real life intrudes, New Berne House can accommodate business travelers as well.

All respondents were struck by the pleasant and charming personalities of innkeepers Joel and Shan Wilkins. The couple opened the New Berne House in 1987 after completing the restoration themselves. Rooms are furnished primarily with antiques, including many accent pieces original to the house. Rates include a full breakfast, brought to your room or served in the dining room, and afternoon tea.

"Joel and Shan have made the house very comfortable while preserving its historic feeling. It's fun to look through the old books and magazines they found in the house, and the pictures of the original family." *(Stacey Blazer)* "My room was kept cool by the window air-conditioning unit. The inn is on a busy street but I was never bothered by any noises." *(LM)* "Fresh new wallpaper and paint; everything immaculately clean." *(Donna McFall)*

"Shan welcomed us on arrival and gave us helpful information on area activities. Joel's breakfast was fantastic. We had fruit crepes with cream cheese and sour cream sauce, country ham, blueberry muffins, lots of coffee, tea, and orange juice—all brought to our room at the time of our choosing, along with the morning paper. Parking is adequate. We had plenty of privacy but knew that we were welcome to mingle with the other guests. New Bern's historic sights are all within walking distance." *(Janet Pittman)* "Good accommodations at a reasonable price. Convenient location right next to Tryon Palace. Fabulous breakfast, though we would have preferred it a little earlier than 8:30 A.M.. *(D.J. Farrington)*

Open All year.
Rooms 6 doubles—all with private bath and/or shower, telephone, radio, air-conditioning, fan. TV upon request.
Facilities Parlor with baby grand piano, fireplace; dining room with fireplace, library with fireplace, porch. Formal gardens. Tandem bicycle. Tennis, golf nearby. Sailing, fishing charters, aerial tours of Outer Banks arranged. Off-street parking.
Location SE NC. Historic district. 1 block N of Tryon Palace; go left on Broad St. to 3rd house on left.
Restrictions No smoking.
Credit cards Amex, CB, Choice, DC, Discover, MC, Visa.
Rates B&B, $75 double, $55 single. Extra person, $15. Children under 12 free in parents' room. 10% discount when 2 or more rooms are rented together. 10% senior, AAA discount. Golf, sailing, flying, history packages.
Extras Wheelchair access. Airport/station pickup. Federal Express pickup; fax machine. Pets allowed with prior arrangement. Crib; babysitting with prior notice. Mystery weekends, holiday candlelight tours.

OCRACOKE

Ocracoke is on the Outer Banks of coastal North Carolina, about 1½ hours south of Nags Head, and 40 minutes by ferry from Hatteras village.

"Come to Ocracoke to heighten your awareness of the incredible forces of nature. Violent summer storms sweep through in minutes, and the pounding of ocean waves never ceases. The island is mercifully undeveloped, since most of it is part of the Cape Hatteras National Seashore. There's not a great deal to do but relax and enjoy the beautiful uncrowded beaches, fish and swim, rent a bicycle, and explore. The seafood is delicious; some of it familiar, some unusual to Yankee tastebuds." *(MS)*

Also recommended: Although not really suitable for a full entry, we received an enthusiastic report from frequent contributor *James Utt* about the **Pirate's Quay Hotel** (Ocracoke 27960; 919–928–1921), a small condominium hotel overlooking Silver Lake, in the village of Ocracoke. Each unit has a full kitchen, 1½ baths, and at least one balcony, if not two. Limited covered parking and a private dock are available. "It has an unparalleled view of the lake. You can relax in your room and watch the comings and goings of the fishing and pleasure boats." Double rates range from $84–134, depending on season.

Berkley Center Inn ¢   *Tel:* 919–928–5911
On the Harbor, P.O. Box 220, 27960

The Egan family has restored the Berkley Center, originally built as a center for employees of the Berkeley Machine Tool Company, as an inn, refurbishing its hand-carved fireplace mantels and the beautiful fir, cypress, and cedar-paneled walls and ceilings. Rooms are highlighted with over-stuffed Queen Anne wing chairs and sofas, quilts, baskets, and the work of local artists.

"Our spacious suite was beautiful, with a nice bath and a large sitting area. The inn is roomy and the grounds are well kept, with chairs for sitting and reading in the yard. The innkeepers, Ruth and Wes Egan, were helpful and really seem to love the building and its history." *(Ellen Olbrys)* "Cedar panelling gave our large room a lovely fragrance. The common areas were both handsome and homey, and the hospitable owners made the breakfast room a friendly place." *(Daniel Nash)*

Open April–Nov.
Rooms 11 doubles—9 with private bath and/or shower, 2 with a maximum of 4 people sharing bath. All with air-conditioning.
Facilities Living room with fireplace, dining room, gift shop. 3½ acres.
Location On the harbor, next to ferry landing.
Credit cards None accepted.
Rates B&B, $65–80 double.

ORIENTAL

Tar Heel Inn   *Tel:* 919–249–1078
205 Church Street, P.O. Box 176, 28571

Named after a 19th-century ship wrecked on nearby Hatteras Island, Oriental claims to be the sailing capital of North Carolina, having more world class boats than people in the village. The Tar Heel Inn, built in 1899 (about the time the town was founded) has been purchased and restored by Dave and Patti Nelson in 1987. They've decorated the rooms with a mixture of antiques and contemporary furnishings, English country wallpaper and fabrics, pencil-post, canopy, four-poster, or cannonball beds, and plenty of fresh flowers. With the sailing atmosphere of the community in mind, the Nelsons have begun offering a "sail and stay" package that includes a ½ day or sunset sail, with a picnic, on a 40-foot ketch-rigged sailboat. Patti's culinary skills have gotten a lot of attention, having been included in two cookbooks, so guests are sure to be in for a treat at breakfast.

"Dave and Patti are outgoing, warm, and friendly. They are delighted to help you plan local trips by car or boat. The inn is immaculate, furnished with personal flair. Guest rooms have comfortable beds, soft chairs, and good reading lamps. You can sit by the living room fire and relax with a book. There is a charming patio with umbrella tables, lounge chairs, and a beautiful tree-shaded back yard: perfect for croquet. The area is very quiet and pleasant to explore on the inn's bicycles." *(Mrs. Joseph Ziemba)*

"The breakfasts are marvelous. Our favorite was Patti's Puffcakes, which covered a dinner plate and were smothered with delicious fresh fruit." *(Beverly & Dick Dalton)* "I like to run early, but coffee was always brewed before I got up. Patti's breakfast feasts are always beautifully presented, with flowers on the table." *(C.J. Lambertsen)* Additional comments welcome.

Open March 1 to Nov. 30.
Rooms 7 doubles—all with private bath and/or shower, air-conditioning, fan. Some with telephone, radio, desk.
Facilities Dining room with piano, coffee bar; living room with fireplace, TV/VCR, stereo. Horseshoes, croquet, bicycles. Golf, tennis, swimming, sailing, fishing nearby.
Location On Pamlico Sound. 24 m SE of New Bern. Take Hwy. 70 to New Bern, then Hwy. 55 for 24 m E to Oriental. Across street from town hall.
Restrictions No smoking. Children by prior arrangement only.
Credit cards MC, Visa with 4% surcharge.
Rates B&B, $65–80 double, $55–60 single. Extra person, $20. No tipping. 2-night weekend minimum, holidays and in season. "Sail and stay" packages.
Extras One guest room equipped for the disabled. Airport/station pickups. Crib, babysitting. Some Spanish, Turkish spoken.

PINEHURST

Pinehurst is home to 34 golf courses and the Golf Hall of Fame. Beginning in 1895, the area was developed as a warm-weather refuge by a wealthy Boston industrialist, who hired the famed Frederick Law Olmsted, landscape architect of New York's Central Park and Asheville's Biltmore Estate. Pinehurst soon developed into a golfer's paradise, with the Pinehurst Hotel and Country Club its headquarters. Less-than-fanatic golfers will be happy to note that the area offers other recreational opportunities, including tennis, swimming, horseback riding, skeet and sport shooting, bicycling, hiking, and sailing.

Pinehurst is in the Piedmont Sandhills region of south central North Carolina, 70 miles southwest of Raleigh, and 45 miles northwest of Fayetteville.

Also recommended: Although the Pinehurst Hotel is too big for the guide at 400 units, *Betty Norman* reports that "the service in the dining room is outstanding. We felt that we were the only guests. The delicious food is graciously served in a beautiful setting. My waitress brought me a taste of two desserts to help me in a difficult decision, and the piano music enhances the dining experience."

Received too late for a full write-up was an enthusiastic report on the

Inn at the Bryant House (214 North Poplar Street, Aberdeen 28315; 919–944–3300), just south of Pinehurst. "This 1913 inn has been graciously renovated. The rooms are large and comfortable and the breakfast features fresh-baked breads and muffins with homemade jellies and jams. Every effort is made to make guests feel relaxed and at home. Picnic facilities under the pecan trees, and flower and vegetable gardens add to the southern charm of this historic community. Delightful owners." *(Ann Milton)* **Information please:** Dropped for lack of reader feedback, the **Holly Inn** (Cherokee Road, P.O. Box 2300; 919–295–2300 or In NC: 800–682–6901 or Outside NC: 800–533–0041) was built in 1895 by James Walker Tufts, the original developer of Pinehurst. This inn is listed on the National Register of Historic Places and guest rooms are decorated with handsome reproduction furnishings, although the decor is more Chippendale and Queen Anne than high Victorian. Comments please.

Pine Crest Inn ¢ ♙ ✕   *Tel:* 919–295–6121
Dogwood Road, P.O. Box 879, 28374

Owned by the Barrett family for over 25 years, the Pine Crest was founded in 1913 and was previously owned by Donald Ross, architect of more than 600 American golf courses. Although rooms are clean and comfortable, the inn is especially known for its bar and restaurant. The former, a local gathering place called Mr. B's Old South Lounge, is the domain of bartender and local golf columnist Bill Jones, CBS golf funnyman Bob Drum, and pianist Bob Israel. The inn's fine southern cooking is just as popular; Bob Barrett notes that the chef has been with the inn for over half a century, and "he surely knows what's cookin' in the kitchen." Barrett also describes the Pine Crest's business as being "80 percent repeat, with March, April, May, October, and November being the busiest times," and further suggests that "you leave your stuffed shirt at home." *(MW)*

"The food is excellent. Charming, small inn with very pleasant staff. Peter Barrett is an excellent host. Casual atmosphere during the day; coat and tie for dinner. Very low key, though. Rooms are spacious and colorful." *(MDS)* "We've always loved this inn and now its better than ever, combining elegance with country charm. The lobby has been totally redecorated in English style, and the food is great." *(Theresa Boyd)*

Open Jan. to Sept.
Rooms 4 suites, 34 doubles, 2 singles—36 with private shower and/or bath, 4 with maximum of 4 people sharing bath. All with telephone, TV, desk, air-conditioning.
Facilities Dining rooms, bar/lounge, piano bar, lobby/game room. 5 acres with patio, terrace, porch. Use of Pinehurst Country Club for heated swimming pool, health club, tennis courts, access to lake for fishing, swimming, boating. 5 Pinehurst Country Club golf courses in walking distance; 12 more nearby.
Location Sandhills, "Golf Capital of the World." 1 block from village.
Restrictions Casual attire not permitted after 6 P.M.
Credit cards Amex, DC, MC, Visa.
Rates MAP, $114–126 suite, $102–110 double, $84–95 single. 15% service. Reduced rates for children sharing parents' room. Senior discount. Alc dinner, $20–25. Golf packages.
Extras Wheelchair access. Airport/station pickup. Crib, babysitting.

PITTSBORO

The Fearrington House 🍴   *Tel:* 919–542–2121
2000 Fearrington Village Center, 27312

Just eight miles from Chapel Hill, Fearrington Village is a small complex consisting of a well-established first-class restaurant, a number of small quality shops, and, most recently, a country inn. Developed and owned by R.B. and Jenny Fitch, The Fearrington House features rooms decorated with English pine antiques and carefully matched Laura Ashley wallpapers and fabrics. The Fearrington House restaurant, which opened in 1981, is known for its innovative southern cuisine; a recent dinner included braised rabbit over homemade sage pasta, seared pork tenderloin with apricot glaze, and warm apple tarts, custard sauce, and caramel ice cream.

"Like all Relais et Chateaux establishments, this one is class A-1, luxurious and exquisite down to the last detail. The rooms, almost too perfect, are warm and extremely comfortable. The gardens are breathtaking and the restaurant shockingly good." *(Deborah Reese, also Robert Lenz)* "The rooms and grounds were beautiful, and the service superb." *(MM)* "Exquisite southern cuisine, excellent service, beautiful rooms, relaxing setting." *(Jeanine Kuczik, also Robert Lenz)*

Open All year.
Rooms 9 suites, 4 doubles—all with private bath and/or shower, telephone, radio, TV, desk, air-conditioning.
Facilities Living room, restaurant, bar/lounge, wine bar, tea room, specialty shops. 60 acres with bike trails, swimming pool. 8 m to Lake Jordan for swimming, boating, fishing. 15 min. to golf, tennis.
Location Central NC. 8 m SW of Chapel Hill, 20 m to Research Triangle Park. From Chapel Hill, go S on Rte. 15/501 toward Pittsboro & Sanford.
Restrictions Smoking permitted in lounge only. No children under 12.
Credit cards MC, Visa.
Rates B&B, $155–185 suite, $125 double and single. Alc lunch, $5–7; prix fixe dinner, $42.50.
Extras Wheelchair access; some rooms equipped for disabled. Airport/station pickup, $30. Spanish, French, German spoken. Member, Relais et Chateaux.

RALEIGH

Also recommended: Located 45 miles east of Raleigh, is the little town of Tarboro. Received too late for a full write-up was *Michele Palamountain*'s recommendation for **The Barracks Inn** (1100 Albemarle Avenue, Tarboro 27886; 919–641–1641). "This stately home was built as a replica of the capitol building in Raleigh. The innkeepers, transplanted Washingtonians, offer gracious hospitality."

Also in Tarboro is the **Little Warren B&B** (304 East Park Avenue, Tarboro 27886; 919–823–1314) set on the second oldest town common in America, in Tarboro's historic district. Rooms are filled with antiques, collectibles, and artifacts gathered by Tom and Patsy Miller during their worldwide travels. Breakfasts range from casual continental to elegant Southern or English repasts.

The Oakwood Inn   *Tel:* 919–832–9712
411 North Bloodworth Street, 27604

Pressured business travelers with appointments in North Carolina's capital city will find a welcome respite at The Oakwood Inn, opened in 1984. Built in 1871 as the Raynor Stronach House, the inn is listed on the National Register of Historic Places, and is located in the historic Oakwood District, home to twenty blocks of Victorian buildings, ranging in style from Greek Revival to Steamboat Gothic, some have been restored while others are rundown. Rooms are furnished entirely in period, and innkeeper Diana Newton describes her inn as an "exquisite example of careful historic restoration and vintage Victorian decor." Guests are greeted with refreshments on arrival, and are served a full breakfast, including fruit, juice, home-baked breads or muffins, breakfast meat, and a changing menu of hot dishes, ranging from quiche to pancakes, from asparagus and almond strudel to cheese-stuffed French toast with apricot glaze.

"The inn is quiet and restful, the neighborhood full of beautifully restored homes, a lovely place for a late afternoon walk." *(Ron Simblist)* "Home-baked breads or cakes await your arrival. Fresh fruit fills the silver bowl in the hallway. The dining room is complete with a lace tablecloth and fresh linen napkins, beautiful china, and silver service. Breakfasts are unsurpassed, with no repetition of dishes during a three- or four-day stay. The meal includes fresh fruit, homemade muffins or bread, and entrées varying from French toast stuffed with three cheeses and topped with homemade sauce to a light cheese, egg, and sausage casserole." *(Leigh Farver)*

"Our room had a comfortable bed, sofa, and rocking chair, with ample storage space in the closet and dresser. Our bathroom was well supplied with fresh soap, shampoo, and conditioner. Parking is provided behind the inn as well as on the street in front. We had a key to the front door, so we could come and go as we chose." *(Penelope Elliott)* "Diana served us an enormous breakfast, and then in the afternoon brought out a huge tray of wine, cheese, and other snacks. She was charming and helpful, supplying us with information on activities. Our bath, though tiny, was immaculate." *(Elisabeth McLaughlin)*

Minor niggles: "Our room got too cold at night, but there was no in-room control for the air-conditioning." Also: "There seemed to be no one on site at night, which made me feel a bit uncomfortable."

Note: The inn was for sale as we went to press; inquire further when booking.

Open All year. Closed Christmas.
Rooms 5 doubles, 1 single—all with private bath and/or shower, air-conditioning. Many with fireplace. TV on request.
Facilities Dining room, parlor with fireplace, porches. 1/2 acre with rose gardens.
Location In historic district. Between Oakwood and Polk Sts.
Restrictions Smoking in designated guest rooms only. No children under 12.

Credit cards Amex, Discover, MC, Visa.
Rates B&B, $75–100 double, $65–90 single. Weekday rates.
Extras Limited wheelchair access. Some French spoken.

ROBBINSVILLE

Snowbird Mountain Lodge ¢   *Tel:* 704–479–3433
275 Santeetlah Road, 28771

Snowbird is an informal and relaxed place, set atop a low mountain at 2,880 feet. It is built of chestnut logs and native stone, and rooms are paneled in butternut, cherry, and other native woods, with matching custom-made furniture. In 1990, the lodge was purchased by Jim and Eleanor Burbank, who had enjoyed Snowbird as guests for many years and they have done a little sprucing up here and there. As Jim puts it: "We're not for the 'country club set'—there's not even a golf course in the whole county. What is popular are the spring wildflower walks through the Nantahala and Joyce Kilmer forests, led by a naturalist, and other outdoors activities, like the hiking week held in June." Although most readers are delighted with Snowbird's isolated setting, it's not for everyone. Accommodations are comfortable but basic; windows are not sealed and you can expect that the odd bug or two will find your room inviting. Come here for the fabulous views, glorious mountains, and beautiful woods at very reasonable prices—but not for mounds of thick towels or bedtime mints.

"Many guests return again and again, and wonderful friendships develop. We enjoy the peaceful, quiet atmosphere, wonderful view of the mountains, and interesting walking trails, particularly the Joyce Kilmer Virgin Forest." *(Laura I. Smith)* "The location and view exceeded our expectations—as magnificent as one could possibly expect in mountains of such moderate altitude. The inn is far from other dwellings and secluded from the road, making for a cozy retreat. We greatly enjoyed sitting in the large common room with ancient hand-hewn wooden posts and beams, awaiting dinner-time. " *(FJH)* "Located miles from anything but natural beauty, with spectacular views in all directions. Limitless hiking. We have always found clean pleasant rooms, great meals, and have met a lot of wonderful guests. The Burbanks can't do enough to please their guests." *(Phil Young)*

Minor niggle: "Our room was adequate but lacked sufficient lighting for reading in bed."

Open Mid-April–early-Nov.
Rooms 23 doubles—21 with private bath and/or shower, 2 rooms with a maximum of 4 sharing bath. All with desk, fan. 7 rooms in 2 cottages.
Facilities Dining room; sitting room/library with games, fireplace, piano, books. Shuffleboard, Ping-Pong, pool, lawn games. 100 acres with stream swimming, trout fishing, hiking. Canoe rental, white-water rafting on Nantahala River. Spring wildflower walks with naturalist.
Location W NC. 100 m W of Asheville, 80 m S of Knoxville, TN, 160 m N of Atlanta. 10 m NW of Robbinsville; follow Rte. 129 to Joyce Kilmer Virgin Forest.

Restrictions No smoking in dining room. No alcohol served, BYOB. No children under 12.
Credit cards Amex, MC, Visa.
Rates Full board, $110–130 double, $85–90 single. Extra person, $38. 10% service additional. 2-3 night weekend, holiday minimum.
Extras Wheelchair access.

SALISBURY

Information please: About 20 miles west of Salisbury is the town of Statesville, home to the **Cedar Hill Farm B&B** (Route 1, Box 492, Statesville 28677; 704–873–4332). A preliminary recommendation noted that it is a working farm, with a welcoming atmosphere, friendly owners, comfortable rooms, and a delightful private cottage.

Visit the small town of Hiddenite, 40 miles northwest of Salisbury, where you can stake a claim and dig for emeralds or semi-precious stones, or buy a bucket of already mined soil and pan it (like gold). Named for a type of tourmaline found here, it is a rockhound's dream—you can find 60 different minerals: rubies, aquamarine, amethyst, moonstone, rose quartz, or emeralds. The **Hidden Crystal Inn** (School Road, Hiddenite 28636; 704–632–0063) was created from a plantation-style home by Hiddenite native Eileen Sharpe. An extensive arrangement of minerals is displayed in the emerald-green library, and the five guest rooms, with private bath, are named for gems, with coordinating fabrics and wallcoverings; the Amethyst is pink and lavender, and the Hiddenite is yellow. Rates include a full breakfast of country ham, eggs, buttermilk biscuits, homemade jams, fruit, and pastries; a swimming pool and lawn games are available.

Rowan Oak House ¢
208 South Fulton Street, 28144

Tel: 704–633–2086
800–786–0437

A Scottish-Celtic legend tells of a magical tree that symbolized beauty, hospitality, privacy, peace, and sanctuary—the Rowan Oak. So, when Bill and Ruth Ann Coffey sold their house in Texas and moved to Salisbury to start their retirement career as innkeepers, they decided the Rowan Oak symbolized everything they hoped to achieve with their inn. Built in 1901, their home was constructed in the Queen Anne style and has been furnished by the Coffeys in high Victorian decor. The house features seven fireplaces, each different, as well as the original combined gas and electric light fixtures. A recent paint job returned the inn to its original appearance—a soft blue-gray and cream. Ruth Ann reports that "we strive to provide a touch of the past with the comforts of 1991. We appeal to the romantic." Breakfast includes homemade breads and muffins, fruit and juice, and an entrée such as a French toast Lorraine with bacon and sausage, or a Dutch baby with bacon, or the Rowan Oak breakfast soufflé; afternoon refreshments are served in the living room; fresh fruit and flowers are placed in each guest room.

"Beautiful, comfortable furnishings which matched the inn's Victorian atmosphere. Bill and Ruth Ann provided friendly, personable service; a delicious breakfast was served on fine china and crystal." *(Franklin Bryan)* "Enjoyed a warm greeting from the Coffeys, and everything else about the Rowan Oak. This is a big old house with huge bathrooms, all furnished beautifully." *(Elisabeth McLaughlin)*

"Our hosts, well-traveled and interesting people, pampered us but also respected our privacy. Furnishings are impressive, with very fine antiques throughout. The atmosphere is congenial, very much class and refinement, yet not stuffy." *(Janet Beck)* "Lots of reading material of general interest as well as about local historic area. Nice common room upstairs. The Coffeys' experience as guests at other B&Bs have given them insight in what makes a good one. Excellent food." *(Margaret Stanley)*

Open All year.
Rooms 3 doubles—all with private bath and/or shower, telephone, radio, desk, air-conditioning, fan. 1 room with whirlpool bath, fireplace.
Facilities Dining room, parlor with fireplace, game room with TV, wraparound porches. 1/2 acre with gardens. Tennis, golf, boating, fishing nearby.
Location Central NC. 42 m N of Charlotte. 39 m S of Winston-Salem. 3 blocks to center of town. In historic district. From I-85 take Exit 76B. Go W on Innes St. Turn left on Fulton St. Inn on right.
Restrictions Smoking in living room, lounge only. No children under 10.
Credit cards Discover, MC, Visa.
Rates B&B, $65–85 double, $60–80 single. Extra person, $15. No tipping. Reduced rates for extended stays. 10% senior, AAA discount. 2-night minimum stay some weekends.
Extras Local airport/station pickups. Crib. Some Spanish spoken.

The 1868 Stewart-Marsh House ¢　　　　*Tel:* 704–633–6841
220 South Ellis Street, 28144

The Federal-style Stewart-Marsh House, built in 1868 by J.J. Stewart, is one of many restored homes in the West Square Historic District of Salisbury. Geraldine Webster has owned the inn since 1988 and has decorated with antique furnishings and collectibles, as well as with some of her own artwork. Guest rooms have simple tie-back curtains, antique walnut and maple beds, and comfortable reading chairs. Breakfast includes an entrée, maybe a grits and sausage casserole, or a baked ham, cheese, and turkey sandwich, accompanied by fruit compote, homemade muffins and breads, coffee, tea, and milk; fresh fruit, mints, and flowers are in every room.

"Breakfast is served in the dining room at the hour of your choice. Gerry served a beautifully prepared meal and was kind enough to share her recipes with me."*(Jeanne Schember)* "Gerry and Chuck are not only gracious hosts but also interesting people who are involved in the area, well informed about local activities." *(Scottie Baker)* "Comfy library with fireplace, TV, and lendable paperbacks. Modern bath, comfortable bed." *(Vincent Lindgren, and others)*

Open All year.
Rooms 2 doubles—both with private bath, desk, air-conditioning, fan.
Facilities Library with TV, books, games. Dining room, breakfast room, living room, screened porch. Off-street parking. Tennis, golf nearby.

Location Rowan County. From I-85, take Exit 76B. Follow East Innes Street to South Ellis Street. Take left onto South Ellis Street and inn is near end of road.
Restrictions No smoking. Children under 6 accepted at innkeeper's discretion.
Credit cards MC, Visa.
Rates B&B, $50–55 double. Extra person, $15. 2-day minimum stay during local events. No tipping.
Extras Airport/station pickups.

SALUDA

Saluda is a quiet, small town in the foothills of the Blue Ridge Mountains of western North Carolina, 30 miles south of Asheville, near the South Carolina border. There are many antique and craft shops in the area, along with restaurants serving good mountain cooking, and lots of good hiking trails. The Carl Sandburg National Historic Site is also nearby.

Information please: A Queen Anne Victorian home built in 1894, **The Oaks** (Greenville Street, P.O. Box 1008, 28773; 704–749–9613) offers period decor, heart pine flooring, and a breakfast of homemade croissants and muffins. Five guest rooms are available, most with private bath, and rates are reasonable.

The Orchard Inn ✗
Highway 176, P.O. Box 725, 28773

Tel: 704–749–5471

In the early 1900s the Southern Railway Company built a summer mountain retreat, at an elevation of 2,500 feet, for railroad clerks and their families; it is now known as The Orchard Inn. Kenneth and Ann Hough renovated the inn in 1982, and have decorated the rooms with antiques and casual country charm, including brass/iron and four-poster beds, rag and Oriental rugs, and baskets and other craftwork.

"The setting is spectacular, the foothills visible for miles, with the premier view from the rear sunporch. A large living room has several conversational groupings to allow guests to visit as they wait to be escorted to dinner. The fireplace is the focal point but books and many interesting art objects occupy those who would rather browse. The area has a spacious, bright air, with light hardwood floors and Oriental rugs. Dinner is the evening's entertainment, served by candlelight, with the innkeepers visiting from table to table. We had a choice of entrée—prime rib, chicken, or trout—and all were excellent. The innkeepers were really likeable." *(SHW)*

"The living room has maps, walking sticks, and nooks for everyone. Ken sings opera (sometimes for guests), and has an extensive music collection. Breakfast is wonderful, with blueberry pancakes one morning, eggs and granola the next. They will keep and uncork your wine for you; my husband did not bring the required jacket for dinner, but Ken had a closet full for him to choose. Everyone staying at the inn was friendly, yet there was plenty of room to be alone.

"Our room was pleasant and quiet, even with the inn full, with a very good bed, and lots of blankets and excellent pillows. On the upstairs landing were more books, magazines, and antiques. Ken gave good suggestions for other places to dine, and for art galleries and boutiques. When we had to leave abruptly due to a family emergency, he was wonderfully understanding." *(Louise Brown)*

Open All year. Restaurant closed Sundays.
Rooms 1 suite, 9 doubles, 2 cottages—all with full private bath, radio. Some with desk, air-conditioning, deck.
Facilities Restaurant, large living room, extensive library, game room. 20 acres with nature walks. Tennis, golf nearby.
Location SW NC. 20 m S of Hendersonville. 30 m E of Asheville. 1 m from town. On Hwy 176, 2 m S of I-26, Exit 28.
Restrictions No smoking in dining room or guest rooms. No alcohol is served; BYOB. Jackets required for gentlemen for evening meal. No children under 12.
Credit cards None accepted.
Rates B&B, $125 suite, $85–95 double, including service. Extra person, $20. 2-night minimum. Prix fixe dinner, $20–30.
Extras Airport pickup, $20. French spoken.

SPRUCE PINE

Also recommended: Too late for a full write-up, we received a report from *Betty Norman* on the **Big Lynn Lodge** (Route 226A, P.O. Box 459, Little Switzerland 28749; 704–765–4257) listed in many earlier editions of this guide, and once again recommended under its new ownership. The lodge is set at an altitude of 3200 feet, and most of the 40 rooms have beautiful views; many were recently refurbished. "While we were not in one of the refurbished rooms, we enjoyed our time here. Our dinner and breakfast were outstanding. The fresh trout from a local hatchery was delicious and we were surprised when the owner and chef came to our table to see if we would like seconds. We think the Big Lynn Lodge is an exceptional value."

Reader tip: "Ask your innkeeper for restaurant advice; there's not a whole lot available in this area. Saturday nights can be busy and slow, and many restaurants are closed on Sunday and Monday. Our favorite was the Little Switzerland Cafe, with delicious lunches of pastries, breads, soups, and chili. Also acceptable was the Cedar Crest in downtown Spruce Pine, with reasonable prices and good trout." *(Virginia Henke)*

The Fairway Inn ¢   *Tel:* 704–765–4917
110 Henry Lane, 28777   Off-season: 904–724–7379

Pierce and Margaret Stevens, owners of the Fairway since 1985, welcome guests to their comfortable mountain home, overlooking an 18-hole golf course. The spacious white clapboard house is decorated eclectically with traditional and contemporary decor; one guest room is done in rattan, another with iron beds. Rates include a full breakfast featuring such entrées as baked cheese blintzes, sausage and egg casserole, or French toast made with homemade bread.

"Our room was large, with a sun porch and private entrance, on the first floor. We had a pretty bathroom, good closet, plenty of chairs, a good-sized table, large chest of drawers, good lamps and bedside tables, ample pillows, and fresh flowers; the color scheme was quiet and tasteful, and everything was very clean. Pierce is an architect, and Margaret paints; they are warm, considerate, capable, tactful, and fun. Attention to detail was apparent in small touches—from different linen napkins each morning to the wine and cheese hour every evening. Breakfast was an event. Every day we had delicious, imaginative dishes, fresh fruit prettily served, two kinds of home-baked muffins and toast, cereal if desired, homemade jams, our own carafe of tea or coffee. The other guests were interesting and friendly. There was one large table, so we all talked. There's a TV in the living room but the signals are few and the quality poor because of the mountains. We didn't mind because the surroundings are so enticing. The inn is just three miles from the Blue Ridge Parkway, which led us to many interesting spots. There are dozens of gem stores nearby and some antique shops, but it is an unsophisticated area. We loved the quiet beauty of the grounds and giant spruces, the birds and rabbits." *(Janet & Clifford Nelson)*

"Margaret and Pierce are terrific, friendly people providing outstanding service and an immaculate home." *(Donna Sinclair)* "This is a comfortable place where you feel free to come in, take off your shoes and put your feet up on the friendly couch in the big living room and watch a ball game or read. Service is first-rate with many homey touches. They put a piece of candy on your pillow every night and make the beds promptly in the morning. They also have an evening happy hour with crackers, home-made spreads, and wine or spiked cider. Breakfast is delicious, with egg-based dishes and pancakes with raisin-based toppings." *(Virginia Henke)*

Open April through Dec.
Rooms 1 apartment, 1 suite, 4 doubles—all with private bath and/or shower, desk. 5 with fan. Apartment with equipped kitchen.
Facilities Dining room, living room with TV, fireplace, library with games, porch. 1½ acres with lawn. Golf, tennis nearby, $2 discount on greens fee. 30 min. to lake for fishing, boating.
Location W NC, Blue Ridge Mt. region. 45 m E of Asheville, 100 m NW of Charlotte, 30 m W of Boone. 1 m from town. From Blue Ridge Pkwy. take Rte. 226 N to Spruce Pine Shopping Ctr., then turn left on Fairway Ln., which becomes Henry Ln., to inn on left.
Restrictions Smoking permitted only in living room during cold weather.
Credit cards None accepted.
Rates B&B, $65–75 suite or double. Room only, $55. Extra person, $15. Weekly, monthly rates for apartment. Reduced rates for families.
Extras Wheelchair access; some rooms equipped for disabled. Crib, babysitting.

SYLVA

Mountain Brook   *Tel:* 704–586–4329
Route 2, P.O. Box 301, 28779

The Mountain Brook dates from the 1930s when Hardy Clark built cottages from logs felled on the property, and others from the stone of nearby quarries. Electricity came via an enormous overshot water wheel, powered by the mountain brook for which the resort is named. Gus and Michele McMahon bought Mountain Brook in 1979, and have slowly upgraded the dozen cottages built of log, stone, brick, and board and batten, to enhance their rustic charm with modern amenities and comfortable appointments. Michele notes that "we are a favorite with honeymooners—romance for lovers of all ages is our specialty."

"Mountain Brook is located off the main highway between Sylva and Franklin. It is far enough from the main road that traffic noise does not disturb anyone, but close enough to allow easy access to nearby towns and shops. The cottages are staggered along a slight hillside, and are fairly close together, but because of natural landscaping, some are quite private. The cottages are decorated with country warmth and coziness—pictures on the walls, quilts, rocking chairs, and dried flowers—combined with microwave ovens, electric heat, and clean, up-to-date bathrooms. No food is served, but kitchens are well supplied with utensils and appliances; a restaurant is within walking distance. There is no maid service during your stay, although soiled linens and towels may be exchanged anytime at the office.

"The owners and staff try to honor guests' privacy by being as inconspicuous as possible. Information and help is always close at hand (such as the information binder placed in every cottage), but the guest generally has to make the first move. Staff members are polite and helpful and always willing to answer questions or stop and chat, but only if approached. A recent improvement was the renovation of two of the larger cottages into honeymoon retreats, with especially luxurious appointments." *(Geoffrey & Lauraine Murray, also Barry Gardner)* More reports appreciated.

Open All year.
Rooms 12 1-2 bedroom cottages—all with private bath and/or shower, radio, fireplace, fully equipped kitchen, deck. 3 with desk, 2 with air-conditioning, or fan, 3 with whirlpool tub.
Facilities Game room with pool table, board games; sauna/spa bungalow, hot tub. 33 acres with stocked trout pond (rods provided), nature trails, playground and children's play equipment, picnic area.
Location W NC, 1 hr. W of Asheville. 9 m S of Dillsboro, 2/10 m off Rte. 441.
Restrictions No maid service.
Credit cards None accepted.
Rates Room only, $70–90 cabin (for 2 people). Romance packages, $120.
Extras Wheelchair access; 1 cabin partially equipped for disabled. Station pickup by arrangment. Crib, babysitting. Some French spoken.

TRYON

Tryon is in the heart of Carolina fox-hunting country; the climate is mild, with golf and horseback riding available year-round.

Pine Crest Inn ¢ 🏇 ✗   *Tel:* 704–859–9135
200 Pine Crest Lane, 28782   800–633–3001

Established by Michigan equestrian Carter Brown in 1917, and listed on the National Register of Historic Places, the Pine Crest was purchased by Jeremy and Jennifer Wainwright in 1990. Originally from Great Britain, the Wainwrights have renovated the main building to evoke the feeling of an English country inn, with leather chairs and richly upholstered furnishings, and a traditional hunt and steeplechase decor. Plans are to continue this renovation process to all the guest rooms; by 1992, all should be re-done. The restaurant is open to the public, serving two meals daily; sample entrées might include rack of lamb with mustard and Madeira sauce, filet mignon with green peppercorn sauce, and grilled mountain trout with lemon parsley.

"A wonderful metamorphosis has taken place at Pine Crest. The rustic tweeds have given way to sporting prints, a reincarnation suitable to the North Carolina horse country. The atmosphere is posh, but practical, with Ralph Lauren decor supplementing the antiques. The dining room is evocative of Colonial Williamsburg, with small dining rooms of just four to six tables. My favorite selections are the lamb and crabcakes, classically prepared, and not over-sauced. Beautiful desserts are presented on a silver tray, and some of the waiters have been here at least fourteen years. The full breakfast includes entrées such as eggs Benedict or Florentine.

"The Front Pine room has a half-tester paisley canopy, down duvet, and a hunting print over the bed, accenting the dark paneling and shutters and the hunt green and red color scheme. The West suite is a dramatic contrast, with celadon green and pink floral fabrics, but equally attractive. The Gold room should surely be called the Audubon, for the print hanging over the red-tiled fireplace commands your attention. All rooms have thick towels and robes, English soaps and gels in oversize portions. Even the unrenovated rooms are lovely, though not lavish, and economically priced at $60. And all are worth the price when you consider the wonderful breakfast." *(SHW)*

"This inn is close to the center of a lovely small town just at the edge of the Blue Ridge Mountains, but so secluded you'd swear you were in the middle of a forest." *(Sandra & Berge Heede)*

Open All year.
Rooms 4 cabins, 8 1–3 bedroom suites, 12 doubles—all with private bath and/or shower, telephone, TV, desk, air-conditioning. Rooms in 10 buildings and cabins, most with fireplace.
Facilities Restaurant, lobby, den with fireplaces, TV, books, games, puzzles, piano; facsimile, copier, word processing equipment available. 3 acres. Swimming pool, golf, tennis, hiking nearby.
Location W NC, 1 m from the SC border, halfway between Asheville and Spartanburg, SC. ½ m to town; 4 m from I-26.
Credit cards MC, Visa.
Rates B&B, $50–135 double, $40–125 single. Extra adult, $25; extra child age 6–17, $15; children under 6 free in parents' room. Corporate rates. Alc dinner, $20–35.

VALLE CRUCIS

Named for the three streams that cross in this high mountain valley, Valle Crucis is the home of the Mast General Store, dating back to 1883, and several interesting craft stores; it was founded by Scottish Highlanders, and hosts the largest gathering of the clans in the U.S. each summer. The village has been designated a National Historic District, the first rural one in North Carolina, and it encompasses 1,000 acres. Valle Crucis is located in the High Country of northwest North Carolina, midway between Boone and Banner Elk, 100 miles north of Charlotte, and 93 miles west of Winston-Salem. Within a short drive are such activities as golf, tennis, horseback riding, hiking, fishing, canoeing, downhill and cross-country skiing.

The Inn at the Taylor House 👥   *Tel:* 704–963–5581
Highway 194, P.O. Box 713, 28691

Describing an inn is easiest when we can clearly label the decor as Victorian, Williamsburg Colonial, Arts & Crafts style, or perhaps contemporary—and is hardest in the case of an inn like this one, where phrases like "elegant good taste" are more than empty adjectives. In the case of the Inn at the Taylor House, Chip and Roland Schwab, who opened the inn in 1988, have done an exceptional job of renovating and decorating their 1911 home. The living room is done with Oriental carpets and lamps, period antiques and reproductions, and lots of overstuffed chairs and couches. Each bedroom is different, one done in soft flowered corals and white wicker, another crisp with striped wallpaper and soft green fabrics. Imported duvets combine handsome appearance with real comfort. Guests enjoy relaxing on the plant-filled porch, looking out on a field of cattle, or assembling in the dining room for one of the Schwabs' hearty breakfasts. Roland is Swiss, and a fifth-generation innkeeper; his specialties include Birchermuesli—a Swiss cereal of local fruits and berries combined with oats, nuts, and yogurt—followed by omelets, corned beef hash, or blueberry pancakes.

"Only one thing rivals the lovely decor of the Taylor House—the caring, gracious innkeepers, Chip and Roland Schwab. They made us feel at home from the moment we arrived. Each morning of our stay was something to look forward to. Coffee is put out early, and we couldn't resist strolling through the gardens with a steaming fresh cup. (Chip has planted lovely herbs and flowers to explore.) We stayed in the main bedroom downstairs, with a down comforter on the bed and a large private bath. The colors used in the room are striking—a deep forest-green carpet with terra-cotta walls and complementing drapes." *(Valerie Vogler-Stipe)*

"The inn provides an ideal blend of sophisticated elegance and continental flair, with a genuine concern for guest comfort. A strong background in professional food preparation makes breakfast one of the day's highlights."*(Henry and Val Egem)*

Open April 15 to Jan. 1
Rooms 1 suite, 5 doubles, 1 cabin—all with private bath and/or shower, desk, fan.
Facilities Breakfast room, living room with fireplace, library with fireplace, TV room with VCR, games; wraparound porch. 2 acres with gazebo, herb garden.
Location 5 m W of Boone. On Hwy. 194 between Banner Elk and Valle Crucis.
Restrictions No smoking.
Credit cards MC, Visa.

Rates B&B, $135 suite, $90 double or single. Extra person, $25. 2-night weekend minimum.
Extras Airport/station pickup. Crib, babysitting. German, Italian, French, Spanish spoken.

Mast Farm Inn ✕
P.O. Box 704, 28691

Tel: 704–963–5857

The Mast Farm began as a log cabin in 1812, and grew to include a blacksmith shop, meat house, spring house, wash house, apple house, and barn. The main house was completed in 1885 and served as a thirteen-bedroom, one-bath (!) country inn through the first half of this century, but it fell into disrepair and was sold by the Mast family. Francis and Sibyl Pressly, who left very different careers in Washington, DC, bought the inn late in 1984; they spent nearly a year restoring it and all the outbuildings.

Reporting after a return visit, *Sibyl Nestor* wrote: "This is our very favorite inn—a very friendly place. The Presslys make an effort to seat guests in compatible groups at meals. The food is something special—much of it is grown on the grounds, and after a big meal you can walk alongside the immense garden."

"Staying here is like visiting good friends in their well-restored, but not fancy, old country farmhouse. The principal activity, aside from eating, is rocking on the porch and watching the cars go by, and making the acquaintance of fellow guests. The rooms are airy, large, and clean, with adequate lighting, at least one easy chair, comfortable beds and appropriate decorative touches. Service is mostly provided by the Presslys themselves (except at meals), and is unfailingly gracious. Sybil Pressly oversees the kitchen, house, and cutting garden (lovely dried flowers are for sale). Her recipes form the basis of memorable meals, served family-style in two dining rooms. Breakfast is simple—juice and coffee, fresh fruit and home-baked muffins, breads, honey-pecan rolls, pancakes, homemade apple butter, and locally made preserves. Dinner is a major event, with a set menu for every day of the week. Thursday is chicken and dumplings, Friday is sautéed trout with vegetable strudel, and Sunday brings outstanding fried chicken and country ham with biscuits and gravy. All the superb entrées are accompanied by home-style vegetables (corn, beans, potatoes, black-eyed peas, carrots, and more), fresh salad, and savories. No alcoholic beverages are served, but the staff is happy to chill your wine and serve it at dinner." *(Beth & Vaughn Morrison)*

"Our spacious room was furnished with country antiques, fresh-cut flowers, and an old-fashioned dried blossom sachet in the bureau." *(Robert Folger)* "The baths are equipped with tubs from the era, painted to go with the color scheme of the room." *(Chuck & Linda Shore)* "Each guest room is named after a different member of the Mast family. Guests are encouraged to come back to the kitchen for coffee anytime after dinner. Most gather on the large wraparound front porch to rock, sip their coffee, and chat." *(Mrs. Carolyn Hemric)*

"Although it was a busy time (Sunday dinner), we felt the inn's warmth and friendliness the moment we walked in. Throughout our stay, the hosts took time to visit with guests and make them feel like part of the family.

Our room was squeaky clean and extremely comfortable; we liked the lemon soap in the bathroom. The owners' restoration of this farmhouse was clearly a labor of love. The food was wonderful—fresh from the garden when possible." *(Mrs. Louis Haynes)*

While truly wonderful, the Mast Farm is not perfect; some minor complaints noted in otherwise glowing reports: Parking is tight when the inn is busy with outside and resident dinner guests; the third floor can be hot in summer, despite plenty of fans; and there is some road traffic noise, mostly caused by "motorists whizzing past the inn much too fast on their way to the Mast General Store, a wonderful place."

Open May–Oct., Jan.–Feb.
Rooms 1 suite, 10 doubles, 1 cottage—10 with private bath, 2 with a maximum of 4 people sharing bath. All with radio, fan. 5 rooms with desk. 3 rooms in out-buildings.
Facilities Restaurant, parlor with fireplace, sun porch, library/game room. 18 acres with river for trout fishing; pond for fishing, swimming.
Location On SR 1112, 3 m from NC 105.
Restrictions No smoking. No children under 12.
Credit cards MC, Visa.
Rates MAP, $80–145 double. Children under 12, $17. Extra person, $33. Sunday prix fixe lunch, $13.50; prix fixe dinner, $13.50. 2-night weekend minimum.
Extras First-floor bedroom equipped for disabled. Airport/station pickups. Portuguese spoken.

WAYNESVILLE

Waynesville is a popular mountain resort, set between the Great Smoky Mountains National Park and the Pisgah National Forest. Summer activities include hiking, fishing, horseback riding, white-water rafting, golf, and tennis, while downhill and cross-country skiing are available nearby in the winter. Waynesville is 25 miles west of Asheville, 130 miles southeast of Knoxville, and 190 miles north of Atlanta.

Information please: If you're traveling with the family, there's little doubt that your school-age kids will prefer staying at the 5000-foot-high **Cataloochee Ranch** (Route 1, Box 500F, Maggie Valley 28751; 828 926–1401). About 10 miles northwest of Waynesville, this 50-year-old dude ranch, bought when land bordering the Smoky Mountains National Park cost $10 an acre, offers comfortable accommodations in its rustic mountain lodge and cabins. Rates are reasonable, and activities include trail rides, tennis, hiking, and trout fishing; downhill skiing is available nearby in winter. Meals are hearty and rooms highlighted by fieldstone fireplaces, classic or primitive antiques, and quilts.

We'd also like to hear from any of our readers who have recently visited the **Mt. Pisgah Inn** (Milepost 408.6, Blue Ridge Parkway, P.O. Drawer 749, 28786; 704–235–8228), a motel-like structure, set on a mountaintop a mile high, with 360° panoramic views and cool nighttime temperatures. Rooms are plain but clean, with contemporary decor, and a balcony or deck to take in the vistas. All food is home-cooked "from scratch," including desserts and bread; freshly caught mountain trout is a specialty and prices are reasonable. Be sure to eat in the restaurant if you'd like the view to compliment the cuisine; the cafeteria is fine if it's foggy or you're on a tight budget. "Wonderful views, convenient location; food mediocre on our last visit." (JS)

Hallcrest Inn ¢ ♦♦   *Tel:* 704–456–6457
299 Halltop Circle, 28786   800–334–6457

Built as a private home in 1880, the Hallcrest sits atop Hall Mountain with views of Waynesville and the Balsam Mountains, in a quiet setting at the end of a gravel road. Long-time owners of the Hallcrest, Russell and Margaret Burson note that their inn has a "relaxing home-like atmosphere. You can come for early morning coffee in your bathrobe. Most guests are out during the day, taking in the area's many attractions, but a few prefer to stay in and enjoy the quiet." Rooms are simply furnished, highlighted by family antiques; four rooms are in a motel-type annex called the Side Porch. The extremely reasonable rates include a breakfast of eggs, grits, juice, fruit, biscuits, breakfast meat, and beverage. A typical dinner might include roast beef, brown rice, squash casserole, lima beans with herbs, marinated cucumbers and tomatoes, home baked rolls with strawberry preserves and apple butter, and homemade ice cream. Apples in some form are served at each meal.

"Come to the Hallcrest to slow down and relax, make new friends, and eat excellent food. We loved all the friendly folk we met, and the breakfasts and dinners were always taken at the same table with new-found friends. The food is placed on lazy Susans in the center of each table, enabling one to select (again and again) all the different dishes. Our room on the second floor of the main building was clean and comfortable with good reading lights. We rocked slowly on the porch, reflecting on what would be served at the next delicious meal, and whether we should take another walk around Halltop Circle." *(April Burwell)* More reports welcome.

Open Late May through Thanksgiving.
Rooms 12 doubles—all with private bath and/or shower, fan. Some with fireplace. 4 rooms in motel-style annex.
Facilities Dining room, living room with TV, sitting room with TV, games, library; porches with rockers. 4 acres with lawns, woodland, children's play equipment.
Location W NC. 25 m W of Asheville. 3 m from town. Take Rte. 276 N from Waynesville, then turn left on Mauney Cove Rd. Follow signs to inn.
Restrictions No smoking in dining room.
Credit cards MC, Visa.
Rates MAP, $75 double, $55 single. Extra person, $30. Tipping of housekeeper, dining room staff appreciated. Discount for children under 6.
Extras Airport pickup, $15; station pickup. Crib, babysitting.

Heath Lodge ¢ ♦♦   *Tel:* 704–456–3333
900 Dolan Road, 28786   800–HEATH–99

Set at 3,200 feet, Heath Lodge offers pure mountain air, to be enjoyed on wide porches that have high-backed rockers. The buildings are constructed of native poplar and stone, and rooms are rustic but comfortable. David and Bonnie Probst have owned the inn since 1980; Bonnie notes that Heath Lodge attracts "couples and families interested in both active and idle country vacations—golfers, hikers, rafters, sightseers, and those whose only desire is to rock or lie in the hammock between meals." The full country breakfast includes eggs cooked to order, bacon or country sausage, grits, homemade biscuits, and hot applesauce. Dinners are served family-style at lazy-Susan tables, and include two meats and five vegetables with homemade breads and desserts.

"Secluded mountain setting, away from city sights and sounds. Warm days and cool nights, great for sleeping." *(Clyde & Hilda Vaughn)* "Country touches with class: miniature soaps in a basket, potpourri in the closet, a ribbon wrapped grapevine wreath, and fresh white country curtains, attractive quilted handiwork, and fresh flowers. Sleep with the windows open, and listen to the birds." *(Mr. & Mrs. Robert Ogg)* "The parking lot has ample room and is well lit, and the recreation room is large and comfortable, with a good reading and TV area, and several corners for doing jigsaw puzzles and playing cards." *(Mr. & Mrs. H.M. Hoff)*

"The food and dining room service is outstanding—all of the food is home-cooked American-style with quality ingredients and healthy preparation. Rooms are comfortable but simple, with plenty of closet and drawer space in which to unpack for a week-plus stay. Everything is clean and well maintained; rooms are made up very well and quickly, right after breakfast. David and Bonnie are very knowledgeable about the area and its many attractions." *(Norm & Carol Proffitt)*

Open Late April through Oct.; breakfast only April through Memorial Day.
Rooms 2 suites, 20 doubles—all with private bath and/or shower, TV, desk, fan. 2 rooms in main lodge, 20 in 7 outlying buildings.
Facilities Dining room; great room with library, card tables, TV, piano. 6 wooded acres with hot tub, stream. Golf, fishing nearby.
Location 1 m to town. From I-40, take Exit 27, Hwy. 19/23. Go 6 m to Waynesville exit and take Hwy. 276 S. Go about 1/4 m to Phillips 66 station (opposite Pizza Hut), turn right onto Love Lane. Turn right again onto Dolan to inn on left.
Credit cards None accepted.
Rates B&B (April to Memorial Day weekend), $50–60 double, $45 single. MAP, $85–95 double, $55–60 single. Extra person, $30–35. Reduced rates for children, 4 week or longer stays. Prix fixe dinner, $12.
Extras Wheelchair access. Airport/station pickup. Crib, babysitting.

The Swag   *Tel:* 704–926–0430
Route 2, Box 280-A, Hemphill Road, 28786

Long-time owner Deener Matthews reports that a "swag" is a dip between two knolls on a high mountain ridge. It is the traditional term used by our mountain neighbors for as long as anyone can recall to designate our particular site." The Matthews family has created their inn from an old hand-hewn log and rock church and five other buildings, some dating back 200 years. They've decorated the inn with furniture, art, crafts, and handmade quilts of western North Carolina and eastern Tennessee. Each evening a different four-course dinner is served (happily adapted for dietary restrictions); the menu might include snow pea mushroom soup,

267

NORTH CAROLINA

fresh fruit salad with poppyseed dressing, chicken teriyaki with herb couscous and stir-fried zucchini, and lemon daffodil cake; or French onion soup, fresh spinach and artichoke salad, trout amandine with mushroom stroganoff, and melon with fruit glaze and almond meringue cookies.

"Perched at 5,000 feet, The Swag is a unique mountain inn. Through the years the Matthews family has crafted the structure from hand-shaped beams, wood, and stone. Our room, high under the eaves, was cozy, comfortable, and had a remarkable view. The bath was luxurious and complete down to the soft terry cloth robes. Meals are distinctive and delicious, served with care. For recreation you can step out the door and hike in the Great Smoky Mountains National Park, engage in activities from racquetball to croquet, or sit by the fire and enjoy a book from the extensive library. Finally, you will find no more charming and helpful host than Deener Matthews." *(Sheila & Joe Schmidt)* "Just as good on a return visit as it was the first time. Several times during the summer naturalists, musicians, and other experts offers programs for the guests. We were fortunate to hear an excellent performance of country music." *(JS)*

Open May through Oct.

Rooms 2 cabins, 12 doubles—all with private bath and/or shower. Many with balcony, refrigerator. 7 with steam shower, 9 with woodstove or fireplace. 1 cabin with whirlpool tub, refrigerator, wet bar, fireplace.

Facilities Dining room, living room with fireplace, player piano, games, library; porch. 250 acres with woodland, wildflowers, hammock, swing, hiking trails, badminton, croquet, underground racquetball court, sauna, private entrance to Great Smoky Mt. National Park. Golf nearby.

Location W NC. 12 m from Waynesville, 5 m from Maggie Valley, 30 m W of Asheville. From Waynesville, take I-276 N toward Knoxville. Go 2.3 m past intersection with Rte. 19 to Hemphill Rd. Turn left on Hemphill Rd. to inn.

Restrictions No smoking. No children under 7. Dry county, BYOB.

Credit cards MC, Visa.

Rates Full board (for 2 people), $238–258 cabin, $138–228 double. Extra person, $70. Prix fixe lunch, $10; prix fixe dinner $30. 15% service. Box lunches. Nature, painting, writing workshops. 2-night minimum.

Extras Wheelchair access; some rooms equipped for the disabled. Airport pickup, $36. Crib; babysitting can be arranged.

WHITTIER

The Fisher House B&B ¢
Tel: 704–497–5921
Camp Creek Road, Route 1, Box 219, 28789
Mailing address: P.O. Box 108, Bryson City 28713

The Fisher House, an 1881 farmhouse, was home to five generations of the Fisher/Kinsland family before it was purchased in 1985 by Beverly and Gary Means. While the Means have respected the careful restoration accomplished by the last resident, the great-granddaughter of Bartlett Clingman Fisher, they have added their own personal touches, as well.

"The Means are hospitable innkeepers, who ask you upon arriving if they can get you anything—I felt at home immediately. The decor is largely contemporary, with an emphasis on wood—the lovely oak dining set is a good example. The cozy den with overstuffed sofa and stone fireplace is especially inviting. Bev has accessorized effectively with the work of local artisans—we remarked on an American Indian basket and a prayer doll. Each of the guest rooms has its own temperature control, a welcome feature. Equally thoughtful was the built-in hair dryer in the bathroom and the large fluffy towels. Gary was also helpful in arranging dinner reservations on a busy evening when they were hard to come by. Breakfast is served in the dining room around 8:30 A.M., with everyone generally eating together, but the Meanses are willing to make it earlier or later if needed. We had an excellent egg, sausage, and cheese casserole and parsley potatoes. The homemade biscuits had us all in ecstasy—I think four of us polished off a dozen of them. There were preserves, butter and margarine, a choice of coffee (regular and decaf), hot tea, plus orange juice and fresh fruit. There's a big porch out front with a rocking chair and an old-fashioned swing for a good view of the rolling hills and neighboring farms. The setting is isolated and quiet, yet is less than half an hour from Bryson City, Dillsboro, and the southernmost entrance to the Great Smoky Mountains National Park, making it an excellent base for touring the area." *(Virginia Henke)*

Open All year.
Rooms 3 doubles—all with full private bath, fan. 1 with fireplace.
Facilities Dining room, den with fireplace, piano, TV, stereo, books. 2 acres with picnic area. Swimming, boating, fishing, rafting, hiking, bicycling nearby.
Location W NC, 50 m W of Asheville. Midway between Cherokee, Bryson City, & Dillsboro; 5 min. to entrance to Great Smoky Mts. National Park & S terminus of Blue Ridge Pkwy. Just off Rte. 441 at intersection of Camp Creek & Beck Branch Rds. From I-40, take Exit 27 & follow Rte. 74W past Sylva. Take Rte. 441N to Cherokee exit and go 1/2 m to Camp Creek Road & turn right.
Restrictions No smoking. No children under 6.
Credit cards None accepted.
Rates B&B, $45–65 double, $35–45 single. Extra person, $10. 10% discount for 3-night stays. Full, half-day bicycling trips.
Extras Airport/station pickups, $.22/mile.

WILMINGTON

Located in southeastern North Carolina, on the Cape Fear River, Wilmington is the state's largest port and a major trading center. Its historic district has been restored in recent years, and is now home to several B&Bs. The city has plenty of charm and several museums of interest, including the U.S.S. *North Carolina* Battleship Memorial; it's just a short drive to the ocean beaches and to several restored plantation homes. The city has also become a major movie-making center in recent years, and a number of major films have been made on its streets and sound stages.

Information please: The **Worth House** (412 South Third Street, 28401; 919–762–8562) is a century-old Victorian home, offering period decor, hearty breakfasts, and evening goodies. It's been highly recommended for its graceful architecture, charming decor, and lovely grounds;

one respondent felt that the hospitality was not up to the same standard. We've heard that the inn is for sale; let us know of your experiences.

Catherine's Inn on Orange ¢   *Tel:* 919–251–0863
North 410 Orange Street, 28401   800–476–0723

Whether traveling for pleasure or business, a small inn like this one can really make a difference in the quality of your trip. Owner Catherine Ackiss offers guests a full breakfast, afternoon refreshments, a bedtime liqueur, along with such extras as terry cloth robes. Summertime visitors will enjoy a cooling dip in the backyard swimming pool.

"The inn is conveniently located in the historic, restored area, a short and walkable distance to waterfront restaurants, shops, and museums. The inn is charming, decorated with a variety of antiques. Our room had a king-sized bed with a firm mattress, abundant towels and bathrobes laundered daily, and a fabulous breakfast served on fine china, silver, and crystal. The service, cleanliness, and hospitality were impeccable." *(Diane Mrva)*

"Our room had twin beds—Catherine told us they were the only ones in the Historic District—and the room was nicely done. Lots of southern charm, warmth, and hospitality in the inn, and a great breakfast." *(Dianne Crawford)*

Minor niggle: "Our bathroom was tiny, with old-fashioned fixtures that were hard to regulate."

Open All year.
Rooms 1 suite, 3 doubles—3 with private bath and/or shower, 1 with shared bath. All with telephone, radio, desk, air-conditioning. 3 with fireplace.
Facilities Dining room, living room, library with TV, stereo, guest refrigerator; porch. ½ acre with swimming pool, bicycles.
Location Historic area. From highways 74, 76, 17 take 2nd St. to right on Front St. Go 6 blocks and turn right on Orange St. From I-40, take 17 south to the historic district. Turn left on Third St. Go two blocks and turn left on Orange.
Restrictions Light sleepers should request rooms away from street. No smoking in guest rooms, dining room, or library. No children under 12 unless by prior arrangement.
Credit cards Amex, MC, Visa.
Rates B&B, $110–120 suite, $55–60 double or single. AARP discount (not available with credit card payment). Minimum stay required during special events.
Extras Airport/station pickups.

The Five Star Guest House ¢   *Tel:* 919–763–7581
14 North Seventh Street, 28401

This turn-of-the-century Victorian home was purchased by Ann and Harvey Crowther in 1987. "The family who built the home, the Taylors, really believed in plumbing and adequate space for a large family," Ann reports, "so the house really lends itself to being a B&B. They also put in all the expensive details, like an elaborate oak staircase, stained glass and leaded windows, and twelve-foot ceilings. We encourage people to enjoy the house as if it were their own, and it thrills us when someone feels comfortable enough to play the piano in the parlor." Rooms are furnished with antiques, and plants, and breakfast includes fresh fruit, juice, cereal, hot bread, muffins, eggs, cheese, and a specialty dish; refreshments are served in the parlor every afternoon.

"This is a lovely, homey inn on a quiet street in the historic port city of Wilmington. The owner, Ann, delivered home-baked cookies and wine on our arrival, making us feel right at home. Our room was comfortable, peaceful, and roomy, with a huge Victorian claw-foot tub (with plenty of hot water and bath salts) and a separate shower. Breakfast was spectacular—my husband who never eats breakfast ate plentifully of the muffins, eggs, bacon, croissants, and fresh fruit." *(Connie Clark)* "Pleasant place, excellent breakfast." *(William MacGowan)*

"You made me feel like a princess. I loved my room, especially the lamp with its little feet." *(Elisabeth Leonard—age 7)*

Open All year.
Rooms 2 suite, 2 doubles—all with full private bath, radio, air-conditioning, fan, fireplace.
Facilities Dining room with fireplace, living room, music room with piano, front porch with rockers, swings. Walled rear garden with pond. Tennis, golf nearby. 10 m to beaches.
Location Downtown. In historic district. 3 blocks to center. Follow Rte. 17/74 into town. Inn is at corner of Rte. 17 Bus. and N. 7th St.
Restrictions Children by prior arrangement only.
Credit cards Amex, Discover, MC, Visa.
Rates B&B, $75 suite, $60 double, $50 single. Extra person, $10. 2-night minimum for holiday weekends. No charge for children under 3.
Extras Crib, babysitting.

The Inn at St. Thomas Court

101 South Second Street, 28401

Tel: 919–343–1800
800–525–0909

The Inn at St. Thomas Court opened in 1988, to provide the privacy and business facilities of a hotel with the ambiance of an inn. The suites have been created in two reconstructed turn-of-the century commercial buildings, and combine individualized decor and polished hardwood floors with skylights, lofts, and everything from twin four-posters to king-sized French campaign beds. Seven of the suites are in Dram Tree House, while the other eight are in the Clarendon House. Rooms in the latter have a more contemporary feel, with one done in a Southwestern motif, and another in the tropical mood of Nassau. Rates include a welcome basket, with information about local events, a continental breakfast basket, and a morning newspaper."Lovely apartments, beautifully decorated and very comfortable; *(JD)* "Wonderful rehabbed old buildings in downtown Wilmington, an interesting small city on the Cape Fear River, now undergoing a renaissance. My suite had a well equipped kitchen, living-dining room, bedroom, and bath. It would be easy to prepare a simple meal, since there were adequate pots and pans. The decor was most attractive, and the innkeepers were cordial and interesting." *(Betty Richards)*

Open All year.
Rooms 15 1-2 bedroom suites—all with full private bath, TV, telephone, air-conditioning, fully equipped kitchen or microwave oven, refrigerator. Some with washer/dryer. Suites in 2 adjacent houses.

Facilities Conservatory, billiard room, conference room, balconies, courtyard. Bicycle rentals, business services, yacht charter. Sailing school.
Location In historic district. 2 blocks from river; at corner of Dock St. Half-block from St. John's Museum. Walking distance to business district.
Credit cards Amex, MC, Visa.
Rates B&B, $85–125 double. Extra adult, $10; child age 12–17, $5; child under 12, free. AARP, corporate, senior discounts. Weekly, monthly rates.

WINSTON-SALEM

Winston-Salem is known for its attention to the arts, and is the home of Old Salem, a restored eighteenth-century Moravian village. Other sites of interest include Reynolds House, the estate of the late R.J. Reynolds, founder of the tobacco firm that bears his name. The residence and gardens are open to the public; the house has an excellent collection of American art. If all that culture makes you thirsty, we suggest a free tour of the Joseph Schlitz Brewing Company; their Winston-Salem facility produces 4 million barrels of beer annually.

Winston-Salem is in central North Carolina, 144 miles east of Asheville, 80 miles north of Charlotte, and 104 miles west of Raleigh.

Also recommended: Received too late for a full write-up was an enthusiastic report on the **Colonel Ludlow House** (Summit & West 5th Street, 27101; 919–777–1887), a century-old inn decorated with period charm; the seven guest rooms combine Victorian decor with such luxuries as a double Jacuzzi, stereo system, VCR, and a stocked refrigerator; each has an in-room telephone and a desk to accommodate business travelers. "Loved the luxuries. Lighting at the bed was great. Parked right in front in a very safe neighborhood for walking. Very clean, and with such nice people. Mark, the afternoon manager, was super in helping us plan our 'attack' on the area. The breakfast was served in our room on a silver tray with linen and lace napkins and placemats, using nice china and flatware. A very personal inn." *(Dianne Crawford)* Another option is the **Wachovia B&B** (513 Wachovia Street, 27101; 919–777–0332) a rose-and-white Victorian cottage with wrap-around porch and white wicker rockers. Three of the five bathrooms have private baths; the $45–55 double rates include a breakfast of fresh fruit and juice, yogurt, and home-baked breads and pastries, plus afternoon wine and cheese, and evening tea. "Only five minutes from the Moravian Village, with a helpful, congenial hostess. Our spacious room was beautifully decorated. The porch rockers were ideal for reading and relaxing, and the breakfast was good; the living room was cozy and comfortable." *(Pat Torpie)*

Information please: About 12 miles west of Winston-Salem is the **Tanglewood Manor House** (919–766–0591; Highway 158, P.O. Box 1040, Clemmons 27012). Once the private estate of William and Kate Reynolds, Tanglewood is now operated by Forsyth County as an 1150-acre park. As a result, rates for all park facilities are very reasonable. Accommodations are available in the Manor house, a motel lodge, and cabins; a restaurant is also available. Recreation facilities include 3 golf courses, 9 tennis courts, a swimming pool and lake, horseback riding, and more.

In Greensboro, about 20 miles east of Winston-Salem is the **Greenwich Inn** (111 West Washington Street, Greensboro 27401; 919–272–3474), a 27-room luxury inn, built in the restored 1895 headquarters of Cone Mills. Rooms are elegantly furnished in period decor, and rates include continental breakfast and newspaper, brought to your door, evening wine and cheese, bedtime chocolates, and turndown service. A more intimate option is the **Greenwood B&B** (205 North Park Drive, Greensboro 27401; 919–274–6350) in a historic neighborhood a short walk from downtown. The five guest rooms in this 1905 home are air-conditioned, with queen- or king-sized beds and private baths; rates are a reasonable $45–75, including breakfast.

High Point, about 15 miles southeast of Winston-Salem, is the furniture capital of the country, and is home to **The Premier** (1001 Johnson Street, High Point 27262; 919–889–8349), a 1907 Colonial Revival home, renovated as a B&B in 1985. Rates include a welcoming glass of wine and a full breakfast.

For an escape to the woods, consider the **Pilot Knob Inn** (P.O. Box 1280, Pilot Mountain 27041; 919–325–2502), on the eastern slope of Pilot Mountain, about 20 miles northwest of Winston-Salem, via Route 52. Jim Rouse has painstakingly restored five century-old tobacco barns for overnight accommodations, combining rustic charm with antique furnishings, Jacuzzi tubs, and a swimming pool.

Brookstown Inn 🏃 ✖   Tel: 919–725–1120
200 Brookstown Avenue, 27101

The Brookstown Inn is based in an old cotton mill complex dating back to 1836. After a century of industrial operation, the mill had become obsolete, and was scheduled for demolition in the 1970s, when historians identified it as the city's first factory. The mill was placed on the National Register of Historic Places, and was restored as an inn, surrounded by shops and a restaurant.

Many rooms at the Brookstown are exceptionally large, with loft ceilings, exposed, handmade brick walls, and rough-hewn beams. The decor is an eclectic mixture of Appalachian handmade quilts, traditional pieces, antiques, and twentieth-century industrial chic. Rates include a continental breakfast of coffee, orange juice, fresh fruit, cereal, and Moravian buns. Wine and cheese are served in the parlor in the early evening. The Brookstown is located between Winston's commercial center and the restored colonial village of Old Salem.

"Some of the largest bedrooms and bathrooms imaginable, with furnishings that reflect its history: the cotton mill, the countryside, and the Moravian crafts. Excellent." *(William MacGowan)* "The front desk advised us on the best way to see Old Salem in a very limited time. Everything in the inn was sparkling clean, and the Caswell-Massey soap was a nice touch. Daryll's is a bistro in the same mill complex, serving excellent hamburgers and fries at a reasonable price, with friendly waitresses." *(Perri & Michael Rappel)* "Our room was well decorated, with period furnishings, and breakfast was far above the ordinary—pastries, muffins, and even sausage biscuits. Old Salem Village, a healthy walk away, is worth seeing." *(Ben & Peg Bedini)* "A cozy haven after a long day on the road. Wine and cheese in the early evening and a fine continental-plus breakfast." *(Betty Norman)*

This inn is a real reader favorite, and all noted that they'd be happy to return. At the same time, there was consensus that the inn was missing a personal touch, the concern for guest comfort that separates excellent inns and hotels from outstanding ones. Some examples: "Our room, which had plenty of space, had only one comfortable reading chair, while both of us would both have liked one. The lighting could have been brighter in both the bedroom and bath." Also: "Beverages (though not food) were promptly removed from the dining room at 10 A.M. sharp; doing it the other way around would have made more sense to us." And, although one respondent commented on the helpful staff, other readers found the staff to be "curt, minimally pleasant" or "impersonal." And we must admit that we've not had a response to our repeated mailings to the inn's management since 1986.

Open All year.
Rooms 71 suites and doubles—all with private bath and/or shower, telephone, radio, TV, air-conditioning. Some with whirlpool bath, fireplace, microwave, coffee maker, or wet bar. 12 rooms in annex.
Facilities Parlor, dining room. Free parking.
Location Central NC. 4 blocks to downtown. From I-70, take Cherry St. Exit to Marshall Ave. Follow signs to Brookstown Ave.
Restrictions Noise from central heating/cooling unit in some annex rooms.
Credit cards Amex, CB, DC, MC, Visa.
Rates B&B, $90–115 suite, $80–105 double. Extra person, $10. Children under 12 free in parents' room.
Extras Wheelchair access; some rooms equipped for disabled. Crib.

We Want to Hear from You!

As you know, this book is only effective with your help. We really need to know about your experiences and discoveries. If you stayed at an inn or hotel listed here, we want to know how it was. Did it live up to our description? Exceed it? Was it what you expected? Did you like it? Were you disappointed? Delighted? Have you discovered new establishments that we should add to the next edition?

Tear out one of the report forms at the back of this book (or use your own stationery if you prefer) and write today. *Even if you write only "Fully endorse existing entry" you will have been most helpful.*

Thank You!

South Carolina

Rhett House Inn, Beaufort

South Carolina's major area of tourist interest is the Low Country, extending from Charleston down along the coast from Beaufort and Hilton Head to Savannah. This area's original wealth came from shipping and rice plantations, and later from cotton. For an interesting side trip, take Route 17 north from Charleston to Mt. Pleasant. A highlight of this drive is the stands lining the highway where sweetgrass baskets are sold. Using skills brought from Africa on slave ships, the local basketmakers create intricate pieces from simple trivets to large lacy baskets.

Inland, visitors will find deep forests, the foothills of the Blue Ridge mountains, and the Santee Cooper Lakes. In Aiken, visit Hopeland Gardens' flower-lined paths; in Abbeville, see a play in the restored Opera House; or snap photos of the colorful fields at Greenwood's Park Seed Company gardens.

Although wine is sold by the bottle in South Carolina restaurants, liquor can be sold only in mini-bottles (outside of package stores), tending to produce skimpy libations at relatively high prices and leading one reader to campaign for reform: "The state of South Carolina should change its laws so you can buy a reasonable drink at a reasonable price!" *(WB)*

Information please: In the northeast part of the state, about 70 miles east of Columbia and 7 miles north of Florence and the intersections of Interstates 95 and 20 is the century-old **Croft Magnolia Inn** (414 Cashua Street, Darlington 29532; 803–393–1908) set on a tree-lined street in the historic district, just a mile from the Darlington Speedway and Museum. The six guest rooms have private baths, and children are welcome; the $55 double rate includes a full breakfast.

A newly opened inn in northwestern South Carolina, about 70 miles north of Columbia is the **Inn at Merridun** (100 Merridun Place, Union 29379; 803–427–7052). Peggy and Jim Waller spent over a year (and probably more time and money than they ever intended) renovating their Greek Revival antebellum home. There are very few—if any—inns in these areas so your comments would be especially welcome.

Rates do not include 7% state sales and accommodation tax.

ABBEVILLE

The Belmont Inn ¢ 👫 ✗   *Tel: 803–459–9625*
106 East Pickens Street, Court Square, 29620

A major transportation hub through much of the 19th and early 20th centuries, Abbeville was once a very prosperous town—"where the Confederacy began and ended." Bypassed when the interstate highways were built in the fifties and sixties, its once handsome structures were neglected and even abandoned. Restoration began in the late sixties with the Abbeville Opera House, and has since spread to historic structures throughout the downtown area. Listed on the National Register of Historic Places, The Belmont Inn, a historic hotel, was built in 1903 and was fully restored in 1984 by owners Allyson and Joe Harden.

"Big, bright, high-ceilinged rooms, convenient off-street parking, all in the heart of a delightful piece of the small-town South. We had a lovely corner room overlooking the town square. Clemson University is nearby, and the weekend football package is a real value. On game day be sure to walk up the hill from 'Death Valley' stadium and visit 'Fort Hill,' the home of antebellum South Carolina Senator John C. Calhoun. The home and grounds are authentically restored and the Duncan Phyfe Empire furnishings are original to the house." *(Nancy Harrison & Nelson Ormsby)* "The inn adjoins the famed Abbeville Opera House (built in 1908), one of the finest little theaters in the country. Abbeville also has many historic buildings and great antique shops." *(Jane Simms)* "Lovely old hotel in a backwater town. The dining room features high ceilings and pleasantly prepared food. The poem on Court Square's Civil War monument is a must for any first-time visitor to the South." *(Andrew Hoffman)* "After a cordial, but impersonal check-in, we were shown to the John C. Calhoun Suite, a large room with two queen-sized poster beds—neat, fresh, attractive, and comfortable. Our dinner was highlighted by a spectacular soup of collard greens and black-eyed peas swimming in a rich, succulent stock." *(John Blewer)*

Areas for improvement: "Our breakfast consisted of a plastic-wrapped store-bought pastry and wax-like fruit." Also: "My sole stuffed with crabmeat tasted like an institutional portion microwaved to order." Hopefully, by the time this book is in print a new chef and manager will be back on staff to re-establish this inn's culinary reputation. Comments please.

Open All year.
Rooms 1 suite, 23 doubles—all with private bath, telephone, TV, air-conditioning. 1 with balcony.

Facilities Restaurant, bar with TV, parlors, meeting rooms, theater, courtyard garden. Live weekend entertainment. Hickory Knob State Park nearby for golf. 12 m to Lake Russell for swimming, fishing, boating. Tennis nearby. Off-street parking.

Location NW SC. 50 m S of Greenville; 137 m E of Atlanta, GA. In historic district, on Court Square.

Credit cards Amex, Discover, MC, Visa.

Rates B&B, $60–85 suite or double. Corporate rates. Theater package, $160. Extra adult, $6; child under 10 free. Alc lunch, $8; alc dinner, $27. Senior, AAA discount.

Extras Limited wheelchair access. Airport/station pickup. Small pets by prior arrangement. Crib, babysitting.

AIKEN

The Willcox Inn ✕   *Tel: 803–649–1377*
100 Colleton Avenue at Whiskey Road, 29801

The Willcox Inn was built in 1898, soon after sportsman Thomas Hitchcock established the Winter Colony to take advantage of the city's mild winter climate. He introduced steeplechase racing to Aiken, now the home of the Aiken Triple Crown.

The Willcox is listed on the National Register of Historic Places and has been recently restored to its original elegance. Guest rooms are individually furnished with reproduction furniture, and the wood-paneled pub and restaurant both offer a relaxed atmosphere.

"A charming inn, located in a quiet, beautiful setting, with spacious, clean, well-lighted rooms. The large bathrooms all have new plumbing. Our dinner was delicious and was served by people who were genuinely interested in our complete satisfaction. A young man with a marvelous touch played the piano while we ate." *(George P. & Louise I. Thorne)*

"First-class all the way! Dinner was extraordinary, our room exceptional with such extras as bath sheets rather than bath towels. Considering their quality, both were reasonably priced. Can't say enough about Aiken; make sure you take a stroll down Colleton Avenue to marvel at the homes there." *(Wayne Braffman)*

And a different experience: "Impersonal hotel atmosphere. The night I was there the dining room was closed to guests to accommodate a corporate function." Reports required.

Open All year.

Rooms 6 suites, 19 doubles, 5 singles—all with full private bath, telephone, radio, TV, desk, air-conditioning. Some with fireplace.

Facilities Restaurant, pub, lobby with fireplace, piano. Tennis, golf, fishing nearby.

Location SW SC. 60 m SW of Columbia, 125 m NW of Charleston, 125 m NE of Atlanta, GA. From I-20, take Rte. 19 to Rte. 78, Richland Ave. Turn right onto Whiskey Rd., then right onto Colleton Ave.

Credit cards Amex, MC, Visa.

Rates Room only, $113–131 suite, $98–113 double, $78–98 single. Extra person, $18. Weekly, government, corporate rates. Weekend, honeymoon packages. Alc lunch, $7–10; alc dinner, $25–33.

Extras Wheelchair access; some guest rooms equipped for handicapped. Crib. French, Italian, German spoken.

ANDERSON

Evergreen Inn ¢ ✗   *Tel:* 803–225–1109
1109 South Main Street, 29621

The Evergreen Inn and the neighboring restaurant, "1109 South Main," have been owned by Peter and Myrna Ryter since 1982. B&B rates include a continental breakfast and a welcoming cocktail.

"The inn and restaurant occupy two adjacent historic white Greek Revival buildings. Some of the guest rooms are elegantly decorated, one in French country style and another with a mirrored ceiling, while others are more simple but still comfortable. A buffet breakfast is set out in the kitchen with home-baked breads and muffins, fresh fruit, juices, teas, coffee, and cereals. Best of all is the top-notch restaurant. The chef-owner, Peter, is Swiss-born and trained, but has worked in restaurants from the South Pacific to California. Our meals were exquisite, with a fine wine selection and desserts that tasted as good as they looked." *(Celia McCullough)*

Open All year.
Rooms 2 suites, 5 doubles—6 with private bath, 1 with shared bath. All with air-conditioning, 3 with TV.
Facilities Restaurant, kitchen, parlor with TV. 10 min. to Lake Hartwell.
Location NW SC. Halfway between Atlanta GA & Charlotte NC (2-hr. drive). Walking distance to downtown.
Restrictions No smoking in suites. No children under 7.
Credit cards Amex, DC, MC, Visa.
Rates B&B, $65 double, $52 single. Corporate rate, $46. Restaurant discount.
Extras German, French, Swiss-German spoken.

BEAUFORT

The second oldest town in the state, Beaufort (pronounced BUE-fort) was founded in 1711. Overlooking the Intracoastal Waterway, this historic port town has beautifully restored 18th and 19th century antebellum homes shaded by century-old trees. Although Beaufort's emergence from the 1930s Depression was long and gradual, its economy has been given quite a boost by travelers discovering its charms, and a recent jolt from the movie industry; *The Great Santini, The Big Chill* and, more recently, *Prince of Tides* have been filmed amidst the town's carefully reconstructed beauty. Beaufort is located in the Low Country of coastal South Carolina, 50 miles northeast of Savannah, Georgia, and 62 miles southwest of Charleston.

Information please: Built in 1898 in the "Beaufort style," **Old Point Inn** (212 New Street, 29902; 803–524–3177) is furnished with antiques, lace curtains, and reproductions. Located in the historic district, all rooms have a private bath; there are river views from the second-floor porch. The $55–75 rates include a continental breakfast.

Bay Street Inn ¢
601 Bay Street, 29902

Tel: 803–524–7720

A Greek Revival home built in 1852, the Bay Street Inn has been owned by Eugene Roe since 1985 and is listed on the National Register of Historic Places. The inn is beautifully furnished with period antiques and Oriental carpets, and two of the guest rooms have especially lovely views of the bay. According to Mr. Roe, "The inn has one of the finest collections of Americana in the Southeast, including a large library on the subject. We appreciate our guests, and we hope they appreciate their surroundings." Movie-going readers will see the inn featured in the movie, *Prince of Tides*, which was filmed on location in 1990. Rates include full breakfast, in-room sherry and fruit, and evening chocolates.

"The exterior and lawns are well maintained with rockers on the veranda for relaxing. Gene's lovely whippets [dogs which look like small-size greyhounds] look almost ornamental. Housekeeping was excellent, with attention to detail. We filled up on a hearty breakfast of silver dollar pancakes with blueberry sauce, bacon, juice, and coffee." *(Shelley Mathews)*

Open All year.
Rooms 6 doubles—all with private bath and/or shower, radio, desk, air-conditioning, fan, fireplace. 2 with balcony.
Facilities Dining room with fireplace, breakfast room with fireplace, living room with fireplace, TV room, library, music room with grand piano, porch. ½ acre with seating. Bicycles. Off-street parking. Tennis, golf nearby. Beach nearby for swimming, boating, fishing.
Location 50 m S of Savannah, 60 m N of Charleston, 35 m S of Hilton Head. Historic district. From Hwy. 21 turn left on Bay St. to inn on corner.
Restrictions No children under 12.
Credit cards MC, Visa.
Rates B&B, $70–80 double. Extra person, $15.
Extras Station/local airport pickup. Crib, babysitting. Pets permitted by prior arrangement.

The Rhett House Inn
1009 Craven Street, 29902

Tel: 803–524–9030

If you feel like you're experiencing déjà vu when you see this inn, then maybe you've purchased a box of Shredded Wheat, which featured The Rhett House on the back of 11 million cereal boxes. Innkeepers/owners Steve and Marianne Harrison moved to Beaufort from Connecticut, and opened the Rhett House in 1987, after a complete renovation. Their background in the New York textile and fashion business helped them plan the decoration of this antebellum house, done in period antiques. Rates include a full breakfast of eggs or French toast, homemade breads and muffins served with preserves and fresh fruit, plus afternoon tea and evening sherry. Reader raves continue to arrive on this first-rate inn:

"The Rhett House is a very imposing, two-story white home that features a wraparound piazza. The inn is located one block from Main

279

Street in a quiet historic section. A family-style breakfast is served at a long pine table in the dining room. After breakfast, guests relax in the parlor, furnished with comfortable antiques, including a pool table." *(Dr. & Mrs. Henry Price)*

"The inn is polished to the nth degree. Marianne Harrison has a real eye for color. Each room is attractively turned out, and most are larger than in a typical B&B; I looked hard to find some fault, but failed—it's all so well done. The staff is knowledgeable and courteous. Although the area is primarily residential, there's a small business across the street from the inn, so the rooms with the best views are those that face the garden and courtyard." *(Jeanne Smith)*

"Silent paddle fans, quiet heating and air-conditioning systems, fine linens, extensive reading material, and other amenities contributed to a relaxing stay." *(Nancy & Joe Lipton)* "Live oaks, gracefully draped with Spanish moss, rocking chairs on the porch, designer bedrooms with plumped-up pillows and fresh flowers, and delicious morning wake-ups to the smell of baking bread and fresh coffee make The Rhett House a place you never want to leave. Innkeepers Marianne and Steve, both well-polished New Yorkers, warm the inn with their sense of humor and meticulous care of both guests and inn." *(Claudia & Gerry Venable)*

"The inn comes close to that ideal of making you feel you're the guest of a wealthy friend." *(Stephan Wilkinson)* "The veranda was a wonderful place to sit and sip sherry; the gardens, bursting with azaleas, Spanish moss, flowers, and herbs, were a visual and aromatic delight." *(Bob Kolton)* "The hammock and wicker chairs on the upstairs porch are wonderful for reading and dozing away the afternoon." *(Bev & Susie Carter, also Tom & Mary Minges)*

"Fully endorse existing entry. Inn is beautifully appointed, with gracious hosts and a delicious breakfast. The bedrooms are comfortable, supplied with good lighting, thermos of water, sherry, and chocolates." *(Ina Ross, also Andrew Hoffman)*

Open All year.
Rooms 1 suite, 7 doubles—all with full private bath, telephone, radio, air-conditioning, fan, hair-dryer, deck. 3 with fireplace.
Facilities Dining room, living room with pool table, fireplace, library; gift shop, veranda, gardens, patio with fountain picnic area, off-street parking. Club privileges for tennis, golf, and swimming. 15 m to ocean for fishing, boating.
Location 1 block from Beaufort marina on Intracoastal Waterway. Take Exit 33 off I-95 to Beaufort. Inn is 1 block N of Bay St. (on waterfront), at corner of New Castle and Craven Sts.
Restrictions No smoking. No children under 5.
Credit cards MC, Visa.
Rates B&B, $200 suite, $80–125 double, $70–115 single. Extra person, $15. Corporate rates. Minimum stay requirements some weekends.
Extras Limited wheelchair access. Station/marina/airport pickups. Babysitting.

Trescot Inn   *Tel: 803–522–8552*
500 Washington Street, 29902

Just about every family has moved twice, but how many houses do we know that have moved as often? The Trescot Inn, an 1850s plantation house, is one of them: in its history it has been completely disassembled, floated down the river, and rebuilt once; the second time, in 1975, it was lifted off its foundations and moved through the streets of Beaufort before coming to rest at its present (and, we hope, final) location in the historic Point District.

According to JoAnne Mitchell, who's owned the inn since 1989, the Trescot Inn provides a warm, homey atmosphere in a bright and "sunshiney" environment; guests may be as sociable or as quiet as they wish. JoAnne provides home baked bread and muffins, fresh fruit, and a special blend of coffee for breakfast; rates also include bedside sherry each evening.

"We were welcomed like a member of the family and made to feel completely at ease in this grand home. We loved the tranquillity and came away rejuvenated and relaxed." (John & Annette Tompkins) "JoAnne is charming, witty, and helpful. The tempting breakfast included poached pears and freshly baked blueberry muffins. From our room there were French doors to a large second floor veranda with rocking chairs and a park-like view." (J.P. & Betty Dunston)

As we went to press, we learned that the inn is for sale; inquire further when booking.

Open All year.
Rooms 6 doubles—all with private shower and/or bath, radio, air-conditioning, fan. Some with fireplace, veranda.
Facilities Dining room, living room with stereo, veranda. 1.4 acres with lawn. On-site parking.
Location Historic "Old Point" district. 6 blocks from center. From I-95, take Hwy. 21 to Washington St. Turn right and continue to inn at corner of Washington and East Sts.
Restrictions No smoking. No children under 12.
Credit cards Amex, MC, Visa.
Rates B&B, $85–100 double, $70–85 single. Extra person, $10. 2-night holiday/special weekend minimum.

TwoSuns Inn   *Tel:* 803–522–1122
1705 Bay Street, 29902

TwoSuns Inn, which sits just across the street from the bay, gets its name from the view at sunrise, when the sun appears doubled by its mirror image on the water's surface. This 1917 Neoclassical Revival building, complete with veranda, was built as a private home, then was used as the "teacherage," providing housing for seventeen female teachers in the Beaufort schools. When purchased by Carrol and Ron Kay in 1990, it had been virtually abandoned. After extensive renovation and restoration, which included the rebuilding of a landmark skylight, the inn opened in October, 1990. Oriental rugs accent the inlaid oak floors in the living and dining rooms, and Carrol's weaving looms reside in the adjoining parlor. Guest rooms are comfortably furnished with antiques and period reproductions, with fluffy comforters or quilts on the beds. Rates include a full breakfast and a "tea and toddy hour" every afternoon.

"Beautiful inside and out, with a magnificent view of the bay from its location in the historic district. We stayed in Chamber B, with access to a semi-private second floor porch filled with white wicker. The room itself was done in a Victorian theme of garnet red and white. The inn is immaculate and parking is ample. The hospitable Kays made us feel right at home, providing maps, and ideas for things to do. Breakfast was served in the warm, sunny, and inviting dining room. One morning we had a fresh fruit compote, homemade muffins and rolls, juice, cereal, and crepes filled with cheese, mushrooms, and turkey." *(Mr. & Mrs. Jerry Hammel, and others)* "The large bathroom had the original 'body' shower, with brass piping in a semi-circle to produce spray all around, set in new tiles." *(Patricia Swift)*

Open All year.
Rooms 5 doubles—All with private bath and/or shower, radio, air-conditioning, fan; telephone and cable TV available on request. 3 with balcony/deck.
Facilities Dining room, living room with fireplace, piano, books, games; parlor with TV/VCR, porch. Bay-front city lot with croquet; bicycles. Tennis, golf, boating, fishing, swimming nearby.
Location Beaufort County SC. 45 m N of Savannah, GA. 65 m S of Charleston, SC. 5 short blocks from downtown.
Restrictions No smoking except on veranda and 2nd floor porch. No children under 12.
Credit cards Amex, MC, Visa.
Rates B&B, $168 suite, $85–93 double, $77–85 single. Extra person, $8. No tipping. 10% senior, AAA discount. 10% discount for stays of 3-days or more. Special events packages available for 1–3 nights.
Extras Wheelchair access; 1 room equipped for disabled.

CAMDEN

The oldest inland city in South Carolina, Camden was the focus of numerous battles in the Revolutionary War. Today, "Historic Camden" re-creates several homes of that period as well as period fortifications. It also attracts many people in the horse world with two major steeplechase events, six thoroughbred training tracks, and the Camden Hunt. Camden is 30 miles northeast of Columbia.

The Carriage House   *Tel: 803–432–2430*
1413 Lyttleton Street, 29020

"Run by Appie and Robert Watkins, the Carriage House was built in 1840, and it sits neatly behind a white picket fence. It is fully decorated in antiques and beautiful fabrics with a lovely English garden in back. Mrs. Watkins grows her own herbs and serves a wonderful breakfast of grits, cheese souffle, along with her homemade jellies and sausages. I don't think I've ever met nicer people." *(Pam Harpootlian)* More comments please.

Open All year.
Rooms 2 doubles—both with private bath, telephone, clock/radio, desk, air-conditioning, fan.

Facilities Breakfast room with TV; deck, patio. $\frac{1}{2}$ acre with English gardens. Park and tennis court nearby.
Location 4 blocks from center.
Restrictions No smoking. Children over 5 preferred.
Credit cards None accepted.
Rates B&B, $50 double. Extra person, $10.

The Greenleaf Inn ¢ ⱨ ✕
1310 North Broad Street, 29020

Tel: 803–425–1806
800–848–4031

Composed of two houses, the Colonial-style Reynolds House, built in 1840, and the Victorian McLean House, the Greenleaf was purchased by Alice Boykin and Virginia Isham in 1989. Rooms are furnished with antiques and period reproductions, and the inn tries to offer a particularly hospitable environment for business travelers. William's, the inn restaurant, is run by William H. Murphy, former chef to two South Carolina governors. His creative menu includes such entrées as tuna grilled with Dijon mustard and capers; salmon sautéed with corn, jalapeños, and mint, and breast of duck sauced with a zinfandel and green peppercorn sauce. "Our room had a king-sized bed and quality reproduction furnishings; the bathroom had an ample supply of thick towels."*(MA)* More reports required.

Open All year. Restaurant closed Sun.
Rooms 2 suites, 8 doubles, 1 single—all with private bath and/or shower, telephone, TV, air-conditioning. Some with desk, fan. Additional 2-bedroom cottage with sitting room, kitchen, 2 baths. Rooms in 2 adjacent houses.
Facilities Restaurant, bar, wraparound porches. Sporting clays course. Revolutionary War archives and historic district nearby. Nature walks, gristmill, and syrup mill tours available. Carolina and Colonial Cup steeplechases, Camden Hunt, and other equine events nearby.
Location Center of town. From I-20 (Exit 98), go 2 m N on Hwy. 521 to Camden. Inn on the right between DeKalb and Lauren Sts.
Credit cards Amex, MC, Visa.
Rates B&B, $65 suite, $58 double, $45–50 single. Extra person, $10. Children under 12 free in parents' room. Senior discount. 2-night minimum during spring, fall steeplechase season. Alc lunch, $8; alc dinner, $30.
Extras Two rooms have ramp access. Some pets permitted by prior arrangement. Airport/station pickups for fee. Crib, babysitting. French spoken.

CHARLESTON

Charleston, founded in 1670, was at one point the wealthiest city in Colonial America. Many think that it is still the most beautiful. The Civil War brought major devastation and poverty to the city and halted development. Efforts to preserve the city's priceless heritage began in the 1920s. Restoration work progressed slowly until around 1975, when the American Bicentennial, followed by the founding of Spoleto Festival U.S.A., sparked the restoration and conversion of numerous homes and commercial properties into bed & breakfast inns and restaurants.

Sights of interest in Charleston and the surrounding area include the many restored houses and museums, antique shops, the city market, tours of the river and harbor, the public beaches and resorts (with full golf and tennis facilities) at Folly Beach, Seabrook Island, and Kiawah Island. Last but far from least are the beautiful gardens of Middleton Place, Magnolia Gardens, and Cypress Gardens. Although all three gardens bloom year-round, many think that they are at their most magnificent from late March to early April, when the azaleas are in full bloom.

The peak season in Charleston runs from March to mid-June, and from September through October. The times of highest demand are in late March and early April for the azaleas, and in late May and early June for the Spoleto Festival. Charleston is located midway along the South Carolina coast, at the confluence of the Ashley, Cooper, and Wando rivers and the Intracoastal Waterway. It's 106 miles northeast of Savannah, GA, 113 miles southeast of Columbia, SC, and 94 miles southwest of Myrtle Beach.

Budget tip: If you're traveling along the coast, and Charlestown prices are tough on your wallet, considering spending a night or two in **Georgetown**, about an hour away, where prices are about 50% less. See listings for details.

Information please: Listed in many past editions is the **Vendue Inn/ Vendue West** (19 Vendue Range, 29401; 803–577–7970 or 800–845–7900), long owned by Evelyn and Morton Needle. Once an abandoned and dilapidated nineteenth-century warehouse, they renovated it and furnished the rooms with Oriental rugs and Charleston reproduction furniture, wallcoverings, and fabrics. Rooms are individually decorated, some with rice beds, others with canopy, brass, or cannonball beds. We've had rave reports on the inn's restaurant, Chovinards, but more information on the inn's staffing and service is needed. **The Elliott House Inn** (78 Queen Street; 803–723–1855 or 800–729–1855) was originally a private residence built in the mid-1700s. The structure was expanded over the years and now encircles a central courtyard where guests can enjoy breakfast and afternoon refreshments. The **Church Street Inn** (177 Church Street, 29401; 803–722–3420 or 800–552–3777) has 31 1- and 2-bedroom fully equipped suites. Amenities include champagne on arrival, continental breakfast, and morning paper, and evening wine in your room. Most of the rooms are done in eighteenth-century reproductions, with mahogany furniture, Audubon prints, and solid brass lamps; some have first-quality American folk art reproductions.

We'd also like to hear more about the **Rice Hope Plantation**, 39 miles north of Charleston. A meeting place since Revolutionary War days, it has been open for B&B accommodation and afternoon tea since 1987. It's right on the Cooper River for fishing and river tours, and even has a tennis court (P.O. Box 355, Moncks Corner, 29461; 803–761–4832).

Barksdale House Inn   *Tel:* 803–577–4800
27 George Street, 29401

George Barksdale, a wealthy Charleston planter, built this elegant house in 1778; some 200 years later, it was unoccupied and in a state of considerable disrepair. Restored as an inn in 1985, it was purchased by

George and Peggy Sloan in May, 1990. Decorated with antiques, inspired color schemes, and luxurious fabrics from Scalamandre and other top-quality firms, the rates include a continental breakfast, afternoon tea and sherry, and evening wine and chocolates.

"You can walk from the inn to Charleston's shops, marketplace, restaurants, but I suspect you'd drive. I was able to see a number of the rooms; numbers 3, 5, and 6 were my favorites." *(Jeanne Smith)* "The Barksdale House is not a typical Charleston house, with a piazza down the side, but a regular square frame house, with a center entrance and hallway. The parking lot behind the garden is a real convenience in this city. Flanking the inn are a large pay-parking lot on one side, and a house on the other; the City of Charleston College is across the street. The inn is located on the northern edge of the historic district, on a narrow, quiet street. The first-floor rooms are huge, with separate sitting areas, bay windows, hidden bars, and double Jacuzzis, but they face directly onto the street. I especially liked rooms 3 and 4 on the second floor. The third floor is a bit of a climb, and the rooms generally smaller. The only public area is a small parlor in the back corner downstairs; this also serves as a reception area. Breakfast is served on a tray in the your room or small garden." *(SHW)* More reports required.

Open All year. Closed Christmas Day.
Rooms 2 suites, 16 doubles—all with full private bath, telephone, radio, TV, desk, ceiling fan, air-conditioning. Some with double whirlpool tub, fireplace, dry bar.
Facilities Parlor, courtyard with fountain, porch. Off-street parking. 3 blocks from market area, 2 blocks from Charleston Museum.
Location N edge of historic district, between King and Meeting Sts.
Restrictions Street noise "on nights of college games only." No children under 7.
Credit cards MC, Visa.
Rates B&B, $150 suite, $95–135 double, $75–95 single. Extra person, $10. Children's, corporate rates.
Extras Airport/station pickups.

Brasington House   *Tel:* 803–722–1274
328 East Bay Street, 29401   800–722–1274

The Brasington House is a 1790s "single" house, meaning it's one room wide, two rooms deep, and three stories high, with a corresponding three-story piazza (Charlestonian for porch). Rates include a continental breakfast and afternoon refreshments.

"Charming, warm, and cozy B&B was bought by Dalton and Judy Brasington in 1988. They've rescued it from a ramshackle state and have restored it to its original 1790s style. Their 'before-and after' albums are fun to peruse over wine and cheese. Liqueurs are served upon returning from dinner. Breakfast was exquisite: grapefruit, cereal, croissants, coffee cake, baked peaches, juice, and coffee. Judy and Dalton are fascinating and make their home a friendly and comfortable place to stay." *(Belinda King)*

Open All year.
Rooms 4 doubles—all with private bath, telephone, TV, air-conditioning.

Facilities Dining room with fireplace, living room with fireplace. Off-street parking.
Location Ansonborough historic district.
Restrictions No smoking. Children over 12 preferred.
Credit cards MC, Visa.
Rates B&B, $89–98 double. Extra person, $25.

Indigo Inn
1 Maiden Lane, 29401

Tel: 803–577–5900
800–845–7639

The Indigo Inn is furnished with eighteenth-century antiques and period reproductions. It's been owned since 1978 by Mr. and Mrs. H.B. Limehouse, and is managed by Larry Deery. The Limehouses also own the Jasmine House, an 1843 Greek Revival inn across the street. Rates include a light breakfast of a quickbread and ham biscuits, the morning paper, plus afternoon hors d'oeuvres. Readers report unanimously that the high point of a stay at the Indigo is the staff:

"The inn, which resembles a windowless warehouse from the outside, and which seems to be in a redevelopment area, was a real surprise inside. The rooms all face a lush central courtyard. Our room, on the second floor, was rather long and narrow. We had two queen-size four-poster beds. The decor was subdued and restful—blues, browns, and beiges—with beautiful chintz fabrics and excellent mahogany Chippendale reproductions. The inn is located at the edge of the Old Town, near the market; most of Charleston's tourist sights are within walking distance. *(MFD, also Jack & Sue Lane)* "Best service ever by desk staff, with perfect meal and sightseeing suggestions." *(Carol Moritz)*

"Breakfast is served in the well-designed 'chinoise' front hall buffet-style. It can be consumed there, or taken to one's room or to the New Orleans–style courtyard. Because the rooms face this courtyard they are quiet, away from the traffic of busy Meeting Street. In the afternoon, drinks and hors d'oeuvres are also set out here (there's a charge only for small bottles of spirits). The desk staff was exceptionally friendly, welcoming, and helpful." *(Ann Baxter)* "Rooms in the Jasmine House are lovely, with antiques and tester beds. Best feature of the Indigo was the staff—professional, helpful, and extremely courteous to visitors." *(Elliott Kagen)*

A word to the wise: "I'd like to stay at the Indigo again, but would ask for a room on an upper floor for greater privacy." Also: "We were disappointed in our room in the carriage house of the Jasmine House; it was adequate but ordinary, and had none of the period charm we expected for the price."

Open All year.
Rooms 40 doubles—all with full private bath, telephone, radio, TV, desk, air-conditioning, balcony. Most rooms with two queen-size beds, down pillows, and comforters. Additional rooms in Jasmine House & carriage house.
Facilities Breakfast room, courtyard, honor bar, lounge, lobby. Off-street parking. 10 m from ocean.
Location Historic district. At corner of Meeting and Pinckney Sts. 1 block from the market.
Restrictions No smoking in some guest rooms.

Credit cards Amex, MC, Visa.
Rates B&B, $85–130 double, $75–105 single. Extra person, $10. Family rate. Senior, AAA discount. 2-night holiday/weekend minimum.
Extras Wheelchair access; 2 rooms specially equipped. Cribs, babysitting. French spoken.

John Rutledge House Inn 🏃
116 Broad Street, 29401

Tel: 803–723–7999
800–476–9741

The John Rutledge House Inn, built in 1763 by one of the fifty-five signers of the U.S. Constitution, John Rutledge (also Chief Justice of the U.S. Supreme Court), can almost claim that "George Washington slept here"; an entry in his diary records show his breakfasting with Mrs. Rutledge in 1791. Much of the history of South Carolina and the U.S. can be traced to meetings and writings which took place in the ballroom and library here; reminders of Rutledge's service is visible in the Federal eagle and South Carolina's emblem, the palmetto tree, forged in the antebellum ironwork. Of equal significance to some is the fact that Charleston's famous she-crab soup was supposedly invented here.

Meticulously restored and stylishly updated in 1989 by Rick Widman, rooms are furnished in antiques and period reproductions; it is the first historic landmark to receive the "historic hotel" designation by the National Trust for Historic Preservation. Readers should be aware that one of the two carriage houses is a new building, constructed to duplicate the original. Rates include continental breakfast in your room, brandy and chocolates at your bedside each evening. A full breakfast is also available for $5 extra. "We stayed in Mrs. Rutledge's Room, and were impressed by its beauty, spaciousness, and comfort." *(Donna Jacobson)* "Excellent location; friendly helpful staff. A good compromise between a true B&B and a big hotel." *(SK)*

Under the same ownership is the **Kings Courtyard Inn** (198 King Street; 803–723–7000, 800–845–6119), constructed in 1853 and restored in 1983, incorporating unusual Egyptian design elements into the Greek Revival style of the building. Double rates of $105–145 include wine or sherry on arrival, brandy and chocolate at bedtime, and a continental breakfast of juice, croissant, home-baked muffin, and coffee or tea.

Open All year.
Rooms 3 suites and 16 doubles—all with private bath and/or shower, telephone, radio, TV, desk, air-conditioning, fan, mini-refrigerator. Some with fireplace, deck. Rooms in inn and 2 carriage houses.
Facilities Parlor with fireplace, ballroom with fireplace, games, library. Off-street parking. Ocean nearby for swimming, boating.
Location Historic district. From King St. turn right on Broad St. to inn.
Restrictions Smoking restricted in some guest rooms.
Credit cards Amex, MC, Visa.
Rates B&B, $180–220 suite, $105–185 double, $90–170 single. Extra person, $15. Children under 12 free in parents' room. 10% senior, AAA discount. Minimum stay requirements.
Extras Limited wheelchair access; some rooms equipped for disabled. Crib, babysitting. Spanish, French spoken.

Lodge Alley Inn 🏃 ✗
195 East Bay Street, 29401

Tel: 803–722–1611
Inside SC: 800–821–2791
Outside SC: 800–845–1004

Originally built as a series of warehouses, the Lodge Alley offers the amenities of a small luxury hotel, combined with the feeling of a historic inn. Rooms have the exposed brick walls and pine flooring of the original warehouses, but have been decorated with Oriental rugs and elegant period reproduction furniture.

"The location is great—right in the heart of the city. Some of the rooms overlook a courtyard, and have a small sitting room with comfortable couch and chairs." *(Jeanne Smith)* "Our one-bedroom suite overlooked a charming courtyard. We didn't have dinner here but breakfast in the restaurant was good." *(Ruth Tilsley)*

Open All year.
Rooms 63 1-2 bedroom suites, 34 doubles—all with full private bath, refrigerator, telephone, radio, TV, air-conditioning, fireplace. Most with kitchenette; 8 with whirlpool tub, some with fireplace. 12 rooms in annex.
Facilities Restaurant, lounge, parlor with fireplace, meeting rooms, courtyard. Valet parking.
Location In historic district. On East Bay St., between Cumberland St. and Vendue Range.
Credit cards Amex, MC, Visa.
Rates Room only, $125–290 suite; $115–130 double. Extra person, $15. Children under 13 free in parents' room. Monthly, group rates. Full breakfast, $5–7; alc lunch, $10–14; alc dinner, $37–40.
Extras Small pets permitted by prior arrangement; fee charged. Crib, babysitting. French, Italian spoken.

Maison Du Pré
317 East Bay Street, 29401

Tel: 803–723–8691
800–662–INNS

One of Charleston's newest "old" inns, the Maison Du Pré opened in 1987. It's composed of five adjacent buildings, dating as far back as 1804; two of the buildings had been slated for demolition, and were brought to this site by owners Lucille and Robert Mulholland as part of the renovation process. Rooms look onto the flower-bedecked courtyard, and are individually decorated with Oriental carpets, reproduction furnishings ranging from four-poster rice beds to country pine sleigh beds, and Williamsburg colors. Rates include the morning paper and a continental breakfast of croissants, pastry, cereal, and fruit and juice; plus afternoon refreshments with tea, wine, soft drinks, cheese, fruit, and sandwiches; carriage tour; and turndown service with chocolates.

"A first-rate experience from the courteous and informative phone call to the goodbye handshake. The welcoming owners and staff were friendly and warm, making us feel very welcome. Their knowledge of area sights and restaurants was extremely helpful. Our room was exceptionally clean, and graciously decorated with quality antiques. The breakfast of fresh juice, croissants, and coffee was enough to start the day. Afternoon tea provided a great opportunity to meet the other guests." *(Fran Mazarella, also SK)* Reports required.

Open All year. Closed New Year's Eve.
Rooms 3 suites, 12 doubles—all with full private bath, telephone, TV, desk, air-conditioning, fireplace, deck. Rooms divided between 5 separate buildings.
Facilities Lounge/lobby with fireplace, parlor, breakfast room with fireplace, TV, art gallery, game room with books, fireplace. ½ acre with courtyard, fountain, flower garden. Tennis, boating, fishing nearby. Private lot across street.
Location Ansonborough historic district, adjacent to Gaillaird Auditorium. Walking distance to market. On East Bay St., between George and Laurens Sts.
Restrictions Traffic noise might disturb light sleepers in 2 front rooms. No smoking inside. Parents with small children should request "kitchen suite."
Credit cards MC, Visa.
Rates B&B, $145–200 suite, $98–145 double. Extra person, $15. 3-night holiday weekend minimum.
Extras Crib, babysitting. Some French spoken.

Middleton Inn at Middleton Place ¢ 🛏 ✕ 🦃 Tel: 803–556–0500
Ashley River Road, 29407

Middleton Place was the plantation home of Henry Middletown, President of the First Continental Congress, and son Arthur, signer of the Declaration of Independence. Laid out in 1741, its formal, landscaped gardens, reminiscent of earlier ones in England and France, were the first in America, with sweeping terraces and vast plantings of camellias, magnolias, and roses. Constructed on the grounds in 1986, Middleton Inn won American Institute of Architects 1987 National Honor Award for its vine-covered cement, glass, and wood design. Rates include continental breakfast and a tour of the plantation. A short walk from the inn is the Restaurant at Middleton Place, open for lunch and specializing in "Southern plantation cooking."

"A classy hotel, and a strikingly unusual sight as you approach. Nordic interior design; bright and comfortable guest rooms with fireplace, gigantic bathtub, and a wall of windows providing a beautiful view of the nearby Ashley River and wildlife, with many birds. The buffet breakfast in the central building included cereals, fruits, muffins, Danish, teas, juices, coffees, and milk. The diverse international clientele gave us the feeling of being overseas—the setting, the buildings and furnishings, and the people. The front desk staff made dinner recommendations and gave directions. Peaceful, natural location convenient to other plantations and to Charleston." *(Celia McCullough)*

Areas for improvement: The inn has been under several different managements since its opening, and some minor glitches have yet to be ironed out. "We had to call twice to get a brochure; when it finally came, the rates were scrawled on the back, and listed the 'exucutive' *(sic)* rates."

Open All year.
Rooms 55 suites & doubles—all with full private bath, telephone, radio, TV, refrigerator, fireplace.
Facilities Common area, cafeteria, lobby, restaurant. Heated swimming pool, 2 tennis courts, jogging track, golf, horseback riding.
Location 14 m N on Rte. 61.
Credit cards Amex, MC, Visa.
Rates Room only, $99–129 suite, $69–89 double. Senior discount. Extra person, $10.
Extras Crib, babysitting.

Two Meeting Street Inn   *Tel: 803–723–7322*
2 Meeting Street, 29401

In 1992, Two Meeting Street Inn celebrates its 100th birthday and its 60th anniversary as a guest home. Built as a father's wedding present to his daughter, this Victorian mansion has been run by the Spell family since 1946; recently Karen Spell took it over as innkeeper, and reports that she is enjoying "the pleasure of sharing our home and making new friends part of our extended family." Heavily damaged by Hurricane Hugo in 1989, the building was fully refurbished and all rooms now have private baths. Fortunately, the Spells' marvelous collections of antique furniture, china, and silver remained largely intact. Breakfast includes home-baked "Texas-sized" muffins, fresh fruit, four kinds of juice, coffee, and a selection of teas, served in the dining room. Though not an inn for families or budget travelers, the widespread consensus of our readers is that Two Meeting Street is Charleston's best inn:

"An excellent location with beautiful views; staying among the historic houses gives you a real Charleston feel. The main floor of the house has a huge entry hall, fireplace, and staircase, all with the most beautiful English oak paneling. The living room and dining room are equally fine, with Victorian furnishings, more paneling, built-in cabinets, and seven stained glass windows. It is my understanding that Louis Comfort Tiffany himself installed the windows in the living room. Family silver, crystal, and mementos are displayed everywhere, but the display is tasteful, not cluttered. A fine breakfast, different each morning, is served in the dining room. Although all guests share the table, they come and go at will and are served individually on china and silver. Guests share restaurant and tourist experiences, and we've found many excellent restaurants that way.

"We recently returned here for another visit, and found the inn to be as fine as ever. A new downstairs bedroom has been added, with a stately queen-size bed with half-canopy, rich decor, and a modern bathroom. The Spells are generous and trusting to allow their guests to be 'at home' with their wonderful antiques, but this is not an inn for children, nor for people who aren't at ease with antiques." *(Susan Waller Schwemm)*

"My favorite in Charleston; worth every penny for a true Charleston feel." *(Betty Norman)* "Fabulous inn, with lovely rooms, in a beautiful neighborhood across from a park and the river. Breakfast served in the garden was a delight. Very friendly innkeeper, too." *(Pat Borysiewicz)* "Sitting on the wide piazzas, one can enjoy the view of the Charleston Harbor and the Battery. This inn has the unique attribute of combining fine architecture and beautiful antiques while preserving the warm intimacy that makes each guest feel special and welcome." *(Sammy Feehrer)*

Open All year. Closed Dec. 24, 25, 26.
Rooms 9 doubles—all with private bath and/or shower, radio, TV, desk, air-conditioning, fan. 2 with fireplace. 3 with balcony/deck.
Facilities Dining room with fireplace, breakfast room, lobby with fireplace, parlor with fireplace, guest refreshment bar, piazzas, formal garden. Tennis, golf, picnic area, beaches nearby.
Location Historic district, opposite Battery Park. Exit I-26 or Rte. 17 onto Meeting St. Inn is at end of Meeting St., the corner house at the Battery, near Battery Park.

Restrictions No smoking. No children under 9.
Credit cards None accepted.
Rates B&B, $85–150 double. Extra person, $20. Suggested tip: $5 per day. 2-3 night weekend/holiday minimum.
Extras German spoken.

COLUMBIA

Capital of South Carolina for over 200 years, Columbia is located in the center of the state. Over three-quarters of the city burned to the ground when General Sherman entered the city in 1865. Columbia is home to the University of South Carolina. Children will enjoy visiting the Riverbanks Zoo and the Criminal Justice Hall of Fame, while history and architecture buffs will prefer seeing the Hampton-Preston Mansion, a restored antebellum home, and the State House.

Claussen's Inn at Five Points
2003 Greene Street, 29205

Tel: 803–765–0440
800–622–3382

Originally constructed in 1928 as Claussen's Bakery, the structure was rebuilt in 1986 as a small luxury inn. It is owned by Richard T. Widman (owner of the King's Courtyard and John Rutledge House in Charleston) and managed by Dan Vance. While the bakery's aromas once tempted passersby, now only guests are greeted with the good smells of the inn's breakfast of coffee, juice, homemade blueberry muffins, and croissants from a neighborhood bakery. Rates also include evening wine and sherry, and turndown service with chocolates. Many of the building's original architectural features were preserved in the renovation, while skylights and terra-cotta tiling were added. Rooms are decorated with lots of plants, overstuffed furniture, four-poster or iron and brass beds, and traditional furnishings, along with all modern amenities.

"Quiet, elegant atmosphere. Staff is eager to serve guests' needs from ironing boards, dry cleaning services, and Xeroxing, to restaurant recommendations." *(David Ransdell)* "Spotlessly clean, with friendly, helpful staff. The inn is interesting architecturally and ideally located within easy walking distance of the University of South Carolina. The Five Points area is a mixture of sidewalk cafés, small shops, and good restaurants." *(Pam Harpootlian)* Additional comments welcome.

Open All year.
Rooms 8 suites, 21 doubles—all with full private bath, telephone, radio, TV, desk, air-conditioning. Some with fan, balcony, or loft.
Facilities Lobby with breakfast area, bar. Hot tub. Off-street parking.
Location Five Points section, near intersection of Saluda, Greene, and Harden Sts., in SE section of city. 4 blocks to center.
Restrictions No smoking in some guest rooms.
Credit cards Amex, MC, Visa.
Rates B&B, $100 suite, $95–100 double, $68–90 single. Extra person, $10. Children under 12 free. 10% AAA discount. AARP discount.
Extras Wheelchair access; some rooms accessible to handicapped. Crib. Spanish spoken.

The Whitney ¢ 👫   *Tel:* 803–252–0845
700 Woodrow Street at Devine, 29205   800–637–4008

Looking more like an apartment building than a hotel, the Whitney offers handsome spacious rooms that are furnished traditionally with American and English antique reproductions in a beige and blue color scheme.

"In a quiet residential neighborhood, the Whitney was first built as a condominium, then was converted into an exceptionally livable hotel. Devine Street has lots of nice restaurants, along with fast-food places and many dress boutiques. Breakfast includes sweet rolls, Danish, sausage and steak biscuits, juice, and coffee—all served in the Club room, furnished much like a living room with comfortable chairs and sofas. Marble-floored halls and gilt mirrors add to the hotel atmosphere. Rooms are spotlessly clean and the staff very pleasant." *(Pam Harpootlian)* More comments appreciated.

Open All year.
Rooms 72 suites—all with full private bath, telephone/answering machine, clock/radio, TV, desk, air-conditioning, kitchen with microwave, washer/dryer, balcony.
Facilities Living/breakfast room with fireplace, piano, stereo, books. Swimming pool.
Location Five Points Section; at corner of Woodrow and Devine, about ¼ m from Five Points intersection. 5 min. drive from downtown, government offices, university.
Restrictions No smoking in some guest rooms.
Credit cards Amex, DC, Discover, MC, Visa.
Rates B&B, $105 2-bedroom suite, $85 1-bedroom suite. No charge for children under 18 in parents' room. Weekend, weekly, corporate rates.
Extras Wheelchair access. Airport/station pickups. Crib, babysitting. Grocery delivery service.

GEORGETOWN

Originally settled in the early 1700s by indigo and rice planters, Georgetown has long been a major port. A variety of tours is available to explore the town: walking, horse and carriage, tram, and water tours cover the historic district, area plantations, the port, and other sights of interest. Beautiful beaches are in nearby at Huntington State Park and Pawley's Island, while most of the rice plantations, the area's original source of prosperity, have largely been replaced with golf courses. Georgetown is located on the South Carolina coast, about 10 minutes from the beach, about 30 minutes south of Myrtle Beach and one hour north of Charleston.

Reader tip: "Georgetown is a perfect place to settle in for those who prefer a quieter location than Myrtle Beach. It's a historic town in the midst of redevelopment and growth." *(Betty Richards)*

Information please: A charming raised cottage just a short walk from the main part of town and the waterfront, the **1790 House** (630 Highmarket Street, 29440; 803–546–4821) offers the historic charms of a 200-year-old house combined with such modern comforts as private baths and central air-conditioning. A full breakfast is served in the keeping room or on the veranda, and rates are very reasonable. Reports?

Five-Thirty Prince Street ¢   *Tel:* 803–527–1114
530 Prince Street, 29440

Different people like different things when they go to a B&B. If a warm, welcoming, and spontaneous hostess with a good sense of humor, a casual family atmosphere, and spacious Southern home are high on your list of desirables, the Five-Thirty Prince Street will suit you to a "T." The inn opened in 1988, and owner Nancy Bazemore says that "I love people, and enjoy telling them about everything Georgetown has to offer. The people who stay here are guests in my home and are treated like family."

The building is about 75 years old, with a tiled roof and a southern flavor to its "hodgepodge" architecture. Nancy has decorated it with originality and charm, combining early American antiques with contemporary furnishings, original modern art with old hand-stitched quilts. She's done the living room with raspberry-colored walls; the dining room has white wainscotting and green walls with white lattice-work; and the wicker-filled sunporch is always a favorite spot for relaxing. Breakfasts are different daily, but might include popovers and herb-cheese omelets, French toast made with raisin bread and pure maple syrup, or crustless quiche made with sausage and apples, accompanied by fresh fruit and juice, and homemade jams and jellies. Guests are welcome to help themselves to refreshments, settling down on the porch rockers to watch the world go by.

"Nancy welcomed me warmly, even though she was busy serving breakfast to her guests when I stopped by. I felt very much at home with a cup of coffee and historic book on the area until Nancy was free to chat with me and give me a tour of her most attractively decorated home. Reasonably priced, an outstanding value." *(Betty Norman)* More reports welcome.

Open All year.
Rooms 3 doubles—1 with private bath, 2 with a maximum of 4 people sharing bath (1 with ½ bath in room). All with radio, desk, air-conditioning, ceiling fan, fireplace. 1 with deck.
Facilities Dining room, living room, sun porch, veranda, patio.
Location In historic district. 2 blocks from center of town. At the corner of Prince & Queen Sts.
Restrictions "Well-behaved children welcome."
Credit cards None accepted.
Rates B&B, $60 double, $50 single.

The Shaw House ¢   *Tel:* 803–546–9663
8 Cyprus Court, 29440

Owned by Mary Shaw since 1974, she describes her B&B as "a recently built two-story Colonial with a large front porch and rocking chairs. Rooms are spacious, furnished with antiques, and our location is ideal—close to town yet very quiet. We serve a little refreshment upon arrival, and a full home-cooked southern breakfast each morning. We turn back beds at night, and always send guests on their way with 'a little some-thing'—perhaps a recipe, a prayer, or a little jar of jam or jelly."

"We ate breakfast in the den, which overlooks the beautiful Willow-bank salt marsh, and watched the soft play of water and clouds. Although beautiful antiques fill the house, it seems the opposite of formality and stuffiness. Each guest room is furnished for comfort, with tons of pillows. Mary and Joe's warmth made us feel that this was our second home." *(Leslie & Pat Rowell)* "The Shaw House is located in a very picturesque part of Georgetown, a delightful area for bird lovers. Mary Shaw exudes Southern hospitality and I left feeling that I had known her for years. " *(Betty Norman)*

Open All year.
Rooms 3 doubles—all with full private bath, telephone, radio, TV, air-condition-ing.
Facilities Living room with piano, den with TV, games; kitchen, porch. Golf, tennis, marinas nearby.
Location Coastal SC. 30 m SW of Myrtle Beach, 10 m S of Pawley's Island, 60 m NE of Charleston. 4 blocks from center of town. From Hwy. 17, turn W on Orange St. and continue to Cyprus Ct. Turn left on Cyprus to inn.
Credit cards None accepted.
Rates B&B, $50 double. Extra person, $10. 10% senior discount.
Extras Airport/station pickups. Crib, babysitting.

MYRTLE BEACH

Serendipity, An Inn ¢   *Tel:* 803–449–5268
407 71st Avenue North, 29577

Cos and Ellen Ficarra built this Spanish mission–style inn in 1985; they offer comfortable motel-style accommodations, just 300 yards from the beach. A breakfast of juice, fruit, cereal, hard-boiled eggs, and different home-baked bread or muffins is served in the breakfast room, decorated with white wicker; its walls and ceiling are adorned with Ellen's collection of country collectibles.

"The units are spacious, sparkling clean, comfortable, and quiet, each with a motel-style layout, but individual decor—one has white wicker, another has four-poster beds and wing chairs. Breakfast is a great time to meet and become acquainted with the other guests." *(Richard & Angie Davis, and others)* "Friendly, hospitable owners, spotless decor, good light-ing." *(Betty Norman)*

Minor niggle: "Many chairs and sofas are covered in plastic; under-standable at a beach resort, I suppose."

Open March to mid Nov.
Rooms 3 suites, 12 doubles—all with private bath and/or shower, TV, desk, refrigerator, air-conditioning. Some with radio, fan, balcony. 8 rooms in annex.
Facilities Living room with TV/VCR, fireplace, books; garden room, patio with fountain. Heated swimming pool, Jacuzzi, gas grill, shuffleboard, garden, Ping-Pong, bicycles. 300 yds. to ocean beaches, fishing, water-skiing. Tennis, 60 golf courses nearby.

Location N coastal SC, Horry County. 90 m NE of Charleston, SC; 40 m NE of Georgetown, SC; 60 m SW of Wilmington, NC. Center of town. Take Hwy. 17 to 71st Ave. N. Turn E toward ocean; inn is just off Hwy. 17.
Restrictions No smoking in common rooms. No children under 12.
Credit cards Amex, MC, Visa.
Rates B&B, $65–85 suite, $50–65 double. Extra person, $10. Tipping encouraged.
Extras Crib. Spanish, Italian spoken.

PENDLETON

Liberty Hall Inn ¢ ✕   *Tel: 803–646–7500*
621 South Mechanic Street, 29670

Pendleton was founded in 1790, and grew to some prominence in the nineteenth century as a local center of commerce, and an attractive place for Low Country planters and politicians to build their summer homes. The town is now one of the largest historic districts on the National Register of Historic Places, extending to Lake Hartwell. There are several plantations and historic homes worth seeing, plus craft and antique shops; a Spring Jubilee Festival is held each year during the first weekend in April.

Liberty Hall was built in 1840 by Thomas Sloan, and was totally rebuilt and refurbished as an inn in 1984, with all new bathrooms, period antiques, and quality bed and bath linens. Tom and Susan Jonas bought the inn in 1987, and have decorated it with period antiques, Susan's collection of antique glass lamps, and the work of a local potter, quilter, and basket maker. Along with their two sons, they have adjusted well to the country life after many years in St. Louis. Limited-choice dinners are served: a sample menu might include hot soup, marinated beef tenderloin, salad with poppy seed dressing, and apple crisp with vanilla ice cream.

"Pendleton is near Clemson and the university there. The inn is charming—a very lovely, restful, and pleasant place to stay. It has been beautifully and appropriately decorated to suit its 1840s origin. The breakfast of fruits, cereals, and homemade quick breads is a treat. The dinners are very tasty and attractively served, and the dining rooms and patio are pleasant and comfortable." *(Katherine Dunham)*

"Quiet but friendly atmosphere. Tom and Susan Jonas made us feel totally at home here, and went out of their way to accommodate our every wish." *(Sherril & Charles Cuzzell)* "Outstanding dinner, with fresh flowers and candlelight. A well-cared-for B&B." *(Betty Norman)*

"Each guest room has its own personality and style, beautifully coordinated down to the small details. Bathrooms are modern, towels thick and plush. All facilities were very clean, the neighborhood quiet. The Jonases suggested places to visit and explore in the area. Food was delicious, especially the cinnamon rolls." *(Angela Anderson)* "Rooms interesting and clean; good food served at candlelit tables." *(Joe & Sheila Schmidt)*

Open All year. Restaurant closed Sun. and holidays.
Rooms 10 doubles—all with private bath and/or shower, TV, air-conditioning, ceiling fans.

Facilities Dining room, upstairs lounge, deck, porches with hammock, verandas. 4 acres with gardens, walking paths. Lake swimming, hiking, fishing, golf, tennis, white-water canoeing and rafting nearby.

Location NW SC, Up Country. 30 m SW of Greenville, 130 m NW of Columbia, 88 m S of Asheville, NC. ½ m from town on Business Rte. 28, just off U.S. Route 76/28. 7 m from I-85.

Restrictions Smoking in public rooms only. Overhead footsteps audible in first floor guest rooms.

Credit cards Amex, DC, Discover, MC, Visa.

Rates B&B, $57–67 double, $52–62 single. Extra person, $15. Prix fixe dinner, $17, plus 15% service.

Key to Abbreviations and Symbols

For complete information and explanations, please see the Introduction.

¢ Especially good value for overnight accommodation.

♦ Families welcome. Most (but not all) have cribs, baby-sitting, games, play equipment, and reduced rates for children.

✗ Meals served to public; reservations recommended or required.

♠ Tennis court and swimming pool or lake on the grounds. Golf usually on grounds or nearby.

Rates: Range from least expensive room in low season to most expensive room in peak season.

Room only: No meals included; European Plan (EP).

B&B: Bed and breakfast; includes breakfast, sometimes afternoon/evening refreshment.

MAP: Modified American Plan; includes breakfast and dinner.

Full board: Three meals daily.

Alc lunch: À la carte lunch; average price of entrée plus nonalcoholic drink, tax, tip.

Alc dinner: Average price of three-course dinner, including half bottle of house wine, tax, tip.

Prix fixe dinner: Three- to five-course set dinner, excluding wine, tax, tip unless otherwise noted.

Extras: Noted if available. Always confirm in advance. Pets are not permitted unless specified; if you are allergic, ask for details; *most innkeepers have pets.*

Tennessee

Edgeworth Inn, Monteagle

Music (from country to bluegrass to rock 'n' roll), whisky, horses, Davy Crockett, and Appalachian mountain crafts are sounds and images evoked by the name of this state. A major attraction (perhaps too much so) is the Great Smoky Mountains National Park, the most visited national park in the country. Although we think of Tennessee as a rural state, its major cities—Nashville, Memphis, Knoxville, and Chattanooga—are key manufacturing centers, while Oak Ridge is home to National Laboratory and other high-tech industries. The key to Tennessee's development dates to the 1930s, when the Tennessee Valley Authority built huge dams all over the state, creating inexpensive electricity for homes and business.

Rates do not include Tennessee sales tax of 7¾%.

DANDRIDGE

Sugarfork Bed & Breakfast ¢   *Tel: 615–397–7327*
743 Garrett Road, 37725

Dandridge is the second oldest town in East Tennessee and has the distinction of being the only town in the U.S. named for George's wife, Martha Dandridge Washington. A walking tour of historic Dandridge includes 29 historic homes, shops, and taverns, most dating to the mid-1800s or earlier. The Sugarfork B&B is a contemporary two-story home overlooking Douglas Lake, with a view of the English and Great Smoky Mountains. Rooms are decorated with lots of personal touches, from the wild bird pillows mounded on one of the beds to the oversize watch on

297

the wall of one of the bathrooms. Full Southern breakfasts, served from 8–10 A.M., include country ham or beef tenderloin and eggs, with milk or red-eye gravy or quiche with bacon.

"Very clean, quiet, and homey, with great water views. The Prices are friendly and gracious, and we felt like we were visiting friends." *(Margaret Semones)* "Excellent food, with plenty of variety. We ate on the deck, overlooking the lake." *(Dan Lohr)* "Mary and Sam were attentive to our needs yet gave us absolute privacy." *(Durward White)*

Open All year.
Rooms 3 doubles—1 with full-private bath, 2 with a maximum of 4 sharing bath. All with air-conditioning.
Facilities Dining room, breakfast room, living room, family room with TV, guest kitchen, laundry facility. 2 lakefront acres with picnic area, dock, float boat, swimming, boating, fishing.
Location 30 m E of Knoxville. 1/2 m from Dandridge. From I-40, take Exit 417 to Hwy. 92 S. Go E on Hwy 25/70 through Dandridge. Turn right on Sugar Fork Rd. & go .6 m to inn on right.
Restrictions No smoking in rooms. Children welcome by prior arrangement.
Credit cards MC, Visa.
Rates B&B, $55–65 double, $45–55 single. Reduced rates for families/children. Senior discount.
Extras Limited handicapped access.

GATLINBURG

People come to Gatlinburg because it is a convenient starting point for explorations of the Great Smoky Mountains National Park. Unfortunately, the road from Knoxville to Gatlinburg is littered with one tourist trap after the next. Gatlinburg itself is no better, with dozens of tacky souvenir shops, no-go traffic, and non-stop people. Leave the town and then your car behind as soon as possible, and spend your time exploring the beauty and peace of the park—you won't have to go far on foot to leave the crowds behind.

Gatlinburg is located in southeastern Tennessee, 50 miles southeast of Knoxville.

Best Western Fabulous Chalet Inn   *Tel:* 615–436–5151
Sunset Drive, P.O. Box 11, 37738   800–528–1234

"The Fabulous Chalet is set high on a quiet hillside above the hustle and bustle of narrow downtown Gatlinburg, which runs along the Little Pigeon River. Our room was one of the largest we've ever stayed in. It had two queen-sized beds with good reading lights, a free-standing fireplace, cathedral ceiling, floor-to-ceiling windows with a view of the Smokies, a large sitting area with two couches and two reclining chairs, and a big dressing area. The large bathroom had a wonderful high-pressure shower, built-in hair dryer, marble-topped vanity, and heated tile floors. Furniture was generic motel modern, but clean, attractive, and comfortable. Our room also had a deck overlooking the swimming pool and mountain." *(SHW)* More comments needed.

Open All year.
Rooms 2 1-2 bedroom townhouses, 38 suites and doubles—all with full private bath, telephone, TV, refrigerator, air-conditioning, hair dryer, coffeemaker. Some with balcony, fireplace, whirlpool tub, king-size waterbed. Rooms in 3 buildings.
Facilities Lobby, heated swimming pool, garden. Fishing, horseback riding, golf, tennis, skiing nearby.
Location Southside; 4 blocks off Hwy. 441. Follow signs from traffic light #9.
Credit cards Amex, DC, Discover, MC, Visa.
Rates B&B, $125–175 townhouse, $91–155 suite, $45–105 double. Extra person in room, $5. (No breakfast served off-season). 3-night minimum holiday weekends & October. Ski packages.
Extras Crib, rollaway bed, babysitting.

Buckhorn Inn ✗
Tel: 615–436–4668
Route 3, Box 393, 37738

Away from the cacophony that is Gatlinburg, the Buckhorn's white-columned porch overlooks a panorama of Mount LeConte and the blue-gray Smoky Mountains. Enter the inn to find a spacious living room and dining area furnished with antiques and country-comfortable sofas. Guest rooms in the inn are furnished simply, with spindle beds and some antiques; the nearby rustic cottages all have a fireplace and porch. Rates include a full breakfast with a choice of French toast or eggs with fresh fruit, juice, hash browns, and biscuits. A typical dinner might include vegetable soup, stuffed chicken breast with cream gravy, herbed orange rice, fresh broccoli, salad, and strawberry shortcake. The Buckhorn has been owned by the Young family since 1979, and is managed by John and Connie Burns. John is the grandson of the inn's architect, and great-nephew to the original owner.

"The inn overlooks the Greenbriar section of the Great Smoky Mountains National Park. The atmosphere is homey, relaxed, and friendly, reflecting the hosts' nature." *(Betty & Ed Sternberg)* "The Buckhorn is located in a secluded spot; the accommodations are comfortable, with magnificent views." *(Mrs. Creed Reagan)*

"Gracious living and dining areas, highlighted by antiques, a fireplace, piano, and books. The grounds are lovely, with ducks and geese you can feed. Our room was comfortable, but best of all was the excellent food and service provided by the attentive, energetic innkeepers." *(Robert Ziek, also BG)* "We stayed in one of the newer cottages, with 60s decor, and a nice view from the back windows. We went elsewhere for dinner, since no vegetarian entrées were available, but enjoyed breakfast. The area is quiet and pleasant, with beautiful autumn colors." *(Celia McCullough)*

Open All year. Closed Dec. 24, 25. Dinner weekends only Dec. through March.
Rooms 5 cottages, 6 doubles—all with full private bath and/or shower, air-conditioning. Cottages with TV, fireplace, refrigerator.
Facilities Dining/living room with fireplace, piano; library. 35 acres for hiking, fishing. 1 m to swimming, trout fishing. 8 m to downhill skiing.
Location 5 m from town. From Gatlinburg, take Hwy. 321 N 5 m; turn left at Buckhorn Rd. Go 1 m and turn right on Tudor Mt. Rd. to inn.
Restrictions Smoking "permitted without enthusiasm" in cottages only. Children welcome in cottages; no children under 10 in main house or at dinner.
Credit cards None accepted.

Rates B&B, $115–140 cottage, $75–130 double, $67–130 single. Extra person, $20. 5% service. 2-night weekend minimum. Prix fixe dinner, $18.
Extras Limited wheelchair access.

Butcher House ¢   *Tel: 615–436–9457*
Route 2, Box 750, 37738

The Butcher House is a stone and cedar "Swiss chalet-style" home with views extending for miles around, elaborately decorated with period antiques and reproductions. Former executives Hugh and Gloria Butcher opened a B&B after choosing early retirement from years of travel throughout the U.S. and abroad. "We welcome guests from all walks of life and feel that a potpourri of people is conducive to pleasurable social interaction," reports Gloria. Judging from their guests' comments, that formula works. Breakfast begins with French roast coffee, mini-muffins, fresh fruit, almond granola, and fruit yogurt, and is served on the mountain-view deck, weather permitting, or in the dining room; crepes or an egg dish is the second course.

"An antique lover's paradise, with a spectacular view and delicious food to boot." *(Jill Brasfield)* "Very clean and well-kept. The Butchers are friendly, thoughtful, and made us feel right at home. They assisted us with area information, and in getting reservations for two shows. We breakfasted on eggs Florentine, hot croissants, and a fresh fruit compote, served with real linen tablecloth and napkins, and crystal water glasses." *(Lorraine Koenig)* "They agreeably prepared a special meal for a diabetic member of our party." *(TH)* "While only a ten-minute ride from downtown Gatlinburg, after driving up to the top of their mountain you feel like you're on top of the world and no one else is around." *(Keith & Mary Ann Schulte, and others)*

"A lovely deck allows you to sit outdoors and enjoy the views of the Smokies. A wonderful late night snack was provided." *(Carole Jean Adkisson)* "Everything was in perfect working order, service was excellent, and the hosts were delightful." *(Wendy Libby)*

A suggestion: "Parking was a little tight, and more lighting in that area would be helpful."

Open All year.
Rooms 1 suite, 4 doubles—3 with private bath and/or shower. 2 with maximum of 4 people sharing bath. All with TV, air-conditioning.
Facilities Dining room, living room with fireplace, family room with fireplace, TV, books. Guest kitchen, deck. 2 m to cross-country, downhill skiing.
Location 3 m NW of Gatlinburg. From US-441 go S to Gatlingburg, turn right at traffic light #10 on Ski Mtn. Rd. Turn right on Wiley Oakley Rd. At 4-way stop turn left on Ski View Rd., then right on Wiley Oakley Rd. Go N to Garret Dr., turn left. Turn right on gravel road to inn on right.
Restrictions No smoking. No children under 10.
Credit cards MC, Visa.
Rates B&B, $55–70 double, $50–65 single. 2-night minumum stay.
Extras Crib. Italian, some French, Spanish spoken.

LeConte Lodge ¢   *Tel: 615–436–4473*
Atop Mt. LeConte in the Great Smoky Mountains
National Park P.O. Box 350, 37738

LeConte Lodge is not going to be a "wonderful" choice for everyone. There's no electricity, no indoor plumbing, and no way to get there by motorized vehicle of any kind! Five trails lead to the lodge, ranging in length from 5½ to 8 miles. Set in a sheltering saddle near the 6,593-foot summit of Mt. LeConte, the lodge was built four years before the Great Smoky Mountains National Park was created in 1930. The LeConte is self-sufficient, with propane gas for cooking, and kerosene for heating and lighting. Fresh food is brought in three times a week by llama (really!). Accommodations are provided in little cabins, each with a bunkbed and daybed with striped wool blankets, a basic table and chair, and a kerosene lamp. Although last-minute cancellations are always possible, advance reservations are strongly recommended. Reservations for each spring opening begin on Oct. 1 of the previous year.

"Our visit to LeConte was an unforgettable experience. To get there, you park in one of the lots at the beginning of each of the trails. All we took were a knapsack with a canteen, a jacket, and clean clothes. The hike was long but beautiful—especially the wildflowers. It felt great to get out of over-commercialized Gatlinburg and into the quiet of the mountains. Although it was very hot when we started, it was surprisingly cool in our tiny cabin that night. Dinner was simple but good, as was breakfast the next morning—of course we were ravenous. Don't miss the short hike to Clifftops for a gorgeous sunset!" *(Diane Gayles, also NMC)* Your comments welcome.

Open Late March through mid Nov.
Rooms 15 1-3 room cabins with outdoor flush toilets and outhouses.
Facilities Game room, porch with rocking chairs. Cross-country skiing in early spring and late fall.
Location E TN. 45 m S of Knoxville. In Great Smoky Mountains National Park.
Restrictions Guests must bring their own towels. No smoking in dining room.
Credit cards None accepted.
Rates MAP, $50–55 per person. Children under 10, $45; no charge for children under 3.
Extras Special diets accommodated with advance notice.

The Wonderland Hotel ¢ ✗   *Tel:* 615–436–5490
RFD 2, Box 205, 37738

In 1912, when the Wonderland Hotel was built, this area was owned by lumber companies and was accessible only by logging train or horseback. Eventually, a road was built, and the surrounding lands were sold to the government when the Great Smoky Mountains National Park was created, but not a great deal changed at the Wonderland. Recent improvements include a new water system, painting of the interior, and the addition of smoke detectors, emergency lighting, and fire escapes. Rooms are carpeted and have twin or queen-size beds. The hotel is managed by Mr. and Mrs. Darrell Huskey; Mrs. Huskey grew up in and around the hotel, and her grandmother cooked at breakfast. The inn is leased from the park service, and is scheduled to be torn down at the end of 1992; inquire further when booking.

"A rustic inn with few modern conveniences and less than pristine accommodations . . . but we loved it! The hotel is away from the commercialism of Gatlinburg, one of only two hotels located inside the park. The old-fashioned rocking chairs on the veranda overlooking the Little River

Gorge provide a delightfully relaxing evening after a day in the mountains. The hotel also has an adequate restaurant providing three meals daily." *(GB)*

"Very basic accommodation—more tacky than rustic—with simple tasty meals and a great front porch." *(MA)* "Though far from plush and not for everyone, we love it for its wonderful atmosphere. Right across the road is the Little River, excellent for trout fishing and tubing." *(Deborah Farrington)*

Open May through Oct.
Rooms 3 suites, 20 doubles with private or shared bath.
Facilities Restaurant with fireplace, lobby, veranda. Sat. night square dances. River in front of hotel for fishing, tubing, swimming. Hiking, skiing, horseback riding nearby.
Location 20 m S of Knoxville. From Gatlinburg, follow Hwy. 73/441 to the point where it divides. Continue 4 m on Hwy. 73 to a sign for the inn. Turn left and go 1 m to the inn.
Credit cards MC, Visa.
Rates Room only, $70 suite, $38–70 double. Extra person, $4.
Extras Crib.

GREENEVILLE

Big Spring Inn ¢   *Tel:* 615–638–2917
315 North Main Street, 37743

The historic town of Greeneville, birthplace of Davy Crockett (though not on a mountaintop) and President Andrew Johnson is also home to a delightful B&B. This well-shaded, turn-of-the-century brick manor house has been restored by owners Jeanne Driese and her daughter Cheryl Van Dyck, assisted by resident artist Deedee Harruff. Those for whom Victorian means dark and somber will be delighted to know that the Big Spring Inn is anything but. Since 1985, when they bought the inn, they've furnished it with antiques and reproductions; the guest rooms are bright and cheery, with soft floral papers and pastel-colored trim, and such extra touches as fresh flowers and terry cloth robes.

Cheryl notes that "we feel our caring service and exceptional food make the inn special. We love every aspect of the kitchen—from setting a beautiful table with antique dishes to fresh and innovative recipes, using herbs from our own garden. We also provide information on hikes and local day trips to places guests would rarely find on their own."

Rates include a full breakfast, perhaps herbed eggs with French breakfast muffins, or cheese-stuffed French toast with ginger peaches; the dinner menu (by advance reservation) might be salad with herb vinaigrette; chicken breast with lime butter, Parmesan potatoes, peas with walnuts and scallions, and buttermilk rolls; and puff pastry berry hearts with cinnamon coffee.

"Arriving on a damp, dreary afternoon, we were greeted with a warm welcome, literally; there was a fire burning in the sitting room, and tea was served with freshly made cookies, still warm from the oven. Even though the home is on Main Street, we found it very quiet and peaceful. Our room was tastefully decorated and very clean, with good attention to detail. Our candlelit dinner was presented beautifully, and lots of fresh herbs were used in cooking—an unexpected treat was the arugula in our salad. The inn accepts pets—our dog was warmly welcomed, not just tolerated." *(Lillie & John Galvin)*

One area for improvement: "Better bedside lighting would be appreciated."

Open All year.
Rooms 1 suite, 5 doubles—5 with private shower and/or bath, 1 room with shared bath. All with radio, desk, air-conditioning. Some with fan. Telephone, TV on request.
Facilities Dining room, breakfast room, parlor with fireplace, TV, games; library. 2 acres with swimming pool, gazebo, flower and herb gardens. Swimming, hiking, golf, tennis nearby.
Location E TN. 68 miles east of Knoxville. From I-81 take Exit 23 to Greeneville, Bulls Gap. Follow Bus. Rte. 11-E to Main St. and turn left. Go 3 stoplights. Inn is 7th house on left after 3rd light.
Restrictions Occasional train noise. No smoking. No children under 10.
Credit cards Amex, MC, Visa.
Rates B&B, $130 suite, $60–78 double, $55–70 single. Extra person, $10. MAP, $160–170 suite, $90–118 double, $70–110 single. Extra person, $25. 10% senior discount. 10% discount for rental of all rooms. Picnic baskets for 2, $15. Prix fixe dinner, $20.
Extras Airport/station pickup, $15 each way. Pets by prior arrangement. Crib.

KNOXVILLE

Once an outpost of the western frontier, Knoxville is today a manufacturing center and home of the University of Tennessee. Its location in eastern Tennessee, about 50 miles northwest of Gatlinburg, makes it a common starting point for visits to the Smokies.

Information please: The Middleton (800 West Hill, 37902; 615–524–8100) served as student housing until late in 1981, when it was restored as a 15-room hotel. Rooms are individually decorated with original art and antiques; some have canopied beds and Jacuzzi tubs. Listed in earlier editions, more feedback is needed to reinstate it as a full entry.

Compton Manor   *Tel:* 615–523–1204
3747 Kingston Pike, 37919

Compton Manor is a Tudor mansion built in 1925 and modeled after Compton Wynyates, a English Tudor manor house built in 1520. Built entirely of stone, this B&B comes complete with coat of arms, castellated tower, great hall with stone mullioned and transomed windows, leaded glass, and slate roof. Surrounded by giant oaks, black walnuts, dogwoods, stone walls and paths, it even has a private swimming pool and tennis court. Inside you'll find a cathedral-ceilinged great hall with a carved stone fireplace and paneled library. Rooms are decorated with a variety of antiques and comfortable traditional furnishings. The inn has been restored by Brian and Hala Hunt, who have owned it since 1987.

"Impressive mansion with delightful atmosphere and gracious hosts,

who made me feel as though I were a welcomed guest in their home."
(Chester McCullough)

"The Hunts were delighted to share the history of their unique home.
Our room was comfortable with a lovely view of Knoxville's night lights.
We returned from dinner to find a variety of fresh fruit in our room, and
enjoyed a breakfast of hot breads, cereal, juice, coffee, tea, and breakfast
condiments." *(IJ)*

Open All year.
Rooms 3 doubles—all with private bath and/or shower, radio, air-conditioning,
fan. 1 with balcony or deck.
Facilities Dining room, breakfast room, living room with fireplace, games. 3 acres
with swimming pool, tennis court, croquet, lawn games.
Location SW Knoxville, 1 1/2 m W of Univ. of TN. From I-40 East, take Exit
383—Papermill Drive. Go to 2nd light, turn left on Kingston Pike. Go 1 1/2m to
inn on left.
Restrictions No smoking. No children under 12.
Credit cards MC, Visa.
Rates B&B, $65–85 double, $60–80 single. Extra person, $10. No tipping.
Extras Airport pickup, $10. Arabic, some French spoken.

The Graustein Inn ¢   *Tel:* 615–690–7007
8300 Nubbin Ridge Road, 37923

As its name implies, the Graustein, owned since 1986 by Darlene and Jim
Lara, is made of gray stone. The interior features a cathedral-ceilinged
great room, and guest rooms are highlighted with 18th- and 19th-century
antiques. The three-course breakfast includes a hearty entrée, homemade
granola, fresh fruit, and home-baked rolls and pastries. Dinner selections
change frequently, but a recent meal included mushrooms stuffed with
walnuts and cheese; roast beef tenderloin with peppers and onions and a
brandy Dijon sauce, accompanied by vegetables and salad; and poached
pears glazed with chocolate set on raspberry sauce.

"First, the setting is beautiful—secluded, lovely woods and paths, quiet
and very natural. Second, nothing was spared in the decoration of the inn.
The quality of the furnishings, wall coverings, bed linens, and pillows was
excellent. My bathroom was well appointed with such luxuries as special
soaps, shampoos, and fluffy towels." *(Sydney Summers)* "The many extras
include a robe and magazines in your room, homemade candy on the
nightstand, fresh flowers, and the smell of baking bread in the early
morning." *(Mr. & Mrs. David House)*

"Only a dozen years old, the inn has all the atmosphere of an old-timer
with none of the drawbacks. Lighting, plumbing, heating, air-conditioning
are all modern but the furnishings are antique." *(John A. Hoyer)* "The stone
patios and decking outside the inn make for a relaxed area to enjoy the
out-of-doors or an informal breakfast. A hike on the nature trails was a
welcome change. Inside, the great room is equipped with a large variety
of music and reading materials, and the fire was set for our enjoyment. The
free-standing stairway that reaches three floors is a work of art. Retiring
to our room, we found our fire blazing and easy chairs ready for some
quiet reading. Breakfast in the morning was another highlight and included fresh fruit and juice, the inn's own granola, omelets, freshly baked

muffins, and coffee that Jim and Darlene blend for use at the inn." *(Joseph & Wanda Krause)*

"Our room, 'Der Grey,' was nicely furnished, but on a second visit, we would choose 'Der Hunt' or 'La Suite,' which we thought were the best rooms in the inn. Darlene and Jim make a special effort to please their guests, bending over backwards to make their stay as pleasurable as possible." *(Charles & Barbara Sutton)* "We stayed in 'Der Hunt' with beautiful Ralph Lauren designs, and a balcony overlooking acres of woods. The owners were sincerely interested in sharing the warmth of their inn with us, yet respected our privacy. Their two friendly cats made us feel right at home." *(Avalyn Separiak)* "Service is impeccable and the inn is spotless. We used the inn as a base camp for daily hikes into the Smokies, and were aided by the Laras, who provided maps, tips, and friendly advice." *(Terri J. Webster)*

"Fully confirm existing entry. Accommodating hosts, delicious food, and lots of room to relax. Even the lower priced rooms with shared bath are quite comfortable and more than satisfactory. If you're not familiar with the area, take careful note of the directions." *(James Utt)*

Open Closed Dec. 22–25. Restaurant closed Sun.

Rooms 2 suites, 3 doubles—3 with private bath and/or shower, 2 with maximum of 4 people sharing 1 bath. All with radio, air-conditioning. 3 with balcony. 1 with desk, fireplace.

Facilities Great room, library, game room, all with fireplace, TV, stereo; breakfast porch, dining rooms, conference center. 20 acres with patio, gardens, nature trail, forest, basketball court. Golf, lake nearby.

Location 20 min. W of downtown Knoxville. From I-40, take West Hills Exit 380, turn left on Kingston Pike. At 1st traffic light, turn right on Morrell Rd. Go through 4 traffic lights to Stop sign & turn right on Nubbin Ridge Rd. Go exactly 1.5 m to driveway of inn on left.

Restrictions No smoking. No children under 13.

Credit cards Amex, MC, Visa.

Rates B&B, $90–125 suite, $59–125 double, $49–98 single. 2-3 night minimum for special event weekends. 48-hr. notice for prix fixe lunch, $8.50–15.50; prix fixe dinner, $24.50–35.50.

Extras Airport/station pickup, $25. Some Spanish spoken.

KODAK

Grandma's House ¢   *Tel:* 615–933–3512
734 Pollard Road, 37764

Just opened in 1990, Hilda and Charlie Hickman welcome guests to their homey B&B. Hilda notes that "our focus is on rest and relaxation. Our guests like to unwind by walking to the river or riding bikes down a country lane. Our large country porch has swings and rockers, or you can sit high on the balcony and watch the sun set over the mountain. Since our home was built in 1989, we have spent many hours wallpapering the rooms, and planting hundreds of bulbs in the yard." The spotless rooms are furnished with antiques, family heirlooms, and handmade quilts; most are spacious, with comfortable seating in wing chairs or rockers, and wall-to-wall carpeting. Rates include a hearty breakfast of eggs, breakfast meat, fresh fruit and juice, granola or grits, biscuits or muffins, gravy, and homemade jam and jelly.

"Conveniently located near the highway yet quietly secluded on its acreage overlooking the countryside. Hilda and Charlie really make the difference here—they are gracious and relaxed, and make you feel truly welcome. They join you at the breakfast table, and on the porch to talk about local attractions. The house is a happy combination of old-fashioned decor with modern amenities. Each bedroom is named for one of their grandmothers and her furniture is in each room." *(KG)*

"When we arrived, Hilda greeted us with chocolate cake and something to drink, making us feel very welcome. After an evening out, we returned to homemade apple cake." *(Wayne & Carol Lawrence)* "It's great to find that places like this still exist, where people take pride in what they're doing." *(Mr. & Mrs. James Jacob)* "Each room was enhanced with hand-made quilts, crafts, and art work made by Hilda. Location was perfect for sitting on the porch swing and enjoying the evening or early morning sounds." *(Gail & Don Helm)* "Breakfast was a real treat (and I'm not a breakfast person) with a variety of choices, served in a homey setting." *(Mrs. R. Jones)* "A nice distance from Gatlinburg and the drive provided us with more great views of the Smokies." *(Jerry & Phyllis Beers, and others)*

Open All year.
Rooms 3 doubles—all with private bath, radio, air-conditioning. 2 with fan, 1 with telephone, TV, desk.
Facilities Dining room with fireplace, living with TV/VCR, games, sitting room with books. 3 acres. Golf, TVA Lake nearby for water sports. 15 m to downhill, cross-country skiing.
Location E TN. 10 m E of Knoxville. From I-40, take Exit 407. Immediately turn right onto Dumplin Valley Road. Go 1 m past stop sign, inn on right.
Restrictions No smoking. No drinking. No children under 15.
Credit cards MC, Visa.
Rates B&B, $55 double, $50 single. Extra person, $10.

LOUDON

River Road Inn ¢   *Tel: 615–458–4861*
River Road, Route 1, Box 372, 37774

Framed by century-old trees and boxwoods, the River Road Inn is an antebellum brick mansion built in 1857 and listed on the National Register of Historic Places. Owned by Pam and Kent Foster, it's furnished with Victorian antiques and Oriental rugs. Special features include the original cabbage rose wallpaper, and a winding staircase connecting three of the four floors. Rates include a breakfast of sourdough coffee cakes or plantation pie, and evening refreshments.

"Kent Foster was most gracious—he showed us around and did what he could to make us feel welcome. His wife and two children were away at the time and he was subbing for the job that his wife Pam usually does. This antebellum mansion has lots of stories connected to its role in the

Civil War. General Sherman's troops camped here, and the cannon balls and rifle shot found on the property indicate that battles were fought here. There is one room for guests in the main house, furnished with antiques and with a most attractive private bath, and the converted slave quarters in the back with two bedrooms, both large. We enjoyed a sumptuous breakfast with delicious homemade breads." *(Bettye Whitney)*

"Every part of the house is tastefully decorated with antiques. Kent and Pam made us feel at home immediately, and several of our evenings ended with all of us in the den listening to the history of the home. We stayed in one of the former slave quarter rooms. It was the largest, with a fireplace, kitchenette, and Jacuzzi. We found Loudon to be a nice little town with a a convenient location." *(James & Melissa Dirmeyer)*

Open All year.
Rooms 3 doubles—all with private bath, fireplace. 1 with kitchen, Jacuzzi.
Facilities Living room with fireplace, piano; dining room, garden room. 15 acres with swimming pool, farm animals, nature trails, hiking, fishing, boating. Golf, tennis, horseback riding nearby.
Location E TN. 24 m SW of Knoxville. Take I-75 S to Loudon Exit 72. Turn left onto Hwy. 72. Go ½ m. Turn left onto Queener Rd. before Bill's Log Cabin restaurant. Go to end of rd. & turn right onto River Rd. Inn on left.
Restrictions No smoking.
Credit cards MC, Visa.
Rates B&B, $65–85 double. Extra person, $10.
Extras Station pickup.

MEMPHIS

We'd like to see more listings for west Tennessee's major city; the famous Peabody is historic, but very big; the B&B listed below is pleasant, but not in the best of neighborhoods. Reports would be most welcome!

Also recommended: The city's best-known hotel is the **Peabody** (149 Union Avenue, 38103; 800–PEABODY), an American classic. Although attractively restored and generally recommended, at 450 rooms it's too large for this guide, especially when jam-packed with conventioneers. In any case, do stop by at either 11 A.M. or 5 P.M. to see the famous duck march through the lobby. If you decide to stay, ask for a room away from the elevators, preferably one that's been recently refurbished; upper story rooms on the west side are most likely to have river views.

The Lowenstein-Long House ¢   *Tel:* 901–527–7174
217 North Waldran, 38105

The Lowenstein-Long House was built by department-store owner Abraham Lowenstein at the turn of the century and is listed on the National Register of Historic Places. Rates include a full breakfast with entrées such as quiche Lorraine; poached eggs with Hollandaise sauce; or frittata with fresh vegetables and cheeses, accompanied by cereal, fresh fruit, juice, bread, and side dishes of cheese grits, bacon, or sausage.

"Charles and Martha Long restored this B&B in 1985, after it had been deserted and derelict for several years. (Vagrants lived in it and sold off much of the original furniture and fixtures in yard sales.) The exterior is a Victorian stick-style castle, executed in gray stone blocks. You enter through an impressive etched-glass front door into an entrance hall with a handsome fireplace. One of the downstairs sitting rooms is done all in blue, while the other has lovely gilded decorative moldings. Guest rooms are immaculate and decorated in soft, harmonious color schemes, with quilts, attractive wallpapers and fabrics. The location is central; the neighborhood is not wonderful is convenient for sightseeing and to major hotels and restaurants." *(Ann Delugach)*

"We stayed in the Mauve Room, which was spacious and decorated with a comfortable couch, tables with magazines, and a writing desk. The only negative is the neighborhood in which the house is located." *(Vicki Turner)* More reports required.

Open All year.
Rooms 4 doubles—all with full private bath, desk, air-conditioning, fan.
Facilities Dining room, sitting rooms, TV room. Patio, large backyard with garden. Secure off-street parking.
Location SW TN. Center city; residential/light commercial area. 5 min. from downtown Memphis, Mud Island, Victorian Village, Overton Square.
Restrictions No smoking in common rooms.
Credit cards None accepted.
Rates B&B, $60–70 double. Extra person or rollaway, $10; children under age 5, $5. Senior discount.
Extras French, German spoken.

MONTEAGLE

Monteagle is an ideal escape from Tennessee's many high-decibel attractions. Listed on the National Register of Historic Places, its Chautauqua Assembly was founded in 1882 and remains active with lectures, concerts, and movies for eight weeks each summer; it was inspired by the original Chautauqua in western New York state. The South Cumberland State Recreation Area is nearby, with wonderful hiking trails in the Cumberland Mountains, as well as trout fishing and canoeing. Natural attractions include the Great Stone Door, Lost Cove Cave, Cathedral Falls, Fiery Gizard Trail, and Sewanee Natural Bridge. Monteagle is 45 miles northwest of Chattanooga, and 85 miles southeast of Nashville.

Also recommended: An hour of interstate driving will bring you to Chattanooga and the **Chattanooga Choo-Choo Holiday Inn** (1400 Market Street, Chattanooga TN 37402; 615–266–500 or 800–TRACK–29), located in the depot of that memorable railway. While too large at 300 rooms for a full entry, it's worth noting here. Listed on the National Register of Historic Places, the lobby offers seating beneath the soaring dome of the vestibule. "Most of the rooms are in three different motel sections, but the antique-filled rooms in the old railroad cars are charming, spacious, and romantic. Be sure and ask for one facing the gardens. Had an acceptable dinner at the Station House restaurant and enjoyed the live singing." *(Ruth & Derek Tilsley)*

Information please: Six miles west of Monteagle, via Route 64, is Sewanee, home of the University of the South, a neo-Gothic replica of Oxford University, and the **Sewanee Inn** (University Avenue, Sewanee 37375; 615–598–5671). There's been an inn on this site for 150 years, although the current buildings date to the 1950s. A small resort, the inn offers 24 motel-style guest rooms, each with a private patio, 6 tennis courts, a swimming pool, golf, and tennis. Regarding its restaurant, one reader noted that "the setting is pretty, but only two southern dishes were on the menu; I ordered a grilled chicken, which arrived covered with canned mushrooms." *(JS)*

Edgeworth Inn ¢   *Tel:* 615–924–2669
Box 340, Monteagle Assembly, 37356   615–924–2476

Wendy and David Adams, owners of the Edgeworth Inn since 1990, report that "our inn is serene and romantic, a place to relax and unwind, enjoyed by those who love to hike the surrounding mountain trails, and those escaping the city for the quiet calm of the mountains." Strolling the picturesque grounds filled with similar gingerbread Victorian cottages, sitting and rocking on the wraparound porch, or gathering by the library fireplace to chat or read a book from the thousand-book library are delightful options year-round.

The entrance parlor has light poplar walls and white wicker furnishings with flowered cushions, while the library is filled with comfortable antique chairs and lots of well-read books. A collection of European, Asian, and American art lends a cosmopolitan atmosphere to this setting. The country-style dining room has two long tables where guests can help themselves to toasted sourdough bread from a nearby Swiss bakery. Breakfast also includes fresh fruit and juice, coffee cake, homemade muffins, coffee, tea, and hot chocolate. Guest rooms are simply furnished with brass or iron beds, country Victorian fabrics, period dressers and chairs.

"A most pleasant, relaxing retreat. The rooms are tidy, clean, and well equipped. The beds are comfortable and the bathrooms clean and cheerful. The Monteagle Assembly is a quiet, secluded restored Victorian living community with controlled access, few cars, and many quiet walkways and footpaths." *(Leonard Bradley)*

"David and Wendy are doing a fine job. The inn is furnished with family pieces and antiques, and carefully chosen decorative items. It is charming and sophisticated, not cutesy. Your comments about the countryside are true. We went for dinner to the Four Seasons, which is an old barn turned into restaurant. The farmer-owner puts out a steam table buffet of fried chicken and catfish, barbecued chicken, mashed potatoes, blackeyed peas, and seven or eight other dishes plus a salad bar and dessert. You are surrounded by local folks eating farm-style food and it was really fun." *(Mrs. Martin Schwartz, also Polly Noe)*

Open All year.
Rooms 1 suite, 9 doubles—all with private bath and/or shower, fan. (Baths are private but down the hall.) Some with desk, fireplace, refrigerator, deck.
Facilities Dining room, living room, library with fireplace; sun room, guest kitchen. Wraparound porches with hammock. ½-acre surrounded by 93 acre

Victorian Village grounds, with walking trails, tennis. Golf, swimming, hiking, fishing nearby.

Location S central TN, 45 m NW of Chattanooga. From I-24 take Exit 134 to Monteagle. Turn left through gate into Monteagle Assembly. Follow East Circle Drive to #23.

Restrictions No smoking. Children by prior arrangement only.

Credit cards MC, Visa.

Rates B&B, $100–125 suite, $70–80 double, $60–75 single, plus $8 daily gate fee mid June—mid Aug. 3% service charge. Extra person, $10. 2-night weekend minimum July, Aug., Oct. Weekly rate. Midweek off-season discount.

NASHVILLE

Nashville is both the capital and the commercial center of Tennessee, and, as everyone knows, it's the country music capital of the world. It's also home to seventeen colleges and universities and to tourist attractions ranging from the sublime to the ridiculous, starting and ending, of course, with Opryland.

Information please: Recently reopened after a rocky financial startup in 1987, **Union Station** is a Romanesque-style fortress built in 1900 as a showpiece for the Louisville & Nashville Railroad, converted into a 127-room hotel in 1987 (1001 Broadway, 37203; 615–726–1001 or 800–331–2123). Carved woodwork, gilded trim, and stained glass have been restored to their original glory, while its restaurant occupies what was the station's original arched stone entrance. Guest rooms are furnished in period reproductions, some looking into the barrel-vaulted main lobby, others out to the street. The hotel is just blocks from the convention center, Music Row, and Vanderbilt University. Reports?

Also recommended: Although too big at 300 rooms for a full entry *James Utt* noted that **The Clarion Maxwell House** "is a fine hotel, out of the hustle and bustle of Nashville, without being so distant that it's inconvenient. My room was well furnished, the staff courteous and helpful, and the food in the dining room very good" (2025 MetroCenter Boulevard 37228; 615–259–4343 or 800–CLARION).

The Hermitage Hotel ♦♦
231 Sixth Avenue North, 37219

Tel: 615–244–3121
In TN: (800) 342–1816
Outside TN: (800) 251–1908

Built in 1910 at a cost of $1,000,000, the Hermitage boasted the most luxurious rooms of its day, with such amenities as hot and cold distilled running water, private baths, telephones, electric fans, and a device to show the arrival of mail. The Beaux Arts–style decor included velvet upholstered furniture, Persian carpets, and palm trees. Public rooms were lavishly ornamented with marble from Greece, Italy, and Tennessee, while the dining room was paneled in Circassian walnut from Russia. The hotel was the focal point for many political and social gatherings, and scores of famous people dined and stayed here over the years. In 1986 the hotel was restored to its early elegance, after years of decay. Its original 250 rooms were redone as 112 suites. Rates include turndown service, luxury soaps, and the morning paper. The hotel restaurant offers continental cuisine in an elegant atmosphere.

"Our suite was comfortable and quiet, with modern Oriental-style furnishings. The bathroom had a sink in the dressing area, with tub and toilet separate, and a powerful massaging shower. Although the high-ceilinged marble lobby is handsome, it seemed cold and empty. The Oak Dining room is in the basement, with arched beams and plaster ceilings. Some find it pretty; I felt like I was in a cave. Breakfasts were OK, and very reasonable in price." *(SHW)* "Our beautiful suite overlooked the Capitol, and was clean, well-kept, and very comfortable." *(Robin Cranton)* More comments welcome.

Open All year.
Rooms 112 suites—all with full private bath, telephone, radio, TV, desk, air-conditioning, wet bar, refrigerator.
Facilities Lobby with etched glass skylight, dining rooms, bar/lounge with enter-tainment. Concierge service. Parking garage next door.
Location Downtown. 1 block from Capitol. At corner of Union St.
Restrictions No smoking in some guest rooms.
Credit cards All major credit cards accepted.
Rates Room only, $95–129 suite. Extra person, $10. Children under 12 free in parents' room. 10% senior discount. Weekend, weekly rates, theme packages.
Extras Some rooms equipped for the disabled. Pets permitted by prior arrange-ment.

PIGEON FORGE

Information please: Another possibility is **Hilton's Bluff Inn** (1101 Valley Heights Drive, Pigeon Forge 37863; 615–428–9765), a newly built B&B with 10 guest rooms, ample common areas, and mountain views. Reports?

Day Dreams Country Inn 👥   *Tel:* 615–428–0370
915 Colonial Drive, 37863

While it may look like it has been around for generations, the Day Dreams Country Inn is a contemporary cedar log home set amid weeping willow trees and a babbling creek. Owners Yvonne and Mark Trombley feel "that we offer the best of both worlds—a quiet setting to use as a base for exploring nature in the Great Smokies but within walking distance of the Pigeon Forge trolley which takes you into town with its crafts shops, outlet malls, Dollywood amusement park, restaurants, and dinner theater." They have furnished their home with antiques and reproduction pieces, comfortable couches, and country accents. Guest rooms have a more sophisticated decor, and one has a Queen Anne reproduction four-poster bed and highboy chest, period wallpaper, and polished wood floor. A full country breakfast of eggs, biscuits and gravy, breakfast meats, fruit, juice, and coffee is included in the rates.

"All the charm of an older home with the conveniences of a modern one, scrupulously clean and beautifully decorated. Each room is spacious, and some of the bathrooms have antique cast iron tubs—wonderful for a relaxing bubble bath." *(Erin Lotherington)* "A wonderfully homey and restful place. Breakfasts are well planned and served family-style with Mark and Yvonne checking to see if each guest is satisfied and happy." *(Fred & Beverly Holweger)* "The owners are young and energetic and continuously add an air of laughter. Parking is excellent and it's nice to walk to town without worrying about traffic. Wonderful home-cooking in endless quantities." *(Mr. & Mrs. Arthur Douglas)* "We love to relax on the screened porch, sipping iced tea on the two-seater swing. Lou, the cook, ensures that breakfast will keep you fueled all day." *(Dave Gorden)*

Open All year.

Rooms 2 suites, 4 doubles—4 with private bath and/or shower. 2 rooms with maximum of 4 sharing bath. All with radio, desk, air-conditioning. 1 with TV.

Facilities Dining room, living room with fireplace, TV/VCR, books; screened porch with swing. 3 wooded acres with creek, picnic area, children's play equipment. 5 m to downhill, cross-country skiing.

Location E TN, 35 m E of Knoxville. ¼m from town center. From I-40, take exit for Rte. 66 S. Go S 13 m to Rte. 441, turn right into Pigeon Forge. Turn right on Wears Valley Rd, go l block, turn left on Florence Dr. Take 3rd right onto Colonial Dr. to inn on right.

Restrictions No smoking.

Credit cards MC, Visa.

Rates B&B, $110–120 suite, $89–99 double, $79–89 single. Extra person, $15. Family rate. 2-night minimum Oct. 10% discount for 3-night stay.

Extras Limited wheelchair access. Crib, babysitting available.

ROGERSVILLE

Hale Springs Inn ¢ ✗   *Tel:* 615–272–5171
110 West Main Street, Town Square, 37857

Rogersville is one of Tennessee's oldest towns, founded in 1786, when this area was still the western frontier. The Hale Springs Inn was built in 1824 and is the oldest continuously running inn or hotel in Tennessee. Presidents Jackson, Polk, and (Andrew) Johnson all stayed here. Originally called McKinney's Tavern, the inn was used as Union headquarters during the Civil War. Confederate headquarters were located across the street, in Kyle House. In 1982, Capt. Carl Netherland-Brown purchased the inn and began its restoration. Many of the original furnishings are still intact, including several Victorian settees and side chairs, original claw-foot bathtubs, and working fireplaces. The decor also includes comfortable velvet-covered wing chairs, handsome brass chandeliers, canopied four-poster beds, Oriental carpets, and handmade quilts. The Captain says that "we cater to nice people who like places in the style of Savannah, Charleston, and Williamsburg, yet we are small and off the beaten track." He also reports a recent improvement: "The movie theater which had been next door to the inn has been torn down, and the formal gardens which had occupied the site for the preceding 116 years have been restored." Now that's progress!

"The quality of the restoration is very impressive. The inn is located right downtown in a pleasant area; wonderful gift shops and specialty shops are located within two blocks." *(Larry & LaDonna Swain)*

"The self-guided walking tour that the inn provides is one of the highlights of a stay here. We chose the 'Winfield B. Hale' room, which we think is one of the nicest, though all are lovely. It was very clean and beautifully furnished. The restaurant is attractively decorated in period, with good service and outstanding food." *(Dana Lupton Abdella)*

Minor niggles: "We visited on a busy holiday weekend, and personal service was somewhat lacking. Portion sizes in the restaurant were small." Comments?

Open All year. Restaurant closed Sun.
Rooms 4 suites, 5 doubles—all with private shower and/or bath, TV, air-conditioning. Some with desk, fireplace.
Facilities Restaurant, library with fireplace, sitting room with fireplace, lobby, balcony. Formal garden with gazebo. Swimming, boating, fishing, tennis, golf nearby.
Location Upper E TN. 65 m E of Knoxville; 30 m W of Kingsport. 16 m NW of I-81 on Rte 11W. In center of town.
Restrictions Light sleepers should request back rooms; inn is on a main street. Dry county; "brown bagging" permitted. No children under 7.
Credit cards Amex, MC, Visa.
Rates B&B, $55–65 suite, $40–55 double. Extra person in room, $15. Alc lunch, $7.50; alc dinner, $16.

RUGBY

Rugby is located at the southern border of the Big South Fork National River and Recreation Area—a wilderness of high plateaus and rugged river gorges. Contact the National Park Service (P.O. Drawer #630, Oneida 37841) for information about the many recreational opportunities the area affords.

Reader tip: "Big South Fork is an undiscovered treasure with high cliffs, natural bridges, deep gorges, and magnificent views. Adults and children will enjoy visiting the wonderfully restored Blue Heron coal mine, best reached by the Big South Fork Scenic Railway. Food prices in the area are very reasonable and the many outdoor activities make it an ideal family vacation spot." *(Joe & Sheila Schmidt)*

Information please: For a nearby wilderness experience, hike to **Charit Creek Lodge** (P.O. Box 350, Gatlinburg 37738; 615–430–HIKE), in Big South Fork National River and Recreation Area of the Cumberland Plateau. (It's now run by the same national park concessionaire as the LeConte Lodge in Gatlinburg, which accounts for its address, and was recently been transformed from a youth hostel into a full-service lodge.) You can get to the lodge only on foot or horseback, although the shortest trail is less than 2 miles. You'll need to bring your own towel, but everything else is provided, including a hearty breakfast and dinner, bed linens, kerosene lamps, and even flush toilet and showers. There's a library stocked with books, indoor and outdoor games, and a stable and pastures for your horse. Summer is hot here, so we'd recommend spring or fall as

TENNESSEE

the best times to try the area's excellent hiking and riding trails, and rivers for canoeing, kayaking, fishing, whitewater rafting, and swimming. Comments?

Newbury House Inn ¢ ✕
P.O. Box 8, 37733

Tel: 615–628–2430

When English author *(Tom Brown's School Days)* and social reformer Thomas Hughes launched his Utopian colony in 1880, he wrote: "For we are about to . . . create a new center of human life . . . in this strangely beautiful solitude." Unfortunately, his words were more accurate than he had perhaps intended; after reaching a peak population of 450 in 1884, the community foundered, as did most such noble 19th century experiments. A small farming community did survive, and in 1966, Historic Rugby, Inc. was founded to restore the surviving buildings and to encourage historically compatible enterprise. Newbury House, Rugby's first boarding house, was built in 1880, and has been restored as a guest house, decorated with lace curtains and Victorian antiques; additional accommodation is available in Pioneer Cottage, built at the same time and similarly restored. Three meals a day are served at the Harrow Road Cafe, which serves both traditional English dishes and Tennessee favorites, providing a range from bangers and mash to deep-fried catfish with spoon rolls; room rates include a full breakfast. Plan to take a walking tour of the restored buildings, and to browse through the crafts and books at the Rugby Commissary and the Percy Bookshop.

"We imagine Rugby and Big South Fork to be today what Gatlinburg was 50 years ago. We had time for only a short tour, but plan to come back to explore further." *(MW)* "A Victorian inn with small rooms but a large, inviting parlor where we could have coffee or tea. The innkeepers are also the waitress and chef at the Cafe, and the British fare was excellent. The area is quiet, a haven for all kinds of birds. A feeder outside the restaurant hosted a dozen species just during our own meal. Nature trails take you along the river, with its interesting rock formations. The town is quaint, off the beaten path—our favorite place during our tour of the Southeast." *(Melanie McKeever)*

Open All year. Restaurant closed Thanksgiving, Christmas Eve, Day.
Rooms 1 3-bedroom cottage, 5 doubles—3 with private bath, 2 with maximum of 4 people sharing 1 bath. All with air-conditioning, fan. Some with desk, 1 with radio. Cottage with screened porch, kitchen.
Facilities Living room with books. Hiking trails. Canoeing, fishing, swimming nearby.
Location NE TN, 70 m NW of Knoxville. From I-40, take exit for Rte. 27. Go N approx. 32 m to Elgin. Turn left on Rte. 52, go W 7 m to Rugby.
Restrictions Smoking only in living room. No children under 12 in inn. Any age fine for cottage. Light sleepers may wish to request a room at the inn instead of in cottage.
Credit cards MC, Visa.
Rates B&B, $50–60 double, $40–50 single. Extra person, $8. Extended stay discounts. Alc breakfast, $3–4, alc lunch $4–6, alc dinner $8–15.

SEVIERVILLE

Sevierville, along with Pigeon Forge three miles down the road, has very much become part of the strip of "attractions" lining the road from Knoxville to Gatlinburg. In Sevierville you'll find the Forbidden Caverns, once inhabited by Indians, more recently by moonshiners, while Pigeon Forge has so much going on that the ratio of motel rooms to permanent residents is now two to one. Both the carrier pigeons and the forge are long gone, but what you will find here are "six miles of action-packed entertainment" in the form of innumerable shopping outlets, and attractions ranging from Dollywood to the Dixie Stampede, with water parks and water shows thrown in for good measure. If you're traveling with kids, either pass through in the dead of night when they're fast asleep, or put your brain on hold and enjoy the fun. As always, avoid visiting in July and August (especially weekends) unless you're nostalgic for rush-hour conditions.

Information please: Milk & Honey Country Hideaway (P.O. Box 4972, Sevierville 37864; 615–428f–4858) is far from the traffic, offering a big porch for rocking, full country breakfasts, and rooms eclectically decorated with Victorian, country, and Amish decor, along with lace curtains and handmade quilts. Reasonable rates include a full southern breakfast and occasional evening sweets. Listed in previous editions, **Blue Mountain Mist Inn** (1811 Pullen Road; 615–428–2335) is set on a hilltop overlooking meadows and rolling hills with the Smokies as a backdrop. Guest rooms are furnished with country antiques and collectibles, including beautiful old quilts on the walls and beds. Breakfast includes biscuits and gravy, eggs, sausage, bacon, grits, fresh fruit, and coffee cake. Reports most welcome.

Located in east Tennessee, Sevierville is situated 30 miles southeast of Knoxville, and 5 miles north of Gatlinburg and the Great Smoky Mountains National Park.

Von Bryan Inn	*Tel:* 615–453–9832
Wears Valley Rd., Rte. 7,	Outside TN, 800–633–1459
Box 91A, 37862	

The Von Bryan Inn is a magnificent log home with beautiful mountain views from every window, porch, deck, and patio. The cathedral-ceilinged living room has a stacked stone fireplace, and guests can socialize and relax weary bones, after a day of hiking or shopping, in the 12-person garden room hot tub. Guest rooms offer a blend of traditional and antique furnishings, with handmade quilts. Owned by D.J. and Jo Ann Vaughn since 1988, rates include a full breakfast and afternoon refreshments. A typical breakfast might include fresh fruit and juice, biscuits or popovers, and sausage-egg casserole or rice-asparagus casserole. A recent dinner (by advance reservation) offered salad with almonds and honey-mustard dressing, Russian chicken and rice, broccoli casserole, and blueberry cheesecake.

"The inn sits on top of a 2,000-foot mountain, with panoramic views of the Wears Valley, farmland and grazing cows below, and the mountains beyond. D.J. Vaughn welcomed us and showed us around. The guest rooms are spotlessly clean, comfortably furnished with queen- or king-sized beds, nice sitting areas, and ample closet and drawer space. The breakfast buffet is ample in quantity and variety, and the Vaughns are happy to accommodate special dietary needs on request. Dinner is well presented in a lovely atmosphere. D.J. and Jo Ann were always attentive and courteous, making us feel right at home. Guests quickly become friends, laughing over a game of Trivial Pursuit or another activity." *(Doris Waters)* "Lovely home with spectacular views and welcoming hosts." *(Ruth & Derek Tilsley)*

Open All year.
Rooms 5 doubles—all with private bath and/or shower, telephone, radio, air-conditioning. 2 with hot tub. 3-bedroom cottage with private bath, hot tub, living room with fireplace, kitchen, wraparound porch, TV.
Facilities Dining room, living room with fireplace, piano, books, games, TV, stereo; garden room with hot tub. 6 acres with swimming pool, swings, hammock, hiking. Skiing, fishing, rafting, tubing, boating, canoeing, nearby.
Location E TN, 40 m SE of Knoxville. From I-40 take exit for Rte. 66. Go S approx. 8 m to Pigeon Forge. Turn right on Hwy. 321, go W 7.2 m to Hatcher Mountain Rd. Turn right, follow signs to top of mountain.
Restrictions Smoking restricted to garden room. No children under 12 in main house.
Credit cards Amex, MC, Visa.
Rates B&B, $160 cottage, $80–125 double. MAP, $110–155. Full board, $125–180. 15% service charge. Extra person, $12–34.50. 10% discount for 2 or more nights midweek. 2-night minimum in cottage. Prix fixe lunch $10, dinner, $15.
Extras Airport pickup, $25.

TOWNSEND

Old Smoky Mountain Cabins ¢ Tel: 615-448-2388
238 Webb Road; Highway 321, Box 437, 37882

Dubbed "the peaceful side of the mountain," Townsend occupies a scenic valley at the entrance to the Cades Cove loop of the Great Smoky Mountains National Park. Owned and operated by Jim and Bobbie Webb, the Old Smoky Mountain cabin resort is comprised of the Mountain View Inn, with a deck and swimming pool with beautiful mountain views, and a ten-person hot tub. Nearby, in the woods are both "honeymoon" and regular family cabins.

"The signs led us across a creek, onto a gravel road, until finally we came upon a clearing where Jim Webb and his son have built a cabin named 'Paradise.' With a king-size water bed with mirrored canopy, a fireplace, hot tub, complete kitchen, back deck with grill and front porch with mountain views, we thought its name well earned." *(Lynn Fullman)*

Open All year.
Rooms 4 cabins, 5 suites, 12 doubles—all with full private bath, telephone, radio, TV, air-conditioning, fan, refrigerator, deck or balcony. Some with fireplace, kitchen. Cabins have from 1–5 bedrooms. Rooms in inn, log cabins, duplexes, glass houses, and chalets.

Facilities Deck, heated swimming pool, hot tub, golf, children's play equipment, picnic area. River for tubing, kyaking, fishing; horseback riding nearby.

Location E TN. Approx. 30 m SE of Knoxville. 5 min. W of entrance to Great Smoky Mt. Natl. Park at Cades Cove. ½ m from town center. Route 321 N to Townsend. Go left at the caution light and follow signs.

Credit cards Amex, Discover, MC, Visa.

Rates Room only, $45–115. Extra person, $10. Reduced rates for children/families. 2-night minimum preferred; $10 surcharge for 1-night stay.

Extras Limited wheelchair access. Airport/station pickup.

We Want to Hear from You!

As you know, this book is only effective with your help. We really need to know about your experiences and discoveries. If you stayed at an inn or hotel listed here, we want to know how it was. Did it live up to our description? Exceed it? Was it what you expected? Did you like it? Were you disappointed? Delighted? Have you discovered new establishments that we should add to the next edition?

Tear out one of the report forms at the back of this book (or use your own stationery if you prefer) and write today. *Even if you write only "Fully endorse existing entry" you will have been most helpful.*

Thank You!

Appendix

STATE TOURIST OFFICES

Listed here are the addresses and telephone numbers for the tourist offices of the Southern states covered in this book. When you write or call one of these offices, be sure to request a map of the state and a calendar of events. If you will be visiting a particular city or region, or if you have any special interests, be sure to specify this as well.

Alabama Bureau of Tourism and
   Travel
532 South Perry Street
Montgomery, Alabama 36104
205–242–4169 or 800–252–2262 (out
   of state) or 800–392–8096 (within
   Alabama)

Arkansas Department of Parks and
   Tourism
1 Capitol Mall
Little Rock, Arkansas 72201
501–682–7777 or 800–643–8383 (out
   of state) or 800–828–8974 (within
   Arkansas)

Florida Division of Tourism
Collins Building, Room 501 D
107 West Gaines Street
Tallahassee, Florida 32399-2000
904–487–1462

Georgia Tourist Division
Box 1776
Atlanta, Georgia 30301
404–656–3590 or 800–847–4842

Kentucky Department of Travel
   Development
Capitol Plaza Tower, Room 22
500 Mero Street

Frankfort, Kentucky 40601–1968
502–564–4930 or 800–225–8747 (out
   of state)

Louisiana Office of Tourism
P.O. Box 94291
Baton Rouge, Louisiana 70804–9291
504–342–8119 or 800–334–8626 (out
   of state)

Mississippi Division of Tourism
P.O. Box 2825
Jackson, Mississippi 39205–2825
601–359–3297 or 800–647–2290

North Carolina Travel and Tourism
   Division
430 North Salisbury Street
Raleigh, North Carolina 27611
919–733–4171 or 800–VISIT NC (out
   of state)

South Carolina Division of Tourism
1205 Pendleton Street
Columbia, South Carolina 29201
803–734–0122

Tennessee Tourist Development
P.O. Box 23170
Nashville, Tennessee 37202
615–741–2158

MAPS

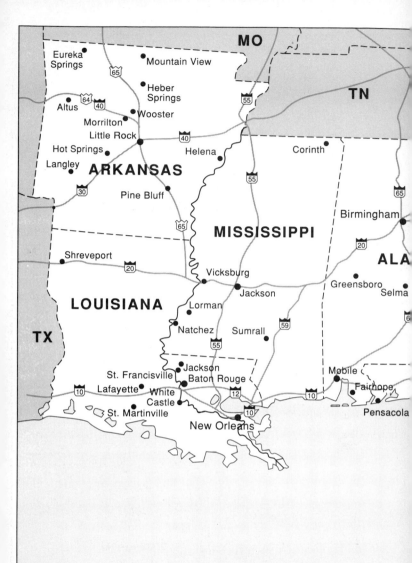

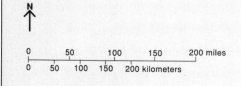

Gulf of Mexico

N

| 0 | 50 | 100 | 150 | 200 miles |
| 0 | 50 | 100 | 150 | 200 kilometers |

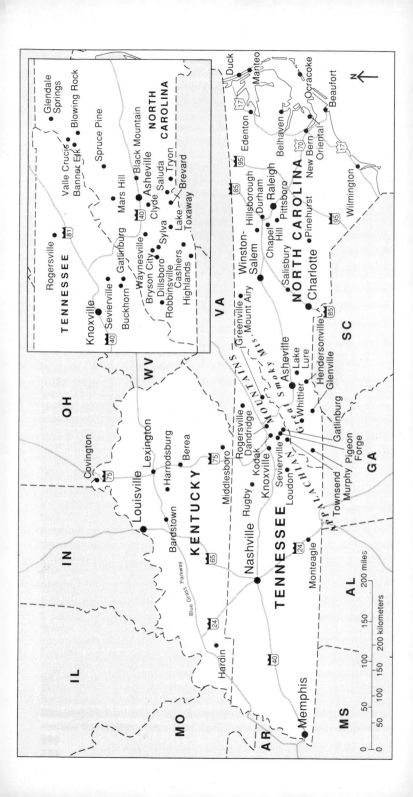

Index of Accommodations

Hotel/Inn Report Forms

The report forms on the following pages may be used to endorse or critique an existing entry or to nominate a hotel or inn that you feel deserves inclusion in next year's edition. Whichever you wish to do, don't feel you have to use our forms, or, if you do use them, don't feel you must restrict yourself to the space provided. All nominations (each on a separate piece of paper, if possible) should include your name and address, the name and location of the hotel or inn, when you have stayed there, and for how long. A copy of the establishment's brochure is also helpful. Please report only on establishments you have visited in the last eighteen months, unless you are sure that standards have not dropped since your stay. Please be as specific as possible, and critical where appropriate, about the character of the building, the public rooms, the accommodations, the meals, the service, the nightlife, the grounds, and the general atmosphere of the inn and the attitude of its owners. Any comments you have about area restaurants and sights would also be most appreciated.

Don't feel you need to write at length. A report that merely verifies the accuracy of existing listings is extremely helpful, i.e.: "Visited XYZ Inn and found it just as described." There is no need to bother with prices or with routine information about the number of rooms and facilities, although a sample brochure is very helpful for new recommendations. We obtain such details directly from the hotels selected. What we are eager to get from readers is information that is not accessible elsewhere.

On the other hand, don't apologize for writing a long report. Although space does not permit us to quote them in toto, the small details provided about furnishings, atmosphere, and cuisine can really make a description come alive, illuminating the special flavor of a particular inn or hotel. Remember that we will again be awarding free copies to our most helpful respondents—last year we mailed over 500 books.

Please note that we print only the names of respondents, never addresses. Those making negative observations are not identified. Although we must always have your full name and address, we will be happy to print your initials, or a pseudonym, if you prefer.

These report forms may also be used, if you wish, to recommend good hotels in Europe to our equivalent publication, *Europe's Wonderful Little Hotels & Inns* (published in Europe as *The Good Hotel Guide*). Reports should be sent to *Europe's Wonderful Little Hotels & Inns*, St. Martin's Press, 175 Fifth Avenue, New York, NY 10010; to P.O. Box 150, Riverside, CT 06878; or directly to *The Good Hotel Guide*, 61 Clarendon Road, London W11. Readers in the UK can send their letters postage-free to *The Good Hotel Guide*, Freepost, London W11 4 BR.

To: *America's Wonderful Little Hotels & Inns,*
     P.O. Box 150, Riverside, CT 06878.

Name of hotel _____

Address _____

Telephone _____

Date of most recent visit _____ Duration of visit _____

☐ New recommendation   ☐ Comment on existing entry

Please be as specific as possible about furnishings, atmosphere, service,
and cuisine. If reporting on an existing entry, please tell us whether
you thought it accurate, and whether you would return. Unless you
tell us not to, we shall assume that we may publish your name in the
next edition. Thank you very much for writing; use your own stationery if preferred:

I am not connected directly or indirectly with the management or
owners.
I would stay here again if returning to the area.

☐ yes   ☐ no

Signed _____

Name _____
                    (Please print)

Address _____
                    (Please print)

_____

SO92

THE INNGOER'S

Europe's Wonderful Little Hotels and Inns, 1992, *Great Britain and Ireland*
◄

Europe's Wonderful Little Hotels and Inns, 1992, *The Continent*
►

America's Wonderful Little Hotels and Inns, 1992, *U.S.A. and Canada*
◄

America's Wonderful Little Hotels and and Inns, 1992, *The Midwest*
►

America's Wonderful Little Hotels and Inns, 1992, *The Middle Atlantic*
◄

America's Wonderful Little Hotels and Inns, 1992, *The South*
►

America's Wonderful Little Hotels and Inns, 1992,*The West Coast*
◄

America's Wonderful Little Hotels and Inns, 1992, *New England*
►

America's Wonderful Little Hotels and Inns, 1992, *The Rocky Mountains and The Southwest*
◄

BEST COMPANIONS!

For up-to-date, accurate, and enjoyable lodging advice across America and Europe, discriminating travelers in all budgets trust the guides written by inngoers for inngoers.

"Entertaining ... always informative."
–*The New York Times*

"Unusual and delightful."
–*The Los Angeles Times*

Please send me:

_____ Europe's Wonderful Little Hotels and Inns, Great Britain and Ireland (063466) @ $14.95

_____ Europe's Wonderful Little Hotels and Inns, The Continent (063474) @ $16.95

_____ America's Wonderful Little Hotels and Inns, U.S.A. and Canada (062850) @ $19.95

_____ America's Wonderful Little Hotels and Inns, New England (062834) @ $15.95

_____ America's Wonderful Little Hotels and Inns, The Middle Atlantic (062818) @ $14.95

_____ America's Wonderful Little Hotels and Inns, The South (062842) @ $13.95

_____ America's Wonderful Little Hotels and Inns, The West Coast (062869) @ $14.95

_____ America's Wonderful Little Hotels and Inns, The Midwest (062826) @ $12.95

_____ America's Wonderful Little Hotels and Inns, The Rocky Mountains and The Southwest (065639) @ $13.95

Plus $3.00 per book for postage and handling (U.S. funds only) for the first book and .75¢ each additional copy. I understand that I may return the book(s), in resaleable condition, within 10 days for a full refund.

Payment is by ___ check/MO ___ Mastercard ___ Visa
For credit card orders only:

_____   _____
  Card Account Number   **Exp. Date**
Signature _____

Send to:
NAME _____

ADDRESS _____

CITY _____ **STATE** _____ **ZIP** _____